STUDIA TRADITIONIS THEOLOGIAE

Explorations in Early and Medieval Theology

Theology continually engages with its past: the people, experience, Scriptures, liturgy, learning and customs of Christians. The past is preserved, rejected, modified; but the legacy steadily evolves as Christians are never indifferent to history. Even when engaging the future, theology looks backwards: the next generation's training includes inheriting a canon of Scripture, doctrine, and controversy; while adapting the past is central in every confrontation with a modernity.

This is the dynamic realm of tradition, and this series' focus. Whether examining people, texts, or periods, its volumes are concerned with how the past evolved in the past, and the interplay of theology, culture, and tradition.

STUDIA TRADITIONIS THEOLOGIAE

Explorations in Early and Medieval Theology

8

Series Editor: Thomas O'Loughlin,
Professor of Historical Theology
in the University of Nottingham

MEDITATIONS OF THE HEART: THE PSALMS IN EARLY CHRISTIAN THOUGHT AND PRACTICE

Essays in Honour of Andrew Louth

Edited by
Andreas Andreopoulos
Augustine Casiday
Carol Harrison

BREPOLS

Cover illustration: *Tabula Peutingeriana* © ÖNB Vienna: Cod. 324, Segm. VIII + IX

© 2011, Brepols Publishers n.v., Turnhout, Belgium

D/20110/0095/85
ISBN 978-2-503-53433-6

Fr Andrew Louth, Durham 2010.

CONTENTS

JOHN BEHR, Andrew Louth   IX

RICHARD PRICE, The Voice of Christ in the Psalms   I

ROWAN WILLIAMS, Christological Exegesis of Psalm 45   17

SARAH COAKLEY, On the Fearfulness of Forgiveness: Psalm
130:4 and Its Theological Implications   33

KALLISTOS WARE, 'Forgive Us ... As we Forgive': Forgiveness in
the Psalms and the Lord's Prayer   53

ADAM G. COOPER, Sex and Transmission of Sin: Patristic Exegesis
of Psalm 50:5 (LXX)   77

JOHN A. MCGUCKIN, Origen's Use of the Psalms in the Treatise
On First Principles   97

MIHAIL NEAMTU, Psalmody, Confession, and Temporality   119

ROBERT HAYWARD, Saint Jerome, Jewish Learning, and the
Symbolism of the Number Eight   141

GILLIAN CLARK, *Psallite sapienter*: Augustine on Psalmody   161

PAULINE ALLEN & BRONWEN NEIL, Discourses on the
Poor in the Psalms: Augustine's *Ennarationes in Psalmos*   181

CAROL HARRISON, Enchanting the Soul: The Music of the Psalms   205

AUGUSTINE CASIDAY, 'The sweetest music that falls upon the ear':
Translating and Interpreting the Psalter in Christian Andalucia   225

NORMAN RUSSELL, The 'Gods' of Psalm 81 (82) in the
Hesychast Debates   243

CAROLINNE WHITE, Allegory and Rhetoric in Erasmus'
Expositions on the Psalms   257

DIMITRI CONOMOS, Elder Aimilianos on the Psalter and the
Revival of Melodious Psalmody at Simonopetra   277

INDEX   299

JOHN BEHR

ANDREW LOUTH

The first time Andrew Louth served as a priest in the chapel of St Vladimir's Seminary happened to be on the Sunday commemorating the Fathers of the First Ecumenical Council. He cut a somewhat incongruous figure, last in priestly line, in borrowed vestments, not entirely sure of his place in the ritual. Standing alone to give the sermon, he was small but composed, in a slightly lopsided phelonion. His voice was quintessentially British, light, precise, and measured. He spoke softly, without notes, directly to the people, who in turn strained to hear him. Yet his years of scholarly research, teaching and mentoring, and pastoral and priestly work, made him not only an eminent theologian, but a persuasive preacher: when he reaffirmed that God is love, he convinced.

Andrew was born in Louth, Lincolnshire, on 11 November 1944, the son of a Church Army evangelist. After various moves, the family settled in Wakefield, where his father began a new career as a prison chaplain and where Andrew went to Queen Elizabeth Grammar School, having won a West Riding County Scholarship. After the death of Andrew's mother (May 1959), his father took a new position at Walton prison in Liverpool, and they moved to Great Crosby, where Andrew and his brother Peter attended Waterloo Grammar School. When his father moved again, this time to Leeds, Andrew stayed as a house-guest of his maths teacher, so that he could complete his studies at Waterloo Grammar and sit the entrance examinations for Cambridge University, which he did with great success.

Andrew went to Cambridge to read mathematics, and after taking a first in part one, he changed to Theology, also gaining a first (1966). After a Masters in Edinburgh (with a thesis on Karl Barth), Andrew was ordained as a curate at Bristol Cathedral in 1968, serving a parish in Southmead, Bristol, for a couple of years. Pastoral experience was not the only thing that Andrew acquired during this time: George's, the renowned bookstore on Park Street, told him of "an old book" that they had and which, being in Greek, they thought might be of interest to him. The "old book" in question turned out to be a first edition of the *Philokalia* (the only two other copies in the UK being those in the British Library and in the library of Metropolitan Kallistos [Ware]).

Andrew began his distinguished academic career in 1970 when he was appointed as Fellow and Tutor in Theology, and Chaplain, at Worcester College, Oxford. He also began driving a Citroen 2CV, his fondness for which is keenly remembered by his brothers (though according to Roger, Andrew has since grown up by developing a taste for Jaguars). In 1985 he began a decade of teaching at Goldsmiths' College, London, as Senior Lecturer (1985-9) and Reader in Cultural Studies (1989-91), and then as Professor of Cultural History (1992-95). Finally, in 1996 he moved to Durham University to assume a post that matched his primary interest and research area, Patristics. Initially appointed as a Reader in Patristics, he was made Professor of Patristic and Byzantine Studies in 1998, in which position he served until his retirement in 2010.

This journey through the fields of higher education, punctuated with numerous publications, paralleled another journey, both intellectual and spiritual. It is evidenced already in his first book, *The Origins of the Christian Mystical Tradition: From Plato to Denys* (1981). Andrew was surprised at the reception this book had within Orthodox circles: on a visit to the Brotherhood of St John the Baptist at Tolleshunt Knights, Essex, he found himself invited to sit next to Archimandrite Sophrony during the meal, for the widely respected spiritual elder was interested in getting to know the author of this book. His next volume, *Discerning the Mystery: An Essay on the Nature of Theology* (1983), besides now being a textbook for many undergraduates hoping to understand the hermeneutics of Gadamer, shows Andrew drawing ever closer to Orthodoxy. Its reflections on the role of tradition and the value of allegory might have been out of step with much academic theology of the period, but now seems to be rather *avant garde*, presaging not only Andrew's own conversion but also many of the directions which are being pursued (or rediscovered) in contemporary theology.

This journey culminated in 1989, when Andrew was received into the Orthodox Church by Metropolitan Kallistos. This was, in fact, the first time I met Andrew, beginning a long and much-valued friendship. His conversion to Orthodoxy should not in any way be misunderstood as an escape into obscurantism or an anti-intellectual fundamentalism, but as an entry into the tradition that enabled him to deploy all his intellectual gifts so as to be able to immerse himself ever more within its riches and to share these with others. Indeed, the year that he was received into the Orthodox Church saw the publication of *Denys the Areopagite* (1989), and this was followed by a series of impressive theological and historical studies: *The Wilderness of God* (1996), followed by his translations of and introduction to St Maximus the Confessor (1996), his magisterial study *St John Damascene: Tradition and Originality in Byzantine Theology* (2002), and then *Greek East and Latin West: The Church AD 681-1071* (2007). These volumes, together with his numerous articles, chapters, and encyclopedia entries, on a remarkably diverse range of topics, his translations and revisions of classic texts, and innumerable book reviews and review essays, are an impressive testimony to a sharp, engaged, and faithful mind, a landmark that none in the field can miss, and an oeuvre for which generations will be thankful.

It was, no doubt, this breadth of scholarship that was one of the key reasons that led to Andrew being invited to become a co-editor of the series "Oxford Early Christian Studies", initially with Henry Chadwick and now with Gillian Clark. It is not an exaggeration to say that under his guidance this series has grown to become the benchmark standard for scholarship in Patristics and early Christianity more generally. More recently Andrew has also been asked to take over the editorship of "The Church in History" series (St Vladimir's Seminary Press) from the late John Meyendorff.

Central to Andrew's work is the conviction that, in the careful discernment of historical sources, truth is to be found, not only historical but also theological. If God acts in history, then it is in the same history that we come to know God. Theological work thus requires both careful and detailed attention to the sources, combined with a hermeneutical self-awareness, and growth. The former aspects are clear from all of Andrew's work, whether it is his discussion of the employment and semantic range of a term such as *hypostasis*, or his care to contextualize Bulgakov's sophiology. The question of hermeneutics and theological methodology was directly tackled in *Discerning the Mystery*, a book that has already become a classic. But it is his insight that the discipline of theology facilitates the students' growth that I would suggest is closest to the heart-beat of his work.

Andrew already makes mention of this in his review essay on recent work in St Maximus (*SVTQ* 42:1 [1998]). Maximus, Andrew suggests, is not so much concerned with providing a definitive "answer" as to responding to the perplexity of the questioner. Maximus, indeed, offers alternative answers, for what is fixed is not some metaphysical framework or theological hermeneutic, "but the pattern of the spiritual life, which is disclosed in Scripture, and leads towards deification. Thus is disclosed a style of theology that is tentative and open at an intellectual level, while being firmly anchored in the movement of all beings – including Maximus and his interlocutors – towards deification." Likewise in his most substantial study, on the life and work of St John of Damascus, Andrew takes a lead from the literary genre of the Damascene's *The Fountain Head of Knoweldge*, that of the monastic centuries, to argue that it should not be understood as "a proto-scholastic textbook" but that it is rather "concerned with shaping and moulding the monastic vocation of its readers, or, more widely, with defining what it is to be Christian, understood less as a set of beliefs (despite the high doctrinal content) than as a way of life" (p.37). In bringing together theology and *praxis*, in this way, Andrew, using all the intellectual resources of the modern academy, rightfully stands in the tradition of the Fathers that he has spent his life studying. I am sure that I'm not alone in hoping to see appear, sooner now rather than later, the results of his research into St Gregory Palamas and late Byzantine theology.

With this insight, and drawing upon the same talents as his editorial work, Andrew has not only taught generations of undergraduates, but also drawn to himself numerous graduate students and supervised numerous doctoral students, and also serving as an examiner for even more (including my own). Under his guidance, students have explored many and diverse topics, the Greek Fathers of course (especially St Maximus, during the years of Andrew's own work on this complex figure), yet also almost any aspect of Christian experience in history, from liturgy and art to asceticism and canon law. More than that, however, his concern to bring the best out in others is shown by the way in which he selflessly reads, comments, and guides, the work in progress of many students and scholars around the word. In a world that has become much smaller through technological advances such as email, communication has become so much easier, but the demands (and expectations) placed upon someone like Andrew have also become much greater, though, characteristically, he has accepted this not as a burden but as an opportunity for greater service and joy: to those to whom much is given, much is expected.

All of these activities as scholar and teacher found new depths when Andrew was ordained as a priest of the Orthodox Church in 2003. Those only knowing him by his scholarly reputation would probably not have expected this of the professor. However, knowing of his family background, of his initial steps upon graduating university, and of the particular quality of his theology, it is no surprise. All the gifts and talents of a theologian, as priest, professor and scholar, are brought together in a particular way by Andrew, and it is a joy and pleasure to be able to write these words of appreciation, shared by all those who have contributed to this volume in his honour.

RICHARD PRICE

THE VOICE OF CHRIST IN THE PSALMS

The Christian exegesis of the Old Testament may be said to have begun on the road to Emmaus: 'Beginning with Moses and all the prophets, he interpreted to them the things about himself in all the Scriptures' (Lk 24:27). Note, however, the wording 'the things about himself in all the Scriptures' rather than 'all the Scriptures as being about himself'. The reference is apparently to early Christian collections of Messianic texts – verses that could be read as prophecies of the coming and work of Christ, of which many are to be found in the Gospels themselves and many more in the immediately post-apostolic writings, such as the Letter of Barnabas and the First Apology of Justin Martyr.

This selective approach could not, however, satisfy for long, for it failed to do justice to the belief that 'all Scripture is inspired by God' (2 Tim 3:16) and St Paul's insistence, as a model for Christian preachers, that 'I decided to know nothing among you except Jesus Christ, and him crucified' (1 Cor 2:2): this made it essential to find 'Christ and him crucified' throughout the Old Testament. This took on a particular urgency in relation to the Psalter, for two reasons. First, the Psalter was recognized as the 'Psalms of David', while King David was seen as a prototype of Christ – as when in the Gospels Jesus is made to cite David's eating of the bread of the presence as a precedent for the behaviour of his own disciples (Mk 2:23–26 and parallels). Secondly, the monastic movement of the fourth century made the recitation of the Psalter the main form of Christian prayer.[1] It followed that, if Christ was to be the focus of Christian prayer, he had to be found in the Psalter.

From Origen onwards many of Greek Fathers wrote commentaries on the psalms, including Didymus the Blind, Apollinarius, Cyril of Alexandria, Theodore of Mopsuestia, and Theodoret. Unfortunately

---

[1] The liturgical use of the Psalter (as distinguished from its place in the lectionary) started only in around 200; see Fischer (1951), 88–89.

the popularity of these commentaries, and a perceived need to supplement them from each other, led to substantial interpolation and the compilation of numerous *catenae* (or anthologies), full of doubtful attributions.[2] There is a dearth of modern critical editions. The material available, however, is perfectly adequate for a general survey such as the one offered here.

A text on this subject that should be a classic but does not appear to be widely known is the 'Letter to Marcellinus on the interpretation of the Psalms' by St Athanasius.[3] He begins by arguing that the Psalter echoes the themes of all parts of the rest of the Old Testament, and in particular that 'in almost every psalm it conveys the message of the prophets', which he has already described as containing in the first place 'prophecies about the coming of the Saviour'.[4] There follows a citation of numerous psalm verses referring to the Lord's coming and the work of the Word. Most of these are familiar enough in early Christian literature, but in some cases the interpretation is more unusual. The verse 'Sion is my mother, a man will say,[5] and a man was born in her, and the Most High himself founded her' (Ps 86:5) is interpreted, through an identification of the two subjects, as expressing the two great themes of the first chapter of the Gospel of John – the creative role of the Word and his incarnation. The bride of Psalm 44 is, perhaps for the first time in an extant text, identified with the Virgin.[6] Several psalm verses are cited as relating to the Passion, not only the obvious Ps 21:16–18, but also 68.4c (evidently with reference to the whole psalm, taken as uttered by Christ on the Cross) and 87.8a, 'Thy wrath has been fixed against me,' interpreted as spoken by Christ as taking upon himself the divine anger directed against mankind.[7] Verses referring to divine judgement are related to the work of Christ, doubtless

---

[2] See Devreesse (1928), 1125–39.

[3] PG 27. 11–46. For a discussion of both content and textual tradition (the work comes in the Codex Alexandrinus) see Rondeau (1968), who demonstrates at length that the concepts and vocabulary of the work, whose authenticity has sometimes been doubted, are genuinely Athanasian.

[4] PG 27. 13C and 12C.

[5] The text as punctuated (surely wrongly) in PG runs: 'Mother Sion will say, A man.'

[6] At this early date this psalm was understood to apply to the Church or the Christian soul, Rondeau (1968), 180.

[7] PG 27. 16C–17A. Further psalms relating to Christ's Passion are listed later in the work, 37C.

in view of Jn 5:22, 'The Father judges no one but has entrusted all judgement to the Son.' The particular significance of these citations for Athanasius is that the Psalter, as he puts it, 'by saying that Christ will become man indicates in consequence that he is possible in the flesh.'[8]

However, despite giving pride of place to the psalms that refer to Christ, Athanasius does not attempt a Christological interpretation of the whole of the Psalter.[9] He is influenced by Origen's treatment of the psalms as the prayers of the Christian faithful: he develops at length and with eloquence the theme that one of the great marvels of the Psalter is that the pious reader can hear in it his own voice in prayer and praise, while it would be presumptuous to attribute to oneself the words ascribed in other books of the Old Testament to patriarchs and prophets.[10] But even here the uniqueness of the Psalter, according to Athanasius, lies in its relation to Christ. He contrasts pagan teaching, consisting purely in exhortation, to the work of Christ, who not only taught but gave an example in his own life: the great glory of the Psalter, he continues, is that it not only exhorts but provides examples of the virtues, for the benefit of 'whoever is hastening towards virtue and wishes to contemplate the life of the Saviour in the flesh'.[11] This makes it possible for anyone who follows the Psalter closely – so closely as virtually to 'become' the Psalter, as Athanasius puts it – to control his body by taking Christ as his leader and overcoming the passions through him.[12] The implication is that the psalms tell us (often in the first person) of the life of Christ.

How extensive after Athanasius was the Christological interpretation of the Psalter? Obvious enough were the passages that Christian tradition, already in the apostolic writings, had always taken to be prophecies of Christ. These included not only the passages cited or echoed in the New Testament, but also such passages as Ps 23:7–8, 'Lift up the gates, your rulers, and be lifted up, eternal gates, and the king of glory will enter in. Who is this king of glory? The Lord strong and mighty, the Lord mighty in war.' These verses were taken to refer

---

[8] PG 27. 16C.

[9] See Fischer (1974) and Sieben (1973).

[10] PG 27. 21–24.

[11] PG 27. 25C.

[12] PG 27. 40B.

to Christ's ascension into heaven.[13] This line of interpretation was vastly assisted by the constant tendency to identify 'the Lord' (*Kyrios*) of so many psalm verses with Christ, partly through the influence of New Testament usage, and partly through the dominance of prayer addressed specifically to Christ in much early Christian devotion.[14] It became natural for Christians to read many of the psalms as addressed to Christ in his divinity. One could cite Eusebius of Caesarea on Psalm 90:[15]

> Note attentively how in 'For you, Lord my hope, have made the Most High your refuge' the word 'Lord' corresponds to the Tetragram in Hebrew, which the sons of the Hebrews say is not to be uttered and are accustomed to understand of God alone. But we have already shown that in many scriptural passages it refers to the Godhead of the Word, as in the psalm in hand.

A striking example is the interpretation of the words addressed to God in Ps 50:9, 'You will sprinkle me with hyssop and I shall be cleansed.' It seemed obvious that 'hyssop' referred to the blood shed on the Cross, and the addressee could be identified as Christ himself.[16] This interpretation led to the circulation of a version of this psalm in which this verse took the form, 'Sprinkle me with the hyssop of the blood of your Cross and cleanse me.'[17] The consequence was that even when a psalm was read as the prayer not of Christ but of a Christian, as indeed most of the psalms were, it was still possible to involve Christ, as the addressee.

It was a weakness in the earliest Christian use of the Old Testament, prior to the appearance in the third century of commentaries on whole books, that individual verses were constantly cited as Messianic prophecies without attention to their context. It was this that spurred

---

[13] See, e.g., Theodoret, PG 80. 1033D, and Augustine, *En. in ps.* 23. 7–10, CSEL 93/1A, 338–43. Hesychius of Jerusalem sought to improve on this tradition by taking these verses (7–8) to refer to Christ's descent into hell and the nearly identical verses that follow (9–10) to refer to his ascension into heaven.

[14] As noted by Fischer (1951), 96–99. In contrast, early liturgical texts (and the continuing western tradition) preferred prayer through Christ to the Father; see Jungmann (1965).

[15] Eusebius, *Dem. evang.* IX, PG 22. 677C.

[16] Athanasius, PG 27. 241B; Cyril of Alexandria, PG 69. 1096D; Augustine, *En. in ps.* 50. 12, CCSL 38, 608.

[17] Fischer (1951), 100, citing a letter of the eighth-century *catholicos* of the Church of the East Timothy I in Braun (1901), 306.

the protest against the Christological reading of the Psalter that we find in the very first work composed by the most independent-minded of all early biblical commentators (apart from Origen) – Theodore of Mopsuestia.[18] It has become wearisomely familiar to say that Theodore rejected the allegorical interpretation associated with Origen in favour of an historical interpretation, which kept to the original and literal meaning in a way akin to modern biblical scholarship. But categorizing patristic exegesis as either 'allegorical' or 'historical' is unhelpful, since it cannot do justice to either of the modes that in fact dominate the Fathers' reading of the Old Testament – the moral and the typological. Moralizing exegesis of texts intended directly to guide and exhort was naturally literal, but what inspired it was not a desire to be literal but a desire to edify, of which the classic statement is 2 Tim 3:16, 'Every scripture is inspired and useful for teaching, for rebuke, for correction, for training in righteousness.' Meanwhile, the recognition of types or anticipations of the themes and realities of the New Covenant in the ordinances, events and prophecies of the Old arose not from a search for allegorical or secondary meanings, but from the obvious and unimpeachable rule that the interpretation of a text must respect its purpose, and for Christians the purpose of the Bible was to reveal Christ.[19] What motivated Theodore of Mopsuestia to reject many of the traditional typological interpretations of Old Testament passages was not some anticipation of the historico-critical method of modern scholarship, but the commonsense principle that exegesis must respect the immediate context of a passage; he argued accordingly that a part of a psalm can only be taken as referring to Christ if the psalm as a whole allows this interpretation.

A verse that raises this problem in a particularly acute form is Ps 21:2, 'O God my God, attend to me: why have you forsaken me? Far from my salvation are the words of my transgressions.' Some relation between the first half of this verse and the Passion of Christ could not be denied, since the Gospels (Mt 27:46; Mk 15:34) place it in the mouth of Jesus himself on the Cross, quite apart from the echoing of many subsequent verses of this psalm in the Gospel Passion narratives. But the second half of this verse, with its reference to 'my transgressions'

---

[18] According to Leontius of Byzantium, PG 86A. 1364C, the *Commentary on the Psalms* was Theodore's first work, written when he was only eighteen.

[19] For the prime importance in patristic exegesis of perceiving the referent of an inspired text see Frances Young (1997), ch. 6.

(in the Septuagintal form of the text), raises a problem.[20] Theodore commented:

> It is beyond doubt that the psalm does not at all fit the Lord, for it was not for Christ the Lord, who 'did not commit sin nor was deceit found in his mouth' [Is 53:9; 1 Pt 2:22], to say, 'Far from my salvation are the words of my transgressions.' But the Lord himself, according to the common law of men, when he was being crushed by the Passion, uttered the words, 'My God, my God, why have you forsaken me?' The words 'They divided my garments between them and over my clothing they cast lots' [Ps 21:19] were manifestly applied to him by the apostles [Mt 27:35], because what had first been said hyperbolically by David on account of ills inflicted on him happened in actuality to Christ the Lord, whose garments they divided and whose tunic they subjected to lots.[21]

This principle of recognizing prophecy of Christ only when this fitted the whole of a psalm was followed so rigorously by Theodore that he reduced the number of psalms referring directly to Christ to a mere four – 2, 8, 44, 109.

In later life Theodore admitted that in this the first of his exegetical works he had gone too far,[22] and even those commentators who were most indebted to him had to agree. This is true of Theodoret of Cyrrhus, whose massive commentary on the Psalter is the best preserved of all early Greek commentaries.[23] In the preface to this work he castigates the extremism (*ametria*) both of those who introduce too much 'allegory' and of those who reduce it to 'ancient history', like (he says) the Jews, and ignore the prophecies it contains 'about Christ the Lord, the Church from the Gentiles, the evangelical life and the preaching

---

[20] Informed commentators were aware that the versions of Symmachus and Theodotion translated the phrase (accurately as it happens) not as 'my transgressions' but 'my groanings' (e.g. Theodoret, PG 80. 1009C; Ps.-Jerome, *Breviarium in psalmos*, PL 26. 931D–932A), but were unwilling to depart from what for them was the canonical text.

[21] This passage is preserved in the Acts of Constantinople II, *ACO* 4.1 (Berlin, 1971), p. 53, 18–27. A similar passage from Theodore's treatment of the same psalm is given in the same context, pp. 53,27–54,14.

[22] Theodore wrote of it in later life: 'We did not exercise as much care over the matter as was due, for, as it happened, we experienced the lot of beginners inexperienced in writing. Our writings of that time have undergone much revision..., because many of our works, especially our first ones, were written negligently' (in Facundus, *Pro defensione trium capitulorum* III. 6.14, CCSL 90A, 96).

[23] PG 80. 857–1997.

of the apostles'.[24] In his commentary on Psalm 21, he mentions the objection by 'other interpreters' to the Christological interpretation of the psalm (without mentioning Theodore by name) and responds as follows:[25]

> May they listen to John exclaiming, 'Behold the lamb of God, who takes away the sin of the world' (Jn 1:29), and the inspired Paul saying, 'Him who knew not sin he made to be sin on our account, so that we might become righteousness in him' (2 Cor 5:21) and again, 'Christ redeemed us from the curse of the law by becoming a curse on our account' (Gal 3:13). Therefore, being a fount of righteousness, he assumed our sin, and being a sea of blessing, he received the curse incumbent on us, and endured the Cross, despising its shame; and so he uttered these words on our account.

Ps 21:2 was an exceptionally clear case, since the attribution of the verse to Christ himself had Dominical authority and since it was scarcely possible to disassociate verse 2b (with its mention of 'transgressions') from verse 2a (with its complaint of Godforsakenness). To what extent did the Fathers think it appropriate to apply a similar interpretation to the famous series of the seven penitential psalms (6, 31, 37, 50, 101, 129, and 142)? In his treatment of Psalm 101 St Augustine provides a Christological interpretation that is conscious of its boldness. Commenting that this text is the prayer of someone in an abject state of poverty, described as eating ashes and weeping into his cup, he continues:[26]

> Already in comparison with the Word through whom all things were made I recognize a dearth of riches; but still, how far is this from ashes and weeping when drinking! I am still afraid to say, 'It is he,' and yet I wish to... He must add poverty to poverty and transfigure our lowly body into himself; he must be our head and we his members; let them be two in one flesh... Thus they will be two in one voice as well, and in that one voice we shall not now be surprised if we hear our own voice saying, 'I ate ashes like bread, and my drink I mixed with weeping,' for he deigned to have us as his members, and among his members there are penitents.

---

[24] PG 80. 860CD.

[25] PG 80. 1009C–1012A.

[26] Augustine, *En. in ps.* 101, S. 1. 2, CCSL 40, 1426.

In general, the Fathers were happy to recognize the voice of Christ in the penitential psalms, but there was a tendency to separate the expressions of anguish, positively inviting interpretation in relation to the Cross, from confessions of sinfulness, which they usually restricted to the penitent Christian. For example, Gregory the Great writes in a most Augustinian vein on Psalm 142: 'In this psalm the head prays for the members...The Church cries out to God, joined to Christ her head in the unity of the Spirit.'[27] But when he progresses to the theme of appeal to God from a sinner, he does not recognize a Christological reference.

A similar case is the third of the penitential psalms (Psalm 37), which is at times immediately reminiscent for a Christian reader of the Passion of Christ, notably in verses 12 and 14, 'My friends and my neighbours have drawn near over against me and taken their stand there, and those nearest to me have stood afar off...But I like a deaf man did not hear, and like one dumb did not open my mouth.' But could the speaker at this point really be the same as in verses 4b–5, 'There is no peace for my bones in face of my sins, because my law-lessnesses tower above my head', or in verse 19, 'I shall declare my lawlessness and be anxious about my sin'? How, then, did the Fathers treat this psalm?

We are fortunate to possess a complete text of Origen's commentary on this psalm in a translation by Rufinus.[28] Origen interprets the whole text as a model of penitence for the sinner to apply to himself; he gives a Christological interpretation to not a single verse, not even verse 14. Another substantial commentary on this psalm survives from the pen of St Ambrose. After an opening remark to the effect that the psalm is a lesson by King David on how to repent of one's sins,[29] he soons proceeds to the coming of Christ 'in the likeness of sinful flesh' in order to destroy human sinfulness in his own flesh.[30] In the verse by verse commentary that follows, however, this theme does not reappear. Verse 7 ('I am afflicted and bowed down by misery') is interpreted with reference to the Passion of Christ, but with an insistence that the latter had nothing to do with penitence.[31] Verses 12–14 are applied to David

---

[27] Gregory the Great, PL 79. 642C, to which I here contrast 645C.

[28] There is a critical edition in Origène, *Homélies sur les Psaumes* 36 à 38, SC 411 (Paris, 1995), 258–326.

[29] PL 14. 1055–88.

[30] Ibid., 1059.

[31] Ibid., 1073AB.

and Job (and through them to penitents generally), but not to Christ himself. Ambrose's treatment is not directly indebted to Origen, and he differs from Origen's reading of the same psalm in stressing the role of David, but it follows the Origenist tradition of reading the psalms as primarily a model of prayer for the Christian. The same interpretation of the psalm by reference not to Christ but to the biography of David and the requirements of penitence is to be found in the Antiochene commentators Theodore and Theodoret, and also in the passages attributed in the *catenae* to Saints Athanasius and Cyril of Alexandria.[32]

There is, however, one striking exception to this consensus, and this is in Hesychius of Jerusalem, a priest of Jerusalem at the time of the Council of Chalcedon, who wrote three complete commentaries on the Psalter and has been described as 'perhaps the most prolific of the commentators on the psalms'.[33] He was a bitter critic of Theodore of Mopsuestia, of whom he wrote in a page of his lost *Ecclesiastical History* that survives in the Acts of the Fifth Ecumenical Council of 553:[34]

> Taking the first principles of his teaching from Jewish prating, he wrote a book on the prophecy of the psalms that denies all the references to the Lord; but when he was accused and in some danger, he contradicted himself, not of his own free will but compelled by the complaints of all. He promised to destroy the book, but secretly preserved this handbook of Jewish impiety; for while pretending to consign his commentary to the flames, he tried perfidiously to hide his snares.

Theodore's virtual rejection of the Christological interpretation of the psalms was especially offensive to Hesychius, since the prime exegetical principle that he adopted in interpreting the Old Testament was that 'the foundation for expounding the words of the law, without which no builder in the Spirit can put anything, is Christ.'[35]

---

[32] Theodore of Mopusestia, *Commentary on Psalms* 1–81 (Atlanta, 2006), 436–62; Theodoret, PG 80. 1137–44; Athanasius, PG 27. 184–88; Cyril, PG 69. 952–69. Cyril remarks on verse 13 ('Those who sought my life used violence') that this happened to many of the saints and even to Christ (PG 69. 964CD), but stops short of deducing what could properly be called a Christological interpretation of the text.

[33] Devreesse (1928), 1134–35. See also Kirchmeyer (1968).

[34] *ACO* 4.1, p. 90, 12–17.

[35] PG 93. 845BC, from Hesychius' commentary on Leviticus, preserved in Latin.

The shortest of Hesychius' commentaries on the Psalter, which is preserved intact, is no more than a series of brief and elementary notes,[36] and offers nothing than can properly be called a commentary of Psalm 37, but a full commentary of this psalm by the same writer has been recovered by Robert Devreesse from the *catenae*, with confirmation from a sixteenth-century Latin translation of a lost Greek manuscript.[37] This text is of exceptional interest, and deserves our close attention.

The heading of Psalm 37 in the Septuagint is 'A psalm of David, for remembrance concerning a sabbath'. Which sabbath is in question, asks Hesychius, and replies, 'Not any one you please, and so the theme of the psalm is not the sacrifices of the sabbath in the law, but the sufferings of Christ' (ll. 2–5). On verse 2 ('Lord, do not rebuke me in your anger...') he comments, 'We have often said that Christ in both his sufferings and in prophecy [that is, in psalms that foretell the Passion] assumed the role of mankind, because of which he now says this, that [human] nature has been rebuked, but not in anger, wishing it to be corrected, but not in wrath but for salvation... Christ assumed our rebuke and correction, he himself both rebuking and being rebuked, rebuking as God and being rebuked on our behalf as man, uniting each role,[38] both of the rebuker and the rebuked' (ll. 15–28). Verse 3 ('Your weapons are fixed in me...') he relates to the punishment for the sin of Adam, while he places on the lips of Christ the words, 'Since I have assumed the sins of the race, I necessarily undergo their correction' (45–47). Verse 4b ('There is no peace in my bones in face of my sins') he relates to Christ's bearing not his own sins but the sins of the human race (ll. 66–76). On verse 18b ('My anguish is continually before me') he comments, 'Clearly his sympathy with us, on account of which he has a continual remembrance of his own Passion' (ll. 280–81). On verse 19b ('I shall be anxious about my sin') he comments, 'The sin of our race he calls his own, being the first fruits of mankind, wishing as the new Adam to reform the old Adam

---

[36] Printed as Athanasius, *De titulis psalmorum* in PG 27. 649-1344. For Psalm 37 see 793–97.

[37] Devreesse (1924). For his text of the commentary on this psalm see pp. 512–21, with the consecutive line numbers that I cite.

[38] Here (and few lines above) I use 'role' to translate πρόσωπον. I avoid the standard rendering, 'person', because a reference to two 'persons' in Christ is for us too reminiscent of the Nestorianism that Hesychius firmly opposed.

within himself' (ll. 290–91). On verse 22 ('Do not desert me, O Lord my God and do not depart from me') he comments, 'This he uttered not on his own behalf but for the Church, or rather on his own behalf, for the Church is one with him, as a bride is recognized [to be one] with the bridegroom' (ll. 324–28). In commenting on verse 23 ('Attend to my help') he adduces Gen 2:18 on Eve as Adam's helpmate to show that Christ's 'help' is his bride, the Church (ll. 330–34). Finally, on the last phrase of the psalm ('O Lord of my salvation') his comment runs, 'He again calls the salvation of the Gentiles his own salvation. For if he made our sins his own, would he not all the more count our salvation as his own?' (ll. 352–58).

If we turn to western exegetes, there is no shortage of examples of the attribution of some of the verses of this psalm to Christ in his Passion; but the penitent in this psalm is not generally identified with Christ himself. The author of the *Breviarium in psalmos* once ascribed to St Jerome says that the psalm as a whole is spoken by a penitent; it is only from verse 12 onwards that he recognizes 'my Lord Jesus Christ being surrounded by the Jews, hung on the Cross, and rising from the underworld'.[39] Verse 19 on the psalmist's 'iniquity' and 'sin' he explains with reference to Christ's carrying our sins in order to rescue us from them.[40] Gregory the Great in his commentary on this psalm likewise takes the psalmist to be speaking in the person of Christ from verse 12. Referring to the way in which Christ speaks in and through the inspired writers of Scripture, he continues 'It should not cause surprise if he [Christ] sometimes speaks about himself, since he presides within... So here too, after enumerating some of the miseries of human weakness, he mentions his own Passion, in order to show that what suits the members applies to the head.'[41] But by the time he gets to verse 19, the speaker has again become a fallen penitent; the theme of Christ's self-identification with sinners does not appear.[42]

Considering Gregory's immersion in the works of St Augustine, it is striking that he does not follow the latter's treatment of this same psalm, which is the most notable of those in the Latin Fathers. Augustine introduces a Christological interpretation not indeed at the very

---

[39] PG 26. 994C and 995D.
[40] Ibid., 997B.
[41] Gregory the Great, PL 79. 575AB.
[42] Ibid., 579.

beginning of the psalm but already at verse 4b ('There is no peace in my bones in face of my sins'), where he launches out as follows:[43]

> The need to understand compels us to recognize here the full and total Christ (*totum Christum*), that is, head and body. For when Christ speaks, he speaks sometimes in the person of the head alone, which is the Saviour himself, born of the Virgin Mary, and sometimes in the person of his body, which is holy Church spread throughout the world...[44] We also are in his body, as his members, and we find ourselves speaking here... If we deny that these words are the words of Christ, the following also will not be Christ's, 'My God, my God, why have you forsaken me?' For there you have 'My God, my God, why have you forsaken me? Far from my salvation are the words of my offences' (Ps 21:2). Just as here you have 'in face of my sins', so there you have 'the words of my transgressions'. Since Christ was indeed without sin and without offences, we might begin to think that the words of that psalm are not his; yet it would be very difficult and wrong-headed to maintain that that psalm does not refer to Christ, when there we have his Passion as plain as if it were being read from the Gospel... What of the fact that the Lord himself, when hanging on the Cross, uttered the first verse of this psalm with his own voice, and said, 'My God, my God, why have you forsaken me?'? What did he intend this to mean, if not that the whole of that psalm refers to himself, since he himself uttered its heading? And when there follows the phrase 'the words of my offences', there can be no doubt that it is the voice of Christ. So what sins are these, unless he is speaking of his body that is the Church? For both the body and the head of Christ are speaking. How can they speak as one person? Because, says Scripture, 'They will be two in one flesh' [Eph 5:31]... There is but one voice, wherever Scripture does not say when the body is speaking and when the head... When you hear the voice of the body, do not separate the head from it; and when you hear the voice of the head, do not separate the body from it; for no longer are they two, but one flesh.

When after this Augustine reverts to treating Psalm 37 as the utterance of a penitent, he has taught us not to separate this from the voice of

---

[43] Augustine, *En. in ps.* 37. 6, CCSL 38. 386–87.

[44] Fiedrowicz (1997) brings out well how Augustine's notion of 'the voice of the whole Christ' in his body the Church enabled 'a comprehensive Christological re-reading of the psalms' (p. 302). For an outstanding treatment of these themes see Borgomeo (1972), 191–234.

Christ. From verse 12 his exegesis is again explicitly Christological, in accordance with the traditional reading of the psalm, but with a reminder that we must not separate our situation from Christ's:[45]

> But again, when the head begins to speak, do not separate the body from it. If the head has refused to separate itself from the voice of the body, would the body dare separate itself from the sufferings of the head? Suffer in Christ, for Christ, so to say, sinned in your weakness... Therefore the Lord's sufferings are our own sufferings.

Likewise on verse 22, 'Do not forsake me, Lord my God, do not depart from me', he comments, 'Let us speak in him, let us speak through him, for he himself is interceding for us.' And here he repeats his interpretation of 'the words of my offences' (Ps 21:2b) when he imagines Christ saying, 'These words in the person of a sinner have been transformed into myself.'[46]

In all, the common tradition of interpreting some of the verses of Psalm 37 as spoken by Christ with reference to his Passion gave two of the Fathers, St Augustine and Hesychius of Jerusalem, a basis on which to construct a Christological interpretation of the whole psalm, not omitting its expressions of guilt and penitence. Christ, though not himself a sinner, takes on himself the sins of the members of his body, and pleads to his Father on their behalf, not as if he were interceding for other persons, separate from himself, but in virtue of his identification with them. Although Augustine expresses the theme more fully and more eloquently than Hesychius, the lesser writer, it is Hesychius alone who offers a Christological exegesis of every detail of the psalm, and it is Hesychius who expresses in a single sentence the full bearing of this line of interpretation: 'Christ assumed our rebuke and correction, he himself both rebuking and being rebuked, rebuking as God and being rebuked on our behalf as man, uniting each role, both of the rebuker and the rebuked.' This is closely paralleled by a passage of Augustine in a different part of his great work on the psalms: 'Our Lord Jesus Christ the Son of God prays *for* us, and prays *in* us, and is prayed to *by* us: he prays for us as our priest, he prays in us as our head, he is prayed to by us as our God.'[47] If Christ is indeed both the utterer of the prayers of the Psalter and the recipient

---

[45] Augustine, *En. in ps.* 37. 16, CCSL 38. 394.
[46] Ibid. 37. 27, CCSL 38. 400.
[47] Ibid. 85. 1, CCSL 39. 1176.

of the prayers of the Psalter, we may recognize his voice throughout the entire book.[48]

Admittedly none of the Fathers, not even Augustine, were so single-minded as to interpret each one of the psalms as addressed by Christ to Christ. Priority was given to the traditional attribution of the psalms to King David, as our representative and model. But what avail would David's prayers have had, what hope would there be for us, if Christ did not adopt our prayers in his humanity and present them to his Godhead? Let us conclude by listening again to Augustine, commenting this time on the last of the penitential psalms (Psalm 142):[49]

> So our Lord Jesus Christ is both head and body. The one who deigned to die for us willed also to speak in us, for he has made us his members. Accordingly he sometimes speaks in the person of his members, and sometimes in his own person, as our head. He has something to say without us, but without him we cannot say anything...
>
> It is not we who are the Word, it is not we who in the beginning were God with God, it is not we who are the one through whom all things were made. But when we proceed to the flesh, there both he and we ourselves are Christ. Let us therefore not be surprised by the psalms. For he utters many things in the person of the head and many things in the person of the members; yet all of it is uttered as though one person were speaking. Do not be surprised that there are two with one voice, if there are two in one flesh.

St Augustine is the most consistently Christological of the commentators on the Psalter, but he does not weary his reader by repeating this theme on every page. In this passage he reminds us, however, that even where it is undoubtedly we ourselves who are speaking, it is Christ, speaking in his members and on behalf of his members, who alone gives us the right to recite the psalms with confidence, as we turn in supplication to our heavenly Father through the one mediator between God and men.

---

[48] To avoid Nestorianism, the relation between the Christ who prays and the Christ who is prayed to must be conceived as an interior dialogue, within the one person and hypostasis of the Word incarnate. When Christ prays, God prays to God in him. Hesychius himself was a fierce opponent of Nestorianism; see *ACO*, 4.1, pp. 90,22–91,3.

[49] Augustine, *En. in ps.* 142. 3, CCSL 40, 2061–2, CSEL 95/5, 52–4.

Bibliography

Borgomeo, Pasquale (1972), *L'Église de ce temps dans la prédication de Saint Augustin* (Paris).

Braun, Oskar (1901), 'Ein Brief des Katholikos Timotheos I über biblische Studien des 9 Jahrhunderts', *Oriens Christianus* 1, 299–313.

Devreesse, Robert (1924) 'La chaine sur les psaumes de Daniele Barbaro', *RBib* 33, 65–81, 198–521.

Devreesse, Robert (1928) 'Chaines exégétiques grecques', *Dictionnaire de la Bible, Supplément* 1, 1084–1233.

Fiedrowicz, Michael (1997), *Psalmus vox totius Christi: Studien zu Augustins "Enarrationes in Psalmos"* (Freiburg).

Fischer, Balthasar (1951) 'Le Christ dans les Psaumes: La dévotion aux Psaumes dans l'Église des Martyrs', *La Maison-Dieu* 27, 86–113.

Fischer, Balthasar (1974) '*Psalmus vox Christi patientis* selon l'Épître à Marcellinus de S. Athanase', in Charles Kannengiesser, ed., (1974) *Politique et Théologie chez Athanase d'Alexandrie* (Paris), 305–11.

Jungmann, J.A. (1965) *The Place of Christ in Liturgical Prayer* (London).

Kirchmeyer, Jean (1968) 'Hésychius de Jérusalem', *Dictionnaire de Spiritualité* 7, 399–408.

Rondeau, M.J. (1968) 'L'Épître à Marcellinus sur les Psaumes', *Vigiliae Christianae* 22, 176–97.

Sieben, H.J. (1973) 'Athanasius über den Psalter: Analyse seines Briefes an Marcellinus', *Zeitschrift für Theologie und Philosophie* 48, 157–73.

Young, Frances (1997), *Biblical Exegesis and the Formation of Christian Culture* (Cambridge).

ROWAN WILLIAMS

CHRISTOLOGICAL EXEGESIS OF PSALM 45

The importance of the psalms in shaping the earliest theological reflections about the nature of Jesus Christ is a subject that deserves full length treatment in its own right (and further discussion will be found in other contributions to this volume); the present essay seeks only to illustrate this by a brief examination of some of the uses of one particular psalm. But this specific text in fact allows some interesting questions to be raised about the general assumptions governing the exegesis of the Psalter, and makes clear the complexities that could arise in relation to this. As we trace the ways in which elements of this text are deployed and argued over, especially in the seminal period of theological development in the Eastern Mediterranean from Origen to Athanasius, we can see how questions belonging to a traditional mode of 'grammatical' interpretation provided the basis for a more strictly theological argument, which had major significance for the finalising of orthodox Christology in the patristic era.

Psalm 45 – 44 in the LXX – first appears as a Christological proof-text in the opening chapter of Hebrews, as part of the lengthy demonstration that the Son is not to be numbered among the angels:

> About the angels, he says: *he makes his angels winds and his servants flames of fire*, but to his [sic; the possessive is not in the Greek] Son he says: *God, your throne shall last for ever and ever;* and: *his royal sceptre is the sceptre of virtue; virtue you love as much as you hate wickedness. This is why God, your God, has anointed you with the oil of gladness, above all your rivals* (Heb. 1:8–9, citing Ps 45:6–7).

The writer to the Hebrews has already, at the beginning of his catena of texts (a catena heavily dominated by the psalms), identified the speaker simply as 'God', a distinctive habit found throughout the epistle where prophetic quotations were adduced. Westcott, in his commentary on

Hebrews,[1] noted long ago that this usage was peculiar to Hebrews: else-where in the New Testament, we can find reference to named prophets or to 'scripture' in general, but not to God alone, with no reference to the human author. And while other passages in Hebrews refer to 'the Holy Spirit' as the speaker of quoted prophecies, and two passages (both related to quotations from the Psalter) identify the speaker as Christ, the catena in the first chapter is by implication referred to *ho theos* as the subject of the opening sentence. The psalm text as quoted is from the LXX, which preserves the ambiguity of the Hebrew as to whether the repeated *ho theos* of the quotation is vocative or not – i.e. whether we should render, 'God, your throne shall last for ever' and 'O God, this is why your God has anointed you' or 'God is your throne / Your throne is God [or 'like that of God'], enduring for ever' and 'This is why God, your God, has anointed you.' There is no obvious way of deciding this in the context of the epistle, though there has been a tendency to treat the first as vocative, but not the second. In the context of Hebrews, the difference to the argument is negligible. The issues become a little more complicated in some later exegetical contexts, as we shall see.

But it seems that the identification of the speaker as 'God' began to set the agenda quite early on for a more extended – and contested – theological discussion; which, incidentally, tells against the assump-tion that premodern exegesis was *systematically* atomistic. When Origen discusses the psalm in his *Commentary on John*, he refers to the 'majority reading'[2] of the opening verse – 'My heart has brought forth [lit. 'belched' in the Greek] a good word' – as being that the words are spoken by God the Father. Origen has already[3] recorded his unease about the conventional exegesis, which in his view risks reduc-ing the Logos to the status simply of an impersonal communication, something brought out for particular purposes from an undifferenti-ated internal divine unity, and thus failing to treat him as having a proper *hypostasis* of his own. Thus he argues here that if we take *logos* in an apparently 'plain' sense to mean only an utterance, we ought to be taking *kardia* in an equally plain (i.e. physical) sense – which is absurd. We know that the heart must rather be interpreted as the eter-nal 'intellectual and universally providential [*prothetike*] power' and so

---

[1] Westcott (1903), 476 ff
[2] Preuschen (1903), 50.9–11
[3] *Commentary* I.24 (Preuschen (1903), 29.21–26)

we should be able to take *logos* as that which actively 'proclaims' this interior power and communicates it,[4] not merely as a passive medium for the manifestation of God's thoughts. This comes towards the end of a sustained argument about the nature of the divine Logos as that which communicates to us the mind of the Father, externalising in the plurality of creation the eternal unity of immanent divine rationality. In a passage which is bound to strike the contemporary reader as faintly comic,[5] Origen solemnly explains the appropriateness of the image of 'belching' as a discontinuous release of hidden wind; perhaps not the most elegant way of characterising the distinction between first and second divine principles as that between unity and a plurality which is, so to speak, an ordered fragmentation of that unity, but undoubtedly an ingenious justification of a vulgar metaphor to the cultivated sceptic of his day.

However, Origen goes on to query whether this is the only or the best way of reading the opening verse. It is perfectly possible, he says, to accept the majority verdict on who the speaker is in this verse; but the rest of the psalm still gives us some grounds for uncertainty. The psalmist refers to God the Father in the third person later on ('God, your God, has anointed you…') in a way which sits oddly with the assumption that the Father is the speaker. While there are passages which still suggest a direct address on the part of God, it may be better to accept that there are often 'changes of person' in the text of the psalms,[6] rather than looking for complete consistency. It would make equal sense of the opening verse, Origen argues, to think of the prophet being unable to hold back the utterance of a 'good word' about Christ through his prophecy.[7] Origen makes a point of this presumably because of what he sees as the risks of the prevailing exegesis in weakening the sense of a genuine subsistent reality in the Logos. We shall see in due course how this bears on the controversies of the later third and fourth centuries. Origen's rather caustic comment that the text is quoted freely by people who 'use it as if they had understood it'[8]

---

[4] Preuschen (1903), 49.31–33

[5] Preuschen (1903), 50.2–9

[6] Preuschen (1903), 50.28. On the whole question of 'person-exegesis', that aspect of grammatical and rhetorical criticism in the ancient world which sought to clarify who was speaking and to whom in any particular text, Drobner (1986) is helpful as regards the theological context.

[7] Preuschen (1903), 50.13–17

[8] Preuschen (1903), 49.22

makes it pretty clear that he has concerns about the possible implications of what 'the majority' say about the verse, and so what he does
is to outline a way in which we *might* accept that the Father is the
speaker in the opening verse without getting entangled in errors about
the impersonality of the divine Word.

Presumably the 'majority reading' owes something to the fact that
words later in the psalm are directly attributed to God by the writer *ad
Hebraeos* (indeed, the very words which Origen himself thinks *cannot*
be rightly ascribed to God).[9] Origen's final position appears to be a
caution against the mistaken hermeneutical principle that the psalms
are spoken in only one voice. He is insisting, in other words, that the
key principles of proper classical rhetorical interpretation should be
applied in scriptural exegesis, including the capacity to ask questions
about *prosopoi* in a text: whose voice is this? to whom addressed? about
whom spoken? And if we turn to his other discussion of the psalm
in the *Commentary on John*, we can see how significant the point is.
This discussion is in fact a few pages earlier in the *Commentary*,[10] and
focuses on v.8 ('Virtue you love as much as you hate wickedness...').
Here Origen begins by noting that the language of the psalm presupposes that something has changed; an event has occurred which
brings about what was not true before. Anointing denotes a change of
status, to become a king or priest; so if this is addressed to the Son (as
Hebrews tells us), does this mean that kingship cannot be *sumphues*
for him, something tied up with his very nature? And how can the Son
'love' justice when he himself *is* justice (Origen will doubtless have in
mind here Paul's language associating Christ with the righteousness of
God or from God, as in 1 Cor. 1:30). The answer is that he is 'anointed'
as man, in respect of his *psuche*; the text refers to the mutable and vulnerable part of his non-material being, which is endowed with kingship by God's perfect indwelling.[11] This reading is reinforced by appeal
to Ps 72:1 ('God, give your own *krima* [judgement] to the king, your
own righteousness to the royal son'): in this case, the king is the Son
to whom God commits authority for judgement, and the Son in turn
bestows righteousness upon *his* 'son', the human individuality united
to the Logos in the incarnation. Royalty belongs to the Son in eternity
but is something realised in time by the outpouring of divine power

[9] Preuschen (1903), 50.19ff
[10] *Commentary* I.28
[11] Preuschen (1903), 35.32–35

upon the human nature assumed by the Son. The model of union between the Logos and humanity that is realised in Jesus is the destiny of all human *psuchai*, if they are obedient in their intellectual nature to the rule or kingship of the Word.[12]

Origen thus uses the psalm to support his – at that point novel – account of the incarnation in terms of the union of the eternal Logos with frail and mutable human nature through the mediation of the Spirit in which all who are being saved partake (in virtue of the *nous*, the spiritual intellect, within them). The important point in relation to the exegesis of this psalm is, again, the careful use of 'person-exegesis' to clarify the theological question. The tension in the psalm between the reference to the everlasting (therefore unchanging) throne of God which belongs to the Son and the apparently temporal nature of the kingship for which the Son is anointed is a particularly clear invitation in Origen's intellectual world to distinguish different *personae*. As we have seen, he is very wary of a use of the opening verses to suggest some sort of modalism; and his discussion of the 'exaltation' verse (v.7) strengthens the same case in that it presupposes the eternal existence of that primary contemplator of the divine mystery who is the Logos, and who then acts, as a distinct *hypostasis*, to transfigure the created spirit animating the soul and body we call Jesus of Nazareth so as to re-establish the possibility for created spirits to triumph in and over soul and body.

However, Origen's incarnational scheme remained an idiosyncracy, poorly understood and not generally supported; which meant that no steady state had been reached in the reading of this psalm, and in the generations after his death it became more than ever a contested text. Although this has not generally been recognised, it is surely overwhelmingly likely that Paul of Samosata has in mind the same (v.7) of our psalm when he discusses who or what is properly to be called 'anointed' in one of the fragments reliably ascribed to him: the Word cannot be anointed, he insists, it is 'the one from Nazareth' who is anointed; the Logos, as he says in another fragment, remains 'above'.[13] The form of the argument is close to the way Origen approaches the question in the John Commentary, underlining the eternal and immutable status of the Logos; what is different is that Paul does not apparently have the complex metaphysical structure developed by Origen.

---

[12] Preuschen (1903), 36.7–17

[13] For the relevant texts, see Bardy (1929), 137–138, 153 and 186, particularly the last on the identity of the 'anointed'.

Thus his reading of the psalm, if that is what it is, is more nakedly 'dualist' in its clear separation of Logos and human individual.

That being said, it does throw some light on the problem of why, at the beginning of the fourth century, Origen appears to have been associated in the minds of some in the Syrian and Palestinian churches with a theology uncomfortably close to Paul's, so much so that he needed to be defended from charges of failing to ascribe a sufficiently distinct existence to the Logos. The *Defence of Origen* composed by Pamphilus early in the fourth century attempts to answer those who accused the Alexandrian of teaching that the Son was 'ungenerated' and that he came forth from the Father simply as an emanation (*prolatio* in Rufinus' translation, our only witness to the text of Pamphilus though, as I have argued at length elsewhere,[14] a very unreliable one in important respects). Behind these charges we can discern an anxiety that Origen's stress on the coeternity of Father and Logos threatened either to posit a second *agennetos* reality in heaven, a 'twin brother' to God's absolute self-subsistence – which would be a logical and theological monstrosity – or to absorb the Logos into the being of the Father. We know from Methodius (not to mention Eusebius of Caesarea, Eusebius of Nicomedia and Arius himself) how strong the objections to the 'two *agenneta*' model were in the theology of the period, and how easily some aspects of Origen's thought could be prayed in support of the objectionable doctrine.[15] Likewise we know that concerns were around in relation to the use of impersonal imagery for the generation of the Logos, evoking for many the spectre of a series of Valentinian emanations from a remote divine source.

The paradox is that Origen himself, in the exegetical texts we have been looking at, specifically foresees and answers these anxieties. His hesitation about the 'majority reading' of Ps 45:1 rests precisely on the risks of some sort of emanation language creeping in to Trinitarian theology; but it may be that his grudging acceptance of this interpretation as possible, combined with the strongly dualist theology in his reading of v.7, encouraged prejudiced critics in the first decade of the fourth century to link his exegesis of the psalm with that of Paul of Samosata, thus providing at least one quite specific and concrete item upon which to base charges against Origen of a kind of Trinitarian monism, in which the second person is understood as less than fully

---

[14] Williams (1993)

[15] Williams (1983), 66–81, outlines some of the issues here; and cf. Williams (2001a), 167 ff.

distinct in eternal subsistence. If we are right to see in the surviving fragments of Paul traces of an interpretation of Ps 45, using the same 'person-exegesis' questions as Origen, it would not be difficult to associate the two.[16] Whether Paul himself was aware of Origen's interpretation, it is impossible to say – but I think it is, all things considered, not that unlikely.

It seems, then, that the interpretation of Ps 45 may have become, by AD 300, a significant element in the theological dispute that was steadily boiling up towards the crisis that finally broke around the figure of Arius. A reading of the opening verse which reinforced a strongly monist Trinitarian doctrine, with the Logos remaining in some sense 'internal' to the Father prior to the incarnation, led Origen to express misgivings about it – misgivings which, interestingly, prompt him also to note the need for caution in handling the *personae* of the psalms. But he also lends his authority to a reading of v.7 which, in establishing a radical division between the eternal and unchanging divine subject (the Logos, who cannot be literally anointed because anointing creates a new status, and he is immutable) and the human subject who is vulnerable to change, tends towards the sort of Christology which is normally stigmatised as 'teaching two Christs'.[17] Like the impersonal account of the Logos, this is popularly associated with Gnosticism. Paul of Samosata was understood (rightly or wrongly) as combining such a dualist Christology with an impersonal view of the Logos, and a theological public in West Asia still concerned to avoid 'Valentinian' emanationism and to assert the distinctness of the Logos as a subject could very easily have been brought to read Origen through the lens of Paul of Samosata. Hence the need for Pamphilus' defence of Origen's stout pluralism in Trinitarian theology.

There is one more intriguing hint of theological dispute over the opening of Ps 45 in one of Arius' letters in the early days of the controversy (depending on varying theories about the overall dating of the controversy, written either in 318 or 321/2). Here Arius, having laid out his objections to the theology of his bishop, Alexander, implies that doctrine such as Alexander's is as bad as that of teachers like 'Philogonius, Hellanikos and Makarios, those untutored heretics, one saying that the Son is an "eructation" [*eruge*] or an "emanation" [*probole*], another

---

[16] Williams (1993), 158–62

[17] Stead (1976) notes some of the ways in which this theme arises in Athanasius' writing; also Williams (2001b), 333–34.

that he is an ungenerated being alongside the Father [*sunagennetos*]'.[18] The reference to 'eructation' can hardly be accidental in this context; Arius appears to be at one with Origen in suspecting the old 'majority reading' of Ps 45:1 as an utterance of God the Father. The Philogonius mentioned here was bishop of Antioch, and it is safe to assume that he was close to those, like his successor Eustathius, who favoured or were seen as favouring a somewhat more 'monistic' approach to the Trinity; it would not be surprising if he had adopted the sort of reading of the psalm with which Origen is so unhappy.

That Ps 45 was disputed territory in the early days of the controversy over Arius, we know from Bishop Alexander's famous letter to Alexander of Byzantium (probably a little earlier than Arius' letter to Eusebius, though some still date it to a later stage in the struggle, perhaps to 324). Along with texts from the gospels implying human weakness on the part of the incarnate Word, and what is probably the most discussed text in the whole controversy, Prov 8:22, Alexander claims that Ps 45:7 was used by Arius and his supporters to argue for divine status being a *gift* to the Logos rather than an innate dignity.[19] It is not clear from this text whether Arius went on to argue that if the Logos has *metochoi*, companions, rivals, fellows, then the Logos must be one among many sharing (*metechon*) an identical nature, and so must be created; but this seems to have been brought into the discussion at some stage. When, some decades later, Athanasius unleashes his formidable polemical armoury against the 'Arians' in his *orationes*, the exegesis of Ps 45, especially v.7, is the focus of a lengthy and very sophisticated discussion,[20] and the point about participated natures has obviously arisen.

The psalm did not play quite such a major role as the famous text from Proverbs, but it is clear that it posed some of the most challenging questions to what was to become the Nicene party. The text appeared to declare that the Son was the recipient rather than the source of grace and (so Athanasius presents the argument) that he therefore shared with the rest of creation a nature capable of change. It is important, as several commentators have noted, not to take either Alexander or Athanasius entirely at face value when they ascribe to Arius and his followers a clear-cut doctrine of election or promotion of the Logos

---

[18] PG 42. 212A

[19] PG 82. 893A

[20] *orationes contra Arianos* I.46-52, PG 26. 105B–121B.

to the status and title of Son on the basis of moral attainment as we might normally understand it;[21] certainly there are no signs of Arius believing in such a promotion on the grounds of the moral excellence of the *human* will in Jesus. As far as we can discern, Arius held that divine honour was bestowed 'proleptically' on the Logos because of his eternally foreseen fidelity to the praise and contemplation of the Father.[22] But Alexander and Athanasius would not have expended so much trouble on the interpretation of Ps 45 if the text had not been used in controversy by real opponents. We must assume that Arius and others used it primarily to stress that the Logos' nature was in principle changeable; and the interpretation of *metochoi* was evidently a key point in establishing that the Logos could not be divine, since the divine nature is *ametochos*, incapable of being shared with any other. Athanasius's task, then, is to explain both the language of anointing in return for fidelity to righteousness and the word *metochoi*.

On this latter, Athanasius turns the flank ingeniously.[23] *Metochoi* is the designation for all who have participation *in* the Logos or Son. The word designates created things in general, and humans in particular – all beings that exist in virtue of their participation in the Father's rationality through the involvement of the eternal Logos in creation, and most especially those who are made holy by the Spirit of Christ. If the psalmist speaks of creatures participating in the Son, the Son quite clearly belongs to a different order of reality. And while Arius elsewhere seems to have argued that the Logos enjoyed divinity by participating in the Father's wisdom (not the Father's substance – i.e. he has a limited and derivative share in one of the Father's active attributes but no more), Athanasius, by identifying the Father's wisdom with the person of the Logos, rules out any such scheme. The Son is not 'one of those who partake' in divine activity, he *is* divine activity in substantive form, and we have our limited share in divine activity by his gift.

It is a bold exegetical move, exploiting the bewildering ambiguity of *metechein* and its derivatives (though in the context of the psalm text, it is hard to believe that any other sense than the simple one of 'companions' was originally intended – as the sense of the Hebrew

---

[21] The case for Arius as a kind of adoptionist was set out very fully by Gregg and Groh (1981), but criticised by Williams (2001a), 19–20 and Hanson (1988), 97–98, among others.

[22] This phraseology is used by Athanasius, *de decretis* 6, PG 25. 425D.

[23] PG 26. 105C–108A

original dictates);[24] and it allows Athanasius to launch into a further interpretative *tour de force* in dealing with the language of anointing. Anointing – as we saw in Origen's argument – normally indicates a change in status, becoming king or priest, and this is impossible for the Logos. But the Logos, as source of the anointing that makes us holy through the gift of the Spirit, is said in Scripture (Jn 17:18) to make himself holy so that we may be made holy. In the incarnation, the Son bestows upon the human nature assumed by him the grace that *all* human nature requires; his anointed or sanctified humanity becomes the instrument whereby anointing and sanctification can be communicated to the rest of us.[25] As Athanasius memorably puts it, we can imagine the Son saying: 'I give my Spirit to myself', so that the Spirit may be given to us.[26] The anointing is not in this instance therefore a change of status: it is the 'oil of gladness' that is mentioned rather than the anointing that simply establishes a new dignity. And this oil of gladness is manifestly the Spirit, poured out by the incarnate Word onto his human and material being, his 'flesh'. In this light, other texts (Is. 61:1, Acts 10:38) mentioning the anointing of Jesus can be read in an acceptable sense.[27]

Athanasius continues with another flank-turning exercise. *If* the Logos did not enjoy an eternal kingly dignity and power, the 'Arians' would perhaps have a point; but precisely the text they want to use to support such a view has already ruled it out, because the psalmist has just affirmed that the Messiah's throne is God's everlasting throne; QED.[28] This can admit of no promotion or advance to glory; glory is the eternal birthright of the Son, as in Phil 2. The only transformation involved in the whole story of our salvation is the transformation of our humanity – the 'garment' taken on by the Logos; which is why the psalmist goes on immediately to speak of the Messiah's garments as scented with myrrh and aloes, as if foreshadowing the anointing of the suffering human body of the Messiah by Mary and Nicodemus.[29] It is a powerful poetic turn to the interpretation of the psalm, introducing a quite new motif, but one that admirably fills out Athanasius's general theological point. This general argument is hammered home further,

---

[24] The Hebrew *chaber* refers simply to companions or 'peers'.

[25] PG 26. 108B–112A

[26] PG 26. 108B–C

[27] PG 26. 109A

[28] PG 26. 110B–C

[29] PG 26. 112A

as Athanasius evokes the pattern of giving and receiving spelled out in the Fourth Gospel: Jesus receives glory from the Father so as to give it to his disciples, the glory he has already eternally received from the Father and which, with the Father, he now gives to himself as a human being.[30]

What about the connecting 'therefore' in the psalm? Does this not indicate a sequence of cause and effect, virtue pursued and then divinely rewarded? No, because the word 'therefore' simply means that the reason for the incarnate Son's reception of the sanctifying Spirit is that only through this means could that Spirit be conveyed to us.[31] The sequence of the psalm is not a story about created ascent to heaven but divine descent: first we are reminded that the Son's throne is eternal; then – *therefore* – since none but the eternal king can bestow holiness on created beings, the Son grants the anointing of holiness to the human body he assumes. The narrative of Ps 45 turns out to be identical to that of Phil 2, which, of course, Athanasius has just discussed at length in the preceding section of *contra Arianos* I.[32] Ps 45 is about the self-emptying of the creator for the sake of the divinisation, through the Holy Spirit, of created beings. The love of justice or virtue and hatred of wickedness spoken of by the psalmist must be read as affirming the eternal *natural* virtue and justice of God the Son (and a number of scriptural texts, some from elsewhere in the Psalter, are adduced in support of this): God does not love justice in the sense that he prefers it over wickedness, chooses it as against an alternative.[33] The Son as perfect image of the Father has the identical and unchangeable love that the Father has towards the Good; by his incarnation, he condemns wickedness and embodies a stable love for the Good that allows mortals to be rescued from their own spiritual instability.[34]

Thus the argument of the contested seventh verse of the psalm for Athanasius is this: the Son shares the royal state of God in eternity and thus shares God's immutable love for the Good – which is the ground of his incarnation, through which he, as incarnate, receives the anointing of the Spirit in his human form so that other humans may also receive the Spirit. It is a brilliantly comprehensive reversal of an

---

[30] PG 26. 114A
[31] PG 26. 114B–117B
[32] Chs 37-45
[33] PG 26.120B–C
[34] PG 26.120C–121A

opponent's argument that would have referred the text to some kind of sustained effort of contemplation and virtue on the part of a heavenly Logos who is not fully divine. Athanasius, as so often, salvages elements of Origenian exegesis to shape a middle way between Trinitarian pluralism and monism, insisting on the distinctness of the Logos as *eikon* and receiver of glory from the Father, but also his unqualified unity with the eternal divine action and status, his share in divine 'royalty' and all that it means.[35] And he offers an unprecedentedly thorough account of how the eternal nature of the Logos and the Logos' relation with Father and Spirit becomes the foundation for the pattern of human redemption and sanctification; one of the most striking features of his interpretation is the prominence given to the transformative work of the Spirit and the relation between the Spirit's role in the Son's incarnate life and how the Spirit works in the baptised.

If we try to identify what general insights emerge from this small slice of exegetical history, the first is probably the simple recognition, already touched upon above, that patristic exegesis of the Psalter, and by implication of other texts, is not always as insensitive to wider literary context as it is often assumed to be. Both Origen and Athanasius in their different ways attempt to interpret a problematic text by looking at what comes before and after. Origen registers his doubts about the ascription of Ps 45:1 to God the Father by noting the problems this would create in reading later verses of the psalm; but he simultaneously allows that diverse readings are possible so long as we allow that there may be changes of *persona* in the text. He treats the Psalter, in other words, as a dramatic text, not as a collage of undifferentiated prophecies. Athanasius, focusing on v.7, is able to refer both to the implication of the opening verse (where he evidently does not share Origen's scruples)[36] and to the necessary connection between the reference to the Logos as sharing God's throne and the subsequent language about the anointing of the Logos: if he shares an eternal throne, then any interpretation of v.7 that ascribes change to the Logos is indefensible. It is a minor point in some ways, but a helpful corrective to what can be a caricature of patristic exegesis. The appeal to the traditional skills of person-exegesis does enforce a reading that is

---

[35] For a thorough and sympathetic survey of what is distinctive about Athanasius' Trinitarian theology, Behr (2004), 231–249, is particularly valuable.

[36] He consistently ascribes the opening verse to 'the Father'; see, e.g. PG 25. 453B, 513B, as well as the uses in the *orations*; though he can at least once ascribe it simply to David, in his *apologia pro fuga sua*, PG 25. 669B.

more than atomistic. There is a recognisable sense of working with a complex literary unit.

Much more significant, however, is the way in which this literary flexibility increasingly works with, shapes and supports what was to be both a crucial and controversial element in the evolution of classical Christology. The danger of the psalm being used to support a monistic view of God and a consequently impersonal doctrine of the Logos means that there is an interest in how the text speaks to and about the Logos as a separate subject; but this language is itself problematic in ascribing to the Logos what seems to be a change of status or dignity, *prima facie* in relation to changes or developments in the Logos' own life. Both Origen and Athanasius insist on a distinction between what is said of the Logos as such and what is said of the incarnate vehicle of the Logos' identity. We are on the way to the debates around the separate assignment of biblical texts to the Logos and the *anthropos* which focused the disagreements between the Antiochene theologians and their Alexandrian critics in the fifth century (though as a rhetorical trope, the issue is already present in Gregory Nazianzen). That there has to be some sense in which the humanity is object and the Logos subject of certain actions within the incarnate reality is beyond question; how this is to be phrased without compromising the union ('teaching two Christs') is a challenge. Athanasius rises to the challenge in a particularly interesting way by connecting the question to the whole biblical theme of the Spirit's work in and through the incarnate, and develops a strongly Johannine account of the inseparability of the work of the Son in the incarnation and the action of the Spirit in sanctifying the humanity assumed by the Son. Athanasius' greatest contribution to the development of Trinitarian theology is perhaps his new stress on the Trinity as united in *act*; and this exegetical foray is a notably vivid illustration of the biblical foundations for such a perspective.

Finally, there is a still deeper exegetical issue never raised in explicit terms in these discussions but beginning to be recognised – the issue so richly developed in Augustine's interpretation of the Psalter.[37] The words of the Psalter are, as Scripture, the utterance of God; yet they are simultaneously words addressed *to* God. We have to find a way of making sense of the fact that God speaks to us in revelation through what human beings say not only about him

---

[37] Cameron (1999) is a very good orientation to Augustine's exegesis of the psalms; see also Williams (2004).

but to him – including their words of protest or doubt. Augustine famously resolves this in the *enarrationes in psalmos* by an incarnational hermeneutic: God the Son in assuming humanity assumes all that humanity says to God, making his own even the cries of pain and doubt uttered by humans, so as to show that the transforming grace of God can work in situations of the gravest human extremity. Revelation in the words of Scripture does not come simply in the words we consider edifying and positive. And because the Son is eternally turned towards the Father in adoration and self-offering, what humans say can be taken up in that movement towards the Source of all, can become part of what the Son 'says' to the Father and so brought into the reality which alone can heal and unite the fractured voices of creation.

Our earlier exegetes have no such comprehensive framework, but the Christology emerging in their work, especially in Athanasius, lays some of the foundation for this. The incarnation brings into being a humanity equipped to speak to God the Father without obstacle or distraction; and to the extent that Scripture is the written witness to the incarnation above all, it is created speech taken up by an uncreated speaker to proclaim unchanging truth. The incarnation is the key to how and why God reveals himself in human words. But this means that the essential drama embodied in the language of Scripture is a story of how humanity is 'activated' by the Word of God, the Son of God, so as to become capable of bearing the divine agency – and so, as we noted earlier, a story in which God is the primary agent. Scripture, including and in some sense especially the Psalter as a text of variegated human outcry to God, embodies the process in which the gift of the Spirit to humanity, the anointing of humanity for its proper dignity, is realised. To distinguish adequately between what is said in God's person in Scripture and what is said in the person of humanity is precisely not to set up a division between holy and revealing words from God and words expressing the weakness of mortal humanity. It is to understand that Scripture is itself inseparably the record of the steady fusion of the one with the other, the drawing throughout sacred history of the utterances of human beings into the eternal work of divine speech and divine gift. It is so because of the single focal point where the voices are in practice and in action one, the person of the incarnate Word.

The wrestling with the sometimes intractable complications of ancient texts so as to bring this into focus does not issue, in an Origen or an Athanasius, in a neat theory of scriptural inspiration; but to watch them in this struggle is to see how the central point gradually emerges with greater and greater clarity. God speaks to us in human words, including the words he gives to human beings to speak to him, so that we may speak with ever fuller boldness to him; and he is able to do this because he is himself eternally a pattern of relation in which that which is spoken, the Word, is also the speaker of love and adoration towards its Source. Into that eternal communication we are brought by grace, and anointed with the Son's anointing. Andrew Louth wrote memorably many years ago that 'the heart of Scripture is the end of Scripture: the love of God in Christ calling us to respond to that love'.[38] In studying this particular bit of the history of interpretation, I hope that this will indeed be what comes to light as the heart of the reading undertaken by the Fathers.

Bibliography

Bardy, Gustave (1929), *Paul de Samosate. Etude historique*, 2nd ed. (Louvain).

Behr, John (2004), *The Formation of Christian Theology, vol 2. The Nicene Faith, Part 1* (Crestwood, NY)

Cameron, Michael (1999), '*Enarrationes in psalmos*', Alan Fitzgerald, ed., *Augustine Through the Ages: An Encyclopaedia* (Grand Rapids, MI), 290–306.

Drobner, Hubertus (1986), *Person-Exegese und Christologie bei Augustinus. Zur Herkunft der Formel Una Persona* (Leiden).

Gregg, Robert C. and Groh, Dennis E (1981), *Early Arianism. A View of Salvation* (London).

Hanson, Richard P.C. (1988), *The Search for the Christian Doctrine of God. The Arian Controversy,318-381* (Edinburgh).

Louth, Andrew (1981), *Discerning the Mystery. An Essay on the Nature of Theology* (Oxford).

Preuschen, Erwin, ed. (1903), *Origenes Werke. Vierter Band. Der Johanneskommentar*, GCS (Leipzig).

Stead, G. Christopher (1976), 'Rhetorical Method in Athanasius', *VC* 30, 121–37.

Westcott, Brooke Foss (1903), *The Epistle to the Hebrews. The Greek Text with Notes and Essays* (London).

Williams, Rowan (1983), 'The Logic of Arianism', *JTS* n.s. 34, 56–81.

---

[38] Louth (1981), 131.

— (1993), '*Damnosa Haereditas:* Pamphilus' Apology and the Reputation of Origen', Hans Christof Brennecke, Ernst Ludwig Grasmuck, Christoph Markschies, eds., *Logos. Festschrift fur Luise Abramowski* (Berlin/New York).

— (2001a), *Arius. Heresy and Tradition,* 2nd ed. (London).

— (2001b), 'Defining Heresy', Alan Kreider , ed., *The Origins of Christendom in the West* (Edinburgh/New York), 313–335.

— (2004), 'Augustine and the Psalms', *Interpretation* 58, 17–27.

SARAH COAKLEY

ON THE FEARFULNESS OF FORGIVENESS: PSALM 130.4 AND ITS THEOLOGICAL IMPLICATIONS

Andrew Louth's contributions to the study of Greek patristic and Byzantine tradition have been marked by a close attention to textual detail, a remarkable interdisciplinary learning, and a rare spiritual insight. He has played an important role in the recent turn back to patristic biblical commentary as a source of doctrinal and spiritual insight, as well as of potential contemporary application. In this arena, the study of the psalms and their reception is a matter of almost paramount significance, as Louth's own work has demonstrated. The importance of such study applies as much to Jewish/Christian understanding as it does to the history of intra-Christian reception; and here too, in Jewish/Christian dialogue, Fr. Louth has been an active participant.

In what follows I offer to Andrew Louth as *Gratulieren* a short comparative study of the Jewish and Christian receptions of Ps. 130. 4, and argue for its significance in the problematic theological nexus of forgiveness – both human and divine. It would seem that on the topic of forgiveness we have an irretrievable divide between Christians and Jews, especially in a post-Holocaust era. However, it is argued in what I present here that a sensitive probing of the Jewish and Christian reception of this particular psalm verse ('For there is forgiveness with thee; therefore thou art to be feared') can excavate a surprising convergence of thought between Jews and Christians – one of considerable spiritual depth and contemporary theological significance.

Introduction: the impossibility of forgiveness

One does not have to go to Israel to learn that forgiveness is impossible: the evidence is everywhere to be seen – from the botched, if seemingly trivial, failures in our own familial or collegial relations through to the unspeakable recent horrors of genocide, terrorism, war and torture. But in Israel the pain of this impossibility is supremely acute and everywhere evident; and here no theological statement can be made on 'forgiveness' that is not simultaneously a political comment. In this paper, then, I shall be taking the *phenomenological* facts of this 'impossibility' of forgiveness as axiomatic, a strategy which initially may seem to fly in the face both of Jewish ritual practice and of Christian dominical command. I engage this strategy, however, deeply aware of the seeming impasse that often confronts post-holocaust Jewish/Christian discussion of 'forgiveness': Simon Wiesenthal's justly-famous *Sunflower* narrative (in both editions) has produced an array of Jewish responses that resist the human granting of forgiveness from anyone else but the victim, and Christian ones that enjoin it unconditionally.[1] The gulf seems fixed. I want to get behind this impasse – and this apparent Jewish/Christian divergence – in order to re-engage the deep theological insight that *only God forgives*; and to re-think that insight through the lens of divine 'fearfulness'.

To the modern Christian mind the conjunction may now seem odd – forgiveness and fearfulness – but I take my cue from the remarkable psalm verse, 130.4: 'For there is forgiveness with thee; *therefore* thou art to be feared' (כִּי־עִמְּךָ הַסְּלִיחָה לְמַעַן תִּוָּרֵא [*Kî-'immĕkā has-sĕlîḥā: lĕma'an tiwwārē'*]). What follows will in fact be my own selective *midrash* on this verse, a collocation of rabbinic, patristic and Reformation responses to its challenge which give the lie to the common suggestion that 'Jewish' and 'Christian' understandings of 'forgiveness' are somehow uncomplicatedly disjunctive. In fact both traditions contain internal tensions and also important points of contact. The systematic theological conclusion that will emerge is that there is a costly *chronology* of forgiveness (when rightly understood as divine prerogative), comprehended only in physically-enacted postures of awe and 'fear'; to know *divine* forgiveness is no less to know purgative terror. In short, for the phenomenological 'impossibility' of human forgiveness to be sublated, I must pass through a transformation well beyond that of a good-hearted *fiat* of the will, let alone of 'cheap grace', to what I might call the *ecstatic* dimension of forgiveness. I must, thereby, in some anticipatory sense, glimpse – eschatologically or christologically – the divine perspective of mercy itself.

---

[1] Wiesenthal (1997).

Psalm 130.4 and its interpreters, I: Jewish tradition

Let me start with a brief autobiographical aside, which may help to explain my own fascination with this topic. I well recall first learning to sing the psalms in Anglican chant when I was about twelve, and feeling the eerie shock, in the Psalter of *The Book of Common Prayer*, of this particular verse: 'For there is mercy with thee: *therefore* thou art to be feared'.[2] Why the 'therefore'?[3] From the perspective of a regnant modern political liberalism, forgiveness or mercy seemed properly associated with letting people off, even with a certain wimpishness – the very opposite, surely, of 'fearful' behaviour? The puzzle stayed with me. Later, when studying the psalms in Hebrew for Cambridge Tripos examinations, I discovered that the root of the noun 'forgiveness' here (סלח [*slḥ*]) is one of the few (like ברא [*br*], to create) reserved for G-d alone; it is, as Jacob Milgrom has put it recently (in his commentary on *Numbers*), 'exclusively a divine gift'. Milgrom goes on: 'Only God can be the subject of *salaḥ*, never man! Thus, the inherent parameters of this word set it apart from anthropopathic notions: It does not convey the pardon or forgiveness that man is capable of extending … Thus when God extends man His boon of *salaḥ*, He thereby indicates His desire for reconciliation with man in order to … maintain His covenant'.[4] The seemingly-equivalent verb root in Akkadian (*salāhu*), interestingly, means 'asperse' or 'sprinkle', the term often used in rituals of healing. Although the connection between the two verb roots remains speculative, it is at least intriguing that the Akkadian parallel is particularly associated

---

[2] This is Coverdale's translation, using the MT.

[3] In biblical Hebrew, the particle לְמַעַן, rendered here as 'therefore,' does possess multiple valences or shades of meaning, including its use as an introduction to purpose clauses - 'in order that,' 'so that.' The latter is indeed a common, even predominant, rendering of לְמַעַן, and one that could resolve something of the theological difficulty raised by Coverdale's translation. But I have chosen to take advantage of the particle's subtle ambiguity in an effort to grapple with that more difficult, theologically challenging reading. As Bruce K. Waltke and M. O'Connor observe, '[i]n Hebrew (as in many languages) expressions of purpose and consequence are not always readily distinguished; the precise sense of the relevant constructions and particles must be determined from context', Waltke and O'Connor (1990), 638. They go on to reference the study of לְמַעַן by Brongers (1973), 84-96, who 'suggests that *lm'n* introduces a result clause in a few cases (Lev 20:3, 2 Kgs 22:17, Amos 2:7; p. 89); he also notes that sometimes the particle is elliptical in sense and a paraphrase is necessary: "the consequence of which will be"' (Waltke and O'Connor (1990), 638-9, n. 25).

[4] Milgrom (1990), 395-6.

with purification or apotropaic protection.[5] But why then the link to 'fear', specifically?[6]

It should be noted, first, that the collocation of forgiveness/mercy and fear in the Hebrew Bible is by no means limited to this instance in Psalm 130. Perhaps the most striking parallel, semantically, is to be found in I Kings 8. 39-40: here, in Solomon's dedication prayer to G-d in the temple, the same logic of forgiveness and fear is enunciated: 'Then hear in heaven, your dwelling place, and forgive (וְסָלַחְתָּ [wĕ-sālaḥtā]) ... so that (לְמַעַן [lĕmaʿan]) they might fear you (יִרָאוּךָ [yirā'ûḵā]) ...'. In this instance, as in the psalm verse, the fear is *consequent* on the forgiveness, note, rather than a precondition of it. But we may also find instances of the opposite logic, where human fear *precedes* divine forgiveness (e.g., Ben Sirach 2. 7-11, 15-18); and we shall shortly discuss the important way in which the penitential rituals of the New Year and Day of Atonement were to spread out this second logic along a temporal chronology of annual transformation. Yet the former motif (more puzzling, as we have noted, to the liberal Christian), keeps us from any easy collapse of the conundrum into the idea that fear is *supplanted* by mercy. For behind both these variations, and one might say more fundamentally,[7] lies the central insistence of Exodus 34. 6-7 on the absolute metaphysical inseparability of divine mercy and judgment: 'The Lord, the Lord, a God merciful and gracious, slow to anger, and abounding in steadfast love and faithfulness ... forgiving (נוֹשֵׂא [nose']) iniquity and transgression and sin, yet by no means clearing the guilty, but visiting the iniquity of the parents upon the children and the children's children ...'

So central, in fact, is this idea of *simultaneous* divine threat and divine forgiveness, and so important for our own discussion systematically, that it is worth reflecting briefly on the rabbinic treatment of this

---

[5] Roth (1984), *ad loc.*

[6] The root ירא (as both noun and verb), when used with God as the explicit object or in the context of an encounter with the divine, is (notoriously) multivalent in biblical Hebrew, with meanings ranging from 'awe' and 'terror' (cf. Gen 28:17; Exod 3:6; Ps 33:8) to 'reverence' and even 'obedience' or 'right conduct' (cf. Gen 22:12; Prov 8:13; 16:6). Robert Murray, S.J., has suggested to me that the better, simpler reading of the verse (in accord with the NRSV) would be: 'But there is forgiveness with you, so that you may be *revered.*' But taking into account the possible ambiguity of ירא, for the purposes of this paper I would like to grapple with a more difficult, discomforting reading ('fear' or 'terror') and its theological implications.

[7] See Moberly (2002) 177-202, for a new exegesis of the centrality of Ex. 34. 6-7 for the future of 'biblical theology'.

theme before turning to the more specific history of Jewish interpretation of Psalm 130.4, to which it is intrinsically connected. Of immediate relevance is the Tannaitic saying in *Sifre* (on Deuteronomy) that '*Only in regard to God* do we find love combined with fear and fear combined with love'.[8] The exclusiveness of this statement is crucial: a lazy or careless extension of this principle to the human realm would be inherently idolatrous. In similar vein, *Midrash Rabbah* on Exodus (3. 14) famously expounds the mysterious and multi-faceted nature of the divine:

> R. Abba b. Mammel said: God said unto Moses: "Thou wishest to know My name. Well, I am called according to My work; sometimes I am called 'Almighty God', 'Lord of Hosts', 'God', 'Lord'. When I am judging created beings, I am called 'God', and when I am waging war against the wicked, I am called 'Lord of Hosts'. When I suspend judgment for a man's sins, I am called '*El Shadday*' (Almighty God), and when I am merciful towards My world, I am called '*Adonai*', for '*Adonai*' refers to the Attributes of Mercy, as it is said: *The Lord, the Lord* (Adonai, Adonai), *God, merciful and gracious* (Exodus 34.6). Hence *I AM THAT I AM* in virtue of my deeds."[9]

As Urbach charts in fascinating detail in *The Sages*, this theme of G-d's simultaneous judgment and mercy (associated with two different names, sometimes hypostasized) was worked out in complex multiple forms in the rabbinic period, not always consistently associating the different names with the different attributes,[10] and not always maintaining the absolute indissolubility of their conjunction.[11] Thus Urbach contrasts the view of Gamaliel, who 'incorporated the attribute of justice into that of compassion' (allowing the possibility of manipulating divine compassion by human compassionate behaviour), with the ingenious idea of the Amora R. Samuel bar Naḥman (that the divine attribute of justice could be *converted* into that of compassion); but he also compares both these opinions with the older, Tannaitic idea that the two divine attributes remain equal (and indeed are necessarily balanced in order that the creation may endure).[12] In

---

[8] Reuven (1986), 59 (Piska 32). My emphasis.

[9] Lehrman (1983), 64 (*Exodus Rabbah* III.6 *ad* Exod 3:14).

[10] Urbach (1979), 452-3, etc.

[11] Ibid, 464ff.

[12] Ibid, 456, 457, 459.

short, it is far from the case that this fundamental theme is consistently interpreted in the rabbinic discussion; but it is indisputable that it is re-visited constantly.

It is when we examine (against this broad background) the specific liturgies of repentance associated with the High Holy Days of *Rosh Hashana* and *Yom Kippur*, and the Ten Days of Repentance between them, that the history of the interpretation of Psalm 130.4 becomes particularly significant. The psalm is woven into the liturgies on both days.[13] And *prima facie* it would seem that the logic of fear *preceding* repentance is here given preeminent emphasis, and indeed is spread out chronologically through the intervening days of repentance. As we read in *Leviticus Rabbah* XXX. 7:

> ... on the eve of the New Year the leaders of the generation fast, and the Holy One, blessed be He, absolves them of a third of their iniquities. From New Year to the Day of Atonement private individuals fast, and the Holy One, blessed be He, absolves them of a third of their iniquities. On the Day of Atonement, everyone fasts, men, women, and children, and the Holy One, blessed be He, says to Israel: 'Let bygones be bygones; from now onwards we shall begin a new account'. ... R. Aḥa expounded: *For with Thee there is forgiveness* (Ps. CXXX, 4) signifies: forgiveness *waits* with thee from New Year. Why so long? *That Thou mayest be feared*; in order to impose Thy awe upon Thy creatures.[14]

It would seem, then, that the time-span of 'waiting' in 'fear' is the necessary *condition* of the coming of divine forgiveness: 'waiting' is, after all, a key theme in the same psalm (see vs. 5), and one commented upon elsewhere in the *Midrash Rabbah* in eschatological vein.[15] But in fact, on closer inspection it is not the case that the conundrum of the 'ordering' of forgiveness and fear is hereby liturgically resolved by a transformation of fear into forgiveness; the reverse logic (from forgiveness *to* fear) is also given a new, albeit subtle, liturgical instantiation. For it is also in the liturgies of the High Holy Days that an exegetical link between Psalm 130 and the book of Jonah (read as the *haftarah* of the afternoon service on the Day of Atonement) becomes part of the

---

[13] See Scherman (1985), 264-5; and Scherman (1986), 324-5. Also see Nasuti (2004), 95-124, at 109-10.

[14] Israelstam and Slotki (1983), 389-90 (*Leviticus Rabbah* XXX.7 *ad* Lev 23:40). This material is repeated in *Ecclesiastes Rabbah* IX.7.

[15] Freedman (1983), Vol. 2, 964-5 (*Genesis Rabbah* XCVIII.14 *ad* Gen 49:18).

exegetical nexus; so that by implication the 'depths' of Psalm 130.1 (*de profundis*) become identified with Jonah's own perilous – but miraculously salvific – descent into the 'depths' of the sea.[16] Since judgment, mercy and repentance (and their wholly unexpected sets of conjunction in Jonah and the Ninevites) are central to the book of Jonah, the puzzle of why – as in our psalm verse – forgiveness might *result* in 'fear' also takes on new meaning. As a recent modern commentator on Jonah, Uriel Simon, puts it with grace:

> Jonah argues on behalf of strict justice against the merciful God, who repents of his sentence. ... To the advocate of strict justice it is clear that wickedness abounds not only because of the viciousness of evil-doers, but also because the Judge of all the earth does not treat them with the full severity of the law. He must learn that the world can exist only through the unfathomable amalgam of justice and mercy, that fear of sin is produced not only by fear of punishment, but also by awe at the sublimity of salvation ... and by fascination with grace and absolution ('Yours is the power to forgive so that you may be held in awe' [Ps. 130.4]). If Jonah is to be rid of the notion that divine compassion expresses weakness of mind and softness of heart, he must experience the Lord's heavy hand directed against himself.[17]

As Simon explains, it appears to be precisely this reading of Jonah that is in play in the afternoon liturgy of the Day of Atonement; for at the end of the reading the last three verses of the book of Micah are appended (Micah 7. 18-20), 'through which Jonah, as it were, recants his condemnation of the attributes of compassion and grace (Jonah 4. 2) by reciting the praise of God'.[18] In short, Jonah *ends* with 'awe'/fear; his earlier views on justice have been dumbfounded. In similar vein, *Exodus Rabbah* I, 6 insists that 'fear' is the outcome, not only the prerequisite, of forgiveness: 'Israel is steeped in sin through the *Evil Yezer* in their body, but they do repentance and the Lord forgives their sins every year, and *renews their heart to fear him*'.[19]

One might say, then, that the exegesis of Psalm 130.4 in early rabbinic context was vitally flavoured by its liturgical setting. It becomes woven intrinsically into the annual, embodied, practices of repentance and forgiveness, in which, as Schechter puts it, 'the prerogative of

---

[16] See Nasuti (2004), 110.
[17] Simon (1999), xii.
[18] Ibid, xiii.
[19] Cited in Schechter (1993), 304. My italics.

granting pardon is *entirely in the hands of God, every mediator being excluded* …'[20] However, this development in no way resolves the conundrum of the ordering of fear and forgiveness, as we have shown; and nor does it relieve the sense of the *human* 'impossibility' of forgiveness, given the necessary divine initiative and the final mystery of the relation of the 'attributes' of G-d. Small wonder, then, that we find later, medieval, discussion of vs. 4 of the psalm still picking at the difficulty of its exegesis. Rashi thinks that the sole point of vs. 4 is that 'You have not given the authority to any agent/intermediary to forgive [he then quotes Exodus 23] … and therefore no person will trust in the forgiveness of anyone else [but God]'.[21] Abraham Ibn Ezra, on the other hand, thinks that the 'fearing' means that 'when You forgive my transgressions, sinners will hear this and repent, putting aside their own sins. If You don't forgive, they will not fear You and will do their pleasure, as much as they like'.[22] Kimḥi, in turn, cites Ibn Ezra but at the same time seemingly expands on Rashi's more fundamental idea: 'God has given power to the higher intelligences to perform his *will* on earth, but *forgiveness* rests not with them but with him. Why is this so? It is in order that men may not say to themselves: if we sin, the angels will be reconciled to us and will forgive our sins. (Therefore Scripture) proceeds to make it known that forgiveness is not with them, *in order that men may fear God*, for with him there is forgiveness and with none other besides him.'[23]

Can we say, then, in concluding this section, that in the biblical and rabbinic witness forgiveness is in some sense *intrinsically* 'fearful'? On the evidence we have surveyed, that would appear now to be a non-hyperbolic conclusion, mandated by the abiding insistence that only God can forgive; yet we must not forget – before passing to a comparison with the strikingly different Christian interpretation of Ps. 130.4 – that at key moments in the Hebrew Scriptures human *participation* in the logic of divine forgiveness also allows that same fearfulness to 'rub off' on chosen human representatives without in any way undermining the divine uniqueness. Most notable and moving here is the story of Joseph (described of late by Jon Levenson as 'the most sophisticated

---

[20] Ibid, 294. My italics. Also see Urbach (1979), 462ff.
[21] Rashi to Ps. 130. 4.
[22] Abraham Ibn Ezra to Ps. 130. 4.
[23] Baker and Nicholson (1973), 37-9. My italics.

narrative in the Jewish or Christian Bibles'[24]); for at the end of the story, when Joseph has finally revealed himself to his brothers, and been reconciled with his father, his pronouncement to his brothers (who naturally fear a continuing resentment) coheres most strikingly with the themes of Psalm 130.4. Both the brothers and Joseph weep as the brothers abase themselves before Joseph and ask for forgiveness (Genesis 50. 16-18); but Joseph replies: 'Do not be afraid! *Am I in the place of God?* Even though you intended to do harm for me God intended it for good ...' (Genesis 50. 19-20). As Gary Anderson concludes, in a remarkable recent study of the Joseph narrative in Jewish and Christian exegesis, 'we are those brothers, and only the Elect One of Israel can speak the words of absolution'.[25]

It is, however, with this challenging thought (to which we shall duly return at the end of this essay) that we now pass on to examine the Christian reading of Psalm 130.4. And here some surprises await us.

Psalm 130. 4 (129. 4 LXX) and its interpreters, II: Christian tradition

The first surprise, which mightily de-railed much of early Christian reflection on our psalm verse in Greek, was a mistranslation by the LXX of the Hebrew of Psalm 130.4b ('therefore thou art to be feared') to read instead 'according to thy law' (and then often run on into vs. 5).[26] In short, the crucial theological 'surd' that we have been considering – the intense collocation of fear and forgiveness – was dissolved in one stroke by the Greek Bible, and so passed its adjustment into early Christian exegesis. We shall consider in a moment (and here one can only speculate) whether this change could perhaps have come about partly for *theological* reasons: did the translator baulk at the idea of the 'fearfulness of forgiveness', or was he merely misled by a variant text? Whatever lay behind the change, however, the effect on Christian exegesis was – one way or another – that of a flattening of the intensity

---

[24] Levenson (1993), 142.

[25] Anderson (2003), 198-215, at 215.

[26] Rahlfs, A. ed. (1931), Ps 129. 4-5: ὅτι παρὰ σοὶ ὁ ἱλασμός ἐστιν ἕνεκεν τοῦ νόμου σου ὑπέμεινά σε, κύριε, ὑπέμεινεν ἡ ψυχή μου εἰς τὸν λόγον σου.

of the paradox that had so exercised rabbinic thinking at precisely this juncture.

The second major exegetical feature we shall outline is doubtless less surprising, but nonetheless of great significance theologically for divergent Jewish/Christian reflections on the theme of forgiveness. For once the idea of 'law' is introduced into vs. 4 by the LXX, it sets off, for Christian exegesis, a stark contrast – *à la* Romans 7 – between the divine 'forgiveness' available now in *Christ*, and the era of Jewish 'law' that has been sublated. In short, the text becomes an opportunity for the enunciation of a Christian (and specifically Pauline) dispensationalism that relegates both 'law' and 'fear' to an era superseded by that of 'forgiveness': 'law' and (Christic) 'forgiveness' are set in opposition. Doubtless this change is also implicitly affected by the gospel materials on forgiveness – which we can touch on only briefly in this paper. Interestingly, however, this move also corresponds with a return to the Jewish liturgical association of the psalm with the book of Jonah; but along with this re-connection, especially in later (medieval) monastic interpretation, comes a Christian intensification of the idea of Psalm 130 as a 'psalm of ascent': it is 'from the depths' – like Jonah – that a pray-er of distinct maturity prays, one whose perception of 'forgiveness' has the quality both of 'profundity' and of increasing closeness to the divine.

Finally, however – and here is our third *novum* or 'surprise', though one perhaps not entirely unexpected – it is Martin Luther who restores the sense of the simultaneity of 'fear' and 'forgiveness' to the exegesis of Psalm 130. Not only does he go back, courtesy of humanism, to the reading of the Masoretic text, and thus recoups the original reading of vs. 4b; but he interprets the psalm existentially, seeing it as a kind of witness to the maelstrom of his own experience of fear, justification and grace: it becomes an essentially 'Reformation' psalm. What is consciously discarded, however, in this Lutheran return to what we might call the 'Tannaitic' perception of simultaneous judgment and mercy in the divine, is the Christian medieval sense of spiritual 'ascent'. Bridling at 'works righteousness', Luther will no longer range the psalms of ascent upon a ladder of spiritual elevation, as had his medieval predecessors. Thus, precisely as the theme of the 'fearfulness of forgiveness' is retrieved in Lutheran thought, it is also seemingly dislocated from any mandated or manipulable *process* of 'ascent'. The simultaneity of fear and forgiveness is *fixed*, both existentially and theologically; it finds no easy resolution in a spiritual 'improvement' that might transmute or resolve that particular fear that is due only to God.

With this brief preview on the Christian exegesis of Psalm 130.4 in mind, let us now fill in some of the exegetical details of these three developments before moving to our systematic conclusions.

First, the special Hebrew word for G-d's forgiveness (הַסְּלִיחָה [has-sĕlîḥā]) is translated in the LXX ἱλασμός (hilasmos), a word with cultic overtones of expiation, and one therefore naturally referred by Christian exegesis to Christ's saving work (in the Latin it becomes *propitiatio*). The textual change in 129.5a in the LXX (130.4b MT) from 'therefore you are to be feared' to 'according to your law' (ἕνεκεν του νόμου σου [heneken tou nomou sou]) is a slip – if it is such – relatively easy to explain linguistically: what we have as the verb in the Masoretic text (תִּוָּרֵא [tiwwārē']) has been read as תּוֹרָה (tôrā – 'Torah/law'), and the preceding לְמַעַן (lĕma'an – 'therefore' in the MT) translated in its prepositional sense as 'for the sake of'. Since all that was written in those days was the consonants, the confusion is understandable enough; on the other hand, the appearance of 'His word' (MT) or 'your word' (LXX, τον λόγον σου [ton logon sou]) in the succeeding – and perhaps parallel – vs. 5b raises the possibility that the LXX is reading a variant text rather than creatively (or defensively) exegeting the Masoretic version. As we shall see, the Greek Christian exegetes tend to flounder at this point, some of them also showing an awareness of more than one reading; and – yet more interestingly – the *Peshitta* seems altogether flummoxed, leaving out the offending two words altogether.[27] In short, this was a psalm verse that defeated a number of readers. The possibility that the change by the LXX might be a defensive reading, resisting theologically the idea of a fear *consequent* on forgiveness, is intriguing for our purposes;[28] but it cannot be said to have any obvious evidential support: there is no such parallel move by the LXX translators, for instance, to effect a similar change to the substance of I Kings 8. 39-40, where – as we have noted above – the nexus of forgiveness and fear is similarly expressed.

The result of this textual *aporia* is, for the early Christian exegesis of our verse, initially something of a disappointment, granted that the interesting collocation of fear and forgiveness has now been

[27] With only one small textual variant showing, the *Peshitta* omits vs. 4b.

[28] See Gunkel (1986), 561, who remarks that the text may have presented an 'Anstoss'.

obliterated.[29] Unsurprisingly, Origen immediately identifies the ἱλασμός /*propitiatio* as Christ, and identifies the 'depths' of vs. 1 as a form of 'deep' prayer only achieved by the Spirit crying out in one's heart.[30] John Chrysostom, however, does not make the explicit Christological identification, but simply interprets 'because with you there is propitiation', as 'It is not in our good deeds but in your goodness that the possibility lies of escaping punishment'.[31] Interestingly, he then shows awareness of *three* possible textual variants for vs. 4b or 5a: 'for the sake of your Law', 'for the sake of your name', and 'so that you may be fearsome'. Ostensibly floundering as a result of this variety of options, he can apparently make no sense at all of the last one: 'Fearsome to whom?' he asks rhetorically, 'To the enemy, to schemers, to my foes?'[32] We note therefore that he has instantly bracketed out the possibility that the divine might be (appropriately) 'fearsome' to *us*. Theodoret of Cyrus also shows cognizance of a variety of possible readings (including the reference to 'fear'), but again he havers, seemingly baffled; but like Origen he explicitly reads the psalm as Christological: on the concluding vs. 8 he attributes the redemption of Israel to 'the Lamb of God'.[33]

The early Greek exegetes, then, make little or no sense of the theme of the collocation of fear and forgiveness, largely for reasons of textual uncertainty. When we get to the Latin tradition, however, several fascinating (and theologically important) changes occur. Although Jerome of course translated both Hebrew and Greek versions of the Psalter into Latin,[34] Augustine is commenting on the Latin that follows the LXX text of vs. 4b. However, in his case this does not mean that he avoids the issue of the relation of judgment to mercy, because he reads the whole psalm now through the lens of the Pauline theology of justification:

> "For there is propitiation with Thee" (vs. 4). And what is this propitiation, except sacrifice? And what is sacrifice, save that which has

---

[29] See Nasuti (2004), 110ff. for a very useful treatment of the exegesis of Psalm 130 in the early Christian fathers. Nasuti however is focusing on vs. 1.

[30] Origen, *Sel. Ps.* on Ps 130 (PG 12: 1647-8).

[31] Hill (1998), 194.

[32] Ibid.

[33] Hill (2001), 303.

[34] The modern Vulgate has parallel texts of *Psalmi Iuxta Hebr. and Iuxta LXX*, even though the 'Gallican' version became standard under Alcuin.

been offered for us? The pouring forth of innocent blood blotted out all the sins of the guilty ... For if there were not mercy with Thee, if Thou chosest to be Judge only, and didst refuse to be merciful, ... Who could abide this? ... There is therefore one hope: "for the sake of Thy law have I borne Thee, O Lord". What law? That which made men guilty ... There is therefore a law of the mercy of God, a law of the propitiation of God. The one was a law of fear, the other is a law of love ...[35]

Alluding then to both Galatians and Romans, Augustine re-introduces the tension of fear and mercy, despite his LXX reading of vs 4b. But the crucial Christian novelty here is that 'fear' is necessarily perceived as negative: it is the slavish 'fear' of failure in the realm of the law, and is therefore presented as that which is dispensationally *overcome* in Christic justification by faith. The possibility of a remaining 'awe/fear' that might intrinsically relate to divine 'forgiveness' is, at least in this context, rhetorically swept aside; and this despite the fact that Augustine also recaptures the identification of the psalm with Jonah's whale. But the 'depths' are read – not as in Jewish liturgy as a place of re-learning 'fear', nor as in Origen as the deep places of the Spirit – but as the 'depths' of *sin*; for 'this mortal life is our deep', says Augustine, from which only Christ can redeem.[36]

It is in the later Western monastic interpretations of Cassiodorus and Gregory the Great, however, that we get an interesting re-reading of this Augustinian set of moves which now stresses the importance of the psalm as one of the highest in what Jerome translated as a 'canticum graduum' (Psalms 120-34).[37] Despite the fact that in both exegetes the connection with Jonah is retained, and vs. 3 interpreted – as with Augustine – as ruling out the possibility of any human merit before God, nonetheless the 'depths' become a place from which a spiritual advance may be made. The 'depths' in Cassiodorus become the purgative place of the learning of *humility*, not – as in Augustine – the unredeemable depths of sin: 'for those who have buried themselves in the bowels of the holy humility are all the closer to the Highest'.[38] Rather differently, Gregory the Great returns to Augustine's insistence

---

[35] Schaff (1994), 613b.

[36] Ibid, 613a.

[37] See Walsh (1991), 311; and Gregory the Great, *Expositio in Septem Psalmos Penitentiales* (PL 49: 630-2).

[38] Walsh (1991), 312-3.

that Jonah's 'depths' *were* sinful as well as marine ones (the language of 'perversity' and 'disobedience' is used), but he continues Cassiodorus's interest in the motif of spiritual advancement and 'ascent'.[39] When Gregory comes to exegete vs. 4, however (again following the LXX reading: *propter legem tuam*), he makes the now-standard identification of the *propitiatio* with Christ; but – unlike Augustine – he does not exclusively press the psalm into the template of Paul's theory of law and gospel, but first stresses that 'the law of God *is* mercy', appealing to the Lukan theology of Christ's forgiveness of those crucified alongside him, and citing from Luke the dominical command to 'love your enemies'.[40] This is a significant shift, once again deflecting Western Christian exegesis of the psalm from a positive reflection on 'fear'.

With Luther, then, all is changed and made new. As Nasuti's recent article underscores, Luther saw Psalm 130 as 'the height of the Old Testament gospel', as a 'Pauline psalm', and as the basis for one of his greatest Reformation hymns: *Aus tiefer Not*.[41] The connection with Jonah is lost; but at the same time all the great Lutheran themes are constellated into his exegesis of this psalm: the unavoidability of divine judgment and human fear, the necessity of justification in Christ, the possibility of salvation (a rising 'from the deep') only through 'grace' and 'faith'. The return to the Masoretic reading of vs 4b is of course partly what enables this re-emphasis on 'fear'; but it is also Luther's particular re-reading of the Pauline gospel, and his own autobiographical experiences of *Anfechtungen*. As he opens his commentary: 'These are noble, passionate, and very profound words [*sc.* 'out of the depths'] of a truly penitent heart that is most deeply moved in its distress. In fact, this cannot be understood except by those who have felt and experienced it. We are all in deep and great misery, but we do not all feel our condition'.[42] Like Augustine, then, Luther not only casts 'the depths' as a generic human condition of wretchedness, but reads 'fear' as that which characterizes the 'cross of the old man'. Nonetheless,

> ... if anyone does not fear God, he does not implore, nor is he forgiven. In order, therefore, to gain God's grace, He and He alone is to be feared, just as He alone forgives. For if anyone fears something besides God, he seeks the favor and mercy of this other thing and

[39] PL 49: 632 and 630-1.
[40] Ibid, 635-6.
[41] See Nasuti (2004), 115-17.
[42] Guebert (1958), 189.

does not care about God. But whoever fears God desires His grace and does not care about anything that is not God; for he knows that no one can harm him if God is gracious to him.[43]

Thus this part of the commentary leads us to identify a crucial two-sidedness in Luther's treatment of 'fear': the cringing, manipulative 'fear' of the 'old man', and the appropriate, distinctive 'fear' of the 'new man'. For we see that Luther does not technically *resolve* (all) fear into hope; the simultaneity of the two existential responses continues in an important sense to co-exist in the justified soul, even as hope in Christ's salvation is fully acknowledged as *theologically* triumphant; that is why Luther can conclude his commentary on Psalm 130 by insisting that 'we should not be merciful to ourselves, but severe and angry, so that God may be merciful to us and not angry'.[44] The *neurotic* 'fear' of Luther's youth has gone ('those who feel that God is angry and unmerciful do not know him aright'); but the appropriate, and appropriately *unique*, sense of deference and unworthiness before God endures even as His 'kindness and mercy' is fully received. Even as 'works righteousness' is decried, then (and hence, too, all hope in purposeful 'spiritual progress' of the sort enunciated in the medieval exegesis of the 'Psalms of Ascent'), even so is right 'fearfulness' before *God* retrieved as an enduring lesson of humility and trust in 'God's grace alone'.

Systematic conclusions: on the fearfulness of forgiveness

I said at the start of this essay that Jewish and Christian exegeses of Psalm 130 are not uncomplicatedly disjunctive, that both traditions are internally complex, but that indeed they also contain important points of contact. Although this essay has provided only a selective account of Jewish and Christian readings of Psalm 130.4, we have proceeded far enough, I trust, to establish sufficient empirical evidence to support that initial claim. In particular, the rabbinic, and especially rabbinic/liturgical, understanding of the implications of the 'fearfulness of forgiveness' represents a startling point of convergence with Luther's thought on the matter; and that the alarmingly anti-semitic

[43] Ibid, 191.
[44] Ibid, 194.

Luther should thereby present us with such a point of agreement is a spiritual irony which I can only note and leave for our reflection. If it be objected that Luther's resistance to 'spiritual progress' (in the sense of 'works righteousness') sets his position ostensibly *against* the Jewish practices of graduated repentance in the ten days between the New Year and the Day of Atonement, it might be worth voicing a reminder that Luther nonetheless carried over from Catholicism both the practices of auricular confession, and a profound commitment to the transformative liturgical experience of entering into the days of the Passion.[45]

However in closing I want to edge a little further towards my bold assertion, also made at the start, that because – humanly speaking – forgiveness *is* 'impossible', it is a vibrant sense of the 'fearfulness of (divine) forgiveness' that needs to be recaptured if we are to move beyond the apparently disjunctive 'Jewish/Christian' alternatives that characterize the post-holocaust period. Whilst a defense of my (implicit) claim that Jesus's own position on 'forgiveness' is entirely compatible with this stress on holy fear goes well beyond the confines of this particular essay,[46] suffice it to say that the more one pursues the insistence on the uniquely divine characteristic of forgiveness, the higher one's Christology is pressed.[47] It is not for nothing that Teresa of Ávila's account of achieved Christic 'union' in the 7th 'Mansion' includes simultaneously a *renewed* stress on holy fear, and the passing comment that to live in such 'union' is for the first time to see what it means to love one's enemies.[48] Nor is it insignificant that Teresa's mentor and friend, John of the Cross (who shared with her a partial

---

[45] See Gary Anderson's treatment of the Lutheran liturgy in his 'Joseph and the Passion of Our Lord', Anderson (2003), 212-5.

[46] It would involve developing my views 1. that Mark 2. 1-12 and paras. does not mandate an easy forgiveness by 'every mother's son' (one possible rendition of the ambiguous title 'Son of Man'), but rather makes an astonishingly high Christological claim for Jesus's identity; and 2. that the Matthean Sermon on the Mount makes demands about forgiveness which remain impossible unless mediated *through* Jesus.

[47] Hence the nice irony that, in this case of 'forgiveness', an agreement between Jewish and Christian perspectives of the sort for which I have been arguing does not result in the whittling down of Christological claims but rather the opposite.

[48] *The Interior Castle*, VII. 2 in Kavanaugh and Rodriguez (1980), 436 (§9 '... much greater fear...'); and VII. 3 (ibid, 439 [§5 the soul's 'love for its persecutors'], 443 [§§13-14 living with fear]). This 'ecstatic' dimension of forgiveness as articulated by Teresa of Avila is echoed in the twentieth century (during the time of the London *Blitz*) by Charles Williams, who, in his *The Forgiveness of Sins* (1942), esp. chs. 6-7), argues that true forgiveness of one's enemies can only occur by means of a mystical union with Christ which enables one to pass over into one's enemies' shoes, and thus to see oneself from their perspective.

Jewish descent), could discourse so unforgettably on the fearful purgations of self-knowledge in the 'night of spirit' preceding 'union' as a death-like transformation equivalent to 'being in the belly of the whale'.[49] The essentially *participatory* vision that the Carmelites give us of 'mystical union' enables a glimpse at the divine perspective on forgiveness perhaps equivalent only to that which we noted in the Joseph narratives of Genesis.[50]

Let us return finally to Simon Wiesenthal and *The Sunflower*. If this reflection on the Jewish and Christian interpretation of Psalm 130.4 has shown us anything, it has revealed a certain nexus of themes that attend the authentic perception of the 'fearfulness of forgiveness': the maintenance of awe at the *uniqueness* of the divine prerogative to forgive; the patient *waiting* on the chronology of that process; the embodied *practices* of repentance, purgation, and self-knowledge; and finally the *participation* in a flow of compassion which can strictly only come from God. Seen now in this light, Wiesenthal's response to the dying SS-man, his wholly silent but compassionate reception of the German's apology, but his refusal to absolve what only God can, was as eloquent an instantiation of the principles of Psalm 130.4 as one could hope for. Against the stark oppositions of the polarized modern 'Jewish' and 'Christian' reactions to the narrative, I therefore cast my vote with the small minority of respondents who see Wiesenthal's silent response as wholly theologically appropriate; indeed, from the perspective of the themes of this paper, it was itself a small, but highly significant, participation in the 'fearfulness of *divine* forgiveness'.[51]

Notes

I would like to express my gratitude to my former Harvard colleague Dr. Jon D. Levenson, to my former parishioner Dr. Aaron Lazare (Dean, U Mass Medical School), and to Mark Nussberger (then a Th.D. candidate at Harvard Divinity School), for conversations on this topic and assistance in gathering materials for this paper. Mark Nussberger also

[49] Kavanaugh and Rodriguez (1991), 404.

[50] See again, Anderson (2003), 212-5.

[51] See for instance the contribution of Friedrich Heer to the original symposium in Wiesenthal (1976), 125-8. Also see the important recent discussion of the nature of apology and its relation to the possibility of forgiveness in Lazare (2004).

helped me substantially with the preparation of the notes for publication, and I am much indebted to him. Before this paper was prepared for Andrew Louth's Festschrift it had had two airings in Jerusalem: once at the Tantur Ecumenical Institute (in 2005), and later – in a revised form – at the Swedish Theological Institute (in 2010). Alon Goshen-Gottstein, Jeremy Milgrom, Joseph Blenkinsopp and Robert Murray, S.J. provided invaluable responses to the earlier version of the essay as given at Tantur; and Bishop Erik Aurelius, Elitzur Bar-Asher, and Jesper Svartvik gave illuminating responses in the discussion at the Swedish Theological Institute. I am indebted to them all.

Bibliography

Anderson, Gary A. (2003) 'Joseph and the Passion of Our Lord', in Davis, Ellen F. and Hays, Richard B., eds. *The Art of Reading Scripture* (Grand Rapids, Mich.: Wm. B. Eerdmans) pp. 198–215

Baker, Joshua and Nicholson Ernest W., eds. and trans. (1973), *The Commentary of Rabbi David Kimḥi on Psalms* CXX-CL (Cambridge: Cambridge University Press)

Brongers, H.A. (1973) 'Die Partikel לְמַעַן in der biblisch-hebräischen Sprache,' *Oudtestamentische Studiën* 18 (1973), pp. 84–96

Freedman, Rabbi Dr. H. trans. (1983) *Midrash Rabbah. Genesis.* Vol. 2 (London: The Soncino Press)

Guebert, Arnold trans. (1958) *Luther's Works*, vol. 14 (St. Louis: Concordia Publishing House)

Gunkel, Hermann (1986) *Die Psalmen* (Auflage; Göttingen: Vandenhoek & Ruprecht)

Hammer, Reuven trans. (1986) *Sifre: A Tannaitic Commentary on the Book of Deuteronomy* (New Haven: Yale University Press)

Hill, Robert Charles trans. (1998) *St. John Chrysostom: Commentary on the Psalms*, II (Brookline, Mass.: Holy Cross Orthodox Press)

Hill, Robert Charles trans. (2001) *Theodoret of Cyrus: Commentary on the Psalms – Psalms 73-150* (Washington, D.C.: The Catholic University of America Press)

Israelstam, Rev. J. [chs. I-XIX] and Slotki, Judah J. [chs. XX-XXXVII] trans. (1983) *Midrash Rabbah. Leviticus* (London: The Soncino Press)

Kavanaugh, Kieran and Rodriguez, Otilio trans. (1980) *The Collected Works of St. Teresa of Ávila* Vol. 2 (Washington, D.C.: ICS Publications)

Kavanaugh, Kieran and Rodriguez, Otilio trans. (1991) *The Collected Works of St. John of the Cross* Revised ed. (Washington, D.C.: ICS Publications)

Lazare, Aaron (2004) *On Apology* (Oxford: Oxford University Press)

Lehrman, Rabbi Dr. S.M. trans. (1983) *Midrash Rabbah. Exodus* (London: The Soncino Press)

Levenson, Jon D. (1993) *The Death and Resurrection of the Beloved Son: The Transformation of Child Sacrifice in Judaism and Christianity* (New Haven: Yale University Press)

Milgrom, Jacob (1990) *Numbers. The JPS Torah Commentary* (Philadelphia: The Jewish Publication Society)

Moberly, R.W.L. (2002) 'How May We Speak of God? A Reconsideration of the Nature of Biblical Theology,' *Tyndale Bulletin* 53.2 (2002), pp. 177–202

Nasuti, Harry P. (2004) 'Plumbing the Depths: Genre Ambiguity and Theological Creativity in the Interpretation of Psalm 130,' in Najman, Hindy and Newman, Judith H. eds; *The Idea of Biblical Interpretation: Essays in Honor of James L. Kugel* (Leiden: Brill) pp. 95–124

Rahlfs, A. ed. (1931) *Septuaginta. X. Psalmi cum Odis* (Göttingen, Vandenhoeck & Ruprecht)

Roth, Martha, ed. (1984) *The Assyrian Dictionary of the Oriental Institute of the University of Chicago* (Chicago: Oriental Institute)

Schaff, Philip ed. (1994) *Augustine: Expositions on the Book of Psalms* in *Nicene and Post-Nicene Fathers* vol. 8 (reprint; Hendrickson Publishers)

Scherman, Nosson (1985) *The Complete ArtScroll Machzor: Rosh Hashanah; Nusach Ashkenaz* (Brooklyn, N.Y.: Mesorah Publications, Ltd.)

Scherman, Nosson (1986) *The Complete ArtScroll Machzor: Yom Kippur; Nusach Ashkenaz* (Brooklyn, N.Y.: Mesorah Publications, Ltd., 1986)

Simon, Uriel (1999) *Jonah: The JPS Bible Commentary* (Philadelphia: The Jewish Publication Society)

Schechter, Solomon (1993 reprint) *Aspects of Rabbinic Theology* (Woodstock, Vt.: Jewish Lights Publishing)

Urbach, Ephraim E. (1979) *The Sages: Their Concepts and Beliefs* (Cambridge, Mass.: Harvard University Press)

Walsh P.G. trans. (1991) *Cassiodorus: Explanation of the Psalms*, vol. III, *ACW* 53 (New York: Paulist Press)

Waltke, Bruce K. and O'Connor, M. (1990) *An Introduction to Biblical Hebrew Syntax* (Winona Lake, Ind.: Eisenbrauns)

Wiesenthal, Simon and symposia (1976; Rev. and expanded ed., 1997) *The Sunflower* (New York: Schocken Books)

Williams, Charles (1942) *The Forgiveness of Sins* (London: Geoffrey Bles; The Centenary Press)

KALLISTOS WARE

'FORGIVE US … AS WE FORGIVE': FORGIVENESS IN THE PSALMS AND THE LORD'S PRAYER

And throughout all Eternity
I forgive you, you forgive me.
As our dear Redeemer said:
'This the Wine, and this the Bread.'
William Blake

The stupid neither forgive nor forget;
the naïve forgive and forget;
the wise forgive but do not forget.
Thomas Szasz

'He is free because he forgives'

In the book by Kevin Andrews, *The Flight of Ikaros*, there is a story that sums up the essence of forgiveness. Andrews was studying medieval fortresses in Greece. The year was 1949. He was travelling through a land devastated by the German occupation during the Second World War, and cruelly divided by the post-war struggle between Communists and anti-Communists that had only just drawn to a close. Arriving one evening in a village, he was given hospitality by the parish priest Papastavros. The priest's house had been burnt down, and so he received his guest in the shed that was now his home.

Gradually Andrews learnt the priest's story. His two eldest sons had joined the Resistance during the German occupation. But some villagers betrayed their hiding-place; they were captured and never seen again. About the same time, his wife died from starvation. After the Germans had left, Papastavros was living alone with one of his married

53

daughters and her baby son. She was expecting her second child in a few weeks. One day he returned home to find his house in flames, set on fire by Communist partisans. 'I was in time', he recounted to Andrews, 'to see them drag my daughter out and kill her; they shot all their bullets into her stomach. Then they killed the little boy in front of me.'

Those who did these things were not strangers coming from a distance, but they were local people. Papastavros knew exactly who they were, and he had to meet them daily. 'I wonder how he has not gone mad,' one of the village women remarked to Andrews. But the priest did not in fact lose his sanity. On the contrary, he spoke to the villagers about the need for forgiveness. 'I tell them to forgive, and that there exists no other way,' he said to Andrews. Their response, he added, was to laugh in his face. When, however, Andrews talked with the priest's one surviving son, the latter did not laugh at his father, but spoke of him as a free man: 'He is free because he forgives.'[1]

Two phrases stand out in this account: 'There exists no other way', and 'He is free because he forgives.'

There exists no other way. Certain human situations are so complex and intractable, so fraught with anguish, that there exists only one way out: to forgive. Retaliation makes the problem worse; as Mahatma Gandhi observed, 'An eye for an eye leaves the whole world blind.'[2] Solely through forgiveness can we break the chain of mutual reprisal and self-destroying bitterness. Without forgiveness, there can be no hope of a fresh start. So Papastavros found, faced by the tragedies of enemy occupation and civil war. Surely his words apply also to many other situations of conflict, not least in the Holy Land.

He is free because he forgives. In the words of the Russian Orthodox *starets* St Silouan of Mount Athos (1866-1938), 'Where there is forgiveness … there is freedom.'[3] If only we can bring ourselves to forgive – if we can at least *want* to forgive – then we shall find ourselves in what the Psalms call 'a spacious place' or 'a place of liberty': 'We went through fire and water, but Thou broughtest us out into a place of liberty' (Psalm 66:12). Forgiveness means release from a prison in which all the doors are locked on the inside. Only through forgiveness can we

---

[1] Andrews (1959), 109-19.

[2] I take this sentence from a pamphlet entitled *The F Word: Images of Forgiveness* (no place, no date).

[3] Archimandrite Sophrony (1991), 341.

enter into what St Paul terms 'the freedom of the glory of the children of God' (Rom. 8:21).

Yet how hard, how painfully hard, it is to forgive and to be forgiven! To quote another Russian Orthodox witness, Metropolitan Anthony of Sourozh (1914-2003), 'Forgiveness is not a little brook on the boundary between slavery and freedom: it has breadth and depth, it is the Red Sea.'[4] 'Do not think that you have acquired virtue,' said the Desert Father Evagrius of Pontus (346-99), 'unless you have struggled for it to the point of shedding your blood.'[5] The same can be said of forgiveness. Sometimes the struggle to forgive is indeed nothing less than an inner martyrdom, to the point of shedding our blood.

Forgiveness Sunday in the Orthodox Church

How shall we set out in our exodus across the 'Red Sea' of forgiveness? Let us consider first the way in which the Orthodox Church offers to its members an annual opportunity to make a fresh start, on what is known as 'The Sunday of Forgiveness'. This will lead us to look more closely at forgiveness in the Psalms and especially in the Lord's Prayer. What, we may ask, is the meaning of the Greek verb used in the Lord's Prayer for 'forgive', *aphiēmi*, 'let go'? Does this mean that to forgive is to condone, or at any rate to forget? Next, taking as our guide the early Fathers, we shall see how the phrase 'Forgive us … as we forgive' underlines the fundamental unity of the human race. Finally, we shall try to appreciate what is signified by the word 'as' in the forgiveness clause of the Lord's Prayer: '… *as* we forgive'. Why should the scope of God's forgiveness be seemingly restricted by my own willingness to forgive? We shall end with four practical guidelines.

The Sunday of Forgiveness occurs immediately before the seven-week Fast of Lent, the 'Great Fast' in preparation for the 'Feast of Feasts', the Lord's Resurrection at Pascha. The human animal, it has been said, is not only an animal that thinks, an animal that laughs and weeps, but much more profoundly an animal that expresses itself through symbolic actions. With good reason, then, the Orthodox Church affords its members the chance each

---

[4] Bloom (1966), 31. See also his perceptive words about forgiveness in Bloom (1972), 104-8.

[5] *On Prayer* 136; tr. Sinkewicz (2003), 207 (translation modified).

year to externalize their longing for forgiveness, through a liturgical rite that is both corporate and personal.[6]

On the morning of Forgiveness Sunday, the appointed Gospel reading is Matthew 6: 14-21, beginning with Christ's words: 'If you forgive others their trespasses, your heavenly Father will also forgive you; but if you do not forgive others, neither will your Father forgive your trespasses.' Then in the evening, at the end of Vespers, there comes a ceremony of mutual pardon. Usually the priest gives a homily, concluding with an appeal to his flock to forgive him for all his mistakes and shortcomings in the past year. Then he comes down the sanctuary steps to the floor of the nave where the people are standing; for there can be no genuinely mutual forgiveness unless I put myself on the same level as the other. Kneeling before the congregation, he says 'Forgive me, a sinner.' The people likewise kneel before the priest, answering 'May God forgive you. Forgive us.' To this the priest responds 'God will forgive', or 'May God forgive and bless us all.' After that the people come up one by one to the priest, and each kneels before him, as he in turn kneels before each of them; and they exchange the same words, 'Forgive me .... God will forgive.' Then, having first knelt before the priest, the members of the congregation go round the church kneeling before one another, each asking and granting pardon. All this, for obvious reasons, is easier to carry out if, as in traditional Orthodox practice, the church is not cluttered up with pews.[7]

There is of course a danger that a ceremony such as this may become over-emotional, in which case the results will probably prove ephemeral.[8] Forgiveness, after all, is not a feeling but an action. It involves not primarily our emotions but our will. It is a *decision*, which then requires to be given practical effect. There is also the opposite danger that some worshippers, growing accustomed to this ceremony year by

---

[6] For the liturgical texts used on the Sunday of Forgiveness, see Ware (1978), 168-83, especially p. 183. Most of the hymnology for the day in fact alludes, not to mutual forgiveness, but to the other main theme of the Sunday, the Casting out of Adam from Paradise.

[7] The details of the ceremony vary in different places. A simpler form of mutual pardon is used daily at the end of Compline: see Hapgood (1922), 162; *The Liturgikon* (1994), 67, 98.

[8] Not that there is anything wrong with the emotions as such, for they are an integral part of our human personhood according to the divine image, and so they can and should be offered up to God in our 'reasonable worship' (Rom. 12:1). I am thinking here, however, of a febrile emotionalism that is artificial and exaggerated.

year, will go through it in a manner that is merely formal and automatic. Ritual can all too easily become ossified.

Nevertheless, when full allowance has been made for the dangers of emotionalism and formalism, it remains true that for very many Orthodox Christians this annual service of mutual pardon is deeply healing. On the basis of my personal experience, after more than forty years of pastoral work in a parish, I can testify that again and again it has a transfiguring effect upon relationships within the local church family. It is an occasion that many of our people approach with the utmost seriousness. Let us not underestimate the power of ritual. Even if there are times when it becomes ossified, on other occasions it can and does act as a potent catalyst, enabling us to give expression to what would otherwise remain unacknowledged and repressed. Those too hesitant or embarrassed to call at one another's homes and embark on a lengthy verbal explanation can make a new beginning within the framework of shared prayer. The Vespers of Forgiveness serves in this way as a genuine breakthrough, the sudden vision of a fresh landscape.

The burden of unhappy memories means, not surprisingly, that the Vespers of Forgiveness is somewhat subdued and sombre. We cry out in sorrow: 'Turn not away Thy face from Thy servant, for I am in trouble; hear me speedily: hearken unto my soul and deliver it.' Yet, along with sorrow, there is also a note of glad expectation. 'Let us set out with joy upon the season of the Fast,' we sing in one of the hymns; and a little later we add, 'Thy grace has shone forth and given light to our souls.' As the mutual pardon is being exchanged between priest and people, in many churches the choir sings the Resurrection hymns that will be used seven weeks later at Paschal midnight: to forgive is to rise again from the dead. St John Climacus, abbot of Mount Sinai in the seventh-century – whose book *The Ladder of Divine Ascent* is specially appointed for reading in Lent – has a phrase that exactly describes the spirit of the Vespers of Forgiveness: *charopoion penthos*, 'mourning that causes gladness' or 'joy-creating sorrow'.[9]

Sometimes people have told me that they find the phrase commonly used at the service, 'Forgive me ... God will forgive', to be problematic and even evasive. Surely, they object, when someone asks for forgiveness, it is not enough for us to assure them that they are forgiven by God, for they already know that; what is required is that *we* should forgive them. This, however, is to overlook an essential point.

[9] *The Ladder of Divine Ascent*, Step 7, title (*PG* 88: 801C), tr. Moore (1959), 113.

Forgiveness is first and foremost a divine act: 'Who can forgive sins but God alone?' (Mark 2:7). If, then, I am to forgive someone else, and the other person is to forgive me, in the last resort this is possible only in so far as we are both of us *in God*. More specifically, we are able to forgive each other solely because we are both of us already forgiven by God. Our forgiveness is rooted in His, and is impossible without it: 'Apart from Me you can do nothing' (John 15:5).

Since, therefore, forgiveness is not primarily our human action but a divine action in which we humans participate, it is vitally important that in the process of mutual forgiveness we should allow space for God to operate. At the beginning of the Eucharistic service in the Orthodox Church, the Divine Liturgy, the deacon says to the priest, 'It is time for the Lord to act' (see Psalm 119:126), thereby affirming that the true celebrant at the Holy Mysteries is not the priest but Christ Himself. The phrase applies equally to our mutual forgiveness: here, too, it needs to be said, 'It is time for the Lord to act.' Our attempts at reconciliation often fail, precisely because we rely too much upon ourselves, and do not leave proper scope for the action of the Lord. With St. Paul we need to say, 'not I, but Christ in me' (Gal. 2:20). Such, then, is the spirit in which we reply at the Vespers of Forgiveness, 'God will forgive.'

Forgiveness in the Psalms

In order to deepen our appreciation of the mystery of forgiveness, let us turn both to the Old Testament and to the New; and let us consider how forgiveness is understood first in the Psalms and then in the Lord's Prayer. Because of the central place that the Psalms have always occupied in the liturgical life of the Church, in both the East and the West, the testimony that they bear to the meaning of forgiveness is particularly significant.

First of all the Psalms contain a number of striking passages in which the worshipper pleads to God for forgiveness. The best known and most eloquent of these pleas is Psalm 51, 'Have mercy upon me, O God, after Thy great goodness', which is recited no less than four times daily in the Byzantine Divine Office, at the Midnight Service, Matins, the Third Hour and Compline. Another such plea is Psalm 130, 'Out of the deep ...':

> If Thou, Lord, shouldest mark what is done amiss,
> O Lord, who could abide it? (verse 4).

The same urgent cry for forgiveness recurs in many other Psalms:

For Thy name's sake, O Lord,
Be merciful to my sin, for it is great (Psalm 25:10).

Deliver me from all mine offences ...
Take Thy plague away from me (Psalm 39: 9, 11).

I said, 'Lord, be merciful unto me:
Heal me, for I have sinned against Thee' (Psalm 41:4).

O remember not our past sins, but have mercy upon us, and that soon:
For we are come to great misery (Psalm 79:8).

In these and similar passages of the Psalms, it is made abundantly clear how greatly we need the healing grace of divine forgiveness. Without God's mercy we are helpless. It is also made clear that we have no claims upon God. Helpless as we are, we can do nothing to earn or deserve God's mercy, nothing to oblige or constrain Him to forgive us. We can do no more than wait in patience and humility for His free gift of pardon. 'I wait for the Lord, my soul doth wait for Him ... A broken and contrite heart, O God, shalt Thou not despise' (Psalms 130:5; 51:17).

In the second place, the Psalms repeatedly insist that these pleas for divine forgiveness do not remain unheard. The Lord is a God of loving-kindness and tender love, ever eager to show mercy and grant healing. This is the theme in particular of Psalm 103, used daily at Matins in the Orthodox Church, and also regularly in the Divine Liturgy:

Praise the Lord, O my soul:
And all that is within me praise His holy name ...
Who forgiveth all thy sin:
And healeth all thine infirmities ...
The Lord is full of compassion and mercy:
Long-suffering and of great goodness ...
Like as a father hath compassion upon his children,
So hath the Lord compassion upon them that fear Him (verses 1, 3,
    8, 13).

In a memorable phrase, it is said that God 'covers' our sin:

> Blessed is he whose unrighteousness is forgiven:
> Even he whose sin is covered (Psalm 32:1).

Elsewhere it is said that our sins are 'blotted out':

> To Thee shall all flesh come to confess their sins:
> When our misdeeds prevail against us, in Thy mercy do Thou blot
> them out (Psalm 65:2).

A *leitmotif* in the 'historical' Psalms is the way in which, again and again in the story of salvation, the people of Israel has gone astray, and yet God in His faithful love has forgiven them (Psalms 78:38; 106: 43-44; 107: 13-16; cf. 85: 1-3). God, it is said elsewhere, is like a shepherd who goes in search of a lost sheep (cf. Matt. 18:12; Luke 15:4):

> I have gone astray like a sheep that is lost:
> O seek Thy servant, for I do not forget Thy commandments (Psalm
> 119:176).

Yet we are not presumptuously to take God's forgiveness for granted, for His mercy goes hand in hand with His justice (cf. Romans 11:22):

> My song shall be of mercy and justice (Psalm 101:1).

Thirdly, if we are in this way forgiven by God, then we in our turn are called to extend forgiveness to our fellow humans. This is not in fact affirmed in the Psalms very clearly or very frequently, but there are occasions in which it is at least implied, in the context of money-lending:

> The ungodly borroweth and payeth not again:
> But the righteous giveth and is bountiful ...
> The righteous is ever bountiful and lendeth:
> And his children shall be blessed (Psalm 31:21, 26).

> It is good for a man to be generous when he lendeth (Psalm 112:5).

This can perhaps be enlarged to include not only generosity over debts but other forms of remission and forgiveness. At the same time a restriction has to be noted. We cannot grant forgiveness on behalf of others, in regard to offences that have been committed not against us but against them:

> But no man may deliver his brother:
> Nor pay a price unto God for him (Psalm 49:7).

Sadly, however, it has to be noted that there are grave limitations in the Psalms concerning the scope of forgiveness. If, as we have seen, there are only a few places where it is suggested that we should forgive others, there are unfortunately many other passages in which the Psalmist curses his enemies and prays for their destruction. God is invoked as a God of vengeance (Psalms 54:1; 94:1). We are to hate our enemies with a 'perfect hatred' (Psalm 139:22). Particularly harsh is the punishment called down upon the daughter of Babylon:

> Blessed shall he be that taketh thy children:
> And throweth them against the stones (Psalm 137:9).

Most notably, Psalm 109 contains an imprecation daunting in its cruelty:

> Let his days be few:
> And let another seize his possessions.
> Let his children be fatherless:
> And his wife become a widow.
> Let his children be vagabonds and beg their bread:
> Let them be driven out even from their desolate places …
> Let there be no man to pity him:
> Or to have compassion upon his fatherless children (verses 7-9, 11).

Such a passage does not stand alone: compare, for example, Psalms 83: 9-17, 129: 5-8, and 140: 8-10. I have noted altogether over thirty passages in the Psalms asking God to inflict pain and suffering upon others, and this figure is almost certainly an underestimate. It is of course possible to explain away such passages by interpreting them symbolically, as referring not to our fellow human beings but to our evil thoughts or to the demons. But such was not their original intention.

'... seventy times seven ...'

When we turn, however, from the Old Testament to the New, we are at once impressed by a manifest and remarkable contrast. Nowhere in the Gospels does Christ instruct us to hate our enemies: He tells us, on the contrary, 'Love your enemies and pray for those who persecute you' (Matt. 5: 44). The law of retaliation is firmly abrogated: we are not to 'resist an evildoer', but to 'turn the other cheek' (Matt. 5:39). There are to be no limits to our forgiveness: we are to forgive our brother 'seven times a day' (Luke 17:4); and not only that, but 'seventy times seven' (Matt.18:22). We do not find such statements in the Psalms. Nor, indeed, do we find in the Psalms the statement that occupies such a prominent place in the Lord's Prayer: 'Forgive us our debts, as we forgive our debtors' (Matt. 6:12). The Lord's Prayer is comprehensive but extremely concise: if, then, in such a short prayer, nearly a quarter – no less than 13 words in the Greek text, out of 57 (or 58)[10] – is devoted to the theme of forgiveness, this shows how crucially important it is in God's sight that we should forgive and be forgiven.

Such, certainly, is the view of Origen (d. 253/4): if Christ, he says, places such strong emphasis upon forgiveness in the model prayer that He has given us, this is because there cannot be any true prayer at all unless it is offered in a forgiving spirit.[11] St Gregory of Nyssa (d.*ca.* 394) goes so far as to claim that the clause 'Forgive us... as we forgive' is the culminating point in the entire prayer; it constitutes 'the very peak of virtue'.[12] He adds, however, that – fundamental though the clause is – its true sense is not at all easy to grasp: 'The meaning surpasses any interpretation in words.'[13]

A valuable insight into the significance of forgiveness is provided by the literal sense of the verb used in the Lord's Prayer for 'forgive', *aphiēmi*. The primary idea conveyed by this word is 'let go', 'set aside', 'leave behind'. It denotes such things as release from captivity, the cancellation of a debt, or the remission of punishment. The unforgiving

---

[10] The Greek text, as used liturgically in the Orthodox Church, contains 58 words; in critical editions of the New Testament there is one word less, as the definite article is omitted before *gēs* ('earth').

[11] *On prayer* 8:1, 9:1, ed. Koetschau (1899), 317; tr. Greer (1979), 97,98. On the Patristic use of the Lord's Prayer, see the systematic study, with detailed bibliography, Stevenson (2004), to which I am much indebted.

[12] *On the Lord's Prayer*, homily 5, ed. Callahan (1992) 59, line 1; tr. Graef (1954), 71.

[13] *On the Lord's Prayer*, homily 5, ed. Callahan (1992) 61: 10-11; tr. Graef (1954) 73. Here (and elsewhere) I have modified Dr Graef's translation.

grasp, retain, and hold fast; the forgiving let go. Yet, if we 'let go' the memory of an offence, does this not suggest that we are condoning the evil that has been done? That, surely, cannot be the correct meaning of forgiveness. In the words of Archbishop Desmond Tutu, 'Forgiveness does not mean condoning what has been done. It means taking what has happened seriously and not minimizing it.'[14] To condone an evil is to pass over it, to ignore it, or else it is to pretend that it is not an evil, to treat it as if it were good. But to forgive is something altogether different from this. There can be no genuine forgiveness that is not truthful and realistic. Let us not practise any evasion. If an evil has been done, then this has to be frankly admitted.

Moreover, if the process of forgiveness is to be brought to full completion, the evil has to be frankly admitted by *both* sides, by the aggressor as well as the victim. It is true that, when we suffer wrong, we should endeavour to forgive the other immediately, without any delay, not waiting for the other to acknowledge the wrong. It was precisely in this spirit that Jesus prayed at His crucifixion, 'Forgive them, for they do not know what they are doing' (Luke 23:24). If, however, the forgiveness is to come to proper interpersonal fulfilment, more than this is required. Forgiveness needs to be accepted as well as offered; and the one who admits no guilt can accept no forgiveness.

If forgiveness, in the sense of 'letting go', is not the same as condoning, should we say that to forgive is to forget? Shall we make our own King Lear's words, 'Pray you now, forget and forgive'? The answer seems to be both yes and no. It all depends on *what* we remember (or forget) and on *how* we do so. Certainly there is no point in clinging to the memory of trivial misunderstandings and injuries. We should rather allow them to slip quietly away into oblivion, for we have better things with which to occupy our minds. There are, however, events in our personal lives, and in the lives of the communities to which we belong, that are far too important simply to be forgotten. It would not be right to say to the members of the Armenian nation, 'Forget the massacres of 1915', or to the Jewish people, 'Forget the Shoah in the Second World War.' These are matters that, for the sake of our shared humanity, none of us should forget, not least so as to ensure that such atrocities may never be allowed to happen again.

More decisive than what we remember is how we do so. We are not to remember in a spirit of hatred and recrimination, or for the sake of revenge. Dr Jonathan Sacks, Chief Rabbi of the United Hebrew

---

[14] Quoted in the pamphlet *The F Word: Images of Forgiveness.*

Congregations of the Commonwealth, has rightly said: 'Remember the past ... but do not be held captive by it. Turn it into a blessing, not a curse; a source of hope, not humiliation.'[15] Our memories are not to be repressed or negated, but at the same time they require to be purified and healed. We need to remember, yet not self-righteously, not with aggressive accusations, but in a spirit of compunction and mourning. We need to remember with love. But that is difficult.

Forgiveness, it can even be said, begins not with an act of forgetfulness, but with an act of mindfulness and self-knowledge. We have to recognize the harm that has been done, the wound that we or the other carry in our heart. Only after this moment of truthful recognition can we then begin to 'let go', not in the sense of consigning to oblivion, but in the sense of no longer being held prisoner by the memory. Remember, but be free.

Responsible for everyone and everything

In the Patristic interpretation of the Lord's Prayer, a dominant theme is the unity of the human race. The early Fathers are in full agreement with the words of Julian of Norwich (fourteenth century), 'In the sight of God, all man is one man, and one man is all man.'[16] They agree equally with John Donne (1571/2-1631), 'No man is an Island, entire of it self.'[17] Our need to forgive and to be forgiven springs directly from the fact that we are all of us interdependent, members of a single human family. Indeed, this insistence upon coinherence is to be seen, not only in the clause 'Forgive us ... as we forgive', but in the Lord's Prayer as a whole. St Cyprian of Carthage (d. 258) notes how the prepositions in the Prayer are consistently in the plural, not the singular – not 'my' but 'our', not 'me' but 'us':

> We do not say 'My Father who art in heaven', or 'Give me this day my bread', nor does each one ask that only his own debt be remitted, nor does he request for himself alone that he may not be led into temptation or may be delivered from the evil one. Prayer with us is

---

[15] *The Times* (London), 17 July 2004, 47.

[16] Quoted by Williams (1942), 16. This brief study, written in the middle of the Second World War, remains one of the most helpful treatments on the subject.

[17] Donne (1624), Meditation XVII.

public and common, and when we pray we do not pray for one but for the whole people, because the whole people are one.[18]

This perception of our human unity, in Cyprian's view, has its foundation in the Christian doctrine of God. We believe in God the Trinity, who is not only one but one-in-three, not only personal but interpersonal; we believe in the communion of Father, Son and Holy Spirit, and so we human beings are saved, not in isolation, but in communion one with another.[19]

This unity that marks us out as human persons, while underlined throughout the Lord's Prayer, is particularly evident in the clause concerning forgiveness. In the words of Clement of Alexandria (*ca.* 150 – *ca.* 215), when we say 'Forgive us ... as we forgive', we are proclaiming that 'all humankind is the work of one Will'.[20] This is a point emphasized by St Maximos the Confessor (*ca.* 580-662) in his commentary on the Lord's Prayer. Unity and mutual love, he says, constitute 'the principle (*logos*) of nature', according to which we human beings have been created. When, therefore, we pray for forgiveness, we are bringing our human will into harmony with the *logos* of our nature. Conversely, to withhold forgiveness is to 'sunder human nature by separating ourselves from our fellow humans, even though we are ourselves human'. Our refusal to live in union with each other through mutual forgiveness is therefore self-destructive: 'Failing such union, our nature remains self-divided in its will and cannot receive God's divine and ineffable gift of Himself.'[21]

St Gregory of Nyssa likewise sees the refusal of forgiveness as self-destructive: 'In condemning your neighbour, you thereby condemn yourself.'[22] Giving a wide-ranging application to the notion of human unity, Gregory maintains that it extends through time as well as space. When saying 'Forgive us' in the Lord's Prayer, we are asking forgiveness not only for our own personal sins but also for 'the debts that are

---

[18] *On the Lord's Prayer* 8, ed. Moreschini (1976), lines 103-18; cited in Stevenson (2004), 33.

[19] *On the Lord's Prayer* 23, ed. Moreschini, lines 447-9.

[20] *Stromateis* 7:81:2, ed. Stählin and Früchtel (1970), 58; tr. Hort and Mayor (1902), 141.

[21] van Deun (1991), lines 662-8; tr. Palmer, Sherrard and Ware, (1981), 301 (translation adapted).

[22] *On the Lord's Prayer*, homily 5, ed. Callahan (1992), 61: 5-6; cf. 69:24; tr. Graef (1954), 73, 80.

common to our nature', and more particularly for the ancestral sin[23] that the whole human race inherits from Adam. Even if we keep ourselves free from personal sins – in fact, as Gregory comments, none of us can claim this of ourselves, even for an hour – we would still need to say 'Forgive us' on behalf of Adam:

> Adam lives in us ... and so we do well to make use of these words *Forgive us our trespasses*. Even if we were Moses or Samuel or someone else of pre-eminent virtue, we would none the less regard these words as appropriate to ourselves, since we are human; we share in Adam's nature and therefore share also in his fall. Since, then, as the Apostle says, 'we all die in Adam' (1 Cor. 15:22), these words that suitably express Adam's penitence are likewise appropriate for all those who have died with him.[24]

A similar line of thought is found in St Mark the Monk (? early fifth century). In his opinion, we are called to repent not only 'for our own sin' but also 'for the sin of the transgression', that is to say, for the ancestral sin of Adam. Repentance is vicarious:

> The saints are required to offer repentance not only on their own behalf but also on behalf of their neighbour, for without active love they cannot be made perfect ... In this way the whole universe is held together in unity, and through God's providence we are each of us assisted by one another.[25]

Even though there is no explicit reference here to the Lord's Prayer, Mark's line of argument can surely be applied likewise to the petition 'Forgive us ... as we forgive.' If we can repent for the sins of others, then we can and should also ask forgiveness on their behalf. The principle of mutual solidarity applies equally in both cases: 'we are each of us assisted by one another'. No one is forgiven and saved in isolation.

These statements by Gregory of Nyssa and by Mark the Monk fall far short of a fully developed theology of original guilt, such as we find in St Augustine (354-430). Mark specifically excludes the

---

[23] The Greek Fathers, and also most present-day Orthodox writers, speak not of 'original sin' but of 'ancestral sin' (*propatorikē hamartia*). There is a subtle difference in meaning between the two terms.

[24] *On the Lord's Prayer*, homily 5, ed. Callahan (1992), 64:23; 65:2; 66:7-15; tr. Graef (1954), 76,77.

[25] *On repentance* 12 and 11, ed. de Durand (1999), 252, 250.

view that, in a juridical sense, we are guilty of Adam's sin, considered as an act of personal choice.[26] Yet, on a level more profound than legal culpability, there exists a mystical solidarity that unites us all one to another; and it is of this that Gregory and Mark are speaking. 'All man is one man', and so we are each of us 'responsible for everything and everyone', to use the phrase of Dostoevsky's *Starets* Zosima.[27] Even if not personally guilty, nevertheless we bear the burden of what Adam and all the other members of the human family have done. They live in us, and we in them. Here as always the vital word is 'we', not 'I'. None of us falls alone, for we drag each other down; and none of us is forgiven and saved alone. Forgiveness is not solitary but social.

How far can the notion of vicarious forgiveness be legitimately extended? Can I forgive or accept forgiveness on behalf of others? So far as asking forgiveness is concerned, it is surely reasonable to request forgiveness on behalf of others, when those others are joined to me in some way, for example by kinship, nationhood, or religious allegiance. If, tracing back our ancestry, we become aware that our family tree is tainted with unresolved tensions and alienation, we can and should pray for the forgiveness and healing of our forebears. By the same token, the descendant of a slave-trader might rightly feel impelled to ask forgiveness in his heart – and perhaps by some external gesture as well – from the families of those whom his ancestor took captive and sold into bondage. Pope John Paul II acted as a true Christian when, during the visit of the Ecumenical Patriarch Bartholomew I to Rome in June 2004, he asked the Patriarch's forgiveness for the sack of Constantinople by the Latin Crusaders eight hundred years previously.[28] How I long for an Orthodox church leader to ask forgiveness in the same way from the Catholics, for the many evils that we Orthodox have inflicted upon them! And all of us, Orthodox and Catholics alike, have to seek forgiveness from the Jews, God's Chosen People, for the heavy sins that, over the centuries, we have committed against them.

Have we the right, however, not only to ask forgiveness on behalf of others, but also to offer it on their behalf? Here there is reason for us to be much more hesitant. For myself, I agree with the late Rabbi Albert

---

[26] *On baptism* 17, ed. de Durand (1999), 392.

[27] Dostoevsky (1991), 320.

[28] *Service Orthodoxe de Presse et d'Information* (*SOP*) 290 (July-August 2004), 1-3.

Friedlander – and with Psalm 49:7 – that one cannot forgive offences that have not been committed against oneself. It would be inappropriate, and indeed presumptuous, for me as a non-Jew to claim authority to forgive the suffering inflicted upon the Jews during the Shoah in the Second World War. It is not for me but for the Jews themselves to decide how those sufferings should be remembered, and how and when they should be forgiven. In the Lord's Prayer, we do not say, '… as we forgive those who have trespassed against others', but '… as we forgive those who have trespassed against *us*'.

Issuing an order to God

What light do the Fathers shed upon the central word in the forgiveness petition – indeed, the most puzzling word in the whole of the Lord's Prayer – the word 'as': 'Forgive us … *as* we forgive'? 'No word in English', states Charles Williams, 'carries a greater possibility of terror than the little word "as" in that clause; it is the measuring rod of the heavenly City, and the knot of the new union. But also it is the key of hell and the knife that cuts the knot of union.'[29] Truly it is a hazardous prayer. We dare to apply to ourselves with unmitigated rigour the principle laid down by Christ: 'The measure you give will be the measure you get' (Matt. 7:2). 'What you do,' warns St Cyprian, 'that you will also yourself suffer.'[30] As St John Chrysostom (*ca.* 347-407) puts it, 'We ourselves have control over the judgement that is to be passed upon us.'[31]

Not only is it a hazardous request to God, but it is also a very strange one. It is as if we were issuing an order to God and instructing Him how to act. 'If I do not forgive others,' we are saying to Him, 'then do You withhold forgiveness from me.' Nowhere else in the Lord's Prayer do we issue orders in this way. St Gregory of Nyssa attempts to spell out the paradox in terms of what may be called 'mimetic inversion'. Under normal circumstances, he observes, it is we who are called to imitate God; as St Paul says, 'Be imitators of me, as I am of Christ' (1 Cor. 11:1). This is particularly the case when we forgive others. Since in the last resort it is God alone who has the power to forgive sins

---

[29] Williams (1942), 66.

[30] *On the Lord's Prayer* 23, ed. Moreschini, lines 440-1.

[31] *On Matthew*, homily 19:6 (*PG* 57: 281).

(Mark 2:7), it is only possible for us to forgive others if we imitate God. We cannot genuinely forgive, that is to say, unless we have been taken up into God and have ourselves 'in some sense become God', to use Gregory's phrase. The one who forgives needs to be 'deified' or 'divinized'; there can be no effective forgiveness without *theosis*.[32] That is the normal pattern. But here, in the case of the Lord's Prayer – and Gregory admits that this is a 'bold thing' to say[33] – the customary order is reversed. On this occasion, it is we who serve as an example to God. Instead of ourselves imitating Him, we are telling Him to imitate us: 'What I have done, do You do likewise; imitate Your servant, O Lord .... I have forgiven; do You forgive. I have shown great mercy to my neighbour; imitate my loving-kindness, You who are by nature loving-kind.'[34]

Yet, in this clause 'Forgive us ... as we forgive', precisely how strong a sense should be attached to the conjunction 'as'? Should it be understood as causative, proportionate or conditional?

(1) Is the sense causative? In that case, we are saying to God, 'Forgive us *because* we forgive'; our forgiveness is the cause of His. This is indeed the way in which some Patristic authors interpreted the phrase. Clement of Alexandria even suggested that, by forgiving others, we somehow *compel* God to forgive us.[35] Yet a causative interpretation of this kind surely presents grave difficulties. As Calvin has rightly insisted, forgiveness comes from the 'free mercy' of God.[36] It is an unmerited gift of divine grace, conferred solely through Christ's Cross and Resurrection; it is never something that we can earn or deserve. God acts with sovereign liberty, and we have no claims upon Him. As Paul affirms, quoting the Pentateuch: 'For God says to Moses, "I will have mercy on whom I have mercy, and I will have compassion on whom I have compassion." So it depends not on human will or exertion, but on God who shows mercy' (Rom. 9:15-16; cf. Exod. 33:19). This is rendered abundantly clear in Christ's parable concerning the labourers in the vineyard: to those who complain about their wages, the master replies, 'Have I not the right to do as I choose with what

---

[32] *On the Lord's Prayer*, homily 5, ed. Callahan (1992), 59:1-11; 60: 15-16; 61: 15-17; tr. Graef (1954), 71, 72, 73.

[33] op. cit., ed. Callahan (1992), 61: 13-14; tr. Graef (1954), 73.

[34] op. cit., ed. Callahan (1992), 61: 23-24; 62: 7-9; tr. Graef (1954), 73, 74.

[35] *Stromateis* 7: 86: 6, ed. Stählin and Früchtel (1970), 62; tr. Hort and Mayor (1902), 153.

[36] Stevenson (2004), 165.

is my own?' (Matt. 20:15). Moreover, the initiative rests with God and not with us. He does not wait for us to forgive others before He extends His forgiveness to us. On the contrary, His act of free and unrestricted forgiveness precedes any act of forgiveness on our part: 'God proves His love for us, in that while we still were sinners Christ died for us' (Rom. 5:8).

(2) If the word 'as' cannot be causative, is it proportionate? Does it signify *'to the same degree'*, *'according to the same measure'*? Once more, this can hardly be the true sense. Between our forgiveness and God's there can be no common measure. He forgives with a fullness and generosity far beyond our wildest imagining: 'For My thoughts are not your thoughts, nor are your ways My ways, says the Lord' (Isa. 55:8). The transcendent and incomparable character of divine forgiveness is underlined in another Matthaean parable, that of the two debtors (Matt. 18:23-35). In relation to God, we are like the slave who owed ten thousand talents (a talent being equivalent to more than fifteen years' wages received by a labourer), whereas in relation to each other we are like the slave who owed a hundred denarii (a denarius being the usual day's wage for a labourer). Even St Gregory of Nyssa, after suggesting that in His act of forgiveness God is imitating us, at once goes on to qualify this by asserting that our sins against God are immeasurably heavier than any sins by others against us.[37] Later he refers for confirmation precisely to the parable of the two debtors.[38]

(3) If, then, our forgiveness is neither the cause nor the measure of God's forgiveness, what further alternative remains? There exists a third possibility: it is the *condition*. Forgiveness is indeed unmerited, but it is not unconditional. God for His part is always overwhelmingly eager to forgive. This divine eagerness is movingly expressed in the story of the prodigal son (Luke 15: 11-32), which is read at the Orthodox Liturgy on the Sunday two weeks before the Sunday of Forgiveness. The father does not simply sit and wait passively for his son to return home. We are to imagine him standing day after day outside his house, anxiously scanning the horizon in the forlorn hope that at long last he may catch sight of a familiar figure. Then, as soon as the

[37] *On the Lord's Prayer*, homily 5, ed. Callahan (1992), 62: 9-11; tr. Graef (1954), 74.

[38] op. cit., ed. Callahan (1992), 69: 26-70: 12; tr. Graef (1954), 80-81. The parable is quoted to the same effect by other early Christian writers, such as Tertullian (*ca.* 160- *ca.* 225), *On the Prayer* 7, ed. and tr. Evans (1953), 12-13; Origen, *On prayer* 28: 7, ed. Koetschau (1899), 379; tr. Greer, 150.

prodigal comes into view, while he is still far off, the father rushes out to meet his son, embracing and kissing him, and inviting him into the feast. Such is God's great willingness to forgive us and to welcome us home. Later in the story the father again goes out, this time in the hope of persuading his elder son to come and share the feast. This double *going out* on the part of the loving father is of primary significance if we are to appreciate the quality of divine mercy.

Yes, indeed, God is always eager to forgive – far more so than we are to repent. In the words of St Isaac the Syrian (seventh century), 'There exists in Him a single love and compassion that is spread out over all creation, a love that is without alteration, timeless and everlasting.'[39] Calling to mind Christ's agony in the garden of Gethsemane and His death on the Cross, we ask ourselves: What more could God incarnate have done to win us back to Himself, that He has *not* done? Forgiveness, however, has not only to be offered but to be accepted. God knocks at the door of the human heart (Rev. 3:20), but He does not break the door down: we for our part have to open it.

Here precisely we find the true meaning of the word 'as' in the Lord's Prayer. It is not that God is unwilling to forgive us. But if, despite God's unfailing eagerness to forgive, we on our side harden our hearts and refuse forgiveness to others, then quite simply we render ourselves incapable of receiving the divine forgiveness. Closing our hearts to others, we close them also to God; rejecting others, we reject Him. If we are unforgiving, then by our own act we place ourselves outside the interchange of healing love. God does not exclude us; it is we who exclude ourselves.

Our forgiveness of others, then, is not the cause of God's forgiveness towards us, but it is certainly the condition without which God's forgiveness cannot pass within us. Divine pardon is indeed a free gift that we can never earn. What concerns us here, however, is not merit but capacity. Our relation to God and our relation to our fellow humans are strictly interdependent. As St Silouan of Mount Athos affirms, 'Our brother is our life.'[40] This is true not in a sentimental but in an ontological sense. Love for God and love for neighbour are not two loves but one.

---

[39] Isaac of Nineveh (Isaac the Syrian), *'The Second Part'*, Chapters IV – XLI, tr. Brock (1995), *Homily* 40: 1, 174.

[40] Archimandrite Sophrony (1991), 47, 371.

'Forgive us … as we forgive': when we say these words, so Metropolitan Anthony of Sourozh has rightly cautioned us, 'we take our salvation into our own hands'.[41]

Four words of counsel

As we begin to cross the Red Sea of forgiveness, let us remind ourselves of certain practical guidelines.

(1) *Do not delay, but do not be in haste.* Do not delay: the time for forgiveness is always *now*. Maximize the moment. The devil's weapons are nostalgia and procrastination: he tells us 'Too late' or 'Too soon'. But, where the devil says 'Yesterday' or 'Tomorrow', the Holy Spirit says 'Today'.

We are not to think within ourselves, 'First, I will change for the better; then I will be ready to forgive.' Still less are we to think (what is far worse), 'First, I will wait to see whether the other is really sorry for the wrong that he has done, and whether he has really changed for the better; then I will decide whether to forgive him.' Let us, on the contrary, be like the loving father in the story of the prodigal. Let us take the initiative, and run out to meet the other. Forgiveness has to come first; it is the cause of the change in ourselves and in others, not the effect. To adapt a phrase of the Romanian Orthodox theologian Fr Dumitru Staniloae (1903-93), 'In so far as I am not forgiven, I am unintelligible to myself.'[42]

Yet there is another side to the question. Forgive *now*, in your heart; but in your outward actions do not be overhasty. Forgiveness signifies healing, and healing often takes time. Premature requests for forgiveness can make the situation worse. If we force ourselves upon the other, without first seeking through imaginative empathy to discover what the other is thinking and feeling, we may widen rather than bridge the gulf that separates us. Without putting things off, often we need to pause – not with passive indifference but waiting with alertness upon God – until the *kairos*, the moment of opportunity, has become clear. The Emperor Augustus was right: *Festina lente*.[43]

---

[41] Bloom (1972), 30.

[42] de Beauregard (1983), 24: 'Moi-même, tant que je ne suis pas aimé, je suis incompréhensible.'

[43] Suetonius, *Lives of the Caesars*, 'Divus Augustus', §25 ('Make haste slowly').

(2) *Forgive the other, but also be willing to accept the forgiveness that the other is offering to us.* It is hard to forgive; but often it is even harder to acknowledge that we ourselves need to be forgiven. Let us be humble enough to accept the gift of another's pardon. As Charles Williams wisely observes, 'Many reconciliations have unfortunately broken down because both parties have come prepared to forgive and unprepared to be forgiven.'[44]

(3) *Forgive others, but also forgive yourself.* Have we not sometimes said, or heard others say, 'I will never forgive myself for that'? Yet how can we accept forgiveness from others, if we will not forgive ourselves? In the words once more of Charles Williams, by remaining in this state of 'half-anger, half-anguish', we each create for ourselves 'a separate hell'.[45] Judas regretted what he had done, but in his case self-knowledge brought him not to fresh hope but to despair; unable to forgive himself, and therefore unable to accept God's forgiveness, he went out and committed suicide (Matt. 27: 3-5). Peter on the other hand took a different path. Brought to self-knowledge by the crowing of the cock, he wept bitter tears of remorse; yet this remorse did not reduce him to despair. On the contrary, seeing the risen Christ at the lakeside, he did not turn away from Him into a 'separate hell', but drew near with hope. Forgiving himself, accepting Christ's forgiveness, he made a new beginning (Matt. 26:75; John 21:15-19).

(4) *Pray.* If we cannot yet find within our heart the possibility of forgiving the other, then let us at least pray for them. In the words of St Silouan, 'If you will pray for your enemies, peace will come to you.'[46] Let us ask God that we may not make the other's burden more heavy, that we may not be to them a scandal and a cause of stumbling. And if, as we pray, we cannot yet bring ourselves to the point of actually forgiving, then let us ask God that we may experience at least the desire and longing to forgive. There are situations in which truly to want something is already to attain it. Like the man who brought his sick child to Christ and cried out, 'Lord, I believe; help my unbelief' (Mark 9: 24), let us also cry out with tears: 'Lord, I forgive; help my unforgivingness.' Slowly, gradually, there will come at last the moment when we are able to remember with love.

---

[44] Williams (1942), 113.

[45] Williams (1942), 77-78.

[46] Archimandrite Sophrony (1991), 377.

By invoking God's help in prayer and by admitting our own help-lessness, we are reminded of the all-important truth that forgiveness is a divine prerogative. It is not simply our action, but the action of God in us. To forgive, in a full and genuine sense, we need to be 'in God'. 'It is God who has shone in our hearts ... the all-surpassing power is from Him and not from us' (2 Cor. 4: 6-7). This 'all-surpassing power' of God is communicated to us above all through the 'myster-ies' or sacraments of the Church; and, in the Patristic interpretation of 'Our Father', at least two of these 'mysteries' are mentioned implicitly in the course of the Prayer. When we say, 'Give us today our daily bread', we are to think not of material bread alone but of the 'bread from heaven', the Eucharist. Then, in the petition that follows, 'For-give us ... as we forgive', we are to recall the forgiveness of sins that we have received in Holy Baptism. The Lord's Prayer, according to St Augustine, is in this way a continual renewal of Baptism: reciting the words that Christ has given us, 'daily we are washed clean'.[47] Our forgiveness, then, does not depend merely upon our feelings, or upon the decision of our will. It has an objective basis, in the sacrament of our baptismal washing.

Flying kites

After Orthodox Christians have knelt before each other at the Vespers of Forgiveness, asking and granting pardon, what do they do on the next day, the first day of Lent, known as 'Clean Monday' (*Kathara Devtera*)? In many places it is still the custom to go out on the hills and have a picnic; and on this, the first open-air festival of the year, both children and grown-ups fly kites in the spring breeze. Such can also be our inner experience when we begin to forgive one another. To forgive is to enter spiritual springtime. It is to emerge from gloom into the sunlight, from self-imprisonment into the liberty of the open air. It is to ascend the hills, to let the wind blow on our faces, and to fly noetic kites, the kites of imagination, hope and joy.

As his son said of the priest Papastavros, 'He is free because he forgives.'

---

[47] Augustine, *Sermon* 59: 7; cf. 56: 11; 57: 8 (*PL* 38: 382, 390, 401). See Stevenson (2004), 82. A similar interpretation is given by Caesarius of Arles (*ca.* 470-542), and by Euthymius Zigabenus (twelfth century): see Stevenson (2004), 90, 108.

Bibliography

Andrews, Kevin (1959) *The Flight of Ikaros: A Journey into Greece* (London).

Antiochian Orthodox Christian Archdiocese of North America, ed. (1994) *The Liturgikon: The Book of Divine Services for the Priest and the Deacon*, 2nd edtn. (Englewood, NJ).

de Beauregard, Marc-Antoine Costa (1983) *Dumitru Staniloae: Ose comprendre que Je t'aime* (Paris).

Bloom, Anthony (1966) *Living Prayer* (London).

Bloom, Anthony (1972) *Meditations on a Theme* (London/Oxford).

Clement of Alexandria (1902) *Miscellanies Book* VII, ed. F.J. Hort and J.B. Mayor (London).

Clement of Alexandria (1970) *Stromateis*, ed. O. Stählin and L. Früchtel, *GCS* (Berlin).

Cyprian of Carthage (1976) *On the Lord's Prayer*, ed. C. Moreschini, *Corpus Christianorum, Series Latina* III/A, Part II (Turnhout).

Donne, John (1624) *Devotions upon Emergent Occasions* (London).

Dostoevsky, Fyodor (1991) *The Brothers Karamazov*, tr. Richard Pevear and Larissa Volokhonsky (New York).

Evagrius of Pontus (2003) *The Greek Ascetic Corpus*, tr. Robert E. Sinkewicz (Oxford).

Gregory of Nyssa (1992) *On the Lord's Prayer*, ed. J.F. Callahan, *Gregorii Nysseni Opera* VII/2 (Leiden/New York/Köln).

Gregory of Nyssa (1954) *On the Lord's Prayer*, tr. Hilda C. Graef *Ancient Christian Writers* 18 (New York).

Hapgood, Isabel Florence tr. (1922) *Service Book of the Holy Orthodox-Catholic Apostolic Church*, 2nd edtn (New York).

Isaac of Nineveh (Isaac the Syrian) (1995) '*The Second Part*', Chapters IV – XLI, tr. Sebastian Brock, *Corpus Scriptorum Christianorum Orientalium* 555, *Scriptores Syri* 225 (Louvain).

John Climacus (1959) *The Ladder of Divine Ascent*, tr. Lazarus Moore (London).

Mark the Monk (1999) *Traités* vol. I, ed. Georges-Matthieu de Durand, *Sources chrétiennes* 445 (Paris).

Mary, Mother and Ware, Kallistos tr. (1978) *The Lenten Triodion* (London/Boston).

Maximos the Confessor (1991) *On the Lord's Prayer*, ed. Peter van Deun, *Corpus Christianorum Series Graeca* 23 (Turnhout).

Origen (1899) *On Prayer*, ed. P. Koetschau, *GCS* (Leipzig).

Origen (1979) *An Exhortation to Martyrdom, Prayer* [and Selected Works], tr. Rowan A. Greer, *The Classics of Western Spirituality* (New York/Ramsey/Toronto).

Palmer, G.E.H. Sherrard, Philip and Ware, Kallistos tr. (1981) *The Philokalia*, vol. 2 (London/Boston).

Sophrony (Sakharov) (1991) *Saint Silouan the Athonite* (Tolleshunt Knights, Essex).

Stevenson, Kenneth W. (2004) *The Lord's Prayer: A Text in Tradition* (London) .

Tertullian (1953) *On the Prayer*, ed. and tr. E. Evans (London).

Williams, Charles (1942) *The Forgiveness of Sins* (London).

ADAM G. COOPER

SEX AND THE TRANSMISSION OF SIN:
PATRISTIC EXEGESIS OF PSALM 50:5 (LXX)

Psalm 50 (LXX) is a psalm which every Orthodox priest must know off by heart. It is the only psalm required to be prayed in its entirety in every celebration of the Divine Liturgy. Just before the Great Entrance and the procession with the eucharistic gifts, as the congregation begins to sing the thrice-holy hymn to the Trinity, at a moment, in other words, right at 'the threshold of theophany',[1] the priest appropriates King David's prayer of confession after his adultery with Bathsheba, acknowledging his own sins and unworthiness, calling on the all-holy, all-merciful God to renew his heart and spirit in preparation for the priestly service he is about to render.

In praying Psalm 50, famously known in the Latin church as the *Miserere* and one of the seven penitential psalms classified by Cassiodorus, the priest embodies every Christian's proper stance before Almighty God. Its words express the solemn joy and penitent confidence typical of every authentic human encounter with the God who has made himself known in Christ. For the closer one comes to the holy, the more one becomes aware of one's own imperfection and lack of holiness. That Apostle who early in his ministry declared himself to be 'the least of all the Apostles' came finally to that deeper knowledge of himself, soon before his death, as 'the chief of sinners.' To the extent that the faithful are prostrate in humble fear at the foot of Christ's cross, which is at the same time his throne of grace, it becomes difficult to cling proudly to any sense of self-righteousness. One could therefore be forgiven for believing that, in the praying of this psalm at least, Christians of east and west stand on level ground, united with one voice, one mind, one faith.

The truth is, however, that one verse in particular of this Psalm has come to symbolise an overstated difference of understanding between

[1] Reardon (2000), 99.

77

Christians of east and west with respect to sin and the human condition. As it is translated in the Revised Version, the verse in question reads: 'Behold, I was shapen in iniquity, and in sin did my mother conceive me.' What precisely does this passage imply? Are all human beings sinful from conception? Are sexual intercourse and procreation agents, channels, triggers of some kind of moral disorder? The answers posed to these questions by early Christian thinkers varied substantially. So much so, that by our own time it has become commonplace to posit two different, even opposing views on the nature of sin and human alienation from God, the one 'eastern' and the other 'western'. Put most simply, it is alleged that the eastern theologians speak only of 'ancestral sin', by which they mean the universal but blameless consequences of the sin of the first human couple. Such consequences include our liability to pain and suffering, our inclination to enslave ourselves to material goods and physical pleasures, and above all, our subjection to death. Western theologians, by contrast, speak of 'original sin', by which they mean not only the first sin committed by Adam in Paradise, but also the real inheritance of guilt subsequent to Adam's fall, an innate condition, present from conception, that is distinct from any additional guilt incurred by personal transgression. As one might expect when it is put this way, the 'eastern' view is deemed to offer a more optimistic anthropology, while the 'western' view is regarded as hopelessly pessimistic.

To those who know Andrew Louth, it hardly needs saying that he is impatient of such simplistic reductions in which 'eastern' and 'western' theologies are opposed in terms of self-contained, delineable doctrinal confessions. My aim in this study, by which I hope to honour my former professor, is not altogether to deconstruct these hackneyed lines of opposition since, as is usually the case with popular falsehoods, there are some elements of truth in them. Rather my intention, which arises from my experience as a student of Maximus the Confessor, is to discover and trace subtleties in the intellectual landscape of early Christian thought about sin and sexuality, subtleties that defy the kind of tribal categorisations just mentioned. Indeed, it was while I was doing my doctoral research on Maximus in Durham that I discussed with my reverend supervisor a cryptic but quite unique exposition of this verse from Psalm 50 in Maximus' own writings. Since that time, I have wanted to return to the history of exegesis of this verse. In what follows, I survey select examples of patristic exegesis of this passage. Starting with Clement of Alexandria and Origen, moving to Cyprian and Augustine, and finishing with Maximus the Confessor, I conclude that Maximus' interpretation of the passage especially precludes us from alleging two opposing doctrines of sin and human nature, one eastern (and 'optimistic') and the other western (and 'pessimistic'). In fact, we discover in the writings of Maximus a theological anxiety about the nexus between sexuality and sin no less pronounced, and, I would want to stress, no more pathological, than has been found in Augustine, even if it is marked by a different set of historical questions and contextual forms.

Psalm 50:5: an initial analysis[2]

Whether we are reading it in the Hebrew of the Masoretic text or the Greek of the Septuagint, the verse of Psalm 50 with which we are dealing raises difficult questions of interpretation. In the Greek, we encounter a verb whose meaning by and large seems to have been accepted by the Fathers as a straightforward synonym of its counterpart in the parallel poetic construct which forms its context. The verb is *kissan*, a *hapax legomenon* in the Septuagint, and an extremely rare word anyway in extra-biblical sources. Lexica variously define it to mean the odd culinary cravings often experienced by pregnant women, or the longing or desire of women to conceive or simply the act of conception itself. In the context of the poetic structure of Psalm 50:5 the verb stands in parallel with the preceding aorist passive of the verb *syllambanein*, which fairly commonly means 'to conceive.' Yet most English translations, facing the problem of translating two words in parallel whose meaning seems identical, render *synelemphthen* as 'I was brought forth' or 'I was shapen' or some such phrase, and leave the English 'conceive' for the more obscure sentence *ekissesen me he meter mou*.

Admittedly, contemporary Bible translators are working from the Hebrew, not the Greek text of the psalter. Scholarly work in the field of biblical poetics, however, has made it clear that there is usually more going on in Hebrew parallelism than simple repetition. Rather, the second strophe in a given parallel form often tends to elucidate,

---

[2] Chapter and verse numeration in contemporary Hebrew critical texts of the Bible differs from that in the Septuagint and other *mss*. To avoid confusion I identify the verse in question as Psalm 50:5 throughout.

amplify, and even intensify the action indicated in the first strophe. Following this approach, we would expect to discover the sense of the first strophe not simply restated but deepened, developed and intensified in the second.

It would be satisfying to find this suggestion confirmed by the existence of an incremental and semantic progression in intensity of meaning from the first verb to the second, but unfortunately their respective meanings are far from certain. Lexica[3] suggest that *hyl*, here in the *polal*, means 'to be made to tremble' or 'be brought to birth', and is perhaps not unrelated to *hwl*, 'to writhe' or 'turn'. Yet the latter is commonly used of the ritual dancing enacted in both Canaanite and Israelite worship. Just as vividly, *yhm* – an alternative form of *hmm* ('to grow hot with sexual passion'; cf. Is. 57:5; Jer 2:23) – in its turn normally describes the state or activity of an animal on heat, as we find in Genesis 30:38-41, where it is translated in the LXX by a close cognate of *kissan*, namely *egkissan*, 'to mate.' To translate *egkissan* in this context with 'conceive', as suggested in the 1992 Deutsche Bibelgesellschaft Lexicon of the Septuagint, seems overly coy.[4] What can be admitted though is that the activity described by the verb seems to be restricted to female animals (see Genesis 31:10 LXX): it is they who come into heat; it is therefore they who, having mated, conceive.

When read within the wider context of the prayer of confession, these words take on quite a striking aspect. The psalmist, pleading to God for mercy and cleansing, is weighed down with the burden of his sins. His confession goes beyond an expression of 'moral impotence';[5] it is rather an expression of total self-disgust. He searches back through his life to his very origins and finds no exception to this bent for acting treacherously. The ascription of a certain 'beast-like element'[6] to his mother's act of sexual intercourse is not intended as a moral condemnation of sexual passion or procreation. Nor is it meant to excuse his own moral responsibility.[7] Instead it magnifies and universalises his sense of wretchedness and self-loathing in the light of his present circumstances, in a manner not unlike the bereaved when they rue and curse the day of their birth (cf. Job 3:3; Jer 15:10; 20:14; 2 Esdr 5:35).

[3] See, *inter al.*, Koehler and Baumgartner (2001).

[4] Lust (1992), 127.

[5] Dalglish (1962), 118.

[6] Dalglish (1962), 119, quoting Delitzsch.

[7] See Dalglish (1962), 119-22.

One more comment: it is profitable to note how the psalmist himself, agonising over his sexual calumny, adopts the typical language of defilement: 'wash me… cleanse me… cleanse me… wash me.' According to Paul Ricoeur, this 'assonance between sin and defilement' opens the way for a 'reactivation… of the ancient tie between defilement and sexuality' with its 'great affective complexity'.[8] However problematic that may seem, it answers to the common phenomenological experience of shame that surrounds immoral sexual behaviour. Thus, while we might disavow any disparagement of sexual intercourse on the part of this verse, the psalm at least provides the hint of the association, explored by the Fathers, between sex and the transmission of sin.

Psalm 50: 5 in Clement and Origen[9]

We should be looking in vain were we to seek in the Fathers the kind of psychological, existential interpretation of the psalm verse I have just elaborated. When it is cited it usually appears along with other biblical passages used in support of the teaching that human beings, even before the conscious exercise of their will, are in some way fundamentally inclined toward sin. As we read in the Old Testament, 'Every inclination of [man's] heart is evil from his youth' (Gen 8:21), or again, 'No one is free from defilement, even if his life should last but one day on earth' (Job 14:4). Moreover, this inclination or corruption stems in some way from the first human couple, and especially Adam, who is the prototype of all humanity. 'Through this one man, sin entered the world, and through sin, death, and in this way death came to all, because all sinned' (Rom 5:12). Later, as is well known, the meaning of this Pauline passage will become a point of controversy. What should be noted at this stage is that those New Testament passages in which human beings are lumped together equally without distinction into such categories as 'the ungodly', 'the unrighteous', 'sinners', or 'enemies of God', have as their main objective the manifestation of God's abundant mercy in Christ, so that the very baseness of our appalling condition as slaves to sin and subject

[8] Ricoeur (1967), 90.

[9] It is impossible here to examine all the extant material, which includes homilies and commentaries on the Psalms by over twenty Latin or Greek authors before the year 600. I have found helpful the overview of patristic texts treating this subject by Feuillet (1944), Yarnold (1971), and Rondet (1972).

to death only serves all the more to magnify the superabounding stature of divine grace and life that has been effectively realised in Jesus Christ.

It wasn't long after the apostolic period that gnostic anthropology required the church to re-contextualise and restate this typically Pauline teaching about sin. Paul often used the term *sarx* to express a kind of egocentric metaphysical power to which all human beings, without God's gracious intervention, are prone. For the gnostics, such expressions were wrongly taken to indicate that sin was an ontological defect of physical human nature. Everything bodily, including sexual desire, marriage, and procreation, was thereby either considered extrinsic to the conditions that make for authentic spiritual life, or else repudiated as morally questionable or even devilish.

In the writings of Clement of Alexandria, for whom this gnostic moralism spelled blasphemy against the creator, we find Psalm 50:5 listed as one of the texts used by the late second century gnostic teachers – Clement names a certain Julius Cassianus as his immediate target – to censure marriage and procreation.[10] Cassianus and his fellows take as gospel an alleged saying of Jesus recorded in *The Gospel according to the Egyptians*: 'I am come to destroy the works of the female', in which 'female' stands for sexual desire and its issue in birth and decay.[11] Clement does not reject this interpretation outright, but argues that the term 'female' in this text ought more properly to be taken to mean disordered sensuality, or those desires which lead to sin and death. His opponents regard woman as 'the cause of death' since she gives birth to mortal beings. Clement, adumbrating the conviction held by many of his theological heirs, concedes this fact. Yet, as he goes on to point out, she is also the mother of life since, through procreation, a married woman participates in the work of the Creator. Thus, as Clement sees it, Psalm 50:5 can in no way mean that procreation and childbirth are evil. The verse instead makes a prophetic statement about Eve, the mother of all the living, and her moral condition at the time of her sexual union with Adam. Even though Clement will entertain the possibility that Adam and Eve's sin may have been partly sexual in nature, it consisted in the fact that, being young and as yet unmarried, they came together before time and did not wait for God to join them.[12]

---

[10] *Strom.* 3.16.10, tr. Ferguson (1991), 319.

[11] *Strom.* 3.9.63, tr. Ferguson (1991), 295.

[12] *Strom.* 3.17.103, tr. Ferguson (1991), 321.

On this score, Eve may well have been 'in sin' when she conceived her son, the primordial representative of physical humanity, but 'it does not follow that he himself is in sin, still less that he is sin.'[13]

The exegesis of Psalm 50:5 takes a somewhat different turn in Origen. From Clement's writings we learn that one of the other texts the gnostics had gathered along with the psalm verse was Job 14:4: 'No one is free from stain, not even if he lives but a single day.' In Origen's writings, this verse also features alongside Psalm 50:7, though not so much in any kind of direct apologia against the gnostics as in his reflections on the practice, since apostolic times, of infant baptism. If the essence of sin consists in its voluntary nature, its character as a deliberate moral act or failure of a responsible individual, then why are babies, who are incapable of such acts, washed in the church's sacrament for the forgiveness of sins?

Origen finds opportunity to answer this question in his comments on the pentateuchal law that prescribes a rite of purification following childbirth (Lev 12:1-8). He admits he is entering into mysterious territory, that 'there are deep secrets in this statement that a woman, become a mother with the assistance of a man, is unclean and must offer a victim for sin, must cleanse herself as though she were guilty.' There is something about sexual union, conception, and birth, feels Origen, that contaminates all the persons involved. It is not difficult to detect here the Alexandrian's penchant for the doctrine of the pre-existence and terrestrial fall of souls into bodies. Even the child, he says, citing Job 14:4, 'is not exempt from stain.' Why else would the saints, in stark contrast to the customs of the pagans, lament rather than celebrate the day of their birth? Why else would David say, 'In guilt I was born, a sinner I was conceived' (Ps 50:5)? In these words David 'shows that by its birth in the flesh every soul contracts a stain of sin and iniquity [*iniquitatibus et peccati sorde polluitur*].... Undoubtedly, if in little children there were nothing that needs forbearance and pardon, the grace of baptism would be superfluous.'[14]

Can the same be said of Jesus Christ, born of Mary? Origen gives us two answers here. The defilement contracted by conception and cleansed by baptism derives, in almost biological fashion, from both father and mother. 'Every human being, on entering this world,

---

[13] *Strom.* 3.16.100, tr. Ferguson (1991), 319.
[14] *Homilies in Leviticus* 8.2-3, PG 12. 493B-496D, tr. Rondet (1972), 74-5.

contracts a blemish…. From the moment that he dwells in his mother's womb, having received from his father the substance of his body, he is already stained in his father and in his mother.' Since Christ was conceived in 'an intact body' without any male involvement, he is free from defilement in this way.[15]

But when Origen encounters the term '*their* purification' in Luke 2:21, and wonders whether it refers to Joseph and Mary only or also includes Jesus, he concludes that Jesus too, since his physical constitution was really like ours, needed purification from the defilement common to every soul clothed with a human body. This is not to say that the Lord was born a sinner. Pointing out that Job 14:4 uses the word 'stain' (*sordes*) rather than 'sin' (*peccatum*), Origen argues that it was 'for our salvation' that Jesus voluntarily appropriated the stain that marks the human condition. Anticipating the later distinction between personal sin and the inherited effects of sin, he notes the parallel in the fact that all babies, incapable of personal acts of sin, similarly carry 'the defilements of birth' necessitating their removal by baptism 'for the forgiveness of sins'.[16]

One further passage in Origen deserves our attention, in which he finds the eschatological 'regeneration of all things' (Matt 19:28) signified by physical birth, baptismal regeneration, and then resurrection. Again linking Psalm 50:5 with Job 14:4, Origen asserts the universality of the defilement contracted by physical conception and birth. Baptism removes that stain, but the purification is not fulfilled until the baptised come to that final rebirth in Christ by which they will be 'completely pure from filth and see "face to face".'[17]

As Henri Rondet has observed, there is nothing in these heuristic applications of Psalm 50:5 or Job 14:4 that bespeaks a 'doctrinal system', nor is Origen intending to address 'the transmission of original sin.'[18] Nevertheless, Origen does seem to discover the basis of personal sin in human origins and lying at some constitutive level of human generation. Somehow, the punishment for Adam's sin has passed on to all people, so that Origen can declare that all human beings were 'in Adam's loins', that is, 'precontained biologically',

---

[15] *Homilies in Leviticus* 12.4, PG 12. 539AD, tr. Rondet (1972), 75.

[16] *Homilies on Luke* 14.3-5, PG 13. 1834A-1835A, tr. Rondet (1972), 77. See also Yarnold (1971), 61.

[17] *Commentary on Matthew*. 15.22-3, PG 13. 1320B-1321B; tr. von Balthasar (1984), 353.

[18] Rondet (1972), 78-9.

when he sinned.[19] One need not put this outlook down to Origen's platonism; for him, all the relevant biblical descriptions of the human condition, not to mention the church's liturgical practice, give rise to the same conclusion.

Psalm 50:5 in the Latin Fathers

It is a matter of debate whether it was Origen or Cyprian of Carthage who first correlated the practice of infant baptism with the teaching of original or inherited sin.[20] However, Cyprian was quite probably the first to coin a striking phrase that clarifies the nature of the distinction, hinted at by Origen, between inherited 'sin' and personal sins. Cyprian only once places Psalm 50:6 together with Job 14:4; it is a bare reference in his catalogue of 'testimonies against the Jews', serving simply to assert the universality of sin's defilement.[21] But it is not altogether unimportant, for around the middle of the third century a council of African bishops, including Cyprian, discussed the question whether the baptism of babies should be delayed at least until the eighth day, in view of the Old Covenant law of circumcision. In the letter by Cyprian that constitutes the bishops' decision, they advise that baptism should by no means be withheld from the newly born. The problem is not that the baby is guilty of committing any particular sin. Rather, 'being born after the flesh as a descendant of Adam, he has contracted from that first birth the ancient contagion of death. And he is admitted to receive remission of his sins all the more readily in that what are being remitted to him are not his own sins but another's [*non propria sed aliena peccata*].'[22]

There is no mention of Psalm 50 in this letter. Indeed, it suggests more the theology of Romans 5 read in the light of the church's *lex orandi*. What connects it to Psalm 50 however is its expression of the universality of sin's effects. Perhaps we may sense something here also of the legacy of Tertullian, both positively and negatively. Tertullian had taught that male semen had become a 'channel' (*traducem*) of damnation, so that from conception every human soul, which Tertullian

---

[19] Rondet (1972), 78-9.

[20] See Pelikan (1971), 291.

[21] *Test.* 3.54, CCSL 3, 141: *neminem sine sorde et sine peccato esse.*

[22] *Ep.* 64.5, tr. Clarke (1986), 112.

believed to be quasi-material, bears an 'irrational element', an inherent tendency to sin, derived from the original fault (*ex originis vitio*) of the first man.[23] Similarly for Cyprian, something is contracted (*contraxit*) by the process of human conception and birth and removed by baptism, something which bears the character of an effect of 'another's sins'. That something is not personal culpability, but mortality ('the contagion of death') which, as a wound arising from the sin of the first human couple, is suffered by all. On the other hand, whereas Tertullian had opined on the inexpediency of baptising infants, even while holding to their innate impurity,[24] Cyprian and his fellow bishops seem to counter any notion that a newborn baby carries some kind of spiritual uncleanness that renders it polluted until cleansed. On the contrary, pious physical intimacy with the baby is commendable, for in kissing this human being 'recently formed and newly born, we are kissing the hands of God.'[25]

Already in both the Alexandrians and in the teaching of the African Latins we see in incipient form the main lines of the so-called doctrine of 'original sin' (*peccatum originalis*), as Augustine came to express it for the first time. Augustine did not invent the doctrine; he took over much not only from Origen and Cyprian but also from Ambrose who, like Origen, posited a causal relation between Christ's sinlessness and his conception from a virgin.[26] Had Christ been conceived by way of normal impregnation, said Ambrose, his body would have been contaminated by the harmful linking of generation and conception. Augustine retains this idea that sin is transmitted physiologically, but adds to it a psychological interpretation which identifies the sensual desire inescapably operative in sexual intercourse as the specific manifestation and instrument of 'the law of sin' that renders each person genuinely culpable before God. While not sinful in itself, and indeed provisionally instituted by God for our good, marital sex is nevertheless a sign and instrumental cause of sin, for no man can have sex without temporarily surrendering to the irrational lead of his penis, and irrationality is the sure mark of internal moral disorder.[27] Still, when referring in Psalm 50:5 to his conception in sin, David was not

---

[23] See the passages reviewed by Kelly (1968), 175-7.

[24] See Jeremias (1960), 81-86.

[25] *Ep.* 64.4, tr. Clarke (1986), 111.

[26] Pelikan (1971), 289, following Joseph Huhn, credits the establishment of this connection to Ambrose.

[27] See *City of God* 14.12-18. For an overview of the pertinent texts and secondary literature, see Rigby (1999).

ascribing any sin to his mother, for 'the sexual act is chaste in a married person and incurs no guilt.'[28] But with sexual intercourse and conception there is necessarily transmitted to the offspring the mortality bound to human nature as a consequence of the first sin. 'Each of us is born dragging punishment along with us, or at any rate dragging our liability to punishment.'[29] To be conceived in iniquity then means 'that there is here a kind of propagation or transmission of death, which every person contracts who is born of the union of man and woman.'[30] That Augustine takes the Latin mistranslation *in quo* ('in whom') of the Greek *eph ho* ('because') in Romans 5:12 as confirmation of this exegesis should not overly disturb us, for he gives equal weight to a parallel phrase in 1 Corinthians 15:22: 'in Adam all died.' His point is that the propagation of death is existentially bound to the procreative act, which is why Jesus, 'born outside this bond of carnal concupiscence', is mortal not as a consequence of sin, but voluntarily.[31]

To what extent did the Pelagian controversy occasion a development in this vision of the human condition?[32] In enunciating this doctrine, Augustine left the door wide open to the charge of Manichaeism on the part of his theological antagonists. Exploiting this weakness, the youthful Julian of Eclanum claimed that Augustine was basically impugning the human sexual drive, thereby implying that marriage is of the devil. His emphasis on human impotence is little short of determinism. If we are to speak of sin's transmission, it can only be by imitation of Adam's sin, not by any kind of involuntary participation in it.[33] Far from contracting any fault in consequence of Adam's sin, every newborn child embodies the 'primal innocence' of prelapsarian man.[34] In advancing this attack, Julian seemed confident of having the Greek theologians on his side. One contemporary, Cyril of Alexandria, indeed spoke of our having become imitators (*mimetai*) of Adam in as much as we have all sinned.[35] For Cyril Psalm 50:5 meant not that that the operation of sin in us is 'natural'; our nature has inherited

[28] *Exposition of Psalm* 50, tr. Boulding (2000), 419.

[29] *Exposition of Psalm* 50, tr. Boulding (2000), 418.

[30] *Sermon* 170.4, tr. Hill (1992), 241.

[31] *Exposition of Psalm* 50, tr. Boulding (2000), 418.

[32] For a sane and lucid account of the Pelagian controversy, see Bonner (1963), 312-93.

[33] See Brown (1988), 408-23.

[34] Bonner (1963), 319.

[35] *In Rom.* 5.12, PG 74. 784BC.

Adam's fall, but this does not mean that there is any in principle detriment to our capacity for self-determination (*autexousion*).[36] While the Pelagian party finally failed to find any sympathy with Cyril,[37] it was determined to preserve this doctrine of human freedom. Julian, like Pelagius and Caelestius before him, accused the aging Augustine of ascribing evil to the Creator: if the newly created human soul is defective, then God must somehow be responsible.

To this last problem, the mature Augustine never quite arrived at a satisfactory solution. He did however seem to modify slightly his exegesis of Psalm 50:5. Already in his reflections on this verse he had linked the reality of original sin with the need to receive baptism, administered even to babies. The Pelagian contest drove Augustine to emphasise more specifically the *salvific* necessity of baptism, in so far as it effectively removes a guilt that otherwise damns. As he argues in his *Enchiridion* of around 423, 'regeneration was only introduced because of a fault in our generation', a fault on account of which even those conceived in legitimate matrimony rightly say with David, 'in sin my mother conceived me.' Noting the text's use of the plural 'sins' (*peccatis*), rather than 'sin', Augustine points out that while Adam's one sin was such that it changed human nature, making it subject to the necessity of death, even the multiple sins of parents are capable of binding their children 'with guilt unless the free grace and mercy of God comes to their help.'[38] And so original sin includes the inheritance not only of mortality, but of real guilt (*reatus*). Partnership in the penalty implies some kind of partnership in the crime.[39]

Psalm 50:5 in Maximus the Confessor

Augustine's idea that the fateful legacy of Adam and Eve includes more than mortality, that it somehow implicates all human beings in some kind of culpable moral disorder in relation to God, each other, and the

[36] *In Psalmum* 50, PG 69. 1089C.

[37] Pelagius, Caeletius and Julian were all condemned by the Council of Ephesus, 431, though primarily for their happenstance association with Nestorius, not for their doctrine of sin and grace.

[38] *Enchiridion ad Laurentium*, tr. Herbert (2005), 302.

[39] Rondet (1972), 107. This is not to suggest a wholly new development in Augustine's doctrine of sin; he had used the term *originalis reatus* as early as 396 (*Ad Simplicianum* 1.2.20). See Wetzel (1999), 798-9.

cosmos, cannot properly be considered an exclusively western concept. Not, at least, if we take into account the theology of Maximus the Confessor (580-662), one of the most erudite of the Greek Fathers. In Maximus we encounter a thinker whose teaching on sin has been said to exhibit a 'disturbing likeness' to the so-called western conception we have found in Augustine. Why disturbing? Because, says Larchet, of its 'dark representation' of fallen humanity.[40] Maximus' doctrine on this subject has been commented on at length, and I do not intend to delve very deeply here.[41] However, Psalm 50:5 does offer Maximus the occasion to make some fairly arresting remarks about marriage and procreation and their role in the unfolding of sin, so it will be helpful to sketch some background against which to interpret his comments.

For Maximus, the biblical account of the fall of Adam and Eve offers a metahistorical illumination of what is true of every human being. His reflections on the situation combine originality and a deep indebtedness to his forebears, often recalling the first person perspective adopted by such figures as Gregory Nazianzen, who speaks of Christ saving 'the whole me, who wholly fell and was condemned because of the disobedience of the protoplast', or Basil of Caesarea, who lamented, 'We were once glorious when we lived in Paradise, but we became inglorious and humble from the fall.'[42] In his treatises on the passions, Maximus often pays tribute to another Cappadocian, Gregory of Nyssa, who found evil inseparably mixed up with our nature in so far as that nature has its origin in sensual passion. By their transgression, Adam and Eve made 'a permanent place for the disease.' Sin therefore does not simply originate in some primordial past, but 'in some way comes into existence together with those who are born.'[43] It was from the Nyssene that Maximus took the view, at first also accepted, but later dismissed, by Augustine, that neither procreation nor the sensual drives on which it depends belonged to God's original plan for human beings; they were only introduced in view of sin. The whole natural cycle of procreation, birth, ageing, and death manifests 'the marks of corruption', at once punitively and providentially put in place by the Creator to humble us and lead us, through the pain that

[40] Larchet (1998), 42.

[41] See further von Balthasar (2003), 179-205; Thunberg (1995), 144-68; Larchet (1998); Cooper (2005), 208-18.

[42] Gregory Nazianzen, *Orationes* 22.13, PG 35. 1145; Basil of Caesarea, *Comm. in Ps.* 114.5, PG 29. 489B.

[43] *The Beatitudes,* tr. Graff (1954), 150-1.

inevitably arises out of the pursuit of pleasure, back to himself as our only true good. In this scheme, Maximus discerns in physical procreation a double significance: on the one hand, it provisionally ensures the overall continuation of the human species; on the other hand, it perpetuates the cycle of mortality. And not only mortality, but sin too: for in acquiring existence through the law of procreation, 'no one is sinless' (*anamartetos*).[44] While he explicitly denies that marital sex is wrong, Maximus still regards procreation as a liability which, since it originally issued from a deviant carnal pleasure, remains the operative source of 'the power of our condemnation.'[45]

What then does Maximus make of Psalm 50:5?[46] He first of all affirms again that the generation of human beings by means of sexual procreation originally lay outside the Creator's purpose (*skopos*). It was Adam's 'disregard for the law given to him by God' that caused marriage to be introduced as a provisional law of propagation. As a result, all of Adam's descendants are 'brought forth in iniquity' in that they have fallen under his condemnation.

The commentary now turns to consider the second clause from the Psalm, 'in sin my mother conceived me.' Taking 'my mother' to mean Eve, Maximus presents a strikingly original interpretation apparently based on the literal meaning of the verb *kissao*, that is, in the sense in which it describes the craving pregnant women often experience for odd foods. However, *kissao* is then explicated further with *orgao*, a verb laden with moral gravity, meaning to swell or become aroused with pleasure. The play on words, recalling the original Hebrew expression, exploits the whole idea of 'swelling' and even of the 'heat' associated with sexual arousal and pregnancy. My translation hardly does it justice:

> And the phrase *and in sin did my mother conceive me* indicates that Eve, the first mother of us all, craved sin, in that she desired sexual pleasure. This is why we also fall under the condemnation of our mother, and so we say we were 'conceived' in sin.

[44] *Quaestiones ad Thalassium* 21.16, CCSG 7, 127.

[45] *Ambigua ad Iohannem* 42, PG 91. 1348C. This treatise, along with *Ad Thalassium* 61, CCSG 22, 85-105, so important for appreciating Maximus' doctrine of sin and salvation, has recently become available in a fine English translation: Blowers and Wilken (2003), 119-122, 131-143.

[46] See *Quaestiones et dubia* I, 3.1-13, CCSG 10, 138-9.

The words 'conceived' and 'craved' translate the same Greek verb, *ekissesen*. Maximus' unique contribution consists in his expansion upon that verb in terms of the phrase: *orgosa ten hedonen* (she desired [sexual] pleasure). Supplementing the Genesis account with metaphors derived from his own theological repertoire, Maximus has us envision Eve's sexual craving as a manifestation of a disorder that lies at the heart of every act of human generation. Her original preference for sensual self-indulgence, which for Maximus lies at the heart of all sin, remains an active force at work in every act of sexual passion.

There is no evidence that Maximus ever read Augustine, but like him Maximus clearly accords to procreation a definitive role in the generation and transmission of sin. It would be convenient for the more enthusiastic heirs of the Greek spiritual tradition simply to overlook this apparently 'Augustinian', even Manichaean-like tendency in Maximus as an unfortunate but momentary lapse. What precludes this option however is that it now seems quite certain that Maximus' interpretation of Psalm 50:5 is not his after all. Rather it is basically a word for word copy of an exegetical fragment on the psalter, a fragment which today has come down to us as part of a catenae of comments on the psalms ascribed to Athanasius of Alexandria and collated by Nicetas of Heraclea in the 11th century.[47] Suddenly Maximus' teaching on sin is thrown into new relief.

Why did Maximus not mention that he copied his comments from elsewhere? Part of the problem for us is that the Maximian text in question, from the so-called *Quaestiones et dubia,* is merely one of a whole staccato-like collection of theological *aporiae*. Who knows what manuscript Maximus had before him at the time? Who knows the original literary setting of these brief dicta? The only noticeable changes he or some earlier redactor makes to the Athanasian text, besides ironing out a few grammatical anomalies, is the substitution of the verb *gennasthai* (procreate) for the original *genesthai* (generate), and again the participle *gennomenoi* (those born) for the original *genomenoi* (those generated). These minor amendments are not without significance. The fact that sexual intercourse and procreation bear within themselves the operative power of sin and death does not exhaust the meaning of sexuality

---

[47] The question of the authorship of these fragments is highly complicated; see Declerck (1982), CLXXIII-CXCV; Quasten, 39. To my knowledge, Montfaucon's text of Athanasius' comments on Psalm 50:5, PG 27. 240 (cf. Geerard (1974), 28), which is littered with typographical errors, has not been critically edited.

for Maximus; if it did, that particular aspect of the incarnation would lack all recapitulatory significance. But for all his platonism, Maximus is too deeply saturated with the Irenaean theological culture to think like that. In a typically important word-play, he teaches that Christ has made his own miraculous 'procreation' (*gennesis*) from a virgin the means of redeeming humanity's congenitally corrupted generation (*genesis*), a redemption personally realised for and participated by us when we are inserted into his birth through baptism. In this way all the pathos surrounding sex and procreation is sanctified, that is, in so far as they come to function as the vehicles not only of God's creative, but also his redemptive economy.[48]

So it is that what for years has been taken as one of Maximus' more radical remarks about marriage and procreation turns out to be a copied text. Curiously, in lifting his comments on Psalm 50:5 from his unquoted source, Maximus left off its final sentence, which perhaps was absent anyway in the manuscript before him, but in which, in what seems undoubtedly Athanasian style, we are blessed with the faintest allusion to the *praeparatio evangeliae* of Genesis 3:15, a passage that heralds procreation as the means by which God himself, 'in man for man' (Newman),[49] will actualise creation's proper end. It follows on from where Psalm 50:5 left off:

> [This passage] shows that, just as from the beginning human nature has fallen under sin by reason of the transgression [conceived] in Eve, so even procreation has fallen under the curse. But from above, [God] prepares the Word, planning to make manifest the greatness of his divine gift.

Conclusion

I should like to conclude by juxtaposing the comments of two celebrated commentators on the life and thought of the Fathers. Referring to Augustine's theology, Peter Brown finds 'sexuality and the grave' bordering every human life. 'Like two iron clamps, they delineated

[48] See *Ambigua ad Iohannem* 42, PG 91. 1317AC.

[49] 'O generous love! That He who smote / In man for man the foe, / The double agony in man / For man should undergo;' John Henry Newman, *Dream of Gerontius* in Connolly (1964), 474.

inexorably mankind's loss of the primal harmony of body and soul.'[50] Meanwhile, as Hans Urs von Balthasar concludes, 'Maximus is not able to admit that sexuality has a final and fulfilling meaning.... [It] is too closely bound to time and corruptibility, and they are too closely bound to sin.'[51] In their comments on Psalm 50:5, which are seen to rely a good deal on traditional sources, both Augustine and Maximus deny us the pleasant surprise of discovering in their theology an unqualified affirmation, as we might find in theological circles today, of marriage and procreation as primordial sacraments of the Trinitarian and Christological mysteries.[52] There are of course significant differences between them. Maximus speaks of 'ancestral' rather than 'original' sin.[53] For him, it is not so much a question of sin's 'transmission' (*tradux*) as our participation in it, given that in Adam our common human nature constitutes a kind of 'concrete universal'.[54]

But my sense is that such differences do not outweigh the commonalities. Despite their vast separation by culture and circumstance, they shared a common faith in Christ and the life-giving power of his death and resurrection. True, they laboured under an intellectual legacy according to which the entire phenomenal order was felt to require radical reconfiguration if it was completely to be rid of the effects of sin's corruption, yet each, in his own unique way, provided an exposition of Psalm 50:5 that sought realistically to account for the tragic dimension of human life and the inescapable ambiguity of sexuality. Augustine, faced with the Pelagian challenge, ended up leading the western church towards a formal doctrine of sin in which, for some centuries at any rate, Psalm 50:5 functioned as one of the chief proof texts. Maximus, responding to specific questions arising from a kind of dialectical contemplation of biblical and patristic catenae, provided his monastic and ecclesial interlocutors with spiritual grist for the mill as it were, in the hope that, considering his reflections and putting them to work, they would become holier and humbler participants in the divine mysteries. And surely any use of Psalm 50 to that end is to be commended, for, as one of Fr Louth's most esteemed colleagues, Augustinian scholar Gerald Bonner, once remarked, we should consider it no

---

[50] Brown (1988), 416.

[51] Von Balthasar (2003), 204.

[52] See John Paul II (2006).

[53] *Liber asceticus* 23, 1014-15, CCSG 40, 7, 119.

[54] See Sherwood (1955), 231 n. 287.

matter for wonder 'that the greatest saints, with that deep spiritual understanding of dogma which is one of the marks of sanctity, have not only been more conscious of their sins than other men but have always professed their own helplessness.'[55] In any case, what this brief journey through early Christian exegesis does teach us, I think, is that any cut and dried division of 'western' and 'eastern' conceptions of sin, with the one invented by a scrupulous sexual neurotic, and the other as a globally optimistic, integrally emerging consensus of minds over the course of several centuries, is little more than a myth.

Bibliography

von Balthasar, Hans Urs (1984 [orig. 1956]) *Origen: Spirit and Fire: A The-matic Anthology of his Writings*, tr. Robert J. Daly (Edinburgh)

— (2003 [orig. 1988]) *Cosmic Liturgy: The Universe According to Maximus the Confessor*, tr. Brian E. Daley (San Francisco)

Blowers, Paul M. and Wilken, Robert Louis (trs.) (2003) *On the Cosmic Mystery of Jesus Christ: Selected Writings from St Maximus the Confessor* (Crestwood, New York)

Bonner, Gerald (1963) *St Augustine of Hippo: Life and Controversies* (Norwich)

Boulding, Maria (tr.) (2000) *The Works of Saint Augustine: A Translation for the 21st Century*, part III, vol. 16: *Expositions of the Psalms 33-50* (New York)

Brown, Peter (1988) *The Body and Society: Men, Women and Sexual Renuncia-tion in Early Christianity* (London)

Connolly, Francis X. (ed.) (1964) *A Newman Reader* (Garden City, New York)

Dalglish, Edward R. (1962) *Psalm Fifty-One in the Light of Ancient Near East-ern Patternism* (Leiden)

Declerck, José H. (1982) *Maximi Confessoris Quaestiones et Dubia* (CCSG 10, Turnhout-Leuven)

Feuillet, A. (1944) 'Le verset 7 du «Miserere» et le péché originel', *Recherches de Science Religieuse*, 5-26

Geerard, M. (ed.) (1974) *Clavis Patrum Graecorum*, vol. II (Turnhout)

Graff, Hilda C. (tr.) (1954) *St. Gregory of Nyssa: The Lord's Prayer and the Beati-tudes* (ACW 18, London)

Herbert, Bruce (tr.) (2005) *The Works of Saint Augustine: A Translation for the 21st Century*, part I, vol. 8: *On Christian Belief* (New York)

Hill, Edmund (tr.) (1992) *The Works of Saint Augustine: A Translation for the 21st Century*, part III, vol. 5: *Sermons 148-183* (New York)

---

[55] Bonner (1963), 316.

Jeremias, Joachim (1960) *Infant Baptism in the First Four Centuries*, tr. David Cairns (Library of History and Doctrine, London)

John Paul II (2006) *Man and Woman He Created Them: A Theology of the Body*, tr. Michael Waldstein (Boston)

Koehler, Ludwig and Baumgartner, Walter (eds.) (2001) *The Hebrew and Aramaic Lexicon of the Old Testament*, vol. 1, tr. and rev. M. E. J. Richardson (Leiden)

Larchet, Jean-Claude (1998) 'Ancestral Guilt According to St. Maximus the Confessor: A Bridge Between Eastern and Western Conceptions,' *Sobornost* 20/1, 26-48

Lust, J. et al. (1992) *A Greek-English Lexicon of the Septuagint* part I (Stuttgart)

Pelikan, Jaroslav (1971) *The Christian Tradition: A History of the Development of Doctrine*, vol. 1, *The Emergence of the Catholic Tradition* (Chicago)

Quasten, Johannes (nd) *Patrology*, vol. 3 (Allen, Texas)

Reardon, Henry (2000) *Christ in the Psalms* (Ben Lomond, California)

Ricoeur, Paul (1967) *The Symbolism of Evil*, tr. Emerson Buchanan (Boston)

Rigby, Paul (1999) 'Original Sin', in *Augustine Through the Ages: An Encyclopedia*, ed. Allan D. Fitzgerald (Grand Rapids), 607-14

Rondet, Henri (1972) *Original Sin: The Patristic and Theological Background*, tr. Cajetan Finegan (Shannon, Ireland)

Sherwood, Polycarp (tr.) (1955) *The Ascetic Life; The Four Centuries on Charity by St Maximus the Confessor* (Westminster, MD)

Wetzel, James (1999) '*Simplicianum, Ad*', in *Augustine Through the Ages: An Encyclopedia*, ed. Allan D. Fitzgerald (Grand Rapids), 798-9

Yarnold, Edward (1971) *The Theology of Original Sin* (Theology Today 28, Hales Corners, Wisconsin)

JOHN A. MCGUCKIN

ORIGEN'S USE OF THE PSALMS IN THE TREATISE *ON FIRST PRINCIPLES*

Origen of Alexandria is a remarkable theologian, one who never ceases to surprise. Reference to the invaluable research tool of the *Biblia Patristica*[1] (that multi-volume collation of all patristic biblical references, with a whole book in the series devoted solely to Origen himself) will demonstrate the impressive (and significant) fact that he commented, over a long and dedicated theological career, on every single psalm in the Psalter. He had his favourites, of course, but the choice to leave absolutely no psalm unremarked upon was surely a policy decision he had explicitly taken, even as a young man. He began his project of a monumental *Commentary on the Psalms* while he was still resident in Alexandria, and before his treatise *On First Principles* appeared. Eusebius tells his readers that while resident in Alexandria Origen had already produced his *Commentary on Psalms* 1-25.[2] Jerome tells his own readers[3] that even as a young child Origen's mother had taught him to recite the Psalms as his personal prayer book.[4] And Jerome's admiration of his (then) hero's monumental work on the Psalms was explicitly noted when he drew his readers' attention to Origen's labours on the Psalms amounting to 46 books in total, and in addition *Scholia* (*Excerpta*) on Psalms 1-15.[5] Nine of Origen's *Homilies*

---

[1] ed. Allenbach (1980).

[2] Eusebius, *Church History*, book 6. In *First Principles* 2.4.4. Origen refers the reader to his *Psalm Commentary* where he has given a fuller interpretation of Psalm 2 which is at issue in this locus. His residence in Alexandria thus saw the production of *Commentary on Psalms* 1-25, First Principles, Commentary on St. John bks. 1-5, *On The Resurrection, Stromata* bks. 1-10, *Commentary on Genesis* (8 books), and *Commentary on Lamentations* (5 books).

[3] Jerome, *Epistle* 39.22.

[4] Thereby indicating that she was either Jewish or Christian herself.

[5] Jerome, *Epistle* 33.

on the Psalms survived intact through antiquity,[6] but in recent times V. Peri[7] has opened our own readers' eyes afresh by restoring to Origen the seventy four *Homilies on the Psalms* which were once attributed to Jerome himself, though it seems the latter was merely the translator and preserver. When he was busy preparing the *Hexapla*, Origen took the extra effort to add another three columns of translations that he had in hand to represent the Psalms, thus making it in reference to this single canonical book, no less than an *Enneapla*.

This determined attempt to have an encyclopaedic coverage of the Psalter in his work as a theologian clearly signals his immense respect for the Psalms, a sense of value which places them below his overwhelmingly authoritative scriptural teachers, John and Paul, but certainly buoyantly high in the ranks of scriptural sources of authority. For him, it was an axiom that the Logos had left direct and clear traces of his presence, his soteriological *paideia*, in the sacred verses he had given to his Church as its continuing prayer book, through the inspired medium of David and Solomon. The Psalter was a special book, however, in so far as it was especially marked throughout with direct utterances of the Lord, especially with reference to his plan of salvation. It is not David who speaks to us in such sacred utterances as Psalm 21, but the Lord himself describing his economy of salvation long in advance, for the eyes and ears of those who would be given the grace of the Spirit. Origen, thus, regularly finds in the psaltic verses marks of a special revelation. For him it is a book in which those who have been given the gift of inspired reading, those whom he designates as 'the priests of the Lord',[8] can read the secret messages of the Logos describing the 'things hidden since the foundation of the world.' We can witness, in his use of the Psalms in the *First Principles,* some of this aspect of his general theological approach, for here he uses the Psalms especially to establish a biblical authority for some of his most daring 'speculations' on the nature of the fall of souls, and to advance his boldest statement of Logos Christology.

The study of the Psalms in the whole extant work of Origen would be a worthy and useful topic of research, but it is one that exceeds the bounds of this present project of *encomium* for another theologian whose life-long dedication to the ways of the Divine Wisdom (ὅπου λόγος ἄγει,

---

[6] Five on Psalm 36; five on Psalm 37; and two on Psalm 38. The references made to Psalm citations in this article, will follow Origen's practice, namely using the LXX numerations rather than those of the Hebrew bible.

[7] Peri (1980); idem, ed., CCSL 78.

[8] Further see McGuckin (1985).

as Origen liked to say) has similarly resulted in a most impressive body of work for the sustenance and defence of the Christian faith. So, let this short note on the use of the Psalms in the Περὶ Ἀρχῶν serve a much more modest, yet double, purpose: to make a merely preliminary sketch of deeper matters, but also to offer a heartfelt tribute of thanks to one who is an example to so many, as priest, scholar, and friend.

The *First Principles* cites the Psalms more than any other Old Testament book; fifty five times in all.[9] Origen's use of Isaiah in the treatise (overall one of his favourite Old Testament authors) then comes the closest to it, with fifty citations, and other major prophetic books averaging ten citations, with lesser Old Testament literature[10] averaging three or less. Many of the psaltic citations apply the Psalms within a cluster of other Old Testament citations, so as to provide what we might call 'generic ballast' to his argument; that is showing to his readers that his ideas have a genuine network of scriptural support sustaining them. In other word, that they are 'traditional' and unarguable (a brave *apologia* in a church, and at a time, where he must have known that the *simpliciores*[11] would react against many of the esoteric aspects of his theology). In these cases the Psalms do their work like bricks in a wall. It is the togetherness of citation that counts. We do not need to dwell over long on individual instances of texts within this category of use. This style of employment would apply to about half the instances of Origen's psalm citations. We can list them quickly, to clear the land, as it were, so that we can get a closer focus on the more fundamental topography of what *dogmata* have struck him as needing a closer and more intimate exegesis of the Psalms, to support his interpretations.

In order of their appearance in the treatise, Origen applies Ps. 145:8[12] as his primary proof in *First Principles* 2.1.5,[13] to show the making of the world *ex nihilo* by the divine Word.[14] To bolster that reference

---

[9] With multiple attestations for Psalms 33, 45, 62,102, 104 and 116.

[10] 'Susannah', Maccabees, Malachi, Amos, Daniel, Lamentations, Sirach etc.

[11] The 'simpler faithful' whose views he so often sets out to correct and rebuke in his work, and whose censure he certainly feared in case (as it actually did, straight after the issuing of the *First Principles*) it called a whirlwind of reproach on his head as a teacher of theology in good standing with his bishop.

[12] 'He spoke and the (heavens) were made, he commanded and they were created.'

[13] Cited hereafter according to the English translation Butterworth (1936), as FP followed by the relevant page number: FP, 80.

[14] He repeats the same argument in *First Principles* 3.5.1 (FP, 237) using Psalm 101:26-27, in parallel with the teaching of Christ himself in Mt. 19:4.

he also adduces 'confirmation' from 2 Maccabees and the *Shepherd of Hermas*.[15] He uses Psalm 8:4. 'When I see the heavens the work of your hands,' to demonstrate, against the Gnostics, that the worlds God made are from his hands, and not the product of an evil force; but also against the *simpliciores*, to show that the scripture says 'heavens' in the plural, and that we are to be careful with the literal meaning of the holy word, but not to think literalistically that the heaven and the earth that we see with our material eyes are the sum total of God's complex creation of world upon worlds. This is an important point for him to establish theologically in the *First Principles* since so much of his argument in that treatise is to be taken up with metaphysical implications of the fall to corporeality by the noetic creation. To establish it in *First Principles* 2.3.6,[16] Origen begins with a cluster of proofs comprised of Genesis 1:1f and Isaiah 66:2, but chiefly turning around Paul's teaching[17] of the distinction between things seen and unseen. In the first of these arguments, that God's goodness is inherent in the created orders, he is arguing that, accordingly, moral corruption (intrinsic evil) cannot be ascribed to the material order *per se*. While this seems to be a broadside rebuttal of typical gnostic attitudes to 'fixed fates', it is actually a double-sided rebuke to the catholic *simpliciores*, reminding them that if the world is founded by the Creator on the basis of not being 'fixed' (because the will of God is such that it expects the created orders to respond in free will, either for the good or the bad), then it follows, as a constitutional part of Christian metaphysics, that created existence is all about moral change: improvement or decline. The world is thus clearly meant to be a place of reform and improvement, ascent to truth. In a very clever argument he has set out his case that a book on *First Principles* that teaches at its core the notion of the Fall and Ascent of Souls, is not as eccentric as some of his critics would have it.

The argument against fixity of fates, and in defence of free will, is substantially repeated in *First Principles* 3.1[18] using Psalm 80:13-14 to demonstrate the people of God's freedom of conscience, where it appears in a cluster comprising Micah 6:8; Deut. 30:15, 19; Is. 1:19-20; and Mt. 5.22, 39. A similar argument appears later in the same section

---

[15] 2 Macc. 7:28; Hermas, *Mandates* 1.1.

[16] FP, 92

[17] 2 Cor. 4:18; ibid. 5:1.

[18] FP, 164.

of the treatise[19] when he explains to his readers how God's 'predeter-mination' of the created order does not imply the abolition of human moral freedom and responsibility, since the divine pre-ordering is based upon God's will for our salvation based upon our obedience. In this case, it is in the context of explaining that the words of Romans 9:16[20] do not bear a gnostic interpretation, that Origen adduces the 'parallel elucidation' of Solomon's Psalm 126:1[21] to show that scripture in each instance speaks about how God has pre-knowledge of our choices, but does not set us in within a fixity of fates that conversion cannot affect.

A similar background of argument can be presumed in *First Principles* 3.2[22] where Origen takes the catholic *simpliciores* to task[23] for believing that a moral fall from grace is always attributable to demonic influence, and is only something to be expected since human psychic abilities, if pitted against demonic powers, will always come up short. Here he uses Ps. 34:6[24] within a cluster of other texts[25] to show from memory how many passages there are in scripture that demonstrate that fallen angels are in opposition to the just on earth; but not that they are given irresistible power over them. The demonic opposition to Christ during his earthly ministry is demonstrated from Psalm 2:2.[26] He brings this argument about the relation of demonic influence to human moral responsibility to a pitch in the same section of his treatise[27] summarizing with his teaching that evil thoughts in a human heart arise from three separate sources: from outside circumstances and influences, from our own inclinations, and from demonic suggestions; and here he

---

[19] *First Principles* 3.1 (FP, 196-97).

[20] 'It is not what human beings want, or try to do, that counts, but the mercy of God.'

[21] 'If the Lord does not build the house, in vain do the builders labour.'

[22] FP, 212-13.

[23] It will become a *cause célèbre* in the late Origenistic crisis, as the 'simple attitude' that demons cause the believer to fall from grace was a major presumption of the desert ascetics. Evagrios will spend much of his theological efforts refining these leads given by Origen in relation to the psychology of repentance.

[24] Describing an evil angel pursuing and harrowing human beings.

[25] 1 Sam. 18:10; 1 Kgs 22:19-23; 1 Chr. 21:1; Sir. 10:4; Zech. 3:1; Is. 27.1; and Ez. 29:3

[26] 'The kings of the earth stood up and the principalities were gathered together against the Lord and his Christ.' In this instance both the 'Kings' and the 'Rulers' designate fallen angels for Origen. Here in *First Principles* 3.3 (FP, 224-25), the Psalm is set within a cluster of other verses, namely: Ez. 28:12-19 (by allusion); 1 Tim. 6:20; and 1 Cor. 2:6-8.

[27] *First Principles* 3. 2 (FP, 216-17).

uses a dyad of Psalm 75:11,[28] alongside Psalm 83:5[29] to make his point. These psaltic verses are once more set within a cluster of other biblical (and apocryphal) passages.[30]

The above represent his 'main' uses of the Psalms, in those cases when the Psalter is not his only, or his major, source of biblical proof-texting. There are five other instances too where he will use a psalm reference as a scriptural support, in what we can classify as passing observations or arguments. In this category we could list first his argument (again one surely addressed to the *simpliciores*) that the 'anger of God' as mentioned in scriptural texts is not meant to be taken literally. He says Psalm 2:5 is the best example of this, and refers his readers, in the *First Principles* 3.2.6,[31] to the *Commentary on the Psalms* he has written where the idea is taken up further. Moreover in *First Principles* 2.5.2[32] he teaches that the corollary of God allowing each person freedom of conscience is that he will also apply to each one the due and exact recompense for their deeds, whether good or ill. Here Origen uses Psalm 61:13 as his chief proof,[33] set within a supportive cluster of other texts,[34] where the Psalm stands at the head of the list, and is cited again to bring that list to a close.

Again, in *First Principles* 2.5.3,[35] Origen uses Psalm 77:34[36] in another medium sized *catena* of texts[37] to demonstrate the unity of the God and Father of Our Lord Jesus Christ, and the God of the

---

[28] In the LXX version: 'For the thoughts of man shall confess you, and the residue of his thoughts shall hold a day of festival to you.'

[29] LXX version: 'Happy is the man whose acceptance is with you O Lord; your ascents are within his heart.'

[30] Mt. 15:18-19; Sir. 10:4; 2 Cor. 10:5; 2 Cor. 8:16; Tob. 5:4; Zech. 1:14 (LXX); Hermas, *Mandates* 6.2; Epistle of Barnabas 18.

[31] FP, 100. He comes back to the same idea in the *Homily on Jeremiah* 18.6: 'If you hear the anger of God spoken about, or the wrath of God, you must not imagine that that this anger, or wrath, are passions of God.'

[32] FP, 102-3.

[33] 'You repay each man according to his deeds.'

[34] Ex. 20:5, 34:7; Deut. 5:9; Ez. 18 :2-3; Mt. 25:41; Mt. 11:21; Mt. 15:22; Mt. 22:1-13

[35] FP, 104.

[36] 'When he slew them, then they would seek him.' Origen's point here is that the ones who were killed by God are the ones the text says sought after him. The scripture, thus, does not advocate an angry and vengeful God as the Gnostics argued (viz., that God killed some in the desert and thereby frightened the others to return to him), but rather depicts a God who uses punishments on earth to stimulate the return to love of the fallen souls. When the soul receives the suitable correction (after it has 'been slain') it turns back to seek its correcting Teacher with love.

[37] Phil. 4:8-9; 1 Pet. 3:18-21; Gen. 19:24; Ezek.16:55.

Old Testament. In *First Principles* 2.5.4,[38] Origen also uses Ps 72:1 and 117:2 to continue to demonstrate his thesis, against the Gnostics, that the God of the Old Testament is one and the same as He who is depicted in the New, and that He is intrinsically good. He begins the scriptural *catena* in this latter case with three Gospel proofs, interleaves the two psalm verses, introduces a *Lamentations* citation, and then concludes with two references to John.[39] Instructively, when he recapitulates his argument at the end of the chapter, he suggests that, though he might offer more evidence in due course, this is quite enough biblical material to stand for the whole Old Testament as well as the New. Psalms and Lamentations, therefore, can be taken as wholly representational of all the Old Testament theology for Origen. A fourth instance of this generic use of the Psalms appears in *First Principles* 2.7.2[40] where Origen teaches that while every rational creature has a generic share in the Holy Spirit, just as they do of the Word and Wisdom of God, only the elect can be said to have the 'special share in the Spirit' and then only after the Ascension of the Lord into heaven. Before that time the gift of the Spirit was restricted to the prophets and a few saints only. To demonstrate this theology, Origen makes a dyad of the (expected) text from Joel 2:28, as derived from Acts 2:16-17, and the unexpected text of Ps71:11.[41] Once more his shorthand seems to be the suggestion that the Psalms can 'stand for' the spiritual heart of the whole Old Testament. Finally, this is a sentiment echoed again at *First Principles* 4.3.14[42] where Origen sums up a long series of esoteric teachings on the nature of the fall of souls and the long ascent back to spiritual communion with God. He knows it to be a controversial teaching, and therefore turns his attention at the end of his exposition to those who might have increasing doubts as to his orthodoxy:

> Nevertheless in all these matters let it be enough for us to conform our mind to the rule of faith, and to think of the Holy Spirit's words, not as a composition depending on feeble human eloquence, but in accordance with the sayings of scripture: 'All the glory of the King lies

---

[38] FP, 106.
[39] Rom. 7:13; Lk. 6:45; Mk. 10:18; Ps. 72:1; Ps. 117:2; Lam. 3:25; Jn. 17:25; Jn. 15:19.
[40] FP, 117.
[41] FP, 117. 'All nations shall serve him.'
[42] FP, 310.

within'[43] and 'a treasure of divine meaning lies hidden within the frail vessel of the poor letter.'[44]

Yet again we note here that the juxtaposition of a single Psalm, with a single Pauline allusion, is enough for Origen to do duty for the entire body of sacred scripture. His use of Paul and John to stand for the 'first fruits' of the New Testament revelation is a well known aspect of Origen's approach to biblical exegesis as a matter of the Spirit's mystics apprehending the Spirit's hidden truth.[45] What is interesting here is his pattern of using the Book of Psalms in a similar way, albeit a mere suggestion, that the Psalter is the heart of the Old Testament in a way that allows it to 'represent' the whole.

So far, then, we have looked at the manner in which Origen has approached the Psalms in the *First Principles* in a generic way. We see, even here, a master exegete who does nothing carelessly, but on the contrary who, even in passing remarks, has a depth and subtlety to this theology that cannot be captured by a superficial or rapid reading. Now I would like to turn specifically to those instances in the *First Principles* where Origen approaches the Psalms in a substantive and conscious way; leaning on them to make up a significant part of a sustained argument. It is in these places that we shall gain, undoubtedly, a clearer sense of what Origen believed the Psalms would offer to him as an inspired exegete who, in his own turn, was seeking out the meanings and messages of the Holy Spirit of God, the 'glory of the King that lies within.' In this respect Origen approaches the Psalms to make two extended theological arguments. The first is the establishment of basic premises about the Trinity (especially Christological doctrine); the second is the foundation of a major argument within the *First Principles*, namely the concept of the whole of the created order as a system of repentance and return, the fall and ascent of the souls.

The two systematic ideas are intimately related, of course. In the first Origen establishes a Logos Christology as the unravelling of the Triune nature of God but makes a massive Christological advance on his predecessors by explaining all of Logos theology as a *paideia* of salvation. Before him, in the main, the Christian Logos theologians had used the scheme to account for the existence of the material order, and

---

[43] Ps. 44:13 (LXX).
[44] Cf. 2 Cor. 4:7.
[45] Further see McGuckin (1995).

the various mediations of revelation; now Origen firmly proclaims Logos Christology as the very heart and meaning of the Christian doctrine of salvation: communion with the Logos as life and salvation in itself, and the whole purpose and substance of the gift of God to the cosmos. In the second exposition, the story of the fall and ascent of the souls, Origen comments on the nature of the divine outreach in terms of its effects on the creation. The unity of God becomes the inner core of all cosmic striving: return to oneness with The One is the human experience of the divine unity within the Trinity. We could sum it up in this way: in his poetic hands the doctrine of God (theology of revelation) becomes a soteriology of deification by love; and thus his account of the metaphysics of creation (the experience of multiplicity) becomes a vast hymn to the unity of God that calls all spiritual life into harmony with it. Let us begin with his doctrine of God.

The first premise of the first chapter of the first book of the *First Principles* is the establishment, on the basis of the foundation stone of Ps 35:10, that God is pure Spirit; not a body even if conceived in the most ethereal terms. To clarify this cardinal principle is, literally, Origen's first thought as a systematic theologian. His intent is to correct the Christians who might erroneously impute a 'divine substance' from an exegetical basis; relying on Deuteronomy to designate God as a 'consuming fire',[46] or using St. John's concept of 'God is spirit'[47] anhypostatically. On the contrary, the true significance of scriptural theology is given by a deeper scrutiny of the sacred text:

> And so I would ask such people what they would say about this passage of scripture, 'God is light and in him there is no darkness?'[48] He is that light, surely, which enlightens the whole understanding of those who are capable of receiving the truth, just as it is written in the 35th Psalm: 'In your light we shall see light.' For what other light of God can we speak of, in which a person sees light, except God's spiritual power, which causes the one enlightened by it to see clearly the truth of all things, or else to know God himself, who is named the Truth? This then is the meaning of the phrase: 'In your light we shall see light.' It means: In your Word and your Wisdom, namely the Son,

---

[46] Deut. 4:24.

[47] Jn. 4:24.

[48] 1 Jn. 1:5.

we shall see you, the Father. For how can we possibly think that just because it is named light, it is the same as the light our sun gives out? How could there be the slightest grounds for thinking that out of this material light the root of knowledge could be derived, or the meaning of truth discovered?'[49]

This is a major systematic argument for Origen. One on which all his subsequent work will depend. It states the fundamental root of Logos theology, and in his hands how that functions both as a revelatory system (the giving of the light of the knowledge of the Father) and the bestowal of life (the 'seeing light' as the gift of divine power, and the discovery of the meaning of truth). Having established it as his corner-stone, he goes on to develop the precise terms of his Logos Christology. In *First Principles* 1.2[50] he makes a brilliant and bold conclusion, once more set on the basis of the Psalms standing for the synopsis of 'the scriptures'. He attacks, head on, the central problem of third century Logos theology, namely: is the Logos 'subsequent' (later and thus inferior) to God the Father, since he is the medium of creation? He answers it in a brilliant fashion that places all subsequent Logos theology on a new footing: the title Maker is itself subordinate in the Godhead to the title Father:

> Since we are dealing with the question of how Wisdom is a pure effluence, or emanation, of the glory of the Almighty[51] it is needful here to give a brief warning, so that no-one might think that the title of Almighty belonged to God before the birth of Wisdom, through which he is called Father. For it is Wisdom (that is the Son of God) which is said to be the 'pure effluence of the glory of the Almighty'. So whoever is inclined to believe this ought to hear what the scriptures plainly indicate, for they say: 'In Wisdom you have made all things',[52] and the Gospel teaches that: 'All things were made by him, and without him there was nothing that was made.'[53] From this we should understand that the title of 'Almighty' (*Pantocrator*) cannot be older in God than that of 'Father', for it is through the Son that the Father actually is the Almighty.

[49] *First Principles* 1.1.1 (FP, 7; translation adapted).
[50] FP, 24.
[51] Wisd. 7:25.
[52] Ps. 103:24.
[53] Jn. 1:3.

This concept he comes back to explicitly in *First Principles* 1.4.5[54] and once more he stands his fundamental Christological argument on the basis of the same Psalm:

> In Wisdom, who ever existed with the Father, the Creation was always present in form and outline; and there was never a time when the prefiguration of those things which hereafter were to be did not exist within Wisdom. It is probably in this way that, so far as our weakness allows, we shall maintain a reverent belief about God, neither asserting that his creatures were unbegotten and coeternal with him, nor on the other hand that he turned to the work of creation to do good when he had done nothing good before. For what is written is true: 'In Wisdom you have made all things.'[55] Indeed, if all things have been made in Wisdom, then (since Wisdom has always existed) there have always existed within Wisdom, by prefiguration and pre-formation, those things which afterwards received substantial existence.[56]

The eternity of the Logos as the creative Wisdom of God, then, is the premise Origen establishes as the reason why all things are contained in Him. All the created orders (he means primarily the spiritual orders, since the material orders exist 'in time' for the sake of the rehabilitation of the former) partake of God's eternity in a type of prefigurement. The pattern of eternity is within them. This is why, when the souls fall away from the communion with the Logos, an imbalance is set at the heart of God's everlasting plan for the destiny of all being: and why the ultimate restoration of the whole is the driving goal and purpose of the Logos' restless energies within the Cosmos. It is for this reason that, in Origen's hands, Christology, Cosmology, and Soteriology, are finally woven as a single theological strand in Christian systematics.

The same Psalm and verse[57] are applied again in *First Principles* 2.9.4,[58] immediately after a Pauline and Johannine pericope[59] to demonstrate that 'all things were made in and through Christ.' The

---

[54] FP, 42.

[55] Ps. 103:24.

[56] The argument is synopsized, for condemnation, in Justinian's *Letter to Mennas*, fragment 10 (Mansi (1763), 528; Butterworth, trans., FP, 43) as follows: 'All genera and species have forever existed, and some would say even individual things; but either way it is clear that God did not begin to create after spending a period in idleness.'

[57] Ps. 103:24.

[58] FP, 132.

[59] Col. 1:16; Jn. 1:1.

Psalm once again is offered to the reader as a harmonization to the twin great apostolic voices, to stand in for the whole of the Old Testament on a matter of the highest revelatory import. At *First Principles* 4.4.3,[60] when he returns to the same theological idea, he applies the same evangelical citations as before, but this time adds in as the third, representative, Old Testament voice, Ps. 32.6: 'And David also points to the mystery of the Trinity when he says, "By the Word of the Lord all the heavens were made strong; and all their power by the Spirit of his mouth."' In this instance he carefully lifts out of the text a stress on the twin agencies of the Word and the Spirit, elevating Logos and Pneuma to the significance of hypostatic titles. On several other occasions Origen takes the Psalms as primary evidence of the deity and power of the Holy Spirit as distinct hypostasis within the Trinity.[61] Setting the evidence of the Psalm, alone as it were, in the balance against: 'The New Testament, on the other hand, where we have proofs in abundance.'[62] The Psalms, standing for the whole Old Testament on a matter of the deepest mystery of God, are here the only source where the mystical light glimmers until the New Testament revelation shows the fuller light.

These psaltic usages we might sum up, then, as his primary Christological argument that all things came into being through the agency of the Logos, and thus hold their being in dependence on him. It will be the great polar node of his theology from which all his other uses extend like variations on a theme. The first of these other uses is what we may call the 'secondary' Christological argument, namely how the Christ of God worked the economy of incarnation to assist the fallen souls. The second is how the fallen souls experienced that decline from being, and their restitution to it, in and through the Logos incarnate. In relation to the first, Origen returns to a summary of his doctrine about the Trinity at the end of the *First Principles,* 4.4.1 and following.[63] This is preceded by a long series of demonstrations in the Fourth Book,

---

[60] FP, 317.

[61] *First Principles* 1.3.2 (FP, 30), applying Psalm 50:13 ('Do not deprive me of your Holy Spirit'); ibid. 1.3.7 (FP, 36), applying Psalm 103:29 ('You take away their spirit and they will die, you send forth your Spirit and they will be created and you shall renew the face of the earth'); and again in ibid. 1.3.7 (FP, 37), applying Ps. 32:6 ('By the Word of the Lord the heavens were made, and all their power by the Spirit of his mouth').

[62] *First Principles* 1.3.2 (FP, 30), listing an exemplary *catena* of Mt. 3:16; Jn. 20:22; Lk. 1:35; 1 Cor. 12:3; Acts 8:18; Mt. 28:19; and Mt. 12:32.

[63] FP, 313f.

about how the scripture is to be interpreted correctly. Not only does he mean here that they ought to be interpreted 'spiritually', but clearly that they have to be interpreted Christocentrically, as an explication of the economy of the salvation given to fallen souls in the Logos incarnate. It is fitting, then, that in this section[64] he turns his attention to how centrally the Psalms unfold clear Christological doctrine:

> Surely we hardly need to speak of the prophecies relating to Christ found throughout the Psalms? In one of the Odes[65] the title is given: 'For the Beloved', whose tongue is said to be as 'the ready pen of a scribe', and who is 'fairer than the sons of men' because 'grace was poured out upon his lips.'[66] Now the proof that grace was indeed poured out upon his lips is the fact that although he spent such a short time in teaching (for he taught not much more than a year and a few months)[67] the world has nevertheless been filled with his doctrine, and with the religion that came through him. For there has arisen in his days 'righteousness and an abundance of peace'[68] which will endure until the consummation, which in this text is what is meant by the reference to the 'failing of the moon'; and he will continue to have dominion 'from the rivers to the ends of the earth.'[69]

Ps. 44 which is first used here, is one of Origen's most common Christological Psalms. He cites it at *First Principles* 2.6.1[70] to demonstrate that the 'grace poured out upon his lips' (Ps. 44:3) is the significance of the 'self-emptying' that Paul speaks of in Philippians 2.7:

> And so, when we consider these immense and marvellous truths about the nature of the Son of God,[71] we stand lost in the deepest wonderment that such a being who towered high above all, should have 'emptied himself' of his majestic state, and become a man,

---

[64] *First Principles* 4.1.5 (FP, 262; translation adapted).

[65] Origen refers to the LXX title of Ps. 44, and cites verses1-3 of the same.

[66] Ps. 44:3.

[67] Based upon Lk. 4:19; cf. Origen, *Homilies on St. Luke*, 32.

[68] Ps. 71:7.

[69] Ps. 71:8.

[70] FP, 109 (translation adapted).

[71] His divinity, his eternity, his mediation between the Father and the Cosmos, his mysterious revelations, and his form and function as Logos, as demonstrated by a *catena* of New Testament texts: 1 Tim. 2:5; Col. 1:15-17; 1 Cor. 11:3; Mt. 11:27; Jn. 1:1; Jn. 21:25.

dwelling among men; a fact which is evidenced by the 'grace poured out upon his lips', and by the witness that the heavenly Father bore him.[72]

The Christ mystery is of such depths that the commentator says explicitly that he stands 'in deepest wonderment', not merely a rhetorical aside, but a signification for this most careful of theologians, that the reader is being conducted to the apex of a revealed mystery, an ecstatic noetic truth. At this moment it is again indicative that the entire scriptural evidence is summated in the 'direct' words of the Father, as given by Mt. 3:17 and Ps. 44. The Psalms once more stand as the synopsis of all the mystical heart of the Old Testament, as they relate to the sacrament of Christ. Psalm 44:8: 'You have loved justice and hated evil, and so God, your God has anointed you with the oil of gladness above your fellows' is also used by Origen at *First Principles* 2.6.4[73] to demonstrate why the Logos poured out 'the oil of gladness', that is the presence and grace of the Holy Spirit, so abundantly on the Only Begotten Son (the Great Soul Jesus), since that soul had never deviated from union with the Logos, but from eternity had clung to the Divine Wisdom in love. In later centuries, when Origen's particular nuances about the distinction between the Soul Jesus and the Incarnate Logos had been set aside, this text seemed above all others to offer ammunition to an anti-Chalcedonian theology; apparently expounding a vision of a Jesus who possessed the Spirit (only) in a higher degree than the prophets; and so was a particular target for condemnation in the Justinianic anathemata.[74] His argument, in context, had been to insist that the Incarnate Christ was ensouled. In fact that it was the soul's presence and mediation that was an 'oil of gladness poured out', making the Incarnate Lord very different indeed from the prophets and the apostles who were bearers of the Spirit's grace. Origen's distinction bears the force that the servants who 'run in the odour of his ointments'[75] are not to be compared with the 'one who is the vessel containing the perfume itself.'[76] This doctrine of the ensoulment of the Word of God

---

[72] Mt. 3:17: 'This is my Beloved Son.' The relation between the two texts being provided, for Origen, by the same designation used in both the Gospel and Ps 44: 'My Beloved.'

[73] FP, 111-12.

[74] The passage is cited in Justinian's *Epistle to Mennas* (Mansi (1763), 528).

[75] *Song* 1.3: 'Your name is an oil poured out,' which makes the Bride run after the fragrance of the odour.

[76] *First Principles* 2.6.6 (FP, 113).

on earth (what most theologians today would describe simply in terms of the word 'incarnation') is a major concept which Origen wishes to clarify so as to remove from it any suggestion that the Logos might be imagined materially. He sees it as both a critical and a deeply mystical conception, and he returns to it several times, using the Psalms as his primary scriptural proofs in each case;[77] but it was the aspect of his Christology that would suffer most damage in subsequent ages, because of the hypostatic difference he underlined between the Soul Jesus and the person of the Logos.

Having thus established, by using the evidence of select Christological Psalms, his primary and secondary Christological argument (that the Word is the supreme and eternal mediator of the Father to the Cosmos and that the Word came to earth for the salvation of his Elect), Origen also uses the psalm evidence to establish his other major corollary to this theology: namely how the fallen souls got into trouble in the first place, and how they were to be rescued by the Logos once they had fallen. If he sees the Christological doctrine as a sublime and elevated revelation, he undoubtedly sees this latter aspect of his teaching as an esoteric mystery. He clearly sensed (and rightly so) that it was an aspect that might get him into trouble with the traditionalists[78] of the Alexandrian church (joining biblical ideas of the Fall, with Middle Platonic notions of the lapse of pre-existent Psyches). For this reason above all, he was particularly concerned with showing how his understanding of the lapse of souls to an embodied existence needing redemption, was something that could be set on the fundament of the irrefutable biblical evidence of the Psalter. He makes this argument carefully, cumulatively, across many parts of the *First Principles*. All in all, it accounts for a major part of his doctrine of the lapse of souls standing on the back of psaltic proof-texting.

In the first instance he approaches the idea in *First Principles* 1.6.1. Here he states (alluding to the Gospel source)[79] that the time of the general consummation is known to God alone. But then he passes on immediately to state, on the basis of a double psalm exegesis woven parallel with Pauline proofs, that this is not all we can state about the consummation; rather

---

[77] *First Principles* 2.6.7 (FP, 114), using Ps. 88:51-52; *First Principles* 2.8.1 (FP, 121), using Ps. 21:20-21; *First Principles* 2.8.5 (FP, 128), using Ps. 43:20 and Ps. 84:6; and *First Principles* 4.4.4 (FP, 318-19), using Ps. 44:7.

[78] Not just the *simpliciores* this time.

[79] Mt. 24:36.

that the concept of 'restoration'[80] is at the heart of it, not vindictive judgement which was an unsupportable idea of the *simpliciores*. The fundamental principle of eschatological judgement as restoration, follows inexorably from the concept of God's essential and philanthropic goodness. He says:

> We believe, however, that the goodness of God, through Christ, will restore his entire creation to one end: even his enemies being conquered and subdued. For so says the Holy Scripture: 'The Lord said to my Lord, sit on my right hand until I make your enemies a footstool under your feet.'[81] If it is not very clear what the prophetic language means in this case, let us learn from Paul the Apostle, who says more openly: 'Christ must reign until he has put all his enemies under his feet.'[82] And if even this clear declaration of the Apostle is not sufficient to inform us what is the meaning of 'putting enemies under his feet', let us hear more of what he says in the words that follow: 'For all things shall be made subject to him.'[83] And what is this subjection by which all things must be made subject to Christ? In my opinion it is that same subjection in which we too desire to be made subject to the Lord, and in which the apostles, and all the saints who have followed Christ, were subject to him. For when used in reference to subjection to Christ, the very word implies that salvation which emanates from Christ, to those who are subject. This is what David also said: 'Shall not my soul be made subject to God? For my salvation comes from him.'[84]

Once again two psalms have stood as fundamentals of his argument in suggesting a critical (and controverted) doctrine. They stand with Paul, as sufficient epitomes of scriptural revelations of mysteries. From their import Origen is able to state the summation of his whole eschatological theology: that in the end lies the beginning; or in other words, that the end of things has to be deduced from the 'first principles' of why God made anything whatsoever; the soteriological imperative revealing all:

> This is why we must, from such an end as this, deduce the very beginning of things. For the end is always like the beginning. Just as there is one end of all things, so we must understand that there is one beginning of all things; and as there is one end of many things, so

---

[80] Further, see Norris (2004).

[81] Ps. 109:1.

[82] I Cor. 15:25.

[83] I Cor. 15:27-28.

[84] FP, 52-53.

from one beginning arise many differences and varieties, which in their turn are restored, through God's goodness, through their subjection to Christ, and their unity with the Holy Spirit, to one end which is like the beginning.[85]

Origen moves on from this axiomatic statement to deduce in the following sections of the treatise, that souls which have fallen from God's unity and grace, must (since they have declined) be able to ascend also. Change in order and status, being proven possible by the very fall, must be operative in the ascent to salvation. At this juncture he takes the Church's ancient theology of repentance, and daringly applies it cosmically and universally: the ascent and descent of the noetic beings takes place in his system, far beyond the limits of this earthly life. This notion of passing into different orders set off the alarm bells all over the ancient Church for many generations to come.[86] What Origen saw as the single reality of noetic existents assuming greater, or lesser, proximity to God, across the vast cosmic scale of their life in God, became for his hostile readers, the notion of changing 'life-forms' or substances, in a series of lives. Nevertheless, at *First Principles* 1.6.4,[87] he defends his premise that the life in God will be a series of great and numerous changes, from the juxtaposition of 1 Cor. 7:31, and Ps 101:26. Even for a highly controversial idea, it is enough, for him, to set these two particular authorities side by side and thereby to have offered an irrefutable 'proof' of the whole revelation.

The idea of the principle of 'change' is demonstrated on a few other occasions in the *First Principles*. We can see it, for example, in the 'more popular'[88] Christian conception of the supervisory duties that are assigned to angels as not being accidental or random things, but rather promotions based on their merits (and thus demonstrative of their ability to improve their status). In making this point at *First Principles*

---

[85] *First Principles*.1.6.2 (FP, 53).

[86] The beautiful classicism of this statement in *First Principles*.1.6.2, of the principle of the One and the Many, is given tendentiously by Jerome in the *Ep.ad Avitum* 3, where he stirs in the text of *First Principles* 1.6.4, and caricatures Origen to say that on this basis, men pass into being daemons and so on.... 'thereby mixing everything up so that one may be changed from an archangel to a devil, and on the other hand a devil may turn into an angel.'

[87] FP, 57.

[88] By which I think he meant to describe this controversial theory in terms not based on the philosophical principle of the One and the Many, but in terms of the belief in Guardian angels that would appeal to the *simpliciores*.

1.8.1[89] Origen offers a long *scriptural catena* in which the psalm text appears as one among other proofs.[90] To this, later in *First Principles* 1.8.1,[91] he added in the more 'esoteric' doctrine (based upon his use of Ps 102:20) that the philanthropic guiding duties which were given to the angels were promotions awarded to them after their lapse; but were glories that did not match the glory that they had lost. The concept of the 'changeability' of souls within the world is re-presented at *First Principles* 2.3.6-7.[92] Here Origen argues that the Christian tradition is agreed that souls can alter their orientation, for good or ill, within 'the world'. But he presses the point to demonstrate (once again making a pairing of the Apostle Paul and the psalm evidence)[93] that the 'world' is often spoken of by Paul as signifying much more than this material world we can see,[94] indeed to signify the transcendental dominions of God; and thus the concept of *post mortem* (and *pre-mortem*) soul-change is a valid exegetical (and thus 'traditional') statement. In *First Principles* 2.3.7, Origen recapitulates this argument, this time pairing the psalm evidence with Dominical words taken from the Gospel.[95] Knowing that he is working over 'esoteric' ground, he is careful to offer what he clearly regards as substantive proofs.

In a Greek fragment of the *First Principles*[96] preserved by Epiphanius and Jerome, Origen also supported this theological doctrine of the spiritual changes that occurred in souls before their embodiment (sin causing the lapse into history), and the potential for great spiritual progress after death; seemingly in a part of the treatise that Rufinus suppressed. It is interesting to note at this juncture that all the exegetical proofs are taken from the Psalms alone. Speaking of the lapse of souls to embodiment Origen says here:

> When the prophet says, 'Before I was humbled, I went astray',[97] the saying is uttered in the person of the Soul itself.[98] It tells us that in

---

[89] FP, 66.

[90] Enoch 41; Rev. 2:1, 8; Acts 12:7-15; Acts 27:23-24; Mt. 18:10; Ps. 33:8.

[91] FP, 68; according to the testimony of Antipater of Bostra, preserved by St. John of Damascus in *Sacra Parallela* 2.770-71 (PG 96. 504-5).

[92] FP, 92-93.

[93] Rom. 8:20-21; 2 Cor. 4:18; 2 Cor. 5:1; Ps. 8:4.

[94] An argument to which he returns in *First Principles* 4.3.10 (FP, 304-5), using Ps. 85:13.

[95] Mt. 5:3-5; Ps. 36:34.

[96] FP, 124. Epiphanius, *Heresies* 64.4; Jerome, *Against John of Jerusalem* 7.

[97] Ps. 118:67.

[98] That is not in the *Vox Christi,* but speaking in the part of the Soul that indicates the 'humbling' is the corrective embodiment, consequent on the pre-temporal lapse.

heaven it 'went astray' before it was 'humbled' in the body. And when it says, 'Turn again my Soul to your rest',[99] it means that whoever here on earth has played a manly part by good deeds, will turn back to the former 'rest' by reason of the righteousness of his conduct.

In a synopsis of this teaching, which Rufinus does preserve in the Latin,[100] Origen uses the same Psalm (114:7) to show the possibility of the *Psyche* rediscovering the 'same degree of fervour which it once had at the beginning'. He concludes his argument with an emphatic stress on the mysterious nature of this teaching, merely adumbrated by the prophet David:

> All these considerations seem to show that when the *Nous* departed from its original condition and dignity, it became, or was termed, a Soul (*Psyche*); and if ever it is restored and corrected, it returns to the condition of being a *Nous*. … Some such fact the prophet appears to point to when he says: 'Turn again my Soul to your rest.'

In this way Origen sets the basis of his doctrine of the Soul's change-ability, and he demonstrates that if this is accepted (as it should be, since it can be clearly demonstrated from Paul and the Psalms) then the concepts of the pre-temporal lapse, the embodiment of souls, and the possibility of post-mortem spiritual progression, are not so 'strange' to Christian tradition as they might at first appear. Later, at *First Principles* 4.4.7-8,[101] he returns to the concept, but this time from a heavily philosophical starting point. Here we can presume that he is not primarily addressing the *simpliciores* anymore. He states the premise straightforwardly in scholastic terms:

> We should note this; that a substance never exists without quality, and that it is by the intellect alone that this substance which underlies bodies, and is capable of receiving quality, is discerned to be matter.

Of course having discussed this as a philosopher among philosophers, he returns to his conclusion theologically:

> Of course, someone may now ask whether we can obtain any sup-port for this view of things from the scriptures? Well, it appears to

[99] Ps. 114:7.
[100] *First Principles* 2.8.3 (FP, 125).
[101] FP, 322-23.

me that some such view is indicated in the Psalms when the prophet says,[102] 'My eyes have seen your incompleteness.' In this passage the prophet's mind, examining with piercing insight the very beginning of things, and by reason and understanding alone separating matter from its qualities, appears to have perceived God's 'incompleteness', a state which we certainly think of as being brought to perfection by the addition of qualities.

He then uses the text of Enoch[103] to offer additional support of this enigmatic meaning. But it is indicative here that he explicitly allows the prophet of the Psalms to bear mystical insights of the 'most piercing' and deductive nature into the very beginning of the patterns of God's creation, before it received varieties of form. We are shown the practical importance of this philosophical-scriptural argument about form and formlessness very shortly afterwards in *First Principles.* 4.4.9[104] when he concludes that this is the basis of his own deduction that if a soul falls from its substantive form (provided by intellective, contemplative, communion with God) it will not necessarily lapse into non-being, since it is eternal by grace. This being so, however, the alternative position is necessary to affirm, namely that it is within the very nature of an eternal Soul, *qua* soul, to have to turn again and thus always receive an everlasting 'reforming':

> Is it not impious to say that the *Nous* which is capable of receiving God, should ever admit of a destruction of its substance? As if the very fact that it can perceive and understand God would not be sufficient to secure its perpetual existence. This is the more likely since, even if the Nous through carelessness should fall away from the pure and perfect reception of God into itself, it nevertheless always possesses within itself some seeds, as it were, of restoration and recall to a better state. These become operative whenever the inner man (who is also called the rational man) is recalled into the image and likeness of God who created him. And this is why the prophet says: 'All the ends of the earth shall remember, and shall return to the Lord; and all the families of the nations shall worship before him.'[105]

---

[102] Ps. 138:16 (LXX).
[103] Enoch 21:1; ibid. 41:1.
[104] FP, 327.
[105] Ps. 21:7.

It is no accident that Origen chooses to end and rest his argument about the fall and rise of eternal souls, not merely once more on the Psalms at this juncture, but precisely, and particularly on this verse of the Psalms: a text which though spoken through the prophet, is attributed by Origen (and the whole Church tradition as he knew) to the *Vox Christi*.[106] Just as the Lord spoke through the Psalms, eliding time and space in the revelation of the mysteries of his Economy, so too, Origen implies, the Psaltic texts are ideally positioned for revealing the great mysteries of God's plan before history, the shape and forms of the eternal plan for eternal souls.

Our study has been limited to one treatise (albeit a central one for him) but it clearly shows a pattern in Origen's application of biblical evidence in the course of his theologizing, and sufficient indication to allow us to make some overall conclusions about his attitude to the Psalms, and their particular value as proof texts. The Psalms hold immense significance for him. They are of sufficient weight to 'stand for' the whole Old Testament revelation if necessary. Origen feels that they possess a dominating force of tradition both for the *simpliciores*, and for the more educated members of the Christian community (including his own *schola*). He uses the Psalms often to balance his reliance on those other 'first fruits' of the scriptural revelation, Paul and John. He sees the Psalms as distinctive in the Old Testament as being able to penetrate the shadows much more effectively, and frequently to serve as the *locus* of the direct teachings of the Logos himself. Accordingly, the 'Prophet of the Psalms' can sometimes see acutely, penetratingly, into the greatest of all mysteries of the cosmos. As we have seen in this study, Origen lists these explicitly as: the divinity of the Word and the Spirit; the form of the Church's Christology (especially how the Logos as agent of creation is the heart and soul of the spiritual orders and all their longing for restored communion with God); and lastly, the manner in which the fallen souls can ascend once more. It is especially in relation to the exposition of his Christology of *paideia*, and his doctrine of the changeability of souls (the possibility of *pre-* and *post mortem* spiritual alteration) that Origen is confident in relying heavily on free-standing Psaltic proof texts. In using the Book of Psalms precisely to ground his controversial doctrine of the changeability of the spiritual orders, he seems motivated by a desire to convince the catholic

---

[106] It is the culmination of the Psalm which the Crucified Lord recites on Calvary: Mt. 27:46.

simpliciores of Alexandria; an audience he seems often to address in the argumentation of the *First Principles*. No better authority could he offer them. What for him was a wondrous and acute revelation at the core of the mystery of cosmic redemption, was at the same time the very prayer book for the unlettered. Origen is indeed a theologian of surprises. No less is this true than in his most subtle approach to the Psalter in his extremely subtle treatise *First Principles*.

Bibliography

Allenbach, J. et al., eds. (1980) *Biblia patristica : index des citations et allusions bibliques dans la littérature patristique*, vol.3: Origène (Paris).

Butterworth, G.W. (1936) *Origen On First Principles* (London).

Mansi, J.D. (1763) *Sacrorum conciliorum nova, et amplissima collectio*, vol. 9 (Florence).

McGuckin, J. A. (1985) 'Origen's Doctrine of the Priesthood,' *Clergy Review* 70.8, 277-86; ibid. 70.9, 318-25.

— (1995) 'Structural Design and Apologetic Intent in Origen's Commentary on John,' in G. Dorival and A. Le Boulluec, eds. (1995), *Origeniana Sexta, Origen and the Bible* (Leuven), 441–57.

Norris, F. (2004) 'Apocatastasis,' in J. McGuckin, ed. (2004), *The Westminster Handbook to Origen of Alexandria* (Louisville), 59-62.

Peri, Vittorio (1980), *Omelie origeniane sui Salmi: contributi all'identificazione del testo latino*, SeT 289 (Vatican City).

MIHAIL NEAMȚU

PSALMODY, CONFESSION, AND TEMPORALITY

1. Individual asceticism and cosmic salvation

The desert fathers were among the most assiduous Christian readers of the Psalter during the fourth-century in Egypt. In this paper I should like to analyze more systematically the hermeneutical practice of psalmody in correlation with the sacramental practice of confession, as they are revealed mostly in the *apophthegmata patrum*.

Psalmody serves as one of the main spiritual tools used for the healing of one's wounded past. Because of its literary richness and spiritual depth, the Psalms attributed to King David offer powerful insights for every Christian individual and ecclesial community in search of self-understanding. This latter knowledge of the self requires the encounter of God in his saints, which can never be achieved without scriptural mediation. Psalmody brings together powerful historical narratives, prayerful lamentations, and doxological chants, against the background of which the whole monastic liturgy unfolds. Confession, on the other hand, is the sacramental practice which helps one cancel out the leanings of the old Adam.

The mutual interaction between psalmody and confession teaches the monastic novice how to accept their belonging to a particular 'time-space' unit of God's economy in Christ.[1] Psalmody

[1] The latter 'time-space unit' could be perhaps equated with Mikhail Bakhtin's notion of 'chronotope,' which aims to reflect the 'intrinsic connectedness of temporal and spatial relationships that are artistically expressed in literature' (Bakhtin [1984]: 84 sq). Each type of narrative-*cum*-practice must belong to a specific time-space unit, which in its turn is constitutive part of the monastic liturgy. With the major exception of Jean-Yves Lacoste (1990), contemporary scholars of theology have not produced a major discussion of the notion of liturgical temporality, in response maybe to the philosophical insights provided by Husserl and Heidegger in the 20th century continental philosophy. One still does not have clear categories which could describe the invisible 'space-time unit' which one enters by performing some specific practices? Even less discussed are the temporal marks of human affectivity, in its various modes of existence within the liturgical framework (to give here only one example, the liturgy requires the heideggerian notion of *Befindlichkeit* to be rearticulated, taking into account the subtle transitions of the inner state of compunction or joy).

presents the universal story of God with man as the cure for any human lapse into oblivion. Confession, on the other hand, looks into the individual past, and searches to empty it from the fruits of disobedience and death. These temporal registers speak to each other, and are blended within the general framework of the monastic liturgy, for which past, present, and future must gradually become one.

Any conceptual reconstruction of the desert fathers' teachings might help us see in their writings some excellent resources for a devotional library. The fathers and mothers of the Egyptian church connected the Psalter to other branches of the spiritual life: the meditation and the practice of pure prayer, just as they related the sacrament of confession to the self-giving of God in the Eucharist, and to the baptismal encounter of Christ.[2] It might then be possible to suggest that past, present, and future become part of one continuum of sanctified time. We might also say that Psalmody encapsulates mainly the wisdom of the past, while prayer focuses on the here and now of the divine presence, with meditation looking forward into the generous promise of the eschatological future. Equally, confession reinforces faith by healing the sins of our individual and collective past; the Eucharist is the celebration of unmediated love; while baptism endorses hope in the future. Since sacramental life and biblical hermeneutics cannot be separated, I suggest that psalmody, with its theological exposition of *Heilsgeschichte*, could indeed be regarded as an invisible counterpart of the confessional approach to one's individual past.

The desert fathers' engagement with the Psalms in the wilderness[3] entailed an almost forgotten practice of memory, which in its turn corresponded to the self-emptying process of daily repentance.[4] Great athletes of God such as St Anthony or St Pachomios had an implicit

---

[2] A clear three-fold division of the contemplative activity of the desert fathers appears in a saying of Abba John the Dwarf 35 (Ward, 35), 'It was said of the same Abba John that when he returned from the harvest or when he had been with some of the old men, he gave himself to prayer (εἰς τὴν εὐχὴν), meditation (μελέτην) and psalmody (ψαλμῳδίαν), until his thoughts were re-established (ἀποκατεστάθη) in their previous order.' See also Bacht (1955) and Wortley (2006) on meditation in the desert fathers' tradition.

[3] Professor Andrew Louth (1991) has dedicated an entire book to this central experience of Christian life, which is related to seclusion, poverty, and solitude, celebrated in paradoxical terms by the desert fathers.

[4] Rousseau (1999), 98, '[R]epentance had to be social and convincing.'

understanding of time, and salvation history, in which the Psalter often was seen as an indispensable compass. The Egyptian monks and nuns pulled out of the broken world for the sake of the 'unseen warfare' held between 'the old man' (Colossians 3, 9) and the 'New Adam' (Romans 5, 14). In order to achieve the goal of salvation in Christ, they performed both sacramental activities (such as the Eucharist, or the confession) and narrative practices (such as psalmody, prayer or scriptural meditation).

Either the individual, or collective participation in divine revelation, always makes references, for example, to the sacred geography of the apostolic Christianity. References such as Gethsemane, Rome, Alexandria, or Jerusalem have an implicit relationship to the temporal categories of past, present, or future. Distinct act of remembrance, meditation, or prayerful reflection in connection to, or beyond these points of reference, also cultivate the virtues of faith, hope, and love. When reading the Psalter, and by associating this practice with bodily actions such as fasting and prostration, one comes to inhabit a specific time zone on the map of divine economy. The virtue of faith is particularly enriched by psalmody (since its grounds one's subjective relationship to the tradition), hope by meditation (since the latter shows the open horizons of the sacred future), and love by pure prayer (since it abolishes discursive reasoning, and brings the experience of God into the *hic et nunc* of gratitude and praise). These virtues, supported by specific practices, are all part of what might be called monastic liturgy.

In confrontations with the 'terror of history'[5], the Christian ascetic builds up his response in three major sequential, or simultaneous, directions. First, it is the recourse to the wisdom of the past. Secondly, it is the exploration of the rich present. Thirdly, there are the unexplored possibilities of the future. The whole dynamics of desert eschatology depends on the synchronisation of the works of faith, hope and love into one great liturgical performance. It is certainly difficult to

---

[5] The phrase belongs to Eliade (1971), 93-162, whose description of the secularised eschatology of modernity in terms of 'terror of history' may refer implicitly to the modern experience of totalitarian revolutions. However, since all generations have their encounter with the apocalyptic dimension of history, I myself take the liberty to use this term with reference to the ancient times as well. For a monastic perception of the terror of history, see the exhortation of Melania the Elder (342-410), as recorded by Palladius, *h. laus.* 54.6: 'Children (παιδία), it was written four hundred years ago, "it is the last hour (ἐσχάτη ὥρα ἐστί)." Why do you love to linger in life's vanities? Perhaps the days of Antichrist will surprise you (μήποτε φθάσωσιν αἱ ἡμέραι τοῦ ἀντιχρίστου).'

compartmentalise too strictly the temporal structures at work in the monastic life. There are, however, clear strategies of coping with the demands intrinsic to this threefold temporality. In this paper, I shall focus only on two practices of great importance.

2. Psalmody and the 'Manifold Wisdom of God'

Nobody can even begin to understand the complex dynamics of deification in the writings of the desert fathers, before the redeeming encounter with the 'manifold wisdom (τῆς ποικίλης σοφίας) of God' (Ephesians 3, 10). The peaks of contemplation and 'one to One' dialogue (μόνος πρὸς μόνος)[6] cannot be seen ahead of the work of purification. One of the most profound books revealing God's plurality of meanings is the Psalter. For St Athanasios the Great this collection of hymns and prayers constituted the best *vade-mecum* for our sanctification.[7] Along with him, all the desert fathers took it to be inspired by Christ in the Holy Spirit, to the extent it was contemplated as a hologram of both the Old, and the New Testament.[8]

Abba Evagrius states that psalmody belongs to the realm of complexity or multiplicity and, thus, precedes the immediate knowledge of God.[9] Evagrius himself used to sing the Psalms in the desert while pacing in his cell or his courtyard.[10] The physical act of moving to and fro reminds one of the Jewish traditions, developed in the rabbinic schools.[11] Bowing reflects, for example, the inner move of the humbled intellect, divided as it is between the representation of the clear past and the intuition of the often dim eschatological promise. Psalmody, supported by the technique of murmuring and recitation *sotto voce*, helps

[6] N 89.

[7] Athanasius, *ep. marc* (PG 27, 11-46). For a critical research, see Kannengiesser (1962), 359-381; Rondeau (1968); Mammarella (1992); Stead (1982) appeases the severity of Dorival's judgment on the Athanasian authorship, for which see Dorival (1980); Rondeau (1982), 79-86 and Fossas (1997).

[8] Burton-Christi (1993), 118 notes, quoting Palladius, that the practice of psalmody was not entirely private. It was 'about three o'clock when the psalmody could be heard proceeding from each cell at the Mount of Nitria.'

[9] Evagrius, *or.* 83. For a commentary, see Bunge (1987), 13-28, and the very informative study of Dysinger (2005), 62 sq.

[10] Palladius, *h. laus.* 38 (Amélineau, 113), quoted by Dysinger (2005), 15.

[11] See Uri Ehrlich and Dena Ordan (2004), *The Nonverbal Language of Prayer: A New Approach to Jewish Liturgy* (Tübingen: Mohr Siebeck, 2004), p. 29-64.

those who cannot easily concentrate on the few words of the prayer of the heart.[12]

The Egyptian monastics did not confuse the reading of the Psalms with engagement in silent meditation[13], or with the gift of pure prayer.[14] Psalmody is more often associated with singing,[15] since it offers the novice different scores for listening to the voice and the music of divine Providence. The Psalms which include historical passages, such as the recounting of Moses' encounter with the Pharaoh's armies, were read spiritually.[16] The literary richness of the Psalter helped to structure and to clean the novice's imagination. The Psalms were read in distinct portions[17] and encouraged identification with the heroes of the past. For example, one was taught how to walk in King David's footsteps, and how to emulate the vigilance of Christ, who on the Cross uttered nothing else but the words of Psalm 22.

Psalmody differed from contemplative meditation on the Scriptures, which took place especially during long night vigils[18], when sitting was necessary.[19] As part of the ancient customs belonging to the scholarly traditions of *ars memoria*, psalmody required the learning by heart of key scriptural texts.[20] These paragraphs were

[12] Guillaumont (1977), 168–183 on the ancient evidence existing for Jesus prayer in the Coptic monasticism.

[13] Abba Arsenius 40 (Ward, 18), 'I have repented of having spoken, but never of having been silent.'

[14] For psalmody and meditation in the alphabetic *apophthegmata*, see Abba Epiphanius 3 (Ward, 57); Abba Theodore of Enaton 3 (Ward, 79); John the Dwarf 35 (Ward, 92); Serapion 1 (Ward, 226).

[15] McKinnon (1994), 505-521.

[16] See Vogüé (1989), draws on the writings of St Benedict, following a brief account of Evagrius' theory. See also, Vogüé (2000), 855-878.

[17] N 229 speaks of the practice of reading twelve psalms in the morning, and in the evening, respectively. For a succinct exposition of this theme, see Davril (1987).

[18] Scrima (1974), 911, points out: 'la scienza acquisita delle veglie riduce la parte delle "tenebre" – dell'incosciente – rese piú fitte da ciò che la tradizione ascetica chiama "sonno" oppure "la morte dell'anima prima della morte corporale", vale a dire l'insensibilità, la leggerezza, la sclerosi dello spirito.'

[19] Meensbrugghe (1957) on the prayer schedule; Rouillard (1960); Gélineau (1953) on psalmody in the writings of the fathers; Taft (1982) on 'praise in the desert'; Kok (1992) with specific reference to St Pachomius' office.

[20] This technique must be done in adequate ways. Abba Poemen 8 (Ward, 167) speaks of a visitor who 'began to speak of the Scriptures, of spiritual and heavenly things. But Abba Poemen turned his face away and answered nothing.' The explanation follows: 'He is great and speaks of heavenly things and I am lowly and speak of earthly things. If he had spoken of the passions of the soul, I should have replied, but he speaks to me of spiritual things and I know nothing about that.'

repeated and ruminated day and night.[21] The great masters of the desert did not encourage artificial rules for memorising the Scriptures.[22] While he affirms the necessity of scriptural reasoning instead of philosophical dialectics, the monk recognises the limited capacities of the Bible *qua* Bible to provide him with the ultimate knowledge of God. Beyond all letters, the Spirit must always be at work.[23]

The therapeutic effects of such hermeneutics were dependent upon the synthesis of narrative and sacramental practices. Psalmody, meditation, and prayer were often conducted in solitude. This experience proved the capacity of demonic powers to tempt and to corrupt the human mind with unclean thoughts (λογισμοί). The holy book was available as helper in this battle with evil imagination. How could the young novice reverse the constant tendency of the human body and mind towards disorder? He could use the scriptural tradition, in tandem with the most ancient patristic commentaries, in search of the sacred webs of meanings (νοήματα) which could indicate the will

---

[21] There is no space here to discuss the role of 'sacred memory' and the ancient techniques of recollection. For the Western understanding of the use of memory in the classical and medieval period, see the invaluable book of Coleman (1992). Among the ancient authors, Aristotle makes the distinction between 'memory' (ἡ μνημή) and 'recollection' (ἡ ἀνάμνησις), for which cf. *On the soul*, 427a-429b and *On memory and recollection*, 451b-452b, with a thorough commentary in Annas (1986). Recollection is an ambiguous term in the Platonic philosophy, which at times is interpreted as supporting the doctrine of metempsychosis. In modern times, however, the Aristotelian distinction is rephrased by Bergson (1912), 86-168, who defines the rapport between the active and passive dimensions of recollection by coining the couple 'mémoire-habitude,' which is mostly involuntary, and 'mémoire-souvenir.' See also the very substantial discussion offered by Ricoeur (2000), 18-37, who suggests that we are what we can remember in the absence of any physical support for that act of recollection.

[22] Bishop Epiphanius II (Ward, 58) is ascribed the following comment: 'ignorance of the Scriptures is a precipice and a deep abyss.' One may recall here Evagrius' technique of responsorial addresses, called 'antirrheticus,' which instructs the monastic to learn by heart short scriptural quotations, used later during the inner battle with the demonic thoughts (Socrates, *h.e.* 4.23). Known and used by a many desert fathers, this method was not recommended in all the circumstances. See Bunge (1997). For Evagrius' text, see O'Laughlin (1990) and (1992); Evagrius' text on the *antirrhetikos* is extant only in Armenian and Syriac (Greek translation: Frankenberg, 472-545).

[23] The modern reader must have in mind also the particular circumstances, which made the text of the Scriptures far more difficult to acquire for the desert fathers than for the Christian teachers of Alexandria. Resorting to the physical text of the Bible was not always the solution at hand, given the value of manuscripts circulating in the fourth century Egypt. See Harmless (2000) on Abba Poemen's technique of memory.

of God even in the most clouded circumstances.[24] At stake here is not only the intellectual purification which replaces the evil λογισμοί with Christological νοήματα.[25] The monk is also called to widen his heart and understand the multiple layers of the Scriptures as one path towards union with the One.

Before that stage of perfection, the Psalter teaches the monk how to wonder at the marvels of divine creation. Psalmody is bound to entertain the need for diversity of references and information. By following the process of purification, one discovers the spiritual meaning of the Scriptures.[26] Only after that, the contemplation of nature leads to the apex of Christian life, which is the understanding of the supreme mystery of the Holy Trinity.[27] As located in the realm of the manifold wisdom of God, psalmody has a preparatory role. It can 'calm the passions (τὰ πάθη κατευνάζει) and curb (ἀπεργάζετα) the uncontrolled impulses in the body.'[28] With the help of this constant digestion of the ancient lessons of faith, the haunting past of sins gives way to the brighter horizons of salvation and freedom. This vision depends on whether the monastic will persevere[29] in reading or singing the psalms 'with understanding and rhythm,'[30] by means of which he avoids distraction.[31] The novice must recognise in the world of 'entertainment' only penultimate or derivative values, and even a trap on the way towards communion with the divine Word.[32] This is why some of the desert fathers suggest that prayer without distraction is easier to practice than psalmody with an undisturbed mind. The Psalms' subject is often the sacred history of Israel, in all its multifarious dimensions. Pure prayer must therefore follow psalmody, and go beyond even the most rarefied type of imagination.

---

[24] Evagrius, *cog.* (Géhin / Guillaumont, 208-210).

[25] GCSF 5.19: 'we don't need to uproot the thoughts, but only to resist them.' In the Old Testament, *logismos* refers to a divine or human plan (Ezek. 38:10). In Romans (2:15), St Paul uses the same noun in the positive sense (with the meaning of 'calculation'). Only in later, the meaning of λογισμοί becomes predominantly negative.

[26] Bunge (1994), with reference to Evagrius.

[27] Evagrius, *sc.* 247 on Proverbs 22, 40 (Géhin, 342).

[28] Evagrius, *or.* 83.

[29] Evagrius, *or.* 87.

[30] Evagrius, *or.* 82.

[31] Evagrius, *pr.* 69.

[32] Lacoste (1990), 39.

Psalmody is meant to have therapeutic effects. Amma Syncletica, a fourth-century hermit from Alexandria[33], thought that grief, which so often darkened the mind of Christian ascetics, could be cast out 'mainly by prayer and psalmody.'[34] Sorrow can be thawed in psalmody, while mental oppression needs to be cured through prayer. It is easy to see that the exorcism of sinful memories requires that mind has an unquestionable authority over other faculties.[35] Like a mill, the noetic intellect grinds the seeds of the Scriptures through psalmody, meditation or prayer.[36] Psalmody prepares the ground for biblical rumination, to be followed by pure prayer.

3. Confession as Kenosis

After the sacrament of confession takes place, one is called to inhabit again the wisdom of the sacred past, which sin has condemned to oblivion. But how exactly does this self-emptying happen through the work of confession? To what extent can it be called an anthropological version of the divine kenosis? Psalmody, as we have seen, requires immersion into the scriptural ocean of meanings. This can heal the soul stricken by the poverty of gossip and idle-talk. The sacrament of confession, in its turn, suspends one's sinful proclivity towards personal judgement, and calls instead for a confrontation of forgetfulness as one of the major sources of alienation. When ignorance steps in, the complex web of passions begin to separate man's conduct of life from God's commandments (Psalm 119). It is then the role of the masters of the Christian desert to offer practical advices for fighting oblivion, and for making the remembrance of the divine economy part of one's daily habits.

How does one lose the desire for God? What can help the novice regain it? Which are the major 'surgical' operations that one has to undergo, when the tempting memories of the corrupted past come back with full power and wipe out the purity of heart, the spirit of

---

[33] For her biography, see Pseudo-Athanasius (PG 28, 1487-1558). Bongie (1995) and Castelli (1990) offer the English translations of this text; Corrigan (1989) compares Amma Syncletica with Saint Macrina, the sister of Basil and Gregory of Nyssa.

[34] Amma Syncletica 27 (Ward, 235).

[35] N 529.

[36] John Cassian, *Conf.* 1.18.

contrition, and the gift of love? The answer to this series of questions is given within the one-to-one encounter between the spiritual father and the novice. Its goal is to enable the disciple to receive the great riches of the Christian tradition, in lieu of the memory of old transgressions. The Psalter read in moderate portions, or recited by heart, brings about a deep sense of connection with the fate of Israel. Biblical wisdom makes the disciple reflect more upon the presence of God in the church, the Scriptures, and the world. This act of transition is meant to 'redeem time,' by retrieving paradise while casting into oblivion the works of evil. Thus, one may be granted a foretaste of eschatological freedom.

However, an intellectual working over the sacred texts is not sufficient. The novice must turn to confession and listen to the multiple voices of his heart, and separate between good and the bad thoughts. In a spirit of repentance, he can ask advice from his spiritual father,[37] who is often seen as the icon of Christ resplendent in the works of his saints. Every monastic in the desert was encouraged to start his career in the vicinity of a mentor, capable not only of giving general instructions, but also of listening to personalized confessions. In the absence of this dialogical institution, the promise of adoption as sons and daughters of the Most High would become only nominally valid. It is only discipleship that can encourage receptivity towards the very words of wisdom uttered during psalmody, meditation, or prayer.

How can one overcome the memories of a troubled past? The most widespread answer given by the desert fathers is 'humility,' against which the spirit of pride always struggles. Confession is what brings light into this otherwise invisible warfare. It gives bold encouragement to those who are bereft of divine grace. It encourages true repentance, and the love for the Word beyond all words. In the words of Abba Matoes, 'the nearer a man draws to God, the more he sees himself a sinner.'[38] This brings the expurgation of all hidden negative thoughts. The practice of confession becomes indispensable in the struggle against laziness, self-regard, and neglect of the divine commandments. The spiritual director must first know from his own

[37] Dörries (1962), 287 points out that the first instance for the acknowledgment of sin is prayer, not confession. In modern spirituality, one comes across confessions without sin and prayers without confessions.

[38] Abba Matoes 2 (Ward, 143).

experience the secret alchemy of repentance.[39] He should be able to show the novice why the vagaries of evil thoughts (λογισμοί) are self-destructive.

The practice of psalmody, seen as an individual dialogue between man and God, cannot substitute for ecclesial conversations among various Christians who find themselves at different stages in their spiritual pilgrimage. This latter dialogue performed in the manner of confession might be seen as an initiation into the deep mysteries of theological knowledge, which were kept pristine from the times of the apostles. The masters in the art of confession are not necessarily learned persons, but must have personal discernment and the authoritative insight of any long-tested experience.[40]

The relationship established between the mentor and the student is personal, though it lacks the over-familiar speech, so common among relatives. As with Christ, what can be seen matters more than what can be heard. The spiritual father is able to help the novice overcome the obsession of failure (which indicates the tyranny of the past) for the benefit of an eschatological optimism (which trusts, above all, God's future). The healing of sinful memories necessitates the knowledge of the deepest self and long term insight.[41]

The practice of confession also brings together the individual consciousness and ecclesial memory. The people of God inhabit the sacred past of a given tradition by first going through the process of self-emptying. Gavin Flood describes this transformation as the recession of the indexical 'I,' related to the sacred text, for the sake of the anaphoric 'I,' through whom tradition can speak.[42] The same logic is at work in the rapport between learning and doing. The confession of sins triggers the painful feeling of shame and remorse.[43] This voluntary acceptance of pain heals the Christian pupil, who participates consciously in the Cross of his Lord. Shame earns tears, and this has

---

[39] N 245 (Ward, 34).

[40] N 252 (Ward, 35).

[41] Papanikolaou (2008) on confession as one practice that enables the purification of human desire.

[42] Flood (2004), 102 *et passim*.

[43] More on the role of shame in the first stage of purification, see Stăniloae (1993), 194-197, drawing on Gaith (1953), 137-142. Shame here is not to be confused with the psychological notion of guilt.

as an immediate effect: the cleansing of the heart.[44] The flow of tears marks the presence of the Spirit and contributes to the unification of mind and heart, in the absence of which one remains split between contradictory desires.[45] In the words of Pachomius the Great, 'even if someone does not weep although he is moved at the time the event happens, there is also the inner weeping.'[46]

The practice of confession frees the monk from his broken past, while it deepens and broadens his heart to the point of universality. Just as the Psalter helps the novice to read the entire Scriptures, repentance through confession makes one capable of compassion towards the entire universe, seen and unseen. Formally, confession takes place during the tutorials between the confessor and the novice, or during the common weekend sessions, when solitary monastics meet with the coenobites in view of celebrating the Eucharistic liturgy.[47] The monk confesses his sin so that he bring no offence to the Body of Christ. Through the Eucharist, he is reunited with the ecclesial body, and leaves behind individualistic drives. Thus, the monk can grow 'to the measure of the stature of the fullness of Christ' (Ephesians 4, 13), being able to 'test the spirits' (I John 4, 1). This whole process of self-transformation leads to the recognition of the universality of

---

[44] For the presence of this theme in the desert fathers, see the abundant references in the *apophthegmata*, such as Anthony 33 (Ward, 8), Arsenius 41 (Ward, 18); and also Evagrius, *or.* 5-8; John Cassian, *Conf.* 9.28; tears, in particular, help the cleansing of memories retained through sexual sin, as N 176 (Ward, 14) as St Symeon the New Theologian has also emphasised it in the 11th century. Thorough research on this theme in the literature of the desert fathers has been carried out by Müller (2000). The role of tears in the monastic spirituality of Christendom has been often discussed in the patristic scholarship. for the modern relation between prayer and tears in modern literature, see Dostoevsky (2002), 359-363, with the famous scene depicting Alyosha's vision of Cana of Galilee. For more recent reference, see Salinger (1991), which relates Franny's weeping and fainting to her involuntary discovery of the Jesus prayer. With reference to Robinson Crusoe, see also the beautiful commentaries of the Romanian philosopher Pleşu (1990); for a *sui-generis* exploration of the theme of weeping in the Christian tradition, one cannot eschew the iconoclast essays of Cioran (1996). On a different note, reading Augustine's tears, see Derrida (1993), reviewed by Caputo (1997), 308-330.

[45] Abba Poemen 119 (Ward, 184), 'he who wishes to purify his faults, purifies them with tears and he who wishes to acquire virtues acquires them with tears, for weeping is the way the Scriptures and our Fathers give us.'

[46] G153 (Veilleux, 334).

[47] *SBo* 25 (Veilleux, 47), 'He [scil. Pachomius] would take the brothers and would go there on Saturday to receive the sacraments.'

Christ.[48] In order to be able to pray for the world, the novice has to be reconciled first with his own tradition, and free himself from the sinful past. Subsequently, in a later stage of his life, he may become himself a confessor, and face martyrdom with zeal and courage. When they are subtly combined, the multiple narratives of the Psalter, and the disciplined practice of confession, bring about a radical understanding of the past, as an open rubric of temporality. When the purity of the heart is achieved, one can truly digest the wisdom of the past, and not just exhibit an external knowledge of the sacred books.[49] Since it is based on the knowledge of the Spirit within the living tradition, spiritual fatherhood can also lead to prophetic insights into the novice's future trajectory.[50] By his own powers, the Christian beginner cannot discover the particular gifts which he was granted on the day of baptism. The spiritual father, on the other hand, can reveal these gifts to him, among which the greatest is love and forgiveness. The latter triggers a renewed celebration of freedom.[51]

The 'ministry of reconciliation' (II Corinthians 5, 18) is most effective in the filtrated transmission of collective wisdom to individual consciousness. We cannot isolate the father-son relationship from an ecclesiastical context.[52] The novice freely accepts the relation of submission to the one who has already earned discernment. It is impossible to understand the fallen human condition without an exploration of the unseen emotions plundering one's own life.[53] There is no manipulation or control in the practice of transparency required by confession.[54] The abba is not scandalised or soiled by hearing even the most shocking confessions, since his heart is attached to the Christ-like humility. For an experienced hermit, the hearing a confession resembles the divine descent into Hades.[55]

In sum, confession brings healing only if the monastic decides to bravely confront the shades of his sinful past. While the Psalter

---

[48] Pachomius, *Instr.* 2.4 (Veilleux, 48), 'May heaven and earth mourn during these six days of the Passover.'

[49] Abba Bessarion 12 (Ward, 42).

[50] N 361, where an elder announced the destruction of Sketis. On this topic, see Krienen (1990).

[51] *SBo* 118 (Veilleux, 173), 'I never corrected any one of you as the one having authority except for the sake of his soul's salvation.'

[52] *SBo* 89 (Veilleux, 119).

[53] N 270 (Ward, 39).

[54] Abba Poemen 23 (Ward, 170).

[55] Abba Joseph of Panephysis 4 (Ward, 103).

encapsulates the wisdom of the whole revelation, which goes back to the stories of Abraham, Moses, and the righteous men and women of Israel, the practice of psalmody uproots the pretence of old Adam which often governs the psychology of the novice.

4. Saving time as past, present, and future

Psalmody and confession are only two of the many types of liturgical performance required by Christian life in the desert. Their goal is to direct the search for the Kingdom towards the realm of reconciliation with God and one's neighbour. The secular rituals of the world do not allow the achievement of this goal. In the absence of Christ, man often yields to dark melancholy (with regard to the past), to shallow enthusiasm (mistaking the present), or to arrogant despair (forgetting the future). Psalmody sets out the conversation with the saints as a cure for any form of self-centered nostalgia.[56] Other practices related to the present time replace the euphoria insured by the excess of bodily pleasures. The fear of the unknown must be replaced also with hope in the divine promise. It is this fullness of time that the secular economy neglects by endorsing all sick attachments to the present, mesmerising reconstructions of the past, or slavish anxiety towards the future.

The writings of the desert fathers teem with stories about the past, parables for the present and prophecies about a more or less distant future. Depending on its context, each anecdote may become a story, a parable or a prophecy. Often, the shift between the past, present and future goes unnoticed. There are abrupt transitions from a deflected knowledge of God to the totalising perception of divine presence. Different time-zones on the map of the monastic liturgy merge softly into one grand landscape of divine providence. One's capacity to maintain the overarching unity of the temporal structures involved by each part of the monastic liturgy is a sure sign of perfection.[57] How this ordering of past, present and future may have functioned in the lives of the desert fathers we can learn by looking at the liturgical coherence

[56] N 273 (Ward, 40), 'every time forgetfulness (ἡ λήθη) comes, it engenders negligence (ἀμέλειαν); and from negligence, carnal desire (ἡ ἐπιθυμία) proceeds; and desire causes man to fall.'

[57] One could develop this temporal typology in parallel with Augustine's distinction between, respectively, *memoria* (memory), *contuitus* (contemplation of the present) and *expectatio* (expectation of future). See Augustine, *Conf.* 11.20.1-7.

of their tradition. Different strategies of reading the Scriptures were paralleled by antiphonal acts of worship and asceticism.[58]

The shift between past and present can occur during the same reading session by using the same text, but changing only the grid of interpretation or the position of the body (*e.g.* from sitting or standing to kneeling).[59] A sudden experience of contemplation can interrupt one's more basic practice of biblical exegesis.[60] An allegorical reading submerges the reference to the tradition into the sphere of apocalyptic discourse.[61] A literal reading of the book of the Torah, for example, allowed the monastics to pay their tribute to the memory of Israel.[62] The vision of the burning bush reminded Abba Cronius of the unceasing toil which he, as an ascetic, owed to God. He dug out the hidden treasure of Christ from the soil of an adulterated body.[63] In the more sophisticated description of the bishop-monastic Gregory of Nyssa, the burning bush symbolises the virginal birth of Christ from the immaculate Mary.[64] The immaterial flames of this theophany suggest the importance of purification from all passions. The story of Moses bears a double significance, serving both the practical and the contemplative needs of the interpreter. In short, when an allegorical reading replaces the literal reading of the Scriptures, the reference

[58] Even a distant encounter with a theological library can at times account for a narrative practice, as bishop Epiphanius of Salamina 8 (Ward, 58) indicates, 'The acquisition of Christian books is necessary for those who can use them. For the mere sight of these books renders us less inclined to sin, and incites us to believe more firmly in righteousness.'

[59] The Council of Nicaea forbade the practice of kneeling during the Lord's Day, making reference to the feast of the Resurrection. The Church indicated thus her desire to shape more clearly and distinguish the 'liturgical chronotopes' of Christian life.

[60] For a comparison of Plato and Origen on this point, see Louth (1981), 70-71. The topic occurs again in the writings of Dionysios the Areopagite, see Moutsopoulos (2002) and Golitzin (2001). For parallels in the Gospel, see Luke 2:13.

[61] Collins (1979), 9, for a definition of the apocalyptic genre. An excellent example of 'inner apocalypse' is the quote ascribed to Gregory the Theologian 2 (Ward, 45), 'The whole life of a man is but one single day for those who are working hard with longing (τοῖς πόθῳ κάμνουσιν).' Compare with Abba Poemen 126 (Ward, 185), and with Augustine, *Conf.* 11.20.26. Evagrius of Pontus points out that the demon of acedia, or the long feeling of torpour, is the opposite of this experience. See Evagrius, *pr.* 12 (Bamberger, 19).

[62] Abba Poemen 67 (Ward, 176).

[63] Abba Cronius 4 (Ward, 116).

[64] Gregory of Nyssa, *V. Mos.* (PG 44, 332 D).

to history is bracketed for the sake of the mystical encounter with God. Finally, the open future of Christian eschatology, which for the desert fathers was beyond doubt, helps the novice understand why the mystical experience occurs only as an anticipation of what is to come. The ancestral tradition, which both psalmody and confession constantly refer to, prevents someone from taking his personal experience as normative for the entire community of the Church.[65] No proper theological contextualisation of any mystical utterance can be achieved without an awareness of the historical past. The wisdom of tradition can justify both the deferral of divine Parousia and the need for constant intercession to God.[66]

At this point in our analysis, one can ask how do the different temporal intervals (past, present, and future) relate to one another in the daily endeavours of the monastic liturgy? The ethical division of theological knowledge into three major steps (faith, hope, love) would suggest that hermeneutical practices such as psalmody, meditation and prayer are hierarchically differentiated. Evagrius' typology of spiritual progress, for instance, was salient in proving that different paths open distinct avenues for the beginner, the contemplative, and the perfect monk, respectively.[67] However, the road to deification requires the complementarity of these aspects, since none of them is privileged against the other. It would be hard to claim that the saints who reached perfection in the victory of the Cross live more in the eschatological future than in the mystical presence of God. The quality of their monastic experience differs from the more fragmented perception of the sacred temporality available to a simple beginner.

An apocalyptic experience of time is always very dense in comparison to the expanded recollection of the past, or the narrative plunge into the future. Such mystical insights bring about an eschatological totalisation on the largest scale of history. At this point, the memory of the tradition invites the sapiential reflex to step in. The individual ascetic will recall that many saints, from Moses the prophet to

---

[65] N 214.

[66] For the ancient character of Christian petitions, see Aristides, *apol.* 16.1.

[67] Evagrius, *pr.*, intr. 9. This division must be contextualised, if one considers that, every day, Abba Pior 'made a new beginning' (Ward, 179). For erudite references to Evagrius see Guillaumont (1971), Bunge (1996), and Sinkewicz (2003), 91-114, with an excellent discussion in Casiday (2006).

Paul the apostle, have received a direct revelation from God.[68] Almost simultaneously, the open ended nature of the eschatological future enables the revision of our theological reading of human history, until the very last minute.[69] There is always more to come, even for those who have already had a foretaste of paradise. The dangers of having an over-realised eschatology (in the apocalyptic mood), or a delayed eschatology (in the political or secular register) are bracketed when the memory of Israel is reconnected to the future of the Kingdom. The present is thus heavily charged with all consuming revelations.[70] At this point of internal unity, 'the whole of history moves towards an apocalypse of meanings,'[71] as the French Catholic theologian Jean-Yves Lacoste has deftly put it. In short, the unpredictable dynamics of desert eschatology involves a therapeutic relationship with the past, a creative expansion of the present, and a visionary preparation of the future. Psalmody and confession are important parts of this dialogical process, in which different sequences of divine time talk to each other.

5. Conclusion

In this paper I have tried to argue that the practice of psalmody and confession constitute an intrinsic part of the monastic construal of the past as redemption from the individual memory of sin, and appropriation of ecclesial wisdom. Psalmody may be seen as as a narrative-bound expansion of the newly baptised self, while confession represents a dispossession of the old sinful ego. The unity of these interrelated practices is rooted in the time-space reality of the cosmic Church, which is radically appropriated by the monastic liturgy. Its role is to build up faith (as inherited from the past), leading to the experience of hope (with respect to the future), and love (in relationship to the present). Psalmody, meditation, and pure prayer

---

[68] *SBo* 114 (Veilleux, 166), 'It happened once that he [*scil.* Pachomius] fell sick and he suffered so much that those sent out to fetch him snatched his soul away and he died. But as he was approaching the gate of life, an order came from God to bring him back to his body once more.'

[69] Pachomius, *ep.* 5.10 (Veilleux, 66), 'Having knowledge of the things to come, let us be united with one another in love.'

[70] Abba Joseph of Panephysis 7 (Ward, 103), 'If you will, you can become all flame.' This anecdote also explains the frequent association between the Burning Bush and the experience of God in prayer.

[71] Lacoste (1990), 43.

dovetail with the sapiential, the prophetic, and the mystical aspects of desert eschatology. Distinct rubrics of time correspond dialectically to specific virtues, making the monastic liturgy appear as a hierarchical construction.

Between the renunciation of the world and the inauguration of the heavenly Father's kingdom, one must contemplate multiple facets of salvation history. Put together, they contrast with the secular understanding of time, which is blinded by the promise of immanence and bereft of redemption in Christ. The desert fathers endowed psalmody with a strong pedagogical connotation, knowing that the Scriptures prepare the encounter with *totus Christus*, who shall gather the lost ones and raise them up in divine glory. Psalter and confession are not used as an end in themselves, but as means that show us Christ's eschatological recapitulation of all meaningful historical events and of all unrecorded personal encounters with God. The art of psalmody and the practice of confession teach us how the saints shall be made co-present in the Kingdom of God, living together as an assembly the eschatological totality of past, present, and future.

Bibliography

Ancient Sources

ATHANASIUS THE GREAT
ep. marc (PG 27, 11-46), ET by R. C. Gregg and intr. By W. Clebsch, *The Life of Anthony and the Letter to Marcellinus*, New York, 1980.

AUGUSTINE OF HIPPO
conf.   *Confessions*, ET by H. Chadwick in Saint Augustine, *Confessions*, Oxford: 1991.

EVAGRIUS OF PONTUS
cog.   *De cogitationibus (Peri logismon)*; ed. P. Géhin / Cl. Guillaumont: Evagre le Pontique, *Sur les pensées*, SC 438, Paris, 1998.
or.   *de oratione* (PG 79, 1165-1200). A better text can be found in *Philokalia*, vol. I (176-89), Athens, 1957, ET by G. E. H. Palmer, Ph. Sherrard and Kallistos Ware in *The Philokalia*, vol. I, 55-71; another English version is offered by J. E. Bamberger, CS 4, Kalamazoo, Mich., 1981.

pr.   *Praktikos*, ed. by Antoine and Claire Guillaumont: *Traité pratique, ou Le Moine*, SC 171, Paris, 1971, ET by J. E. Bamberger CS 4, Kalamazoo, Mich., 1981.

sc.   *Scholies aux Proverbes*, ed. P. Géhin, SC 340, Paris, 1987.

DESERT FATHERS

AP   *Apophthegmata Patrum* (collectio alphabetica graeca) (PG 65, 72-440) ed. J. B. Cotelier, ET by Benedicta Ward, *The Sayings of the Desert Fathers: The Alphabetical Collection* CS 59, Kalamazoo, Mich., 1984.

GCSF   French translation by L. Regnault in *Les Sentences des Pères du Désert: Troisième recueil et tables*, ed. L. Regnault, Solesmes, 1976; Jean-Claude Guy, ed., *Les Apophtegmes des Pères*, I-IX, SC 387, Paris, 1993.

N   The Greek anonymous series of *Apophthegmata Patrum*; N 1-392, ed. F. Nau, 'Histoires des solitaires égyptiens,' *Revue d'Orient chrétien* 12 (1907), 48-68, 171-81, 393-404; vol. 13 (1908), 47-57, 266-83; vol. 14 (1909), 357-79; vol. 17 (1912), 204-11, 294-301; vol. 18 (1913), 137- 46; N 132 A-D were edited by F. Nau in *Revue d'orient chrétien* 10 (1905), 409-14. Unpublished material following N 392 available in *Les Sentences des Pères du désert: Série des anonymes,* French translation by L. Regnault, Solesmes, 1985.

GREGORY OF NYSSA

v. Mos.   ET by Abraham J. Malherbe and Everett Ferguson, Gregory of Nyssa, *The Life of Moses*, Mahwah, NJ, 1978.

JOHN THE CASSIAN

Conf.   *Conférences*, Introduction, texte latin, traduction et notes par Dom E. Pichery (SC 42, 54, 64), Paris, 1955, 1958, 1959; ET by Boniface Ramsey, *The Conferences*, ACW 57, New York, 1997.

PACHOMIUS THE GREAT

SBo   *Sahidic-Bohairic Life of Pachomius*, reconstructed by Armand Veilleux in *Pachomian Koinonia: The Lives, Rules and Other Writings of Saint Pachomius and his Disciples*, vol. i, *The Lives of Saint Pachomius and his Disciples*, ET by A. Veilleux, intr. A. de Vogüé, CS 45, Kalamazoo, Mich., 1980.

Instr.   The Instructions of Pachomius, in Pachomian Koinonia, vol. iii, *Instructions, Letters, and Other Writings of Saint Pachomius and his Disciples*, ET by A. Veilleux CS 47, Kalamazoo, Mich., 1982.

ep.   The Instructions of Pachomius, in Pachomian Koinonia, vol. iii, *Instructions, Letters, and Other Writings of Saint Pachomius and his Disciples*, ET by A. Veilleux, CS 47, Kalamazoo, Mich., 1982.

PALLADIUS

h. laus.   *Lausiac history*, modern edition (of the Greek text): Cuthbert Butler, *The Lausiac History of Palladius: A Critical Discussion, together with Notes on early Monasticism*, Cambridge: Cambridge University Press, 1898-1904, ET by Robert T. Meyer, *The Lausiac History*, ACW 34. For the Greek version see also the critical edition of G.J.M. Bartelink, *Palladio: La storia Lausiaca* (Verona: 1974), 4-292.

SOCRATES

h.e.   *historia ecclesiastica* (PG 67, 9-892), ET by A. C. Zenos, *NPNF* 2nd series, vol. 2.

Modern Authors

Annas, Julia (1986) 'Aristotle on Memory and the Self,' in J. Annas (ed.), *Ancient Philosophy* vol 5: A Festschrift for J.L. Ackrill, Oxford, 99-118.

Bacht, Heinrich (1955) '*Meditatio* in den ältesten Mönchsquellen,' *Geist und Leben. Zeitschrift für Askeze und Mystik* 28, 360-373.

Bakhtin, Mikhail M. (1984) *The Dialogic Imagination: Four Essays*, ET by Michael Holloquist and Caryl Emerson, Austin, Tex.

Bergson, Henri (1912) *Matter and Memory*, ET by Nancey Margaret Paul and W. Scott Palmer, New York.

Bongie, Elizabeth (1995) (ed.) *The Life and Regimen of the Blessed and Holy Teacher Syncletica by Pseudo-Athanasius*, ET by Elizabeth Bongie, Toronto.

Bunge, Gabriel (1987) *Das Geistgebet: Studien zum Traktat de 'Oratione' des Evagrios Pontikos*, Cologne.

Bunge, Gabriel (1994) 'The Mystical Meaning of Scripture – Remarks on the Occasion of the Publication of Evagrius-Ponticus *Scholien zum Ecclesiasten*,' *Studia Monastica* 36, no. 2, 135-46.

Bunge, Gabriel, (1996) '*Praktike, Physike* und *Theologike* als Stufen der Erkenntnis bei Evagrios Pontikos,' in V.M. Schneider and W. Birschin (eds.), *Ab Oriente et Occidente. Kirche aus Ost und West. Gedenkschrift für Wilhelm Nyssen* (Munich) 59-72.

Bunge, Gabriel (1997) 'Commentary on the Prologue of the *Antirrhetikos* by Evagrius of Pontus,' *Studia Monastica* 39, issue 1, 77–105.

Caputo, John D. (1997) *The Prayers and Tears of Jacques Derrida: Religion Without Religion*, Bloomington, Ind..

Casiday, Augustine M. (2006) *Evagrius Ponticus*, New York.

Castelli, Enrico (1971) 'Herméneutique et Kairos,' in Enrico Castelli (ed.), *Herméneutique et eschatologie* (Paris), 15-20.

Cioran, E.M. (1996) *Tears and Saints*, ET by Ilinca Zarifopol-Johnston (Chicago).

Coleman, Janet (1992) *Ancient and Medieval Memories: Studies in the Reconstruction of the Past* (Cambridge).

Collins, John (1979) 'Apocalypse: The Morphology of a Genre,' *Semeia* 14, 1-19.

Corrigan, Kevin (1989) 'Syncletica and Macrina: Two Early Lives of Women Saints,' *Vox Benedictina*, 6, issue 3, 241-257.

Davril, A. (1987) '*La psalmodie chez les pères du désert*,' *Collectanea Cisterciensia* 49, 132-39.

Derrida, Jacques (1993) *Circumfession,* ET by Geoffrey Bennington (Chicago).

Dorival, Gilles (1980) 'Athanase ou pseudo-Athanase,' *Rivista di Storia e Letteratura Religiosa* 16, 80-89.

Dörries, Herman (1962) 'The Practice of Confession in Ancient Monasticism,' *SP* 5, 284-311.

Dostoevsky, F.M. (2002) *The Brothers Karamazov*, ET by Richard Pevear and Larissa Volokhonsky (New York).

Dysinger, Luke (2005) *Psalmody and Prayer in the Writings of Evagrius Ponticus* (Oxford).

Ehrlich, Uri and Dena Ordan (2004) *The Nonverbal Language of Prayer: A New Approach to Jewish Liturgy* (Tübingen).

Eliade, Mircea (1971) *The Myth of the Eternal Return*, ET by Willard R. Trask (Princeton).

Flood, Gavin (2004) *The Ascetic Self. Subjectivity, Memory and Tradition* (Cambridge).

Fossas, Ignasi M. (1997) 'L'*Epistola ad Marcellinum* di Sant'Atanasio sull'uso cristiano del salterio,' *Studia Monastica* 39, 27-76.

Gaith, Jerôme (1953) *La conception de la liberté chez Grégoire de Nysse* (Paris).

Gélineau, Joseph (1953) 'Les formes de la psalmodie chrétienne,' *La Maison-Dieu* 33, 134-172.

Golitzin, Alexander (2001) 'Revisiting the "Sudden": Epistle III in *Corpus Dionysiacum*,' *SP* 38, 482-491.

Guillaumont, Antoine (1971) Introduction to *Evagre le Pontique. Traité pratique ou le moine* (SC 170), edited by Antoine and Claire Guillaumont (Paris).

Guillaumont, Antoine (1977) *Aux origines du monachisme chrétien. Pour une phénoménologie du monachisme*, Bégrolles-en-Mauges.

Harmless, William (2000) 'Remembering Poemen Remembering: The Desert Fathers and the Spirituality of Memory,' *CH* 69, 483-518.

Kannengiesser, Charles (1962) '*Enarratio in Psalmum* CXVIII: Science de la révélation et progrès spirituel,' *RA* 2, 359-381.

Kok, Franz (1992) 'L'office pachômien: psallere, orare, legere,' *Ecclesia Orans* 9, 69-95.

Lacoste, Jean-Yves (1990) *Notes sur le temps* (Paris).

Louth, Andrew (1981) *The Origins of the Christian Mystical Tradition from Plato to Denys* (Oxford).

Louth, Andrew (1991) *The Wilderness of God* (London).

Mammarella, M. (1992) *"La lettera a Marcellino di Atanasio". L'interpretazione cristologica dei Salmi* (Rome).

McKinnon, James W. (1994) 'Desert Monasticism and the Later Four-Century Psalmodic Movement,' *Music & Letters* 75, issue 4, 505-521.

Meensbrugghe, A. van der (1957) 'Prayer-Time in Egyptian Monasticism,' *SP* 2, 435-454.

Moutsopoulos, Evangelos (2002) 'La fonction catalytique de l'*exaiphnes* chez Denys,' *Archaeus* 6, issue 1-2, 45-54.

Müller, Barbara (2000) *Der Weg des Weinens: die Tradition des "Penthos" in den Apophthegmata* (Göttingen).

O'Laughlin, Michael (1990) 'Antirrheticus (Selections),' in Vincent L. Wimbush, *Ascetic Behavior in Greco-Roman Antiquity a Sourcebook* (Mineapolis), 243–62.

O'Laughlin, Michael (1992) 'The Bible, Demons and the Desert - Evaluating the *Antirrheticus* of Evagrius-Ponticus,' *Studia Monastica* 34, issue 2, 201–15.

Papanikolaou, Aristotle (2008) 'Honest to God: Confession and Desire,' in *Thinking through Faith: New Perspectives from Orthodox Christian Scholars,* eds. Aristotle Papanikolaou and Elizabeth Prodromou (Crestwood, NY), 219-46.

Pleşu, Andrei (1990) *Ethique de Robinson* (Paris).

Ricoeur, Paul (2000) *La Mémoire, l'Histoire, l'Oubli* (Paris).

Rondeau, Marie Joseph (1968) 'L'épître à Marcellinus sur les Psaumes,' *VC* 22, 176-197.

Rondeau, Marie Joseph (1982) Les commentaires patristiques du Psautier (IIIᵉ-Vᵉ siècle) I: Les travaux des Pères Grecs et Latins sur le Psautier. Recherche et bilan (OCA 219), (Rome).

Rouillard, Philippe (1960) 'Temps et rythmes de la prière dans le monachisme ancien,' *La Maison-Dieu* 64, 32-52.

Rousseau, Philip (1999) *Pachomius: The Making of a Community in Fourth-Century Egypt* (Berkeley, Calif.).

Salinger, J.D. (1991) *Franny and Zooey* (Little).

Scrima, André (1978) 'Teologia orientale del monachesimo,' in G. Pellicia and G. Rocca (ed.), *Dizionario degli Istituti di Perfezione*, vol. 5 (Rome), col. 1716-1718.

Sinkewicz, Robert D.E. (2003) *Evagrius of Pontus: The Greek Ascetic Corpus*, ET by Robert D.E. Sinkewicz (Oxford).

Stăniloae, Dumitru (1993) *Ascetica şi mistica ortodoxă*, vol. 1 (Alba-Iulia).

Stead, Christopher (1982) 'St. Athanasius on the Psalms,' *VC* 39, 65-78.

Taft, Robert (1982) 'Praise in the Desert,' *Worship* 56, 513-536.

Vogüé, Adalbert de (1989) 'Psalmodier n'est pas prier,' *Ecclesia Orans* 6, 7-32.

Vogüé, Adalbert de (2000) 'Le Psaume et l'Oraison. Nouveau Florilège,' *Regards sur le monachisme des premières siècles* (Rome), 855-878.

Wortley, John (2006) 'How the Desert Fathers "Meditated,"' *Greek, Roman and Byzantine Studies* 46, issue 3, 315-328.

ROBERT HAYWARD

SAINT JEROME, JEWISH LEARNING, AND THE SYMBOLISM OF THE NUMBER EIGHT

The sixth Psalm represents a heartfelt plea for divine mercy and forgiveness: the psalmist, fearful of death, God's anger, punishment, and justice, and the concomitant hostility of enemies, weeps and supplicates before the Lord. No sooner has the poet presented this plea (Ps. 6:2-8) than the Lord's response is made known. The enemies are ordered to depart; the psalmist's supplication has been accepted; and all the enemies are to be confounded (Ps. 6:9-11). The original Hebrew of this brief, impressive prayer has a title which, like many other psalm titles, uses technical terms obscure to the modern scholar: למנצח בנגינות על השמינית מזמור לדוד. A recent Jewish translation of this title felt the need to resort to an element of transliteration in its rendering, to give us: 'For the leader; with instrumental music on the *sheminith*. A psalm of David'.[1] The transliterated word, as the editors noted alongside their translation, means 'the eighth'; and it is found again in the heading of Psalm 12, which is Psalm 11 according to the LXX enumeration. This poem has the same heading as Psalm 6, with the exception of the word בנגינות, translated above as 'with instrumental music'. In the rendering of these two Psalm headings, the association with musical instruments and song of the word *sheminith*, which normally signifies 'eighth', was undoubtedly suggested to the translators by 1 Chron. 15:21. This last verse forms part of a catalogue of Levites deputed to perform in some manner on stringed instruments (לנצח, a verbal form which shares the same root consonants as the first Hebrew word of both Psalm titles) 'upon the eighth', indicating perhaps a particular sort of stringed instrument.

---

[1] See (eds) Berlin and Brettler (2004), 1289. For modern, historical-critical attempts to elucidate the terminology of Psalm headings and of other technical expressions within the body of the Psalms, see Kraus, vol. 1 (1961), xviii-xxx; Mowinckel, vol. 2 (1967), 207-17; Anderson, vol. 1 (1972), 43-51; Beckwith (2005), 153-66.

As we shall see presently, interpretation of the two psalm headings in light of this verse from the Chronicler was often taken for granted in antiquity.

St. Jerome's concern with the Psalter is well known, and continued long after he had completed his Latin translations of the Bible.[2] His *Commentarioli in Psalmos*, however, may be dated with some certainty to the years 386-388; and this comparatively early example of his exegetical work is of great interest for his understanding of the symbolic meaning of the number eight.[3] The heading of Psalm 6 he quotes according to his Latin translation of the Septuagint Psalter, 'Unto the end, for the eighth: A Psalm of David'. Despite his quotation of the whole superscription, he is apparently unconcerned with anything but the phrase 'for the eighth' in his comment, which reads as follows:

> *Unto the end, for the eighth. A Psalm of David*
> This and the eleventh Psalm have the inscription 'for the eighth'; and they contain the mystery of the resurrection and of penitence and, through this, the mystery of our salvation. In this Psalm, human nature requests that we indeed be corrected and judged by God, but not in his anger and wrath. It is a lengthy business to recall more examples of the mystery of this number. The eight souls who were saved in the flood entered into Noah's ark. The eighth son of Jesse was David, who was both despaired of by his father and alone chosen by God. On the eighth day the first-born are circumcised, and cease to be impure. Also Zacharias, the father of John, on the eighth day of the circumcision of his son, speaks forth. And after eight days, or six, for both numbers are read in the different evangelists, the Lord was transfigured on the mountain, so that in this way the eighth might be contained within the number six in the same manner as now, in the sixth Psalm, the superscription is placed with reference to the ogdoad.

Jerome's insight that the words of the Psalm headings point to some 'mystery' is far removed from most modern biblical scholarship,

---

[2] See Kelly (1975), 285-6 on Jerome's *Epistle* 106, dated sometime between 404 and 410, in which Jerome demonstrates his continuing concern over translations of the Psalms.

[3] For the Latin text of this work, I have used the edition of Risse (2005), who discusses the date of the *Commentarioli* (page 15) and makes important observations throughout his discussions of the text on Jerome's links with Jewish sources.

whose attempts at explanation generally envisage the titles as serving a largely functional role, providing information necessary for correct, possibly liturgical, performance of the text.[4] By way of contrast,
his contemporary St Ambrose often records the mystery most chiefly
associated with the number eight: it represents the Lord's resurrection, since Christ arose from the dead on the eighth day.[5] Indeed,
Ambrose relishes the opportunity to expound the symbolic significance of other numbers besides the number eight;[6] this last number,
however, for him represents a degree of perfection he does not
hesitate to celebrate. Some of his regard for this number will most
likely have been derived from Philo's writings: Ambrose's remarks
in *Ep.* xliv.13-14 about the seven physical and irrational components of the human creature, in which the soul occupies the eighth
rational and indivisible part, clearly recall Philo's treatment of the
same topic.[7]

Many of Ambrose's observations will have been known to Jerome;
and at first blush it is tempting to suggest that his comments on the
number eight set out here might owe a good deal to the writings of his
predecessors, most notably to Origen. Indeed, it so happens that Jerome opens his *Commentarioli* with a declaration that he had recently
been reading Origen's *Enchiridion* on the Psalms. The treatment of the
Psalms in that work he had found piecemeal; and the *Commentarioli*

---

[4] A most important exception to this is Childs (1971), 137-50, who alerted scholars
to aspects of the psalm titles until then largely neglected in historical-critical studies.
This article, however, did not address the titles of Psalms 6 and 12, focusing rather on
titles relating to David's life.

[5] See Ambrose, *Ep.* xliv.5; *In Psalmum cxviii Expositio* 2 (where eight is also explicitly linked with Baptism and purity); *Expositio Evangelii secundum Lucam* V.49, and
especially VII.6 on Luke 9:28 (the resurrection took place on the eighth day, whence
several psalms are inscribed *in octavam*); *In Apocalypsin Expositio. De Visione Prima* 1;
De XLII Mansionibus Filiorum Israel 8 (Israel's eighth station departing from Egypt
was the site of the burning bush, which symbolises the freedom from corruption
granted by the resurrection); and *De Abr.* II.79 (the eighth day of circumcision and its
accompanying purification typifies the resurrection).

[6] See, for example, his praise of the mystical numbers three (*Expositio Evangelii
secundum Lucam* I.56) and four (*De Abr.* II.65), along with fifteen (*De Noe at Arca*
xv.52) and the components of 350 (*De Noe et Arca* xxxiii.125). See also *De Excessu Frat-
ris* II.108 (on the numbers associated with the Jewish festivals) and *De Fide* I.3 (on the
318 servants of Abraham).

[7] See Philo, *Quaestiones et Solutiones in Genesim* I.75, and *Quod Deterius* 168.
Ambrose's debt to Philo may be observed in other writings: see, for example, his *De
Cain et Abel* whose dependence on Philo's work was catalogued by Siegfried (1875).

was written in part to remedy this defect, by providing extra material from Origen's more detailed work on the Psalter.[8] Jerome may also have known St. Gregory of Nyssa's recent work on the Psalm titles (*In Inscriptione Psalmorum*), which seems to have been composed during the years 376-378, when Gregory was in exile.[9] Even though this last treatise discussed 'the eighth' in some detail, it did not exhaust Gregory's interest in the topic, since we have from his pen another short essay on the sixth Psalm, *De Octava*.[10] Yet a comparison of these writings with the information that Jerome has given in his *Commentarioli* is instructive. While in both his treatments of the 'octave' Gregory speaks at length about resurrection and penitence, he says nothing about Noah, David, or Zacharias. The surviving works of Origen do not speak of 'the eighth' in the manner of the *Commentarioli*. Noteworthy are Jerome's words about David, the eighth son of Jesse, whose father had seemingly 'given up on him', when he alone was the chosen one of God. This paper will suggest that Jerome's words about David take on a particular significance in the light of contemporary Jewish interest in the heading of Psalm 6.

Jerome's comments on the Psalm headings, moreover, cannot be divorced from his protracted and painstaking labours in his translations of the Psalter, a biblical book which occupied him more than any other. His sensitivity towards the possible range of meanings concealed in the Hebrew of the Psalm headings is clearly revealed when his translations of the superscriptions of Psalms 6 and 12 'according to the LXX' and 'according to the Hebrew' are set side by side.[11] Instructive is his treatment of the first word in both Psalm headings, the Hebrew למנצח. LXX had dealt with this problematic and ambiguous term by translating it as εἰς τὸ τέλος, which Jerome duly rendered as

---

[8] See the Prologue as edited and translated by Risse (2005), 68-9, where Jerome speaks of relaying Origen's material found *in psalterii opere latissimo*. Risse discusses the particular works of Origen which Jerome may have had in mind in his Introduction, pages 29-30.

[9] See Heine (1995), 8-11.

[10] Gregory's discussion of the "eighth" is found at *In Inscriptione Psalmorum* II.52-53, English translation in Heine (1995), 136-137. For the short treatise *In Sextum Psalmum De Octava*, see PG.44.607-616.

[11] Citations of Jerome's Latin translations of the Psalms are given from (ed.) Weber (1994). LXX is quoted from (ed.) Rahlfs (1935); and the translations of Aquila, Symmachus, and Theodotion are given from the text in Field (1875). The English versions of these citations are mine.

in finem, 'unto, for, with reference to the end'.[12] This is the version he selected to introduce his comment on Psalm 6 in the *Commentarioli*; but he will undoubtedly have been aware of another possible rendering of the term, which he went on to incorporate into his translation 'according to the Hebrew'. This is *victori*, 'for the vanquisher': both the versions of Aquila and Symmachus had opted for this general interpretation, the former giving us τῷ νικοποιῷ, 'for the one who makes victory', the latter ἐπινίκιος, 'of victory'.[13] Indeed, in his translation of 1 Chron. 15:21, which we noted earlier, he represented Hebrew לנצח with the Greek word επινικιον, 'hymn of victory', to indicate that the six Levites named in that verse 'were singing a hymn of victory with lyres for the eighth'.[14] Both the sense of 'end' and of 'victory' can properly be referred to the time of salvation, the time when God will decisively act on behalf of His people, the time of the resurrection and the restoration of creation to its pristine perfection.

The number eight in the Psalm headings and in 1 Chron. 15:21 is evidently inseparable from such notions of 'end' and 'victory', which may account for the fact that the Psalm headings hold pride of place in Jerome's exposition of this number eight.[15] The 'end' achieved by Christ is foremost in his exposition of Psalm 6:1, for the number eight brings to his mind not only the great biblical types of salvation pointing forward to Christ (Noah and the flood; the choice of David as anointed chosen one, being the eighth son of Jesse;[16] God's covenant with Israel sealed in the ceremony of circumcision), but also

[12] The Greek translators evidently understood the Hebrew in light of the common Biblical Hebrew expression לנצח, 'for ever': for occurrences of this form in the Psalter, see (*e.g.*) Pss. 9:7, 19; 10:11; 68:17. On the LXX translation of למנצח at Hab. 3:19, see Harl, Dogniez and others (1999), 300-301.

[13] Both Aquila and Symmachus based their translations on the verbal stem נצח as commonly used in Rabbinic Hebrew along with its cognate root in Aramaic to mean 'be victorious, conquer'.

[14] So Weber, 568: *porro Mattathias et Eliphalu et Machenias et Obededom et Ieihel et Ozaziu in citharis pro octava canebant* επινικιον.

[15] Note also Ambrose's somewhat extravagant statement (*Expositio Evangelii secundum Lucam* V.49) about the 'mystic number eight', that *pro octava multi inscribuntur Psalmi*, even though just two of them, Psalms 6 and 12 (11 in LXX and Old Latin), are so described in the Hebrew, LXX, and Old Latin.

[16] So explicitly 1 Sam. 17:12, implicitly 1 Sam. 16:1; yet we read in 1 Chron. 2:13-15 that David was the seventh son. A clear attempt to deal with this discrepancy may be seen in the Syriac Peshitta version of 1 Chron. 2:14, where an extra son of Jesse, named as Elihu, is enumerated as seventh, leaving David as the eighth son: see Weitzman (1999), 118, 311. Jerome's decision to refer directly to David as eighth son at this point in his commentary may reflect wider Jewish concern with the heading of Psalm 6, as discussed below, pp. 150-151.

the realization of those types in the prophecy of John the Baptist's father Zacharias (Luke 1:67-79) and in Christ's transfiguration after eight days (Luke 9:28) or six days (Matt. 17:1), the eight days being incorporated in the six in a manner already prefigured by the sixth psalm with its superscription 'for the eighth'. Either the end or victory is thus appropriate for the number eight in these instances. That said, we may nonetheless enquire further why Jerome has attached so much weight to superscriptions of Psalms when he might legitimately have emphasised the importance of the number eight by treading in Philo's footsteps, singling out passages from the Pentateuch, the Torah of Moses, which bear witness to the excellence of the number.

While space forbids a full consideration of Philo's engagement with number-symbolism, two of his particular treatments of the number eight are worth noting for present purposes.[17] First, the festival known commonly as *Shemini 'Atzeret*, the eighth day following the end of the seven day period which makes up the autumn feast of Tabernacles (Lev. 23:36; Numb. 29:35), Philo depicted as 'sealing' and bringing to completion not only Tabernacles, but the whole annual cycle of festivals. For the number eight, he declares, is the first cubic number, the first of the category of solids, marking the transition from the unsubstantial and conceptual to that which is stable, substantial, and fixed. In practical terms, the autumn festival renders thanks to God for the crops, whose abundance relieves humanity of anxiety and insecurity for the future (*De Spec. Leg.* II.211-213). Second, God's command to perform circumcision on the eighth day (Gen. 17:12) offered Philo the opportunity for his most detailed disquisition on the number eight, set out in his *Quaestiones et Solutiones in Genesim* III.49. His discussion falls into two parts, each carefully structured. The first lists seven observations specifically focused on arithmology, of which we may 'note especially the first four: (a) eight is the first cubic number; (b) it possesses equality, in that its length, breadth, and depth are equal; (c) the composition of eight from odd and even numbers (1+3+5+7 along with 2+4+6+8) produces the number 36, which makes up a harmony called by the Pythagoreans homology, by others harmony or marriage, which the Creator according to Moses employed in the construction of the universe; and (d) 'the form of the ogdoad produces 64, which is the first cube and, at the same time, square, the pattern of an incorporeal,

---

[17] For number symbolism in Philo and his relationship to Pythagorean ideas, see Moehring (1978), 191-227; and Runia (2001), 25-9.

intelligible and invisible and (also) corporeal substance'.[18] In its second part, Philo's discussion applies this to Israel, the nation which sees God and alone is commanded to perform circumcision on the eighth day. Once more we must select material from his application. Israel wishes to be a part of those who are righteous by nature, and of those righteous by choice, Philo maintains. And Israel is indeed so constituted, first by the principle of creation, the first week of which makes up the first hebdomad, 'the festival of the creation of the world' representing those righteous by nature; and second by the ogdoad, the eighth day beginning the second seven-day period, signifying those righteous by choice. Eight is seven plus one; and Israel, the 'adorned nation', reflects this, being righteous by nature in terms of creation (represented by the seven days of the first week), and having an eighth, additional lot of those righteous by choice. The rite of circumcision, carried out on the eighth day, bears witness to this additional righteousness by choice in respect of Israel.

Philo's treatment of the number eight and the ogdoad, however, extends neither to the eight persons saved in Noah's ark, nor to David's position as the eighth son of Jesse. Indeed, even the topic of circumcision, and its association with the number eight, is mainly confined to his *Quaestiones et Solutiones in Genesim*. In his other writings, eight is significant as being profoundly involved in God's creation of the universe as a cubic number producing harmony and equality.[19] It is also important in relation to other numbers, particularly four and ten, the second of which is of interest in light of Rabbinic statements to be investigated presently.[20]

Nonetheless, in what Philo has written, we may easily discern resources which a Christian scholar and exegete as skilled and learned as Jerome might develop to demonstrate how Christ and the events at his coming into the world had fulfilled the Jewish Scriptures. Jerome

---

[18] The translation is that of Marcus (1961), 248. Philo continues by noting that this 'form of the ogdoad' is incorporeal inasmuch as it produces a square plane, but corporeal in its production of a cubic solid.

[19] See, for example, the *De Opificio Mundi* 93, 99, 101, 105-110. Noah's ark is discussed in *Quaestiones et Solutiones in Genesim* II.5, but not with reference to the number of persons saved by it: there, Philo's concern is with the number 300 and the part played by eight as the first cubic number in the dimensions of the ark.

[20] On eight and the number four, see *De Opificio Mundi* 107; *De Plant.* 124; and on ten, see *De Dec.* 22, 28; *De Spec. Leg.* II. 41; and remarks below, pp. 151-153. In one connection, the number eight has bad connotations: a child born after eight months in the womb is said not to be able to survive, *Leg. All.* I.9.

does, indeed, refer to circumcision, and in a wholly positive manner, in his comment on the heading of Psalm 6; yet this solemn ritual, which, like Ambrose and Gregory, he directly associates with purity, is brought to his readers' attention through analysis of a difficult and somewhat obscure psalm heading, which some may even have considered not to be a part of inspired Scripture, but a mere scribal note.[21] This, and other aspects of Jerome's evident interest in this Psalm title, may become clearer when Jewish interpretations of its unusual phrases are introduced into discussion; for since the discovery of the Dead Sea Scrolls it has become clear that the superscriptions of Psalms 6 and 12 had been the subject of Jewish scholarly attention long before the Christian period.

The Qumran document numbered 4Q177, commonly called 4QCatena[a], represents fragments of a work commenting on selected passages of Scripture, and including many citations of the Psalms.[22] It may once, indeed, have formed part of a larger composition along with the *Florilegium* from Qumran Cave 4 (numbered 4Q174), comprising a substantial commentary, a thematic *pesher*, on the divine plan for the times to come, as Annette Steudel has argued.[23] Whether or not this was the case, 4QCatena[a] alone preserves enough in the way of continuous text for us to recognize that one of its main concerns was what would happen 'at the end of days'.[24] This expression, Steudel has shown, was used to delineate a strongly theological view of the world, in which past events as described in the Bible might be envisaged as having a direct bearing on God's provision for the future.[25] The future, the Catena declares, may be discerned through correct interpretation of prophetic texts such as Hos.5:8; Isa. 37:30; 32:7. This last verse is set alongside the heading to Psalm 11, which in its turn leads to an interpretation of the heading of Psalm 12. Sadly, the document is fragmentary at this point, although it clearly preserves the two

---

[21] Jerome's contemporary, Diodore of Tarsus , regarded the headings as uninspired additions made by scribes when the Jews returned from exile: see (ed.) Olivier (1980), 6. In earlier times, by contrast, Hippolytus (died *ca.* 236) had emphasised the connection between the psalms and their superscriptions: see the English translation of his remarks in *Ante-Nicene Christian Library*, vol. 6 Hippolytus, Bishop of Rome I (1868), 497-504; and Braulik (2004), 31-4.

[22] For the *editio princeps*, see Allegro and Anderson (1968), 57-74.

[23] See Steudel (1994). For recent discussion of the genre thematic *pesher*, see Berrin (2005), 110-33.

[24] For reservations about Steudel's thesis concerning the original extent of the document, see J. Milgrom and L. Novakovic (2002), 287.

[25] See Steudel (1993-1994), 225-46.

opening words of the heading, and the first letter of what must be *hashsheminith*, 'the eighth', since this word in particular is the subject of a clear commentary in the following line of text: 'they refer to the eighth period'.[26] In this document, whose scribal hand suggests a date in the late Hasmonean period (75-50 BCE), it would seem that the 'eighth' noted in the heading of Psalm 12 refers to some future time when, if we follow the tenor of the rest of the document, the wicked and their activities will face God's judgment.[27] As we have seen, the only other Psalm heading which contains the expression 'the eighth' is that of Psalm 6: significantly, 4QCatᵃ fragments 12-13 col.1, lines 1-3 go on to cite Ps. 6:2-3 with specific reference to 'the end of days'; and it is quite possible that, if the whole of the Catena were preserved, we should find the heading of Psalm 6 as the subject of some further hermeneutical operation as well.[28] Even without direct documentary evidence, however, the close similarity in wording between the headings of Psalms 6 and 12 strongly suggests that 'the eighth' was taken by the Jews of Qumran to possess an intimate association with the 'end of days' as they understood that phrase.

Some centuries later, and much closer in time to Jerome's own days, the Tosefta, a key document of classical Rabbinic Judaism, gives pride of place to 'the eighth' mentioned in the heading of Psalm 12, and links it to the covenant of circumcision.[29] At the very end of the first tractate

[26] See 4QCatᵃ fragments 5-6, particularly line 12, which quotes what must be the opening of the superscription of Psalm 12, למנצח על השמינית and line 13 with its comment המה העונה השמינית, 'they refer to the eighth period'. For the Hebrew, see Allegro and Anderson (1968), 69. The Hebrew word translated 'the period', העונה is not found in biblical Hebrew, but in Rabbinic texts often has the sense of 'due season' for produce of fruits and grain, as well as the more general sense of twelve astronomical hours: see Jastrow (1967), 1054.

[27] For the date of the scribal hand in which the document is written, I am indebted to Professor Loren Stuckenbruck (private communication).

[28] See Allegro and Anderson (1968), 71-2. For Qumran documents containing Psalm 6, see Flint (2006), 264-5.

[29] For a valuable survey of modern scholarship on the Tosefta, see Mandel (2006), 316-35. The date of the final form of the Tosefta is subject of much current debate. The traditional view, still upheld by many scholars, places it after the final redaction of the Mishnah (*ca.* 210 CE) to which it forms a Tosefta, *i.e.*, supplement; in this case, it may be dated to the mid to late third century CE. Some students, however, date at least substantial portions of it earlier than the Mishnah; yet others place its final redaction after the publication of the Babylonian Talmud, around the late fifth century CE. See also Strack and Stemberger (1991), 167-81, where a probable date is given (pages 175-176) of the late third to early fourth centuries CE, with some possibility allowed for later modifications.

of the first order of the Tosefta, we find in frame position (*tos. Berakhot* 7:25) the following statement:[30]

> R. Meir used to say: You will not find a man from Israel whom commandments do not surround. *Tefillin* are on his head; *tefillin* are on his arm; the *mezuzah* is at his door-way; and the four fringes (on his garments) surround him. And concerning them David says: 'Seven times a day do I praise Thee' (Ps. 119:164). When he enters the bath-house, the sign of circumcision is in his flesh, as it is said: 'For the leader, upon the eighth, etc.' (Ps. 12:1); and it says: 'The angel of the Lord encamps around those who fear Him, and rescues them'. (Ps. 34:8)

So ends the tractate *Berakhot*, which had begun with rules for the recitation of the *Shema*‛ with its command to love the Lord with all one's heart, a command which includes the binding on head and arm of the *tefillin* (phylacteries), the placing of the *mezuzah* at one's door-way, and the wearing of fringes on garments.[31] The number eight in R. Meir's statement is evidently a number of perfection, completing the sacred number seven which is outwardly displayed at all times by the observant Jew on his person and on his property: the *tefillin* of head and arm, the *mezuzah*, and the four sets of fringes at the corners of clothing add up to seven observances in total. These seven items represent a public affirmation of the terms of the *Shema*‛ with its central assertion of God's Unity. More private, however, is the eighth, the sign of circumcision given on the eighth day.[32] There is nothing external about this commandment. It involves a physical mark unique to each individual Israelite and, although others in the bath-house may see it, the circumcision-mark itself is deeply personal. Furthermore, it is the foundation commandment whose observance grants validity to all other observances commanded by the Torah: without it, the individual male, while nonetheless in principle an Israelite by virtue of his

---

[30] My translation of the text edited by Lieberman (5715/1955), 40.

[31] The liturgical recitation of *Shema*‛ consists of three Scriptural sections, Deut. 6:4-9; 11:13-21; Numb. 15:37-41 which detail these individual commandments.

[32] Circumcision may be 'eighth' in another sense, although what follows is not necessary for interpretation of the Rabbinic texts under consideration. To the sons of Noah, that is, to all the nations, God gave seven commandments, according to R. Simeon b. Eleazar in *Mekhilta of R. Ishmael Bahodesh* 5, lines 81-93 (ed. Lauterbach); see also *Gen. Rabbah* 34:8. The next commandment which Scripture records after Noah's days is that of circumcision (Gen. 17:12); it would thus appear to be the eighth commandment given by God, restricted to Abraham's descendants, and to be carried out on the eighth day.

birth, is seriously disadvantaged, and there might be those who would regard his observance of other commandments as otiose and beside the point, since the fundamental mark of God's covenant with Israel is not found in his flesh. In this Tosefta passage, circumcision is the *sine qua non* for offering to God the praise which David uttered; and it leads to divine protection and rescue for those who fear God.[33] The heading of Psalm 12 with its mention of the eighth is given pride of place at the end of tractate *Berakhot* for a clear purpose: for the final redactor of the Tosefta, this psalm heading was bound up with the most essential affirmation of Israel's life and purpose, her unceasing proclamation of God's Unity and uniqueness, and his love for his people Israel, who by virtue of reciting Shema' take upon themselves the yoke of the Kingdom of Heaven and the yoke of the divine commandments (*m. Berakhot* 2:2).

The heading of Psalm 12 makes a further crucial appearance in *tos. 'Arakhin* 2:7. If *tos. Berakhot* 7:25, quite unlike the Qumran Catena, is concerned with 'the eighth' as an aspect of Israel's life in this world, the treatment of Psalm 12 in tractate *'Arakhin* brings us back to an explicit concern with the future and the world to come. There we read:[34]

> R. Judah says: There are seven [*šeba'*] strings to the lyre at present. as it is said: Fullness [*sōba'*] of joy is with your Presence' (Ps. 16:11). For the days of the Messiah, there will eight, as it is said: 'For the leader upon the eighth' (Ps. 12:1), that is, upon the eighth string [of the lyre]. For the time to come – on ten, as it is said, 'Give thanks to the Lord on the lyre: on an instrument of ten strings sing to the Lord'. (Ps. 33:2).

This somewhat terse passage requires explanation. The section of the Mishnah which corresponds to these words in the Tosefta, *m. 'Arakhin* 2:6, provides some necessary background information. There we learn that never fewer than twelve Levites stood on the platform designated for their musical duties in the Temple during the Temple service. The number might be greater, though Levites who were children could only enter the Temple court when the senior Levites were

---

[33] See also *b. Men.* 43b, where the discussion is introduced as follows: 'Our Rabbis have taught: Beloved are Israel, for the Holy One, Blessed be He, surrounds them with commandments – *tefillin* on their heads…'. Following David's utterance of Ps. 119:164, we read what may be intended as further explication of what is written in the Tosefta: 'Now at the time that David went into the bath-house and saw himself standing naked, he said: "Woe to me, that I stand naked without a commandment!" But when he recalled the circumcision which was in his flesh, his mind was settled. Afterwards, when he went out, he uttered a song about it, as it is said, "To the leader upon the eighth: a psalm of David", about circumcision which was given on the eighth.'

[34] My translation of text edited by Zuckermandel (1937), 544.

singing, to join in the chanting to beautify it, but not to play with harp and lyre. Now when the Babylonian Talmud comes to discuss this Mishnah (at *b. Arakh.* 13b), it appears to quote the Tosefta passage we have here before us by way of explanation, as it comments on the relevant sentence of the Mishnah with its ruling about the children of the Levites:

> 'They did not give voice with harp and lyre, but with the mouth (alone), etc.' (*m. Arakh.* 2:6). One might declare that the harp was one kind (of instrument), the lyre another. Would this suggest that our Mishnah was not like that of R. Judah? For it has been taught (in a *baraita*): R. Judah said: The lyre of the Temple consisted of seven strings, as it is said: 'Fullness [*soba'*] of joy is with your Presence' (Ps. 16:11). Do not read 'fullness' [*soba'*] but 'seven' [*šeba'*]. Now the lyre of the days of the Messiah consists of eight strings, as it is said: 'To the leader upon the eighth' (Ps. 12:1) – upon the eighth string. The lyre of the world to come has ten strings, as it is said: 'Upon ten strings and upon the harp: with resounding music upon the lyre' (Ps. 92:4). And it says: 'Give thanks to the Lord upon the lyre: on an instrument of ten strings sing to the Lord. Sing to Him a new song' (Ps. 33:2-3).

Although of interest in itself, the conclusion of the Talmudic discussion showing that the Mishnah may be understood to be consonant with R. Judah's statements cannot detain us here. What emerges clearly in the course of all these deliberations is that the heading of Psalm 12 is to be understood in the light of Levitical duties in the Temple service. Although there is neither direct quotation of, nor indirect allusion to it, 1 Chron. 15:21 with its list of Levites who sing to the lyre 'upon the eighth' informs the whole discussion. Then in the Talmud, R. Judah's quotation of Ps. 16:11, which in the Tosefta appears at first glance to have nothing at all to do with the matter, is fully explained: we are not to read that verse with the word *sōba'*, 'fullness', as it is commonly vocalised in that context, but with the word *šeba'*, seven'.[35] The reader of the Tosefta is, of course, expected to know this, and

---

[35] This kind of hermeneutical procedure introduced by the formula *'al tiqrei*, literally 'do not read', may involve not only changes in the vocalization of a word, but sometimes also require alteration of one or more consonants. In this instance, the Hebrew letter ש, written without a diacritical mark, might be vocalized either as English letter 's', or as English 'sh'; and the Rabbis have taken full advantage of this to exploit the full exegetical possibilities of the Hebrew consonants *sb'*. For further description and examples of this procedure, see Alexander (2003), 32, 138.

to make the necessary adjustments. The exegesis then becomes clear: the number seven refers to the Temple service of this world, with its seven-stringed lyre. Eight is the number reserved for the service in the days of the Messiah; and it is the heading of Psalm 12 with its reference to 'the eighth' which provides the proof for this difference between this present world, and the days to come when the Messiah shall be present.

It should not be assumed that these interpretations of the headings to Psalm 12 were confined to technical discussions within the Rabbinic schools. Two texts in particular indicate that they came to be more widely known. The first is the Aramaic Targum of Psalms. Targum could be, and often was, a medium by means of which Rabbinic exegesis might be disseminated to a Jewish constituency which, while literate, was not necessarily learned in the intricacies of Rabbinic exegesis and its particular specialised terminology.[36] The Targum interpreted the Hebrew phrase *'al ha-sheminith* in the headings of Psalms 6 and 12 as meaning 'upon the lyre with eight strings': the two final words of the headings are then translated as 'a psalm of David', the Targumist staying as close as possible here to the Hebrew original.[37] There seems little doubt that the Aramaic translator was aware of the implications of the Hebrew phrase upon the eighth as set out, for example, in the Tosefta, and chose his words accordingly.[38] Given the widespread use of the Psalms in the service of the Synagogue, questions about the meaning of the difficult words and phrases used in the superscriptions are likely to have arisen at an early period. This suspicion is in part confirmed by the second text, the homiletic corpus known as the *Tanhuma*. This consists of a collection of synagogue sermons or homilies, and should most probably be dated from the fifth to the seventh centuries CE in its present,

---

[36] The best and most recent discussion in English of Targum and its methods is by Alexander (1992), 320-31. See also Taradach (1991), 51-160; especially 113-7 for the Psalms Targum.

[37] The difficulties in dating the Targum of Psalms are well known; for the most recent discussion, see Stec (2004), 1-2, who tentatively suggests a date in the period from the fourth to the sixth centuries CE. That Aramaic versions of individual Psalms were known from a much earlier time is suggested, however, by Matt. 27:46; Mark 15:34.

[38] On the Targumic approach to Psalm headings, see Preuss (1959), 44-54. Rabbinic texts which in their present form date from the post-Islamic period also record the interpretation of 'the eighth' as meaning 'the lyre with eight strings': see *Numb. Rab.* 15:11 commenting on Numb. 8:6, God's command to 'take the Levites'; *Pesiqta Rabbati* 21 beginning, on Exod. 20:2; and see also *Midrash Tehillim* on Ps. 6:1.

final form.[39] *Tanhuma* 7 בהעלותך 7 records the same interpretation of the heading of Psalm 6 which is transmitted in the name of R. Judah; and we may be reasonably certain that synagogue congregations were aware of it, either through the medium of preaching, or some other formal instruction, or simply through private conversations in which observant Jews discussed matters of Torah with one another.

Viewed alongside this evidence from pre-Rabbinic and Rabbinic Jewish texts, Jerome's concentrated exegetical endeavour on the expression 'for the eighth' in the headings of Psalms 6 and 12 (LXX Psalm 11) in particular seems highly significant. The Qumran text 4QCatena[a] shows clearly how at least one group of Jews in the pre-Christian period had perceived in these superscriptions information about the end of days, an eighth period which would involve the judgment of the wicked and the establishing of divine justice. Consequently, for later Jews, and for the earliest Christians of Judaea, an interpretation of 'the eighth' was already in circulation which was patient of further development by both groups; and these two communities could agree that the term as used in the Psalm headings refers to a future when God will act decisively 'in the latter days', a future involving David, who is named in both Psalm titles.

A key text from the Rabbinic period, the Tosefta, twice invokes 'the eighth' in the heading of Psalm 12, first in frame position in its very opening tractate with reference to circumcision, and then to refer to the days of the Messiah. God's choice of Israel, and the ultimate redemption of the Jewish people, are the matters at stake here; and, in the matter of circumcision, there is the added sense of the individual Jew's personal dedication and commitment to the observance of God's commandments at a time when some Christians were speaking lightly of the Torah in general and the commandment of circumcision in particular.[40] In both these passages from the Tosefta, the Rabbis who comment on the Psalm heading are among the most illustrious of the Sages of their days: in *tos. Berakhot* 7:25 it is R. Meir

---

[39] For discussion of the dates of the Tanhuma and its contents, see M. Bregman, article 'Tanhuma'-Yelammedenu' (1997), 673-674 and bibliography there cited.

[40] It should be noted that the Hebrew term ברית, usually translated as 'covenant', is normally confined by the Mishnah and the Tosefta to refer to the 'covenant of circumcision', except where a Scriptural verse speaking of the covenant at Sinai is quoted: see Schiffman (1987), 289-98.

who speaks, and in *tos.* *'Ararkhin* 2:7 we hear the words of R. Judah.[41] The ensuing discussions in the Babylonian Talmud, and the presence in the Targum and homiletic midrashim of comments set out in the Tosefta, indicate the enduring presence of 'the eighth' and the heading of Psalm 12 on the Rabbinic agenda, and its dissemination outside the academies.

At roughly the same time, Christian scholars like Origen, Ambrose, and Gregory of Nyssa were writing expositions of, and commentaries on, 'the eighth'. Jerome's decision to include in his commentary a prominent mention of David, the eighth son of Jesse and the chosen one of God, may well owe something to contemporary Jewish exegesis of the Psalm headings. It will be noted, however, that Jerome concentrates his attention on the Scriptural *datum* of David as eighth son of Jesse, rather than invoking the eighth string of the Levites' lyre as an allusion to the days of Messiah. Well informed as Jerome was about Jewish traditions, his silence on this matter is telling: it results in a greater emphasis on the figure of David himself, singled out and chosen by God, than the Jewish exposition of 'the eighth'; and the personal element is very much to the fore in Jerome's comment. No other Church Father so resolutely and so succinctly lists the personnel who might be related to 'the eighth', such as Noah, David, Zacharias, John Baptist, and the Lord Himself.

The Jewish Sages themselves, moreover, were almost certainly aware of Christian explanations of the eighth, some of which, as we have seen, date from before the time of Jerome. So we must ask: might they in their turn, perhaps, have sought to 'trump' the Church Fathers' interpretations of 'the eighth' by adding to the symbolism of numbers, and going not one, but two better? It will be recalled that R. Judah in *tos.* *'Arakhin* 2:7 does not end his commentary with the eight stringed lyre of the days of the Messiah, but goes on to speak of the future, the world to come, when the Almighty will be praised on an instrument of ten strings. A distinction between the 'days of the Messiah', which would endure only for a limited time, and the world to come which is eternal, is well known in Rabbinic Judaism from such classic texts

---

[41] The mere ascription of these sayings to highly respected Sages, irrespective of the historical reliability of such ascription, is what matters for our purposes. R. Meir was a Tanna of the fourth generation, and thus active around the years 140-165 CE. Some uncertainty surrounds the identity of R. Judah, who may be either R. Judah b. Ilai, a contemporary of R. Meir; or more probably R. Judah the Patriarch, who flourished 165-200 CE.

as *b.Sanhedrin* 99a, but its presence in the Tosefta passage expounding 'the eighth' need not be construed in any polemical sense. From the days before Christianity, Philo had sung the praises of the number ten; and although the Rabbis make no mention of his writings, they had their own tradition of ten as a significant number reaching back into biblical times and persisting into their own day.[42] Even so, by referring the ten-stringed instrument to a period which succeeds the days of the Messiah, the Sages might have seen an appropriate means, given the exegetical circumstances, of reminding their people that the coming of Messiah is not the end of God's dealings with Israel.

It is entirely comprehensible, given the literary evidence we have examined, that Jews and Christians should have shared a common interest in this matter of 'the eighth', and that their interpretations of the relevant Psalm headings should point in the direction of exegetical influences from one religious group to the other. From Jerome's standpoint, one can envisage a fairly straightforward line of thinking. Traditional Jewish understanding of 'the eighth' in the Psalm headings as a reference to the last days, the future as planned by the Almighty, would for him be true: as we have seen, it would be a prefiguration of the Messiah, and of the world to come. For the Christians, Messiah had come, and the resurrection had taken place: the days of the world to come had dawned. We may note how adroitly Jerome has blended the Old and the New Testaments in his words about the heading of Psalms 6 and 11, how very positively he speaks of, even stresses, the Jewish law of circumcision, relating it to Zacharias the father of St. John Baptist and his prophecy. In this little vignette of promise and fulfilment, of Old and New in such harmony, the formal, literary differences from other Christian commentators whose writings he may have known are quite striking. Knowledge of the interpretations which his Jewish contemporaries were placing upon these Psalm headings may go some way towards explaining his hermeneutical approach in the *Commentarioli*. For themselves, the Jewish

[42] For examples of Philo's allusions to ten as a perfect number, see *De Cong.* 111-120 and, naturally, *De Dec.* 29-30; *De Spec. Leg.* I. 178. The place of the number ten in the Bible requires no comment. For the importance of the number ten in the Rabbinic tradition generally, see *m. Avot* 5:1-6, enumerating the ten utterances with which the world was created, the ten generations from Adam to Noah and from Noah to Abraham; the ten temptations of Abraham; the ten miracles in Egypt, at the Red Sea, and in the Temple; and the ten things created on the eve of the first Sabbath. For the last category, see also *b. Pes.* 54a; *Mekhilta of R. Ishmael Vayassaʿ* 6; Targum Pseudo-Jonathan Gen. 2:2; Numb. 22:28; *Pirqe de R. Eliezer* 19:1

Sages are unlikely to have been ignorant of Christian interpretations of 'the eighth', and we have seen some of what they have to say on the subject: it takes on particular force when the Christian sources are set alongside it for comparison. And in this case, as so often, Jerome stands as a crucial witness to the ways between Jews and Christians, which may be said never really to have parted.[43]

This short essay is offered as a tribute to Andrew Louth, friend and colleague, on his sixty-fifth birthday, in appreciation of his erudition and learning both in the writings of the Church Fathers and of the Jewish Sages.

Bibliography

Alexander, P. S. (1992) 'Targum Targumim', in (ed.) Freedman, D. N. (1992) *The Anchor Bible Dictionary*, vol. 6 (New York), 320-31.

Alexander, P. S. (2003) *The Targum of Canticles* (London).

Allegro, J. M. and Anderson, A. A. (1968) *Discoveries in the Judaean Desert of Jordan. V Qumrân Cave 4 I (4Q158-4Q186)* (Oxford), 57-74.

Anderson, A. A. (1972) *Psalms* (London).

Beckwith, R. T. (2005) *Calendar, Chronology and Worship. Studies in Ancient Judaism and Early Christianity* (Leiden).

(eds) Berlin, A. and Brettler, M.Z. (2004) *The Jewish Study Bible* (Oxford).

Berrin, S. (2005) 'Qumran Pesharim' in (ed.) Henze, M. (2005) *Biblical Interpretation at Qumran* (Grand Rapids), 110-33.

Braulik, G. P. (2004) 'Psalter and Messiah. Towards a Christological Understanding of the Psalms in the Old Testament and the Church Fathers' in (eds) Human, D.J. and Vos, C. J. A. (2004) *Psalms and Liturgy* (London).

Bregman, M. (1997) 'Tanhuma' – Yelammedenu', in (eds) Werblowsky, R. J. Z. and Wigoder, G. (1997) *The Oxford Dictionary of the Jewish Religion* (Oxford).

Childs, B. S. (1971) 'Psalm Titles and Midrashic Exegesis', *JSS* 16, 137-50.

Field, F. (1875) *Origenis Hexaplorum Quae Supersunt*, 2 vols (Oxford).

Flint, P. W. (2006) 'Psalms and Psalters in the Dead Sea Scrolls', in (ed.) Charlesworth, J. H. (2006), *The Bible and the Dead Sea Scrolls, Vol.* 1 Scripture and the Scrolls (Waco, TX).

---

[43] On this topical matter, see most recently Salvesen (2007), 233-58. See the editors' introductory essay to this same volume (pages 1-33) for an excellent analysis of recent scholarship on the so-called 'parting of the ways'.

Harl, M., and Dogniez, C. (1999) *La Bible d'Alexandrie. Les Douzes Prophètes 4-9* (Paris).

Heine, R. E. (1995) *Gregory of Nyssa's Treatise on the Inscriptions of the Psalms* (Oxford).

Jastrow, M. (1967) *A Dictionary of the Targumim, the Talmud Babli and Yerushalmi, and the Midrashic Literature* (New York).

Kelly, J. N. D. (1975) *Jerome. His Life, Writings , and Controversies* (London).

Kraus, H.-J. (1961) *Psalmen. Biblischer Kommentar Altes Testament* (Neukirchen).

Lieberman, S. (5715/1955) *The Tosefta according to Codex Vienna* (New York).

Mandel, P. (2006) 'The Tosefta', in (ed.) Katz, S. T. (2006) *The Cambridge History of Judaism, vol 4. The Late Roman Rabbinic Period* (Cambridge), 316-35.

Marcus, R. (1961) *Philo Supplement 1 Questions and Answers on Genesis*, Loeb Classical Library (Cambridge, Mass.).

Milgrom, J. and Novakovic, L. (2002) 'Catena A (4Q177 = 4QCat^a)', in (eds) Charlesworth, J. H. and others (2002) *The Dead Sea Scrolls: Hebrew, Aramaic and Greek Texts with English Translations, vol. 6B: Pesharim, Other Commentaries and Related Documents* (Tübingen).

Moehring, H. R. (1978) 'Arithmology as an Exegetical Tool in the Writings of Philo of Alexandria', in (ed.) Achtemeir, P. J. (1978) *Society of Biblical Literature 1978 Seminar Papers* (Missoula), 191-227.

Mowinckel, S. (1967) *The Psalms in Israel's Worship* (Oxford).

(ed.) Olivier, J.-M. (1980) *Diodori Tarsensis Commentarii in Psalmos* (Turnhout).

Preuss, H. D. (1959) 'Die Psalmenüberschriften in Targum und Midrasch', *ZAW* 71, 44-54.

Rahlfs, A. (1935) *Septuaginta*, 2 vols (Stuttgart).

Risse, S. (2005) *Hieronymus, Commentarioli in Psalmos. Anmerkungen zum Psalter* (Turnhout).

Runia, D. T. (2001) *Philo of Alexandria. On the Creation of the Cosmos according to Moses. Introduction, Translation and Commentary* (Leiden).

Salvesen, A. (2007) 'A Convergence of the Ways? The Judaizing of Christian Scripture by Origen and Jerome', in (eds) Becker, A. H. and Yoshiko Reed, A. (2007) *The Ways that Never Parted. Jews and Christians in Late Antiquity and the Early Middle Ages* (Minneapolis).

Schiffman, L. H. (1987) 'The Rabbinic Understanding of Covenant', *Review and Expositor* 84, 289-98.

Siegfried, C. (1875) *Philo von Alexandria als Ausleger des Alten Testaments* (Jena).

Stec, D. M. (2004) *The Targum of Psalms: Translated, with a Critical Introduction, Apparatus and Notes* (London).

Steudel, A. (1993-1994) 'אחרית הימים in the Texts from Qumran', *RQ* 16, 225-46.

Steudel, A. (1994) *Der Midrasch zur Eschatologie aus der Qumrangemeinde (4QMidr-Eschat.ᵃˑᵇ): Materielle Rekonstruktion, Textbestand, Gattung und Traditionsgeschichtliche Einordnung des durch 4Q174 ("Florilegium") und 4Q177 ("Catena A") repräsentierten Werkes aus den Qumranfunden* (Leiden).

Strack, H. L. and Stemberger, G. (1991) *Introduction to the Talmud and Midrash* (Edinburgh).

Taradach, M. (1991) *Le Midrash. Introduction à la littérature midrashique* (Genève).

(ed.) Weber, R. (1994) *Biblia Sacra iuxta Vulgatam Versionem*, 4th ed. (Stuttgart).

Weitzman, M. P. (1999) *The Syriac Version of the Old Testament. An Introduction* (Cambridge).

Zuckermandel, M. S. (1937) *Tosephta based on the Erfurt and Vienna Codices*, 2nd ed. (Jerusalem).

GILLIAN CLARK

PSALLITE SAPIENTER: AUGUSTINE ON PSALMODY

The choir stalls of Durham Cathedral provided the title of this paper, a few days after I had been given this very welcome opportunity to honour the friend and co-editor from whom I have learned so much. Morning Prayer included the reading of a Psalm, in the form where the minister reads one verse and the congregation the next, with the traditional pause in the middle for singers to take a breath. When a psalm is sung, singers can, with practice, let the sound of the first half-verse fade, then come in together on the second half-verse. When the psalm is spoken, it is more difficult for the congregation to match the minister's preferred pause-length. During the pauses, I wondered about the words inscribed on the choir stalls opposite: *psallite pueri sapienter*. They proved to be an adaptation of Psalm 46(47): 7-8 in the Vulgate translation:

> *Psallite Deo nostro, psallite;*
> *Psallite regi nostro, psallite;*
> *Quoniam rex omnis terrae Deus,*
> *Psallite sapienter.*

> Sing psalms to our God, sing psalms,
> Sing psalms to our king, sing psalms,
> Because God is king of all the earth,
> Sing psalms with wisdom.

'Sing psalms with wisdom': how is that to be done? Many of the Fathers responded to this verse, but Augustine is exceptional in his emotional involvement with the Psalms, the range of his preaching on them, and his interest in the theory of music. How did he bridge the gap between the Psalms that meant so much to him and the socially dubious activity *psallere*, singing with a stringed instrument, that he knew from his classical education and from life in North Africa and Italy? How did his engagement with the Psalms as sung or spoken texts relate to his concerns about music in worship? In salutation from a classicist to a theologian, these are the answers I have found.[1]

To begin with *psallere* as socially dubious activity: Augustine had a conventional late antique education. He read the central works of the classical curriculum, and Terence and Sallust, Cicero and Virgil, often appear in his writings. In *Confessions,* he used Sallust's description of the revolutionary Catiline to help his analysis of apparently motiveless wrongdoing. Catiline's supporter Sempronia does not appear, but Augustine surely did not forget Sallust's brilliant sketch of a Roman lady whose accomplishments included *psallere et saltare elegantius quam necesse est probae*: 'singing to an instrument, and dancing, more stylishly than a decent woman needs'.[2] That is, she came too close to the level of a professional performer; a speaker in the *Saturnalia* of Augustine's later contemporary Macrobius notes that Sallust did not object to her dancing, only to her expertise.[3] This was not just social snobbery, for performers were morally as well as socially dubious. In *City of God*, Augustine included in a rapid survey of Roman history the moment when Asiatic luxury infected Rome: after Gnaeus Manlius held his triumph over the Gallograeci, in 187 BC, 'that was when *psaltriae*, and other lascivious practices, were introduced into dinner parties.'[4] Different kinds of music were known to produce different emotional effects, and evidently the effect of stringed instruments was lascivious, especially when they were plucked by female performers. Moreover, professional *psaltriae* had to earn a living as private or public entertainers, at parties or exposed to the public gaze in the theatre.[5]

Psaltriae and their instruments, then, were known to people who could afford a classical education. They were still familiar in the late fourth century. An imperial law issued in 385 at Constantinople declared 'No one is permitted to buy, teach, or sell a [female]

---

[1] I am indebted especially to colleagues at Bristol: to Emma Hornby, to Alison Pemble who generously shared her postgraduate work in progress on angels who play instruments, and to Stephen D'Evelyn, Pamela King, and Ellen O'Gorman for their advice on music and performance. Carol Harrison's project on transformative listening will also transform understanding: meanwhile, see Harrison (2010), and the perceptive discussion in Burton (2007), 137-51.

[2] Aug. *conf.* 2.5.11; Sall. *Cat.* 25.2.

[3] Macr. *Sat.* 3.14.5.

[4] Aug. *civ.* 3.21.

[5] For an overview of Roman music in performance, see Landels (1999), 172-205.

string-player [*fidicina*], or to summon one to a dinner-party or to a show.'[6] In Milan, Ambrose contrasted the playing of the *psalterium* at drunken parties with the singing of psalms:

> I had passed over the *cithara, psalteria* and *tympana*, which we have often known summoned to parties of this kind, so that lust may be excited by wine and song. [...] Pious people recite hymns, and you hold a *cithara*? Psalms are sung, and you pick up the *psalterium* or the *tympanum*?[7]

Music, parties and shows recur in a famous complaint against Roman aristocrats by the historian Ammianus Marcellinus, who contrasted their neglect of serious study (such as history) with their interest in entertainment:

> Houses echo with the sound of the voice and the noise of wind and strings; the singer is summoned instead of the philosopher, the teacher of theatre skills in place of the orator, and when libraries are permanently closed like tombs, people make water-organs, and huge lyres [*lyrae*] as big as carriages, and weighty properties for stage performances.[8]

Music could have been a serious study because it was a liberal art, a form of expertise suitable for free people who did not have to hire out their skills, and the liberal arts trained people to move from particulars to principles.[9] Augustine followed philosophical tradition when he sought to show, in his early work *de musica*, that the ratios which governed rhythm also governed the order of the universe.[10] But that was music theory, music as audible mathematics, and Ammianus was not alone in thinking that music performance was a frivolous diversion, or worse. His contemporary Jerome warned the widow Furia not to have *psaltriae* in her house at Rome, and urged Laeta to bring up

---

[6] *Cod. Theod.* 15.7.10: the Theodosian Code, compiled in the mid-fifth century, collected laws of general relevance. Laws on showgirls: Evans Grubbs (2001), 234-39.

[7] *De Helia et ieunio* 15.54.

[8] Amm. Marc. 14.6.18. 'noise of wind and strings' attempts to translate *perflabili tinnitu fidium*, a phrase which conflates the three kinds of instrumental sound: wind (*perflabilis*, literally 'blowable through'), percussion (*tinnitus*, literally 'ringing' or 'tinkling'), and strings (*fides*).

[9] Pollmann and Vessey (2005).

[10] Augustine made a start on music in Milan (c.387), and wrote *de musica* after his baptism and return to Africa (c. 391): *Retr.* 1.5.6. See further Harrison (2008).

her daughter not knowing what musical instruments were for.[11] Did Jerome mean only that little Paula should not go to parties, or did he want to rule out any possibility that a girl of good family would learn to play an instrument, of course as an amateur? Three centuries earlier, when Pliny's young wife set some of his poems to the *cithara*, Pliny emphasised that she had not had professional teaching from an *artifex*; love, he said, was her only tutor.[12]

The law of 385 shows that professional *psaltriae* continued to be public as well as private entertainers, in the theatrical performances that caused Augustine so much concern.[13] Too much concern, perhaps: when J. E. C. Welldon, Dean of Durham, wrote his learned but sparse commentary on *City of God*, he added an appendix on the far more sensible attitude of the Church of England, which accepts that plays can be edifying and that actors and actresses can be morally decent people. Some, indeed, are buried in Westminster Abbey.[14] Augustine was troubled because theatre as he knew it offered examples of bad conduct and reinforced them by its emotional impact. He discussed in *Confessions* how theatre enlists meaningless sympathy for fictitious characters.[15] As always, he focussed on the text; he did not mention the emotional effect of instrumental music, even though it was essential to theatre. Long before Augustine's time, a kind of opera and ballet had come to replace, or perhaps to supplement, complete performances of classical drama. A *tragicus cantor* or *tragoidos*, literally 'singer of tragedy', presented great scenes or speeches (rather as in nineteenth-century 'Scenes from Shakespeare'), in song or recitative accompanied by a stringed instrument: not the *psalterium* used by the *psaltriae*, but the bigger *cithara* which was used for public performance. The classic example is the emperor Nero, who entered, and of course won, dramatic contests in Greece, and who, notoriously, took up his *cithara* to sing the 'Fall of Troy' as Rome burned in the Great Fire of AD 64.[16] Nero's famous last words, *qualis artifex pereo*, express the objections of traditional Romans. They are often translated 'what an artist dies in me!', but that imports a later, romantic valuation of artistic genius. 'What a loss to the profession!' conveys awareness that a *cithara*

[11] Jer. *Ep.* 54.13, 107.8. I owe these references, and much else, to McKinnon (1987).

[12] Pliny *Ep.* 4.19.4.

[13] See Quasten (1983), 127 for church canons excluding professional musicians and other entertainers.

[14] Welldon (1924), 659-69.

[15] Aug. *conf.* 1.16.26, 3.2.1.

[16] Nero as musician: Landels (1999), 200-4.

player was a professional, the object of Roman distaste for exposure to the public gaze and for dependence on fees.[17] Nero did not overcome the traditional Roman disapproval of learning a musical instrument. Suetonius, in his brief biography, grouped together Nero's acceptable and even laudable acts, then moved to his bad acts. These began with music:

> He studied music together with the other subjects learned in childhood, and as soon as he became emperor, he summoned Terpnus, who was then the leading *cithara* performer [*citharoedus*], sat by him day after day as he sang after dinner, and gradually himself began to reflect and practise, doing everything this kind of professional does to conserve or develop the voice.[18]

Three centuries later there is no sign that Augustine and his friends had any experience of playing, or that Augustine emulated Nero when he won a prize for a *carmen theatricum*, a song or poem for the theatre.[19] Orators had much in common with actors, both in voice training and in performance skills, and Augustine could have declaimed the *carmen* himself with a vocal range close to singing. But that would probably have been too theatrical, and it is more likely that his text was performed by a *cantor* with a *cithara*.

Music in the theatre was also essential for *pantomimi*, who performed all the roles in a story, as dance solos with musical accompaniment. There was more song and dance in comedy, where the effect was like a twentieth-century musical, including dialogue, solo and chorus. In *City of God* Augustine refers to raunchier performances with a chorus of *meretrices* ('women who earn', approximately 'sex workers'), but it is not clear whether these happened in his own time or four centuries earlier in the time of Varro, his major source of material on Roman religion and especially on theatre.[20] As Augustine frequently reminded the readers of *City of God,* theatre was part of Roman religion, and according to Varro, who was an acknowledged authority on both, the gods themselves had demanded dramatic performances as part of religious festivals. Religious rituals, too, used music in the theatre and other public spaces.[21] Romans thought that in their earliest

---

[17] Griffin (1984), 41-4.

[18] Suet. *Nero* 20.1

[19] Aug. *conf.* 4.2.3.

[20] *Meretrices,* Aug. *civ.* 6.7; on Varro, see further Clark 2010.

[21] Tert. *Spec.*10 noted the connection of theatre and ritual.

history the only musical instrument was the *tibia*, a wind instrument like the Greek *aulos*. It continued to be used at sacrifices to drown out ill-omened sounds; stringed instruments came in with Greek rites, and trumpets were used in purification. *Tibicines* and *fidicenes,* players of wind and string instruments, came together as *symphoniaci.*[22]

Such rituals were banned by law at the end of the fourth century, but they were clearly remembered and in some places they continued.[23] Augustine told the story of a man who had a vision while dancing *ante symphoniacum,* 'before the music', in a place where there were many idols because of some pagan rite. He himself remembered the festival of Berecynthia at Carthage, where as a young man he listened to the *symphoniaci* and to the obscenities which were 'repeatedly sung by lascivious stage-performers' (*cantitabantur a nequissimis scaenicis*).[24] Here his experience came together with his classical education, for Berecynthia was a title of Cybele, mother of the gods, and Virgil offered an Italian prince mocking her Trojan worshippers and their music:

> *Vobis picta croco et fulgenti murice vestis,*
> *Desidiae cordi, iuvat indulgere choreis*
> *Et tunicae manicas et habent redimicula mitrae.*
> *O vere Phrygiae, neque enim Phryges, ite per alta*
> *Didyma, ubi adsuetis biforem dat tibia cantum.*
> *Tympana vos buxusque vocat Berecynthiae matris*
> *Idaeae: sinite arma viris et cedite ferro.*

> You wear clothes embroidered with saffron and dazzling purple; you love idleness and like dancing; your tunics have long sleeves and your caps have ribbon ties. Phrygian women – you are not Phrygian men – go to the heights of Didyma, where the pipe [*tibia*] plays your familiar two-toned song. The *tympanum* and boxwood [flute] of Berecynthia, the Idaean mother, call you: leave weapons to men, give way to iron.[25]

---

[22] Evidence collected in Quasten (1983), 4-10. Livy 9.30 tells the story of the musicians who went on strike, so no ritual could be performed.

[23] Fowden (1998).

[24] Aug. *Gn. litt.* 12.22.47; *civ.* 2.4.

[25] V. *Aen.* 9. 614-20. Augustine's contemporary Servius quoted Varro to explain that the two-toned *tibia* was not a double pipe (like the Greek *aulos*), but had two stops.

Perhaps the ritual Augustine remembered also linked his classical read-ing to the Bible. The rites of Cybele added clashing cymbals to the musical mix of flute and percussion, and later in *City of God* Augustine mocked Varro's attempt to explain them by allegory.[26] Did Paul of Tar-sus (1 Cor. 13: 1) have such rituals in mind when he wrote 'If I speak with the tongues of men and angels, and have not love, I am become as a sounding brass or a tinkling cymbal'?[27] Plato argued that when instru-mental music is used without words, it has no meaning; Paul said that language at its highest and most rational level is sound without meaning if it is used without love.[28]

Ritual and meaning are central to the question of psalmody: how is God to be worshipped, and how shall we sing psalms with wisdom, or, in the translation Augustine used, *intellegenter,* with understand-ing? Throughout the Hebrew Bible music is used in worship; psalms are by definition songs accompanied by stringed instruments. Hilary of Poitiers thought that the headings in the Book of Psalms envis-aged four possibilities: *psalmus*, for instrument alone; *canticum*, for unaccompanied choir; *canticum psalmi* where the choir follows the instrumental line, and *psalmus cantici* where the *psalterium* follows the singers.[29] Yet Christian writers in the early centuries consistently opposed the use of instruments in Christian worship. The expla-nation usually offered is that musical instruments connoted pagan ritual and pagan theatre, and perhaps also Jewish ritual. There is little evidence for music in synagogue worship, but people who dis-approved of music could argue that Christians should distinguish themselves from Jews in their own time and from outdated Jewish tradition, and that Biblical precedent could not justify musical per-formance in the wrong context and with the wrong content.[30] Johan-nes Quasten began his learned survey of music and worship with a quotation ascribed to Cyprian:

> The fact that David danced in the sight of God does nothing to help
> Christian believers who sit in the theatre: he did not perform a story

---

[26] *Civ.* 7.24.

[27] 1 Cor. 13: 1.

[28] Pl. *Laws* 669e.

[29] *instructio psalmorum* 19 (CSEL 22. 15-16).

[30] Quasten (1983), 100 n. 12a on the debate about music in synagogues. John Chrysostom, *adv.Iud.* 4.7.4-5, refers to the Feast of Trumpets (New Year) in synagogue worship at Antioch: I owe the reference to Bella Sandwell.

of Greek lust, distorting his limbs in obscene movements. Harps, cymbals, flutes, drums and *citharae* sang God, not an idol. So let there be no requirement to watch unlawful things: by the devil as *artifex* [*diabolo artifice*] holy things were changed into unlawful things.[31]

If this was written by a contemporary of Cyprian, he lived at a time when Christians could not safely attract attention with the use of music in worship. But when the risk of persecution had ended, why did Christian writers not use the obvious arguments for using instruments in praise of God?

In the twelfth century, when people were no longer familiar with pagan performances, Hildegard of Bingen showed how the case could be made:

> But in order that mankind should recall that divine sweetness and praise by which, with the angels, Adam was made jubilant in God before he fell, instead of recalling Adam in his banishment, and that mankind too might be stirred to that sweet praise, the holy prophets, taught by the same spirit which they had received, not only composed psalms and canticles, to be sung to kindle the devotion of listeners; but also they invented musical instruments of diverse kinds with this in view, by which the songs could be expressed in multitudinous sounds, so that listeners, aroused and made adept outwardly, might be nurtured within by the forms and qualities of the instruments, as by the meaning of the words performed with them.[32]

Hildegard combined Biblical precedent for the use of instruments with philosophical tradition about their use to arouse or to moderate emotion. Her hymn on the Holy Spirit praises the spirit who works in *timpana* and *citharae*.[33] In late antiquity, anyone with some knowledge of philosophy could have produced these and other arguments in favour of instruments: for example, that rhythm and harmony express the order of creation; music allows even inanimate wood and strings to speak the praise of the creator; musician and instrument symbolise the intimate connection of soul and body. Thus Boethius, dividing

---

[31] Ps-Cyprian *De spectaculis* 3 (CSEL 3.3, p. 5), cited Quasten (1983), Introduction (no page-number).

[32] Letter to the prelates of Mainz, tr. Dronke (1984), 198. I owe the reference to Stephen D' Evelyn, who observes that Hildegard may have known Augustine *de musica*: see next note. Contrast the much more cautious approach of Bede, *On Genesis* 4.20a–22b (tr. Kendall (2008), 156-7).

[33] *Carmen* 52: see further D'Evelyn (2007).

music into cosmic, human, and instrumental, put the human voice in the 'instrumental' category with the *cithara* and *tibia*, and interpreted 'human' music as the relationship of the incorporeal soul with the physical body.[34] Augustine himself may have read a passage in which Plotinus used the *cithara* player and his instrument as an image of the soul and body:

> He will care for [it] and bear with [it] as long as he can, like a musician with his lyre, as long as he can use it; if he cannot use it he will change to another, or give up using the lyre and abandon the activities directed to it. Then he will have something else to do which does not need the lyre, and will let it lie unregarded beside him while he sings without an instrument. Yet the instrument was not given him at the beginning without good reason. He has used it often up till now.[35]

In *de musica* Augustine argued that the rhythms of music express the eternal principles of number more effectively than the rhythms of poetry, which depend on local patterns of speech, *loquendi consuetudo*.[36] (He knew this problem well: Africans had trouble with classical metre, because the local accent did not distinguish long and short vowels.[37]) His later contemporary Macrobius, a supporter of traditional Roman religion, wrote that music is the song of the universe, and music in ritual acknowledges this:

> That the priests acknowledged that the heavens sing is indicated by their use of music at sacrificial ceremonies, some nations preferring the lyre or *cithara*, and some pipes or other musical instruments.[38]

Macrobius here offered a philosophical interpretation of the simpler claim that the gods must like music because their rituals include music in offerings meant to please them, and because the *cithara* is ascribed to Apollo and other instruments to the Muses.[39] In Judaeo-Christian

---

[34] Chadwick (1981), 79-80.

[35] Plotinus, *Ennead* 1.4.16, tr. Armstrong (1966); for the context, see Dillon (1994). Porphyry, *v.Plot.* 14, said that Plotinus understood the theory of geometry, arithmetic, mechanics, optics and music.

[36] MacCormack (1998), 59-63.

[37] *Doctr. Chr.* 4.65; Augustine's own accent, *Ord.* 2.17.45.

[38] Macr. *Comm.* 2.3.5, tr. Stahl (1952).

[39] Censorinus, *de die natali* 12.2, cited Quasten (1983), 1.

tradition, Philo thought that Moses on Sinai heard the music of the spheres, though by God's mercy the rest of us do not: we could not bear the longing.[40] In this tradition too, it could be argued, instrumental music acknowledges the song of God's creation. Psalm 150, the last in the collection, includes all the possibilities:

Laudate eum in sono tubae,
Laudate eum in psalterio et cithara,
Laudate eum in tympano et choro,
Laudate eum in chordis et organo.
Laudate eum in cymbalis benesonantibus,
Laudate eum in cymbalis iubilationis.
Omne quod spirat, laudat Dominum.

Praise him with the sound of the trumpet,
Praise him with the psaltery and cithara,
Praise him with tambourine and dance,
Praise him with the stringed instrument,[41]
Praise him with resonant cymbals,
Praise him with jubilant cymbals.
Let everything that breathes, praise the Lord.

So there were many arguments in favour of musical instruments. If, as ps-Cyprian claimed, the devil perverted their use, so that they praise idols and inspire lusts, surely Christians could get them back? In the book of Exodus, the Israelites take from the Egyptians gold and silver and deep-dyed fabrics, and rework them in honour of the true God. Augustine interpreted this story as signifying that genuine treasures can be found in other traditions: truths from non-Christian literature and philosophy can be appropriated for Christians, and rhetorical skill can be used to convey truth.[42] Why did it not follow that instrumental music could be used to evoke love and reverence, penitence and praise, addressed to the true God?

Music is also useful for understanding Scripture, and in *de doctrina Christiana* Augustine included it in the subjects that deserve study. He gave examples: the difference between *cithara* and psaltery; debates on whether the psaltery has ten strings because of a musical principle or because the number ten symbolises the

---

[40] *Q. Gen.* 3.3.
[41] Augustine's interpretation of *in chordis et organo* (*en. Ps.*150. 7).
[42] Clark (2002).

Decalogue or creation; and the musical connotations of the forty-six years it took to build the Temple which symbolises the body of Christ.[43] He emphasised that Christians must not listen to pagan superstition, such as Varro's account of the nine muses. Varro said that there were originally three muses, and a town commissioned three sculptors to make sets of images for an offering to Apollo; unable to choose which was best, they dedicated all nine. Augustine commented that there are three muses, not because someone had a vision, but

> because it was easy to observe that all sound, which is the basic material of melodies [*materies cantilenarum*], is threefold in nature. It is produced either by voice, as in the case of those who sing from the throat without an instrument, or by breath, as in the *tuba* and *tibia*, or by percussion, as in *citharae* and *tympana* and anything else that resonates by being struck.[44]

Christians, Augustine said, should not avoid all discussion of music because music is associated with pagan superstition; on the other hand, they should not be concerned with 'theatrical trivialities' when discussing something that may help them understand spiritual truths. In this context, he probably meant that they should not be preoccupied with musical technique and performance. But if discussion of music can help us to understand the text of Scripture, performance of music can help us even more. In the last book of *City of God* Augustine included the range of musical instruments and melodies, and indeed the marvels displayed in theatres, among the wonders and blessings of human life.[45] Why did he not reflect that in music accompanied by instruments, as the Psalms so often require, the eternal order expressed in the rhythms of music converges with the eternal truth expressed in the words of Scripture?[46]

---

[43] *Doctr. chr.*2.16.26. In *div.qu.* 56 and *trin.* 4.7 the number 46 is reached by complex calculations about human conception and growth (I owe to Mark Humphries the expression 'patristic SuDoku').

[44] *Doctr. chr.* 2.16.26. Green (1997), 152 n. 47 notes that Ausonius 15. 76-7 (*Griphus ternarii numeri*) offers a different triplet: *et genetrix modulorum musica triplex: / missa labris, secreta astris, vulgata theatris*, that is, song, the music of the spheres, and theatre music.

[45] *Civ.* 22.24.

[46] Compare *de musica* book 6 on Ambrose's line *Deus creator omnium:* MacCormack (1998), 60-1.

In later centuries many Christian traditions have used instrumental music for worship, and composers have used the same melodies for sacred and secular purposes. But it seems that in the early centuries AD Christian leaders reacted the other way. Even when churches set out to rival the attractions of theatre and festival, offering expert rhetoric and impressive liturgy, light reflected from mosaic and silver, processions and incense, they competed with song, but not with instrumental music. Of course there are advantages in singing. Almost everyone can contribute, needing no special skill or equipment; God inspires the body with breath and Scripture with truth, and the God-given instrument of the voice expresses the inspired words of Scripture. Different voices join in unison or harmony: Ambrose compared congregational singing to the strings of the *cithara*, producing harmony with their different lengths.[47] But in practising for the heavenly chorus shared with angels and archangels and all the company of heaven, why not add instruments, as in the book of Revelation (5: 8) where the elders who praise the Lamb have each a *cithara*? In *City of God* Augustine quoted a passage from Cicero comparing political concord with the harmony of 'strings and pipes, song and voices' (*in fidibus et tibiis atque cantu ipso ac vocibus*) that would be heard in traditional ritual. Surely Christian voices and instruments could express the harmony of the city of God?[48]

In late antiquity, some people needed convincing even about song. This might be because singing could become riotous, as it sometimes did at festivals: perhaps this was the late antique equivalent of 'Abide with me' or 'Swing low, sweet chariot' surging across a football stadium.[49] Nicetas of Remesiana found it necessary to argue against people who thought that singing was inappropriate in any circumstances.[50] Paul, they said, had told Christians to 'speak to each other with psalms and hymns and songs, singing and *psallontes* in your heart to the Lord' (Eph. 5: 19), and again 'let the word of Christ dwell richly within you, teaching and advising each other, singing to God in your hearts in thanks with psalms and hymns and spiritual songs' (Col. 3: 16). Some people interpreted this to mean that singing in the heart was acceptable, but singing aloud

[47] Ambrose, *en.Ps.* 1: see Quasten (1983) 78 and n. 96, with further discussion of the kind of psalm-singing Ambrose introduced, and 75-87 on the debate about women singing in church.

[48] Aug. *civ.*2.21; Cic. *Rep.* 2.42. I owe to Alison Pemble the information that angels are very rarely represented with musical instruments before the fourteenth century.

[49] On riotous and aggressive chants, see Shaw (2011 fc).

[50] McKinnon (1987), 303, p. 134.

was not. Perhaps some of these people knew the Platonist tradition that speech, being physical and discursive, is not an appropriate offering to the highest gods.[51] Porphyry, for example, said that the proper offering to the One is pure thought, not voiced prayer or the hymns which are appropriate for lesser gods.[52] Apuleius gave a fuller explanation in *The God of Socrates*, in a passage often exploited by Augustine in *City of God* books 8-10. He said that *daimones* are living, rational, eternal beings, with bodies made of air and souls that can feel. So they have life, reason and bodily existence in common with us, and they have eternity in common with the gods, but they differ from the gods in that they are liable to the same emotional disturbances as we are.[53] Augustine did not cite the next comment by Apuleius, that this explains why *daemones* enjoy rituals: 'Egyptian deities like laments, Greek deities like dances, but the barbarian ones like the noise of cymbal-players and tympanum-players and reed-pipe players.'

Nicetas argued in favour of singing, but said that the musical instruments mentioned in Scripture are obsolete physical usages of the old Jewish law, like circumcision and the Sabbath and food rules. Augustine, like many others, took these physical usages as figures of spiritual truths. His exegesis of psalm 32(33) is a classic example:

> *Exsultate, iusti, in Domino:*
> *Rectos decet laudatio.*
> *Confitemini Dominum in cithara,*
> *In psalterio decem chordarum psallite ei.*
> *Cantate ei canticum novum,*
> *Bene cantate ei in iubilatione.*

> Rejoice in the Lord, you righteous;
> Praise comes well from the upright.
> Acknowledge the Lord on the *cithara*;
> Make music to him on the ten-stringed *psalterium*.
> Sing to him a new song;
> Sing well to him in jubilation.[54]

Augustine had some explaining to do, because he was preaching on this psalm in a place where musical instruments had been forbidden.

[51] Quasten (1983), 51-7.
[52] Porphyry, *Abst.* 2.6.34.
[53] Apuleius, *De deo Socratis* 13.
[54] Text reconstructed from *en.Ps.* 32 ser. 2.

Probably it was the shrine of Cyprian, so the instruments may have been forbidden because of Augustine's own effort to make Christian celebrations more decorous.[55]

> Didn't the establishing of these vigils, in Christ's name, get *citharae* driven out of this place? And look, they are told to sound: 'Acknowledge the Lord on the *cithara*,' it says, 'sing to him on the ten-stringed *psalterium*.' Nobody should think of instruments used in the theatre. He has in himself what he is told to do, as it says elsewhere: 'in me, O God, are the vows of praise that I will pay to you'. Those of you who were here before will remember that I explained, to the best of my ability, the difference between the *cithara* and the *psalterium*.[56]

Augustine explained the difference here and in several other sermons:

> The *cithara* has that hollow wood, like a *tympanum* with a tortoiseshell below, on which strings are laid so that they sound when touched. I don't mean the plectrum with which they are touched, but I talked about the hollow wood on top of which they lie, and they lie on it in such a way that when they are touched and vibrate, they take up sound from it and from the hollowness, and are made more resonant. Well then, the *cithara* has this hollow wood in its lower part, and the *psalterium* in the upper part. That's the difference. Now we are told to acknowledge on the *cithara*, and to sing praises on the ten-stringed *psalterium*. It didn't say ten-stringed *cithara*, either in this psalm or, if I'm not mistaken, anywhere else. Our sons the readers should read and think about it better and more at leisure, but as far as I remember, we find the ten-stringed *psalterium* in many places, but nothing comes to mind about a ten-stringed *cithara*. Remember that the *cithara* has the sound-box in the lower part, and the *psalterium* in the upper part. From the lower life, that is earthly life, we have prosperity and adversity, and we should praise God in both.

So playing the *cithara* is praising God in prosperity and adversity. Whatever happens, Augustine said, 'play your *cithara* confidently: touch the strings in your heart, and say, as if on a *cithara* that sounds well in its lower part, The Lord gave, and the Lord has taken away.'

---

[55] *Ep.* 22 urges Aurelius, the new bishop of Carthage, to reform church practices, especially (22.6) *istae in cemeteriis ebrietates et luxuriosa convivia,* and *ep.* 29 shows Augustine taking action.

[56] *En.Ps.* 32 ser. 2, 5, in my translation, which is deliberately close to Augustine's spoken style. For a more elegant version, see Boulding (2000).

The ten-stringed *psalterium*, which sounds in its upper part, corresponds to the higher gifts of God, that is, God's teachings, especially the Ten Commandments. 'Touch your *psalterium*, fulfill the law.' In his exposition of another psalm, Augustine said the *psalterium* shows that words are not enough:

> What is *psallere*, brothers? A *psalterium* is a musical instrument; it has strings. Our work is our *psalterium*: anyone who does good works with his hands *psallit* to God, and anyone who acknowledges God with his mouth sings to God. Sing with the mouth, *psalle* with works.[57]

So it is not enough just to carry the *psalterium*, that is, to have the Law: we must use our hands and play it. To return to psalm 32(33), Augustine said that the new song, like the instruments, is a way of living. 'New man, new testament: new song.'

> If there's a good hearer of music, and you're told 'Sing so he will approve', you are nervous about singing without instruction in the art of music, in case the professional [*artifex*] does not approve, because what someone untrained doesn't notice in you, the professional criticises.[58]

So how can you sing to God, the ultimate expert? Augustine explained that *iubilatio* is a wordless song expressing joy too great for words; you can hear it among people harvesting or working vigorously, when they sing words at first, then move to *iubilatio*.

Psallere, then, is singing to the Lord, whether in the heart or in the congregation, and singing to the Lord is living according to God's will. Everyone in Augustine's congregation knows that *psallere* means 'singing to an instrument', specifically the *psalterium,* and he can explain the spiritual meaning of the *psalterium*; but though he often reminds his congregation of what they have just sung or heard sung, he never reminds them that they have heard the *psalterium* used in worship. The same applies to private worship: in *Confessions, psalterium* means 'psalter', the book of psalms, not 'psaltery'. Augustine's son Adeodatus burst into tears when his grandmother Monnica died, but this was the wrong response to the death of a Christian. So, when Adeodatus had been calmed, 'Evodius seized a *psalterium* and began to sing a psalm,

---

[57] Aug. *en. Ps.* 91.3.
[58] Aug. *en. Ps.* 32. 8.

to which the whole household responded "I will sing to you, Lord, your mercy and justice"'.[59] The response is the first verse of Ps.100, and as so often in *Confessions*, Augustine intended his readers to remember what follows: *psallam et intellegam*, 'I will sing and understand'. Did Evodius seize a psalter to remind himself of the words, or a psaltery to accompany the singing? Philip Burton confirms the general agreement that it was a psalter with the observation that in three other passages of *Confessions* the object of *arripere* is the Scriptures.[60]

Similarly, in the famous passage of *Confessions* which reflects on the pleasures of hearing, Augustine is concerned with the difference between speech and song. He makes no mention of musical instruments, and *davidicum psalterium* means the Psalms of David, not the psaltery that David played.

> *Aliquando autem hanc ipsam fallaciam immoderatius cavens erro nimia severitate, sed valde interdum, ut melos omne cantilenarum suavium quibus davidicum psalterium frequentatur ab auribus meis removeri velim atque ipsius ecclesiae, tutiusque mihi videtur quod de Alexandrino episcopo Athanasio saepe mihi dictum commemini, qui tam modico flexu vocis faciebat sonare lectorem psalmi ut pronuntianti vicinior esset quam canenti.*

> Sometimes, in my excessive concern to avoid this distraction [i.e. attending to sound rather than content] I err on the side of undue severity. I want all the melody of the sweet chants commonly used for the Psalter of David removed from my ears and the ears of the church. I think it is safer to follow the practice of Athanasius bishop of Alexandria, which I have often heard mentioned. He made the reader of the psalm use such moderate inflection of the voice that it was closer to speech than to song.[61]

Melos and *cantilena* both suggest melody, and Augustine was not alone in worrying about the effect of melody.[62] According to a letter he wrote in 408, he had intended to add six or so books on *melos* to the six books on rhythm which formed his *de musica*, but he did not have

---

[59] Aug. *conf.* 9.12.31.

[60] Burton (2007), 144-5.

[61] Aug. *conf.* 10.33.50.

[62] *Melos* and *cantilena*, Burton (2007), 148; Harrison (2008) has 'harmony' for the six proposed books *de melo*. Quasten (1983), 94-9 offers other examples of concern about the emotional effect of singing.

the time.[63] He thought that melody pleases because it is in accordance with the musical ratios that express the order of the universe; but he might reasonably be concerned that the more pleasing the melody, the more it would hold the mind at the level of pleasure rather than enabling the mind to rise to the principles of order. He might also be concerned that melody would make us especially aware of sound moving through time, for when music is based on melody, not on harmony, tempo and syllable-length can be varied as the performer chooses, especially when singing is from memory rather than from musical notation.[64] In *Confessions*, as in *de musica*, Augustine used the example of moving from syllable to syllable of *Deus creator omnium.*[65] We do not know how Ambrose's hymns were set to music, or where exactly he found the eastern practice of hymn-singing, but they look as if they were easy to sing, with one note for one syllable, and a strong rhythm rather than the complicated metres used by Hilary of Poitiers and Prudentius.[66] A psalm sung with melismata, lingering on some words but not on others, might give Augustine an even better example of *distentio* than singing Ambrose's hymn. It could also be a kind of exegesis, interpreting the psalm by focussing on specific words; but this is not a possibility considered by Augustine. The experience of present-day singers confirms that any complexity in the music makes it difficult to attend to the words without losing track of the music.[67]

Music, for Augustine, is measure and harmony that can raise the mind to universal principles. It is not the merely technical skill of performance. Even the theory of music, which studies universal principles, is a childish study in comparison with incorporeal reality. God is music, because God is supreme measure, and in creation gives measure to the universe.[68] Music on earth brings order and calm, but it also arouses emotion and increases awareness of time-bound existence; singing

---

[63] *Ep.*101.3. Hermanowicz (2004) suggests that Augustine returned to book 6 in 408 because the Theodorus who had just been appointed praetorian prefect of the west was the Platonist Mallius Theodorus whom Augustine knew at Milan, and Augustine wanted to renew their connection by sending him *de musica*.

[64] Hornby (2002) on musical notation from the eighth century; Landels (1999), 218-63 on earlier systems, including (262-3) a third-century papyrus of a Christian hymn. Boethius *de institutione musica* 4.3 comments on the notation that could preserve a tune, as well as words, for posterity.

[65] Aug. *conf.* 11.27.35; *mus.* 6.2.2-4.7.

[66] Singing Ambrose, Hilary and Prudentius: Palmer (1989), 58-75.

[67] Melismata as exegesis: Hornby (2002).

[68] Harrison (2008) on book 6 of *de musica*.

enhances the effect of Scripture, but also distracts from it. Musical instruments are a further distraction from the words, because of their association with theatre and with pagan ritual, and because their appeal is to the senses:

> Many people place their blessed life in the song of voices and strings and pipes, and judge themselves wretched when these are lacking, but are transported with joy when they are present: so when the melodious and eloquent silence of truth slips noiselessly into our minds, shall we look for another blessed life, and not enjoy that which is so sure and present?[69]

Augustine's vision of heaven, most fully developed in the final book of *City of God,* does not include elders with *citharae* as in the book of Revelation, or heavenly choirs, or wordless *iubilatio.* The music of heaven is different:

> *erigit auditum in illam vocem Dei internam, audit rationabile carmen intrinsecus. Ita enim desuper in silentio sonat quiddam, non auribus, sed mentibus; ut quicumque audit illud melos, taedio afficiatur ad strepitum corporalem, et tota ista vita humana tumultus ei quidam sit, impediens auditum superni cuiusdam soni nimium delectabilis, et incomparabilis, et ineffabilis.*

> He raises his hearing to that interior voice of God; he hears within him the song of reason. For in this way something above sounds in silence, not to ears but to minds, so that whoever hears that melody feels distaste for physical noise, and all this human life is for him a kind of racket that stops him hearing the utterly delightful, incomparable, ineffable sound on high.[70]

So to sing psalms with wisdom, *sapienter,* or with understanding, *intellegenter,* we need to focus on the words of Scripture and on the way of life they require us to lead. Augustine knew that any public speaker, including a bishop, had much in common with an actor; a cantor leading worship with a *psalterium* would reinforce the effect of a performance, and the congregation might attend to the skill of the speaker and the delights of the music rather than to the message. It still happens, especially in cathedrals and in college chapels. But Augustine was a man

---

[69] *Lib. Arb.* 2.13.35, in a list (similar to that in *Ser.* 391.5) of sensory delights surpassed by awareness of God.

[70] *En. Ps.* 42.7.

of his time, of late Roman culture: would he have thought differently if he had learned to play an instrument so that *psallere* was part of his experience? George Herbert, to end with an Anglican example, lived in a culture where educated people learned to play an instrument and perform together. Like Augustine, he gave up a promising career for life in the service of the church; but he took music with him.

> Awake, my lute, and struggle for thy part
> With all thy art.
> The cross taught all wood to resound his name
> Who bore the same.
> His stretched sinews taught all strings, what key
> Is best to celebrate this most high day.[71]

Bibliography

Armstrong, A. H. (1966), *Plotinus*; vol. 1 (Cambridge MA).

Boulding, M. (2000), *Saint Augustine: Expositions of the Psalms* 1-32 (New York).

Burton, P. (2007), *Language in the Confessions of Augustine* (Oxford).

Chadwick, H. (1981), *Boethius: the consolations of music, logic, theology, and philosophy* (Oxford).

Clark, G. (2002), 'Spoiling the Egyptians: Roman law and Christian exegesis in late antiquity,' in Mathisen, R. (ed.), *Law, Society and Authority in Late Antiquity* (Oxford), 133-47.

Clark, G. (2010), 'Gods behaving badly: Augustine, Varro, and pagan monotheism,' in Mitchell, S. and P. Van Nuffelen (eds.), *Monotheism between Pagans and Christians* (Leuven), 181-201.

D'Evelyn, S. (2007), 'Heaven as performance and as participation,' in Carolyn Muessig, C. and A. Putter (eds.), *Envisaging Heaven in the Middle Ages* (London), 155-65.

Dillon, J. (1994), 'Singing without an instrument: Plotinus on suicide,' *Illinois Classical Studies* 19, 231-8.

Dronke, P. (1984), *Women Writers of the Middle Ages* (Cambridge).

Evans Grubbs, J. (2001), 'Virgins and Widows, Show-Girls and Whores', in Mathisen, R. (ed.), *Law, Society, and Authority in Late Antiquity* (Oxford), 220-41.

Fowden, G. (1998), 'Polytheist religion and philosophy', in Cameron, Av. and P. Garnsey (eds.), *Cambridge Ancient History XIII: The Late Empire A.D. 337-425* (Cambridge), 538-60.

---

[71] George Herbert, 'Easter', second verse.

Green, R. (1997), *Saint Augustine: On Christian Teaching* (Oxford).

Griffin, M. (1984), *Nero: the end of a dynasty* (London).

Harrison, C. (2010) 'Augustine and the Art of Music' in Jeremy Begbie and Steven Guthrie (eds.) *Resonant Theology* (Grand Rapids MI) Resonant Witness: conversations between music and theology, published 2011.

Hermanowicz, E. (2004), 'Book Six of Augustine's *De Musica* and the episcopal embassies of 408,' *AS* 35, 165-98.

Hornby, E. (2002), *Gregorian and Old Roman Eighth Mode Tracts* (Aldershot).

Kendall, C. (2008), *Bede: On Genesis, translated with an introduction and notes* (Liverpool).

Landels, J. G. (1999), *Music in Ancient Greece and Rome* (London).

MacCormack, S. (1998), *The Shadows of Poetry: Vergil in the Mind of Augustine* (Berkeley, Ca).

McKinnon, J. (1987), *Music in Early Christian Literature* (Cambridge).

Palmer, A.-M. (1989), *Prudentius on the Martyrs* (Oxford).

Pollmann, K. and M. Vessey (2005), (eds.) *Augustine and the Disciplines* (Oxford).

Quasten, J. (1983), *Music and Worship in Pagan and Christian Antiquity* (Washington DC).

Shaw, B. (2011 fc), *Sacred Violence: African Christians and sectarian hatred in the age of Augustine* (Cambridge).

Stahl, W. (1952), *Commentary on the Dream of Scipio by Macrobius* (New York).

Welldon, J. (1924), *Sancti Aurelii Augustini De Civitate Dei*; 2 vols; (London).

PAULINE ALLEN & BRONWEN NEIL

DISCOURSES ON THE POOR IN THE PSALMS: AUGUSTINE'S *ENARRATIONES IN PSALMOS*

Introduction

Over a period of some thirty years, from the early 390s to the late 420s,[1] Augustine wrote and preached a series of homilies known collectively as the *Enarrationes in psalmos*, a commentary on the 150 psalms in the *Vetus Latina* version. Those that were presented orally were delivered variously at Hippo, Utica, Carthage, and Thagaste,[2] on a range of liturgical occasions. Seventeen were delivered on the occasion of Vigils or feasts of the African martyrs.[3] Many were delivered at Matins or Vespers, but relatively few were preached at Eucharistic celebrations at Hippo, or during Lent and Easter, and only one, on Psalm 22, in Holy Week.[4] The 205 homilies are of variable quality: those on Psalms 1-32 took the form of brief exegetical notes, rather than full sermons. The thirty-two expositions on Psalm 118 alone were aimed towards the clergy but the majority were directed to a lay or mixed audience. Later, Augustine collected and edited the material he had delivered to form a systematic exegetical commentary on the book of Psalms. This required the production of new 'desk homilies', written in homiletic

---

[1] La Bonnardière (1971), 73-4 dates the *Narrationes* to the thirty-five years from 393. See also Fiedrowicz (1997), 23-24 on the dating and location of individual homilies. We are grateful for the assistance of the Australian Research Council in funding the Australian Catholic University research project from which this paper arose. We are delighted to dedicate this essay to Prof Andrew Louth, an inspiring teacher, colleague and friend.

[2] Rondet (1958 and 1960); La Bonnardière (1971, 1971/72, 1976 and 1977/78).

[3] These included Cyprian (*En. in Ps.* 32 [*Serm.* 2]; 42; 72; 85; 88), Felix (*En. in Ps.* 127) and Crispina (*En. in Ps.* 120; 137). Augustine's works are usually cited according to the texts in NBA, and unless otherwise indicated the translations are taken from WSA.

[4] *En. in Ps.* 21 (*Serm.* 2). See Fiedrowicz's introduction to WSA, 3/15, trans. Boulding (2000a), 17.

style, but never delivered, to fill in the gaps.[5] Olivar estimated that only 119 were actually delivered, while 86 were dictated to scribes in homiletic form.[6] *Enarrationes* are thus a sort of behemoth, covering a wide range of theological, polemical and pastoral themes which reflect Augustine's views as a newly ordained priest, as the bishop of a major North African see, and in his later life as one keen to pass on a written legacy to a church under threat from within, due to the activities of the Donatists, and from without, with Vandal and Hun conquests of the Western empire making Hippo's future look ever more bleak.

Given the long chronological span of this work's production, and its concentration on themes relating to poverty and oppression, we are legitimately able to ask whether Augustine's representation of the poor changed over time. At the same time we must look for consistency between his presentation of poverty-related themes in *Enarrationes* and in other homilies. Finally, we assess the extent to which Augustine's representation of the proper attitudes towards the poor, and poverty, correlated with his behaviour as bishop. Using this method of approach we hope to test Brown's thesis that the bishop was truly a champion and lover of the poor,[7] or was it rather a case of rhetorical representation overshooting reality.

Augustine's Social Doctrine in *Enarrationes*

Fiedrowicz has made a recent study of *Enarrationes* using the method of prosopological exegesis.[8] Following Rondeau, he identified the following six voices or dialogue partners that Augustine attributes as speakers of the psalms: *vox ad Christum, vox de Christo, vox de ecclesia, vox Christi, vox ecclesiae* and *vox totius Christi*.[9] A different voice may be assumed from one verse to the next within the same psalm, or the same voice identified for a whole psalm or part thereof. These voices deliver prophecy about Christ or the church, and therefore signal for Augustine statements of both christological and ecclesiological significance, as well as statements of social doctrine.

---

[5] Mayer (2009), 37-8.
[6] Olivar (1991), 933.
[7] Brown (2002).
[8] Fiedrowicz (1997), 234-378.
[9] Rondeau (1983), 510-516.

Considering the predominance of the voice of the poor in Psalms it is not surprising that in *Enarrationes* Augustine frequently dwells on themes related to poverty and riches, the poor and the rich. We cannot hope to deal with all of them and have limited our attention to those that seemed most relevant to Augustine's social doctrine: injustice and the plight of the poor; spiritualized poverty and riches; almsgiving; usury; direct or indirect giving; support of clergy and discriminate giving. Before we approach the texts, however, let us consider briefly the Jewish antecedents of Christian almsgiving in the fourth and fifth centuries.[10] How did Augustine's preaching on the poor in Psalms differ from contemporary Jewish interpretations of these texts, if at all?

The Hebrew Psalms, compiled by different several authors, comprise both pre-exilic literature (polytheistic) and post-exilic (monotheistic) literature. As such they incorporate features of an ancient model of social relations dating back to Canaanite civilization, which Bolkestein calls the 'Near Eastern' model.[11] According to this model the weak who described themselves as 'poor' could call upon the mercy and protection of a powerful protector. A key feature of this model was the encoding of the rights of the poor in written law codes. Early examples cited by Brown are the laws of Urukagina of Lagish (2400 BCE) and the Hammurabi law code of 1729-1680 BCE.[12] In this ancient model of society, the 'poor' were a judicial category rather than an economic one,[13] and their rights were encoded in Leviticus and Deuteronomy, e.g. keeping a corner of one's field available for use of the poor; cancellation of debts in Jubilee years; gleaning rights for the poor at harvest time, etc. In Psalms, the Lord is described as the refuge of the poor and oppressed[14] and the champion of the needy.[15] Those who wish to be righteous are instructed to give alms and justice to the poor.[16]

---

[10] These sources are dealt with in more detail by Neil (2010), a summary of which is provided here.

[11] Bolkestein (1939).

[12] Brown (2002), 69.

[13] Brown (2002), 69.

[14] E.g. Ps 9:10, Ps 10:14, Ps 10:18, Ps 12:5, Ps 83:1.

[15] E.g. Ps 33:6-7; Ps 69:33-34; Ps 72:12-13; Ps 113:7-8.

[16] E.g. Ps 40:1-2; Ps 82:3-4; Ps 112:9. Other key passages on almsgiving in the Torah include Gen 18:1-8, the Septuagint book of Tobit, the Prophets (e.g. Isa 58:6) and Wisdom literature (e.g. Prov 11:7; Prov 19:17; Prov 22:22-23; Sir 29:12).

The rabbinic sources, especially the *Tosefta*, *Mishnah*, midrashim on Proverbs and Psalms, *Sifre* on Numbers and Deuteronomy, the *Jerusalem Talmud* of c. 200-500 CE and the later, more authoritative *Babylonian Talmud*, contain collections of rabbinic texts on alms, charity and poverty, in which the mandate to give alms was paramount.[17] According to Bolkestein the Near Eastern model came to the fore in the third century CE with the rise of Christianity and the concurrent disastrous collapse of the Roman economy.[18] When the authors of the Torah and its early commentaries mandated helping the poor they were speaking literally of those who did not have the means to feed or clothe themselves. These were the weak, the socially powerless. The power of the image of the disenfranchised poor falling upon the mercy of the powerful, just judge, was a resonant one in Late Antique Christianity. The 'just judge' imagery was adopted by the bishop, who presided over his own ecclesiastical court, the *audientia episcopalis*.[19]

However the Christianization of the Near Eastern model posed some problems for the fourth-century bishop in Christianity's new urban context. The original context of divine reward for generosity to the poor was non-eschatological: prosperity and longevity were the just rewards anticipated by the pious Jew in this life.[20] Over time, and especially after the destruction of the Temple in Jerusalem in 70 CE, the emphasis in rabbinic commentary shifted to future reward. The generous, like the poor, were to be rewarded in the next life.[21] This shift in emphasis made the teaching of self-interested giving much more attractive to Christian preachers, who were familiar with the demands of classical evergetism for social recognition of the giver. The poor had to be reinterpreted, however, as anyone whom the church wished to help. This included the clergy and the bishops themselves, as well as widows and orphans and others on the poor lists.

[17] Babylonian Talmud *Baba Batra* 9a illustrates this idea: 'Almsgiving weighs as much as all the other commandments.' Montefiore and Loewe (1974), 412, no. 1138.

[18] See Brown (2002), 7 n. 18; 68-73; 80-84.

[19] Brown (2002), 68-9.

[20] E.g. Ps 37:37, Ps 41:3, Ps 92:12-14.

[21] This movement is foreshadowed in Ps 37:27-28: *Depart from evil and do good; so you shall abide forever. For the Lord loves justice; he will not forsake his faithful ones. The righteous shall be kept safe forever, but the children of the wicked shall be cut off.*; cf. *En. in Ps.* 38.7; NBA, 25: 898; trans. Boulding, WSA, 3/16: 178: 'I am looking for the genuine "is", the "is" that we shall find in that Jerusalem which is the bridge of my Lord, where there will be no death, no deficiency, where the day passes not, but abides, the day that is preceded by no yesterday and hustled on by no tomorrow. *Make known to me the number of my days*, this number, *the number that is* (Ps 39:4).'

1. Injustice and the plight of the poor

Any discussion of the plight of the poor in the works of Augustine anticipates the question, 'Who were Augustine's poor?'. Augustine composed no single work dedicated to the theme of poverty and, despite the numerous references in his corpus to poverty and the poor, it is almost impossible to discern the numbers or circumstances of the poor people he had in mind.[22] In the *Enarrationes* Christ's commands in Matt 25: 31-46 to take pity on the hungry, the thirsty, strangers, the naked, the sick, and the imprisoned are applied generically to poor relief without any personalization of the recipients, even when the preacher is at his most demanding.[23] The comment that among a crowd of rich people God will be able to find a few poor ones to care for[24] seems at variance with another statement elsewhere that the poor outnumber the rich by far.[25] Against this we have less shadowy references to professional beggars,[26] to a person giving a coin to a pauper,[27] and to a poor person who accosts a presumably better-off person.[28] Widows and orphans are classified as those 'who are bereft of all resources and all help'.[29]

None of this discourse helps us much to identify the poor, especially if, as it seems, by the 'poor' Augustine understood the 'non-rich' generally. A few examples will suffice to bear out this assumption. In exegeting Ps 33:10-11: *Fear the Lord, you his saints, for they who fear him lack for nothing*, the preacher cites the (probably imaginary) rejoinder of those who find it hard to fear the Lord and not cheat. 'How am I to eat, then? Handicrafts need a little dishonesty to succeed, and the business cannot flourish without fraud.'[30] Here we are dealing with artisans or craftsmen, small business people who, while admittedly in constant danger

---

[22] See in detail on this problematic Allen and Morgan (2009), of which part of this section is an abbreviation.

[23] *En. in Ps.* 36 (*Serm.* 3). 7; NBA, 25: 822; *En. in Ps.* 40.2; NBA, 25: 982; *En. in Ps.* 49.11; NBA, 25: 1264; *En. in Ps.*51.9; NBA, 26: 16; *En. in Ps.* 83.7; NBA, 26: 1186; *En. in Ps.* 92.1; NBA, 27/1: 212 and 214; *En. in Ps.* 147.6; NBA, 28/2: 814 and 816; *En. in Ps.* 148.8; NBA, 28/2: 874; *En. in Ps.* 149.8; NBA, 28/2: 904.

[24] *En. in Ps.* 10.8; NBA, 25: 178.

[25] *En. in Ps.* 51.14; NBA, 26: 26. Cf. *Serm.* 114B.9-10 (Dolbeau 5); NBA, 35/1: 106-110.

[26] *En. in Ps.* 125.12; NBA, 28/1: 130.

[27] *En. in Ps.* 36 (*Serm.* 2).13; NBA, 25: 784.

[28] *En. in Ps.* 103 (*Serm.* 3).10; NBA, 27/1: 718.

[29] *En. in Ps.* 145.18; NBA, 28/2: 758; trans. Boulding, WSA, 3/20: 418.

[30] *En. in Ps.* 33 (*Serm.* 2).14; NBA, 25: 650; trans. Boulding, WSA, 3/16: 34.

of becoming penurious, were not destitute. Similar is the adduced case of someone who is on notice from the tax office for outstanding debts and is terrified about the impending appearance of the bailiffs, hoping against hope that his debt will be written off.[31] Although Augustine's discourse concerning poverty here is not about earthly debts but heavenly ones, this real or imaginary fiscally-challenged person clearly does not belong to the class of beggars or to the poorest of the poor, and there must have been some of his listeners who could relate to the man's situation.

Inherent in the Psalmist's work was the idea of the long-suffering poor and just, an idea which Augustine uses to make more palatable the lot of the various strata of the poor inside and outside his congregations. In commenting on Ps 9:19: *Because the poor will not be forgotten forever*, he remarks: 'By this is meant the person who seems to be forgotten here and now, when to all appearances sinners flourish in the happiness of this world, and the just are struggling'.[32] The flourishing sinners are the proud, rapacious rich, living in luxury with their 'folds of fat' (Ps 72:7), but like a plump, sleek bull they are destined for sacrifice, namely for eternal punishment.[33] While such oratory as this may have pleased the downtrodden in the congregation momentarily, their objections to their lot seem to have been constant: the wicked are God's favourites,[34] God does not care about the poor and needy,[35] and even if the downtrodden may get to heaven, they are neglected here on earth.[36] The entire commentary on Psalm 93, over thirty-five pages of it, is devoted to addressing those who believe that God's dispositions are unjust.[37] The corruption that was endemic in Hippo and caused abuse of the just and poor[38] could also be found allegedly in the *audientia episcopalis*, according to Augustine, who gives an example of the reactions of the litigants when a bishop decides in favour of a rich person or a poor person respectively. Bribery is alleged in both cases.[39]

---

[31] *En. in Ps.* 45.3; NBA, 25: 1128.

[32] *En. in Ps.* 9.18; NBA, 25: 150; trans. Boulding, WSA, 3/15: 151.

[33] *En. in Ps.* 72. 10-12; NBA, 26: 834-8.

[34] *En. in Ps.* 91.7; NBA, 27/1: 198.

[35] *En. in Ps.* 74.8; NBA, 26: 920.

[36] *En. in Ps.* 40.3; NBA, 25: 982.

[37] NBA, 27/1: 234-302.

[38] See further Lepelley (2007), 5-6.

[39] *En. in Ps.* 25 (*Serm.* 2).13; NBA, 25: 348-50. Cf. Lenski (2001), 97; 'When a bishop wished, he could enthusiastically abuse his legal powers'.

This brings us to a recurring theme in the *Enarrationes*, namely the fickleness of fate, to which many of Augustine's listeners and readers must have felt themselves prone, particularly after the tumultuous events of the early 400s. Associated with this was the subsidiary theme of the fickleness of wealth. Like Egyptian desert ascetics who dreamed of fresh fruit which disappeared on their waking, a number of North African non-rich dreamed of being rich, only to wake up and find themselves still 'poor'. Such will be the fate of the arrogant in this life, says their preacher: 'When they have awakened from this life everything they possessed here will be like dream-wealth; it will pass away *like the dream of one who awakens*' (Ps 72: 20).[40] On the other hand, Zacchaeus (Luke 19:8) was not dreaming or phantasizing when he promised to donate half his property to the poor; rather he was speaking 'in the faith of those who are wide awake'.[41] Augustine's congregations were alive to the effects of shipwreck[42] and to the shock of a home burglary,[43] but they still needed to be reminded that all wealth is like a rolling coin whose owner never knows where it will end up[44]. Underlying this argument is the fact that all of them are ignorant of what might befall them the next day,[45] perhaps rendering them as helpless as the unfortunate people whose cries they are unwilling to heed today.

In the face of poverty, injustice, corruption, and the fickleness of fate Augustine has repeated recourse to Psalm verses where God is described as looking kindly on the poor (Ps 10:5),[46] and as a refuge and strength for them (Ps 45:2).[47] The congregations are to be comforted, for example, by the words of Ps 68: 34: *For the Lord has listened to the poor, and has not spurned his servants in their shackles,*[48] and of Ps 71: 12: *He has delivered the needy from the tyrant, that poor person who had no other champion.*[49]

---

[40] *En. in Ps.* 72.26; NBA, 26: 850; trans. Boulding, WSA, 3/17: 487.

[41] *En. in Ps.* 75.9; NBA, 26: 948 and 950; trans. Boulding, WSA, 3/18: 62. Cf. *En. in Ps.*125.11; NBA, 28/1: 128.

[42] *En. in Ps.* 36 (*Serm.* 2).13; NBA, 25: 784.

[43] *En. in Ps.* 36 (*Serm.* 2).13; NBA, 25: 784; *En. in Ps.* 38.12; NBA, 25: 906.

[44] *En. in Ps.* 83.3; NBA, 26: 1178.

[45] *En. in Ps.* 100.4; NBA, 27/1: 488.

[46] *En. in Ps.* 10.8; NBA, 25: 178.

[47] *En. in Ps.* 45.2; NBA, 25: 1126.

[48] *En. in Ps.* 68 (*Serm.* 2).18; NBA, 26: 692.

[49] *En. in Ps.* 71.14; NBA, 26: 808.

2. Spiritual value of poverty and riches

Poverty, defined as a spiritual virtue, also assumes a strong eschatological dimension in the *Enarrationes*.[50] By shifting the place of reward into the *eschaton*, as the second- and third- century rabbis had done, and spiritualising poverty and riches, Late Antique bishops like Augustine could sidestep any need to challenge the *status quo*. One's economic status, whether rich or poor, master or slave, could be attributed to the providence of God, for each condition carried with it a specific moral lesson. The poor were made poor to be tested, and to test the rich.[51] For the poor the lesson was patience and humility; for the rich it was generosity and gratitude to God. In this way the rich attained spiritual poverty. The Lord himself was 'the wealth of the poor'.[52]

Indeed, like Pope Leo after him, Augustine usually interpreted poverty primarily in terms of spiritual need. Thus the state of poverty also, somewhat perversely, came to encompass those who were rich in a material sense but had attained spiritual humility.[53] This hermeneutic pervades *Enarrationes*, and we find Augustine explicitly excluding the literal poor from consideration in his exegesis of Ps 12:5:[54]

> Who are the poor? Who are the needy? Those who have no hope, save in him alone who never let us down. You must be quite clear who the poor and needy are, brothers and sisters. When scripture commends the poor, it is definitely not talking about people who have no possessions.

Such a hermeneutic required a highly allegorical interpretation of the explicitly physical language of poverty and suffering in the

---

[50] On this eschatological aspect of the *Enarrationes* see Michael Fiedrowicz's General Introduction to Maria Boulding's translations in WSA, 3/15: 62. *En. in Ps.* 103 (*Serm.* 3).16; NBA, 27/1: 728 and 730, where the cedars of Lebanon are likened to the wealthy, well-born, and well-placed who provide shelter for the sparrows or 'little people', demonstrates that social reform was not on Augustine's agenda. See the discussion in Lepelley (2007), 11.

[51] *En. in Ps.* 124.2; NBA 28/1: 90.

[52] *En. in Ps.* 21 (*Serm.*2).27; NBA 25: 302.

[53] *En. in Ps.* 48 (*Serm.* 1).3; NBA 25: 1196.

[54] *En. in Ps.* 93.7; trans. Boulding, WSA, 3/18: 382. Spiritualised poverty and riches are found at *En. in Ps.* 9.27; NBA, 25: 156; *En. in Ps.* 11:6; NBA, 25: 186; *En. in Ps.* 30 (*Serm.* 3).12; NBA, 25: 502 and 504 ; *En. in Ps.* 36 (*Serm.* 2).13; NBA, 25: 784; *En. in Ps.* 68 (*Serm.* 2).14; NBA, 26: 688 and 690; *En. in Ps.* 71.3; NBA, 26: 790; *En. in Ps.* 73.24; NBA, 26: 898; *En. in Ps.* 93.7; NBA, 27/1: 252.

Psalms, which goes right through *Enarrationes*. The two levels of exegesis, literal and spiritualising, were not in tension for Augustine, a concept that modern commentators may find somewhat difficult to grasp. However, some scholars such as Cohen (1999) see a movement from a more Platonising approach in Augustine's early works (especially *De Genesi contra Manichaeos*) to a more concrete appreciation of the human body in his mature works, such as *De Genesi ad litteram*.[55] We can see this softer approach to human carnality in *En. in Ps.* 58 (*Serm.* 1), which dwells on the physical weakness of the incarnate Christ, a weakness he shared with the rest of humanity:[56]

> *Rescue me from my enemies, O my God, and redeem me from those who rise up against me* (Ps 58:2). This was the experience of Christ in his flesh, and our experience too. Our enemies are the devil and his angels who constantly, daily, rise up against us and try to dupe us in our weakness and fragility.

Was the spiritualized discourse of poverty and riches conducive to a personal connection with the poor through almsgiving? Finn has explained Augustine's lack of provision of detail on the poor in this work and in his sermons generally as a deliberate attempt to foreshorten social distance between giver and would-be recipient.[57] By avoiding any use of specific descriptive terms which might excite contempt in the potential giver, the preacher avoided the alienation of his audience from those in need of alms. According to Finn, 'rather than seeking simply to heighten the visibility of the poor, Augustine seeks to foreshorten social distances, and to present in a certain light those whom the sermons aid among the urban destitute.'[58] Leaving aside for now the question of whether sermons directly aided anyone, can we accept Finn's explanation for Augustine's clear preference for referring to the poor according to general categories of need, such as widows, orphans, the stranger, the sick, and the prisoner, recalling the prescriptions of Matt 25: 31-36?[59] The use of impersonal categories of need might just as

---

[55] Cohen (1999), 29-59 and esp. 56.

[56] *En. in Ps.* 58 (*Serm.* 1).4; NBA, 26: 246, trans. Boulding, WSA, 3/17: 151.

[57] Finn (2006a), 130-40.

[58] Finn (2006a), 131.

[59] *En. in Ps.* 36 (*Serm.* 3).6; NBA, 25: 820 ; *En. in Ps.* 40.2; NBA, 25: 982; *En. in Ps.* 51.9; NBA, 26: 16; *En. in Ps.* 83.7; NBA, 26: 1188; *En. in Ps.* 92.1; NBA, 27/1: 214; *En. in Ps.* 96.15; NBA 27/1: 390; *En. in Ps.* 147.6; NBA, 28/2: 814-816; *En. in Ps.*148.8; NBA, 28/2: 874; *En. in Ps.* 149.8; NBA, 28/2: 904.

well have worked the other way, to increase social distance from faceless persons with whom the better-off had no desire to identify themselves.

3. Almsgiving[60]

In the *Enarrationes* the question of almsgiving is prominent. We find a much stronger promotion, whether direct or indirect, of almsgiving in Augustine's later homilies, with thirty-two such references in the seventy-six expositions of Psalms 33-98, as compared to a single straight-forward promotion of almsgiving in his forty-three expositions of Psalms 1-32.[61] Finn argues that the contrast '... is more likely to be an indication of a bishop's duty to raise alms through preaching, his need to be seen to act in this way as a champion of the poor.'[62] This explanation depends on a secure dating of the latter group to post-396 when Augustine became bishop of Hippo. The findings of Rondet and La Bonnardière challenge the late dating suggested by Finn for the second part of the corpus, homilies on Psalms 33-98.[63] One wonders how we can assume that almsgiving would have been any less important to Augustine the priest than it was to the bishop. Perhaps it is more relevant that his homilies on Psalms 1-32 were merely exegetical notes rather than complete sermons intended for an audience.

In his other sermons too Augustine emphasizes the shrewdness of giving alms to the poor, a strategy which Peter Brown describes as 'something as impersonal as stockbroking – as a judicious transfer of

[60] For this topic in general in Augustine see Fitzgerald (1989), 445-59; Fitzgerald (1999), 557-61; Kessler and Krause (1996-2002), 752-767; Finn (2006), passim; idem (2006a), 130-44, less successfully; Kamimura (2008). For Augustine's vocabulary on the topic of almsgiving see Pétré (1948), 90-96, 134-139, 156-158, 197-199, 219-220; cf. more generally Grodzynski (1987), 140-218.

[61] Finn (2006a), 133. Only thirty-two of these expositions date to 393-395, according to La Bonnardière, and twenty-one of these (*En. in Ps.* 11-32) are dated as early as 391 by Rondet (1960). The second recensions of *En. in Ps.* 18, 21, 25, 26, 30, 31 and 32 date to the later period of 403-415 CE according to both Rondet and La Bonnardière, and the second recension of *En. in Ps.* 29 to the first year of his episcopate: Rondet (1960), 276.

[62] Finn (2006a), 133. About 113 out of 567 other sermons containing some sort of promotion of almsgiving.

[63] Their findings exclude from the latter group *En. in Ps.* 63, which La Bonnardière dated to pre-396 CE, and possibly *En. in Ps.* 69, which she dates to the period 394-405 CE. Rondet has also proposed early dates for *En. in Ps.* 42, 52, 56, 91, and 92 (all ascribed 'early'), and *En. in Ps.* 94 (pre-396 CE), dates unchallenged by La Bonnardière with one exception: she assigns *En. in Ps.* 56 to 405-411 CE.

capital from this unsafe world to the next'.[64] He assures his congregation that by giving alms they are 'making a kind of mercantile loan or investment. You lend or invest here, you get paid back with interest there'.[65] They are instructed to think of their almsgiving as money-lending to God, who is completely credit-worthy and will pay back everything to them, even the interest on the loan.[66] The consistent use of the term *laturarii* and its commercial resonances with inhabitants of the port city of Hippo[67] reinforces the nature of the charitable transaction. However, in the *Enarrationes* this commercial vocabulary is more limited, and the image of porterage is absent, although the poor person who receives alms and in return prays for the donor says to God, as it were: 'Lord, I have borrowed money; please go surety for me'.[68]

Both in his commentary on the Psalms and elsewhere Augustine maintains that all almsgiving involves concomitant obligations, namely fasting, prayer, and forgiveness. Combinations of these are found in a variety of passages, all of which seem to be intended to consolidate the Christian community,[69] including catechumens.[70] Elsewhere it is said that almsgiving is a means of purchasing future rest for the donor's soul.[71] Here we should note both the individual and the eschatological emphases, which have led more than one scholar to conclude that Augustine's main concern lay with the salvation of the almsgiver and not with the actual poor.[72]

---

[64] Brown (2000), 193.

[65] *Serm.* 42.2; NBA, 29: 746; trans. Hill, WSA, 3/2: 235.

[66] *Serm.* 86.3.3; NBA, 30/2: 10.

[67] For other instances of the image of porters in Augustine see Ramsey (1982), 248 n. 110. On the port city of Hippo see Lepelley (1981), 113-25. However, the vocabulary of almsgiving in most authors tends to be commercial: see Ramsey (1982), 247-8.

[68] *En. in Ps.* 36.26 (*Serm.* 3); NBA, 25: 820; trans. Boulding, WSA, 3/16: 134.

[69] See e.g. *En. in Ps.* 42.8; NBA, 25: 1044 and 1046. Cf. *Serm.* 9.17; NBA, 29: 180; *Serm.* 16B.3; NBA, 29: 326; *Serm.* 39.6; NBA, 29: 716 and 718; *Serm.* 56.12.16; NBA, 30/1: 158 and 160; *Serm.* 58.9.10; NBA, 30/1: 194; *Serm.* 150.6.7; NBA, 31/1: 452 and 454 (on the pre-eminence of giving and prayer over fasting); *Serm.* 209.2; NBA, 32/1: 162; and *De doctrina christiana*, prologue 6, 244-246; NBA, 8: 244 and 246. See more generally Ramsey (1982), 244-6, on the nexus between fasting and almsgiving. On almsgiving as a promotion of church unity see Fitzgerald (1999), 558. Fasting by itself is said to be a means of achieving unity in *Serm. de utilitate jejunii*, esp. 57. 7-8; CCSL, 46: 236-7. For the relationship of almsgiving to forgiving see Swift (2001), 25-48.

[70] On Augustine's exhortations to catechumens regarding almsgiving see Harmless (1995), 229, 251 with n. 37, 258.

[71] *Serm.* 86.14.17; NBA, 30/2: 24.

[72] See e.g. Vismara Chiappa (1975), 165; discussed by Canning (1993), 394-5. Hence it is difficult to agree with Fitzgerald (1989), 447, that Augustine 'does not turn the poor into a means of sanctification for the rich'.

Noticeably lacking in this framework, despite its emphasis on ecclesial unity, is any idea of collective salvation through almsgiving – not surprising, given Augustine's theory of predestination for the few. This approach to what might have been termed poor relief has attracted fierce criticism, for example from John Burnaby, who claimed that it resulted in attempting to use not only our neighbour, but also God, for our own advantage.[73]

Consistently in Augustine's discourse on almsgiving in the *Enarrationes* we encounter a decided emphasis on the disposition of the giver, in which humility is crucial. A passage such as the following is typical:

> Someone may have plenty of money and resources, and yet not be haughty about it, and then he or she is poor. Another may have nothing, yet be covetous and puffed up, and then God classes him or her with the rich and reprobate. God questions both rich and poor in their hearts, not in their treasure-chests or their houses.[74]

It follows that while some rich people will get to heaven, some poor people will not.[75] In commenting on the Psalms Augustine repeatedly juxtaposes the humble rich person with the proud pauper, probably reflecting his concern with the spiritual pride or elitist asceticism, of the Pelagians.[76] In conformity with Matt 5:3 the 'poor' are interpreted as being 'poor in spirit';[77] and the rich are designated as proud and self-important people.[78] Job is an example of a humble rich person,[79] so it is not people's wealth that God pays attention to but the nature of their disposition.[80]

If God is interested only in the disposition of the giver, it follows both that the amount given is immaterial and that riches are not to be dismissed outright. Christians, he explains, are allowed to be rich, as long as they realize that, being Christians, they are necessarily poor.[81]

---

[73] Burnaby (1960), 134, apparently endorsed by Ramsey (1982), 254 n. 142. Canning (1993), 351-420, takes issue with Burnaby's position. Fitzgerald (1989), passim, is also defensive of Augustine.

[74] *En. in Ps.* 48.3 (*Serm.* 1); NBA, 25: 1196; trans. Boulding, WSA, 3/16: 352-3.

[75] This is a recurring theme in Augustine; a good sustained discussion of it is found in *Serm.* 114B.9-13; NBA, 35/1: 106-16.

[76] See *En. in Ps.* 39.27; NBA, 25: 968 and 970; *En. in Ps.* 48 (*Serm.* 1).3; NBA, 25: 1196 and 1198. Cf. *Serm.* 85.2.2; NBA, 30/1: 650; *Serm.* 346A.4; NBA, 34: 94. On Augustine's reaction to the Pelagians in this matter see Bonner (1999), 42.

[77] See e.g. *En. in Ps.* 9.27; NBA, 25: 156.

[78] *Serm.* 290.6.6; NBA, 33: 190.

[79] *En. in Ps.* 30 (*Serm.* 4).12; NBA, 25: 502; *En. in Ps.* 71.3; NBA, 26: 790.

[80] See e.g. *En. in Ps.* 36 (*Serm.* 2).13; NBA, 25: 782.

[81] *En. in Ps.* 68. (*Serm.* 2).14; NBA, 26: 688 and 690.

The possession of wealth has to be seen eschatologically in the context of 1 Tim 6: 18-19: *They* [the rich] *are to do good, to be rich in good deeds*, etc.[82] Augustine expects his congregations to give to capacity without burdening themselves: 'What it costs is what you have', he tells them,[83] and they are not to worry if they have only good intentions and no money.[84] On another occasion Augustine urges his hearers to tithe, even though a tenth of their income is not very much.[85]

A further strategy used in the *Enarrationes* by Augustine and by Patristic writers in general to goad their congregations onto almsgiving was the identification of Christ and the poor.[86] While this is indeed a powerful theological construct, it can legitimately be asked whether it runs the risk of subsuming the poor into Christ and thus depersonalizing them even further than they are in much Patristic discourse.[87] To be sure, Augustine's arguments are compelling: 'You must accept Christ as this needy, poor person';[88] 'Try to understand about the needy, poor person that is, about Christ';[89] 'Christ himself is that poor man'.[90] The solidarity that must obtain within the catholic communities of North Africa is spelled out:

> Who is this brother? Christ. If, then, you are giving to Christ in giving to your own brother or sister and giving to God because you give to Christ, it means that God ... has willed to be in need of your gift.[91]

Graphic advice is also meted out to families to the effect that they should identify Christ as one of their children and so assure him of income from the parents' will.[92]

---

[82] *En. in Ps.* 72.26; NBA, 26: 850 and 852.

[83] *En. in Ps.* 49.13; NBA, 25, 1266; trans. Boulding, WSA, 3/16, 394.

[84] *En. in Ps.* 125.5; NBA, 28/1: 116.

[85] *En. in Ps.* 146.17; NBA, 28/2: 796. For instances where Augustine suggests tithing see Ramsey (1982), 234 with n. 46; cf. Finn (2006), 51. Jones (1960), 85, maintains that in fact tithe was very unusual.

[86] *En. in Ps.* 36 (*Serm.* 3).7; NBA, 25: 822; *En. in Ps.* 39.27; NBA, 25: 968; *En. in Ps.* 40.2; NBA, 25: 980 and 982; *En. in Ps.* 147.13; NBA, 28/2: 826. Cf. Merino (1987), 295-311, esp. 299.

[87] See Ramsey (1982), 253; *pace* Fitzgerald (1989), 450 with n. 24. Ramsey's stance is rejected by Kessler (1996-2002), 766.

[88] *En. in Ps.* 40.1; NBA, 25: 980; trans. Boulding, WSA, 3/16: 226.

[89] *En. in Ps.* 40.2; NBA, 25: 980; trans. Boulding, WSA, 3/16: 227.

[90] *En. in Ps.* 39.28; NBA, 25: 970; trans. Boulding, WSA, 3/16: 221.

[91] *En. in Ps.* 147.13; NBA, 28/2: 826; trans. Boulding, WSA, 3/20: 454.

[92] *En. in Ps.* 38.12; NBA, 25: 908. See further below on the 'quota for Christ'.

A similar strategy was the identification of the needy with the giver as beggars in relation to God.[93] Both owed a debt that could never be repaid. Augustine is concerned to stress our common identity as members of Christ's body under a common head.[94] Christ himself was regularly described as poor, recalling Paul's words in 2 Cor 8:9 (…*though he was rich, yet for your sakes he became poor, so that by his poverty you might become rich*), or the poor as standing for Christ, again with Matthew 25/Luke 19 in mind.[95] However, as Ramsey observes, one could interpret the identification of Christ with the poor as a kind of 'social monophysitism that failed to give due recognition to the individual nature of the poor over against Christ'.[96]

4. Usury

For all Patristic writers who dealt with almsgiving, the antithesis of this form of charity, which is a proper if self-interested investment with God, was usury.[97] At least as early as the fourth-century poet Commodian the idea was entertained that almsgiving which resulted from usury would be rejected by God.[98] Although this idea was taken up by Ambrose in *De officiis* 1.145, we do not find it specifically in Augustine, who takes the established line that while usury is permitted by civil law, it is to be condemned by the church.[99] Because of the theme of the oppression of the

---

[93] *En. in Ps.* 39.27 NBA 25: 968 and 970; *En. in Ps.* 39.28 NBA 25: 970.

[94] Finn (2006a), 139.

[95] *En. in Ps.* 30(*Serm.* 3).19, NBA 25: 492; *En. in Ps.* 36(*Serm.* 3).6, NBA 25: 818; *En. in Ps.* 38.12, NBA 25: 906; *En. in Ps.* 39.27 NBA 25: 968; *En. in Ps.* 40:2, NBA 25: 492; *En. in Ps.* 40.4, NBA 25: 986; *En. in Ps.* 75.9, NBA 26: 950; *En. in Ps.* 124.7, NBA 28/1: 98; *En. in Ps.* 147.13, NBA 28/2: 826; *En. in Ps.* 149.10, NBA 28/2: 908.

[96] Ramsey (1982), 254. 'The very concept of the identification of Christ and the poor…tended to work against the poor by swallowing them up in him' (*ibid.*, 259). This notion is firmly rejected by Fitzgerald (1989), 450 n. 24.

[97] See in general for the Patristic period Maloney (1973), 241-65; Ramsey (1982), 229; Moser (1997). For the topic in Augustine, see Hanson (1988), 141-64, and Di Berardino (2003), 257-63 (on canonical literature); on the Greek Fathers see Ihssen (2009).

[98] *Instructiones divinae* 20; CCSL, 128: 59. See further Ramsey (1982), 250-1.

[99] See *En. in Ps.* 36 (*Serm.* 3). 6; NBA, 25: 818 and 820; *En. in Ps.* 54.14; NBA, 26: 100 and 102. Cf. *Serm.* 77 A.4; NBA, 30/1: 550 and 552; *Serm.* 86.3.3; NBA, 30/2: 10; *Serm.* 113.2.2; NBA, 30/2: 414 and 416; *Serm.* 239.5; NBA, 32/2: 626. See, however, *Ep.* 153.24; NBA, 22: 550 and 552, advising that stolen money should not be considered almsgiving when transferred to the poor; *Serm.* 359A.13: NBA, 34: 338, on the point that funds obtained by fraud, robbery, and extortion and given in alms will avail the donor nothing.

poor in the Psalms, there are numerous references to usury in the *Enarrationes*. According to Augustine, usury is rampant and paraded publicly, while its practitioners form themselves into a corporation.[100] This does not prevent him, however, from using all the terminology of usury in describing how rich people must lend to God: '(t)he Lord himself comes forward to ask you for a loan, he who forbade you to be a usurer'.[101] The terminology of usury is used also in a spiritualizing manner in the image of the souls of the poor which are ransomed from their interest-burdened debts, i.e. their sins, by the redemptive blood of Christ.[102] The practice of lending money is put into an eschatological context whereby those who lend without seeking interest will inherit the kingdom of heaven, whereas those who refuse to lend in this manner will depart for the eternal fire.[103] Augustine derides lending on interest as yet another way of piling up money to no avail, and he is deaf to the objection that the money-lender is keeping his ill-gotten gains for his children: 'This sounds like family loyalty, but it is an excuse for injustice'.[104] Refraining, in the Psalmist's words, from swearing an oath to one's neighbour, deceiving him, putting money out to usury or accepting bribes (Ps 14: 4) is not a virtue of any great moment, Augustine says, but people are still incapable of acting properly in such cases.[105] In another place usurers are similarly included in a list of undesirables who frequent the church – the drunks, slave-dealers, soothsayers, 'and those who run to enchanters or enchantresses when they have a headache'.[106]

5. Direct or indirect giving

According to his biographer Possidius, Augustine distributed to the poor 'from the same source on which he and those living with him depended: the income from the Church's property and the offerings of the faithful'.[107] It is clear, however, that other modes of poor relief

---

[100] *En. in Ps.* 54.14; NBA, 26: 100.

[101] *En. in Ps.* 36 (*Serm.* 3).6; NBA, 25: 818; trans. Boulding, WSA, 3/16: 133.

[102] *En. in Ps.* 71.16; NBA, 26: 810.

[103] Ibid. Cf. *En. in Ps.* 54.14; NBA, 26: 100 (where the eschatological aspect is linked to the sincere recitation of the Lord's prayer); *En. in Ps.* 128.6, NBA, 28/1: 204 and 206.

[104] *En. in Ps.* 38.11; NBA, 25: 904; trans. Boulding, WSA, 3/16: 182.

[105] *En. in Ps.* 14.5: NBA, 25: 202.

[106] *En. in Ps.* 127.11; NBA, 28/1: 182; trans. Boulding, WSA, 3/20: 108.

[107] *Vita Augustini* 23.1. Text in Bastiaensen (1975), 188; trans. Rotelle (1988), 95.

obtained in Hippo encompassing both direct and indirect giving. Jesus himself, says Augustine, owned purses and accepted contributions from believers.[108] Brown points out that the laity in fact may have found themselves caught between two donative systems, the one for support of poor and clergy and the other for their own salvation.[109] Although images of beggars standing at people's doors or gates may be rhetorical echoes of the Dives and Lazarus story in Luke 16: 19-31, there are enough specific references to beggars setting their sights on individuals to indicate that some direct giving was practised by, or perhaps forced on, Augustine's congregations.[110] We know that in late antiquity it was particularly in cultic places like churches and monasteries that the hordes of beggars congregated.[111] Church-goers are advised to put aside some portion of their revenues for the poor,[112] suggesting cumulative and indirect giving, the so-called 'quota for Christ' which was a practical and gradual means of achieving salvation for the great majority of people who could not or would not divest themselves of their possessions in one radical act.[113]

6. Support of clergy[114]

Possidius, as we have said, mentions that Augustine, like Ambrose, admonished the faithful for not providing for the needs of the sacristy.[115] Appeals for the support of the clergy, described at one point as 'labouring oxen',[116] are made even more poignantly, a contrast being made between the beggar or needy person who importunes the potential giver and the priest who is silently in need and must be sought out by a donor, whether directly or indirectly is not clear. 'By all

---

[108] *En. in Ps.* 103 (*Serm.* 3).11; NBA, 27/1: 720 and 722; trans. Boulding, WSA, 3/19: 152.

[109] Brown (2005), 12.

[110] *En. in Ps.* 36 (*Serm.* 2).13; NBA, 25: 782 and 784; *En. in Ps.* 75.9; NBA, 26: 950; *En. in Ps.* 102.12; NBA, 27/1: 606.

[111] See Neri (1998), 64.

[112] *En. in Ps.* 146.17; NBA, 28/2: 794.

[113] On the quota see Bruck (1956) (critique in Holman [2001], 14); Vismara Chiappa (1975), 184-8.

[114] On this topic see La Bonnardière (1976), 65-70; Brown (2005), 13 with n. 26 (lit.).

[115] *Vita Augustini* 24.17. Text in Bastiaensen (1975), 194.

[116] *En. in Ps.* 103 (*Serm.* 3).10; NBA, 27/1: 718.

means give to the beggar', advises Augustine, 'but far more to God's servant'.[117] The congregation is told to be alert to the needs of their clergy: perhaps one of them does not need food, but needs clothing, or else a roof over his head, or perhaps he is building a church and needs financial help. The bishop of Hippo denies that bishops hoard money, admonishing the faithful to increase their contributions to their clergy.[118] In one sermon, delivered in the context of the public pagan games, they are given the choice of giving presents to gladiators or supporting the clergy.[119]

7. Discriminate or indiscriminate giving

In numerous passages in his other works Augustine makes it clear that everybody is everybody's neighbour and kin by virtue of their common humanity.[120] For example, in *Serm.* 149.18 he exhorts his listeners to love their neighbour, meaning every human being;[121] in *Serm.* 399.3.3 he says that everyone is a neighbour.[122] In the *Enarrationes* we find the same stress on the common humanity of Augustine's congregations, who are to regard the poor as a brother because all have descended from Adam and Eve. Rich and poor could easily change places, he warns, and in any case their bones will be indistinguishable after they are dead.[123]

In the overwhelming majority of passages in his commentary on the Psalms Augustine advocates giving indiscriminately, in one case even to non-Christians.[124] The very nature of 'almsgiving' itself is so broad for him that it is indiscriminate: the list given in *Enchiridion* 19.72 is extensive and includes giving anything that is needed to anyone who needs it.[125] Elsewhere he proffers the advice that the moneyed should spend their wealth on the destitute, feed the poor, clothe the naked, build a church, and so on; those who have the gift of good

[117] *En. in Ps.* 103 (*Serm.* 3).10; NBA, 27/1: 718; trans. Boulding, WSA, III/19: 152.
[118] *En. in Ps.* 103 (*Serm.* 3).12; NBA, 27/1: 722.
[119] *En. in Ps.* 102. 13; NBA, 27/1: 608. Cf. La Bonnardière (1976), 75.
[120] See in detail Canning (1993), passim.
[121] Cf. *Serm. de disc. christ.* 3.3; CCSL, 46: 209-10, for the same sentiment.
[122] NBA, 34: 736.
[123] *En. in Ps.* 72.13; NBA, 26: 838.
[124] *En. in Ps.* 46.5; NBA, 25: 1154.
[125] Cf. Ramsey (1982), 241.

counsel or of teaching should put it at the disposition of others; others can visit the sick or bury the dead. 'Be sensitive to each person's needs', he counsels, 'to the particular area in which he or she is poor'.[126] Even beggars help each other out.[127] He remarks pointedly that if even pagans and heretics perform corporal works of mercy then what should be expected of Christians.[128] It is unclear to what extent this all-embracing attitude to almsgiving has its roots in Augustine's reaction to Manichaean asceticism, in which all corporal works of mercy were forbidden to their elect.[129] Augustine specifically condemns the Manichean refusal to give bread and water to a beggar who is not a Manichean.[130]

Conclusion

The author of the *Enarrationes* made concessions to human frailty, with a strong emphasis throughout on the giver's attitude: one must give what one can, but pure intention is what counts, rather than the amount given.[131] Concurrently, Augustine gives the contradictory message that self-interest is a valid motivation for generosity. As well as offering comfort, encouragement, and correction to the listeners and readers of the *Enarrationes* who feel themselves disadvantaged, Augustine gave some very practical tools for self-help in his discourses on redemptive almsgiving. An explicit appeal to self-interest is made in Augustine's exegesis of Ps 90:16:[132]

> *I will show him my salvation.* Seek a safe place for your grain, and will you not seek a safe place for your heart? Will you not look for a secure place to lodge your treasure? Do as much as you can with it on earth: give it away. You will not lose it, you will only bank it securely. Who keeps it safe for you? Christ, who keeps you safe as well.

[126] *En. in Ps.* 125.13; NBA, 28/1:132; trans. Boulding, WSA, 3/20: 80.

[127] *En. in Ps.* 36 (*Serm.* 2).13; NBA, 25: 784; *En. in Ps.* 125.12; NBA, 28/1: 130.

[128] *En. in Ps.* 83.7; NBA, 26: 1186.

[129] Cf. Fitzgerald (1999), 560.

[130] *De moribus* 2.15.36: '*Hinc est quod mendicanti homini, qui Manichaeus non sit, panem vel aliquid frugum vel aquam ipsum, quae omnibus vilis est, dare prohibetis…*'; NBA, 13/1: 156. See Kamimura (2008). Cf. *En. in Ps.*140.12; NBA, 28/2: 562, in which Augustine criticises the Manichaean elect for refusing to give beggars bread.

[131] *En. in Ps* 49.13; NBA, 25: 1266 and 1268; *En. in Ps.* 67.41; NBA, 26: 622; *En. in Ps.* 125.5; NBA, 25,:116 and 118; *En. in Ps.* 125.11; NBA, 25: 128.

[132] *En. in Ps.* 90 (*Serm.* 2).13, on Ps 90:16; NBA ,27/2: 182; WSA, 3/18: 344.

This poses a challenge to contemporary scholars like Finn and Fitzgerald,[133] who have sought to play down Augustine's appeal to self-interest, although the latter admits that Augustine is aware of the inadequate motivations that can guide or influence human actions.[134] However, it is only fair to say that we do not find in *Enarrationes* the focus on self-interested giving that characterizes Augustine's other homilies. In commenting on the contents of the Psalms Augustine had to deal not only with the question of poverty but more particularly with that of the oppression of the just and disadvantaged at the hands of the ungodly rich. More obviously than his other works, the *Enarrationes*, which were preached throughout his ecclesiastical career, display a consistent emphasis on the pauperized and downtrodden whose sole refuge is in the Lord. The fact that this refuge can be provided not in this world but only eschatologically results in a spiritualization of poverty which, although present also in Augustine's other works, is striking in these sermons.

Does Augustine's discourse on the proper attitudes towards the poor, and poverty and riches, correlate with his own behaviour as bishop? To put the question another way, was Augustine truly a champion and lover of the poor, as Brown (2002) maintained? As bishop of Hippo Augustine took seriously his responsibilities to provide for his clergy and for the poor of his diocese, as we can tell from his implementation of poor rolls (*matricula pauperum*),[135] and from his constant letters, especially in his later years, petitioning the powerful for funds to ransom prisoners and to buy grain, and protesting against abuses by imperial tax collectors.[136] Like other bishops of his time Augustine co-opted the Psalmist's appeals for justice and mercy as images of his own generosity, and of the generosity he hoped to inspire amongst his hearers. In this way he sought to model giving to the poor according to much older Jewish traditions, especially in his role as arbiter in the episcopal court. The Psalms played an important role in the development of this

---

[133] Finn (2006a), 139, in reference to *Enarrationes*: 'Augustine avoids texts which emphasise redemptive almsgiving in atonement for sin.' See also Fitzgerald (1989), 449-50. Cf. Ramsey (1982), 241-244 on Augustine's frequent appeals to the salutary effects of almsgiving.

[134] Fitzgerald (1989), 449 n. 20, citing *En. in Ps.* 125.14; NBA, 28/1: 132. This is Fitzgerald's sole reference to *Enarrationes* in an article devoted to Augustine and almsgiving.

[135] See Divjak, *ep.* 20*.2; NBA, 23a: 160. This is the earliest instance of this system in Africa.

[136] Lepelley (2007), 6, expanding on Lepelley (2006). See Divjak, *ep.* 22*.3-4; NBA, 23a: 194, a newly discovered letter written c. 420. See also Brown (2002), 63-65.

rhetoric, as Brown suggests: '... an almost subliminal reception of the Hebrew Bible, through the chanting of the Psalms and through the solemn injunctions of the bishop in connection with the *episcopalis audientia*, came to offer a meaning to the word *pauper* very different from the "pauperized" image of the merely "economic" poor'.[137]

The sermons in the *Enarrationes* appear to underpin such rhetoric and activity with a social doctrine that is pragmatic and respectful of the *status quo*, seeking harmony within the church community and suppression of dissent. Augustine supported slavery, as long as respect obtained within the Christian household. He supported suppression of Donatists, Manichees and Pelagians while advocating help for the stranger and the exile. We must agree with Lepelley's conclusion that while Augustine's continual admonitions to his congregation should be read as genuine,[138] his power to intervene on behalf of the destitute was limited by imperial legal and administrative structures, especially in relation to tax collection, that relegated Augustine and bishops like him to the role of petitioners of the powerful 'even though they had no real power to help'.[139] Even in his role as judge in the episcopal court, Augustine was sometimes accused by the wealthy of being biased towards the poor.[140] There is no question that Augustine was a champion of the poor within the limits of his powers, but when poverty was made a spiritual qualification before a material one, it left the identification of deserving objects of charity, 'the poor', very much at the bishop's discretion.

Bibliography

Primary works including translations

Augustine, *Enarrationes in Psalmos*

Editions

Tarulli, V. et al. (eds./trans.) (1982-1993), *Esposizioni sui Salmi* 1-150, NBA, 25-28/2 (Rome).
Dekkers, E. and J. Fraipont (eds.) (1956) CCSL, 38-40 (Turnhout).

---

[137] Brown (2002), 70.

[138] e.g. *serm.* 41.7, 25.8 and especially many of the Dolbeau sermons e.g. *Sermon Dolbeau* 5.11 and 11.14.

[139] Lepelley, (2007), 6.

[140] Lepelley (2007), 10 cites Aug., *Enarr. in Ps.* 72, 12.

Weidmann, C. (2003), *Enarrationes in Psalmos* 1-50, CSEL, 93 part 1 (Vienna).

Müller, H. (ed.) (2004), *Enarrationes in Psalmos* 51-60, CSEL, 94 part 1 (Vienna).

Gori, F. (ed.) (2001-2005), *Enarrationes in Psalmos* 51-100, CSEL, 93-95 (Vienna).

Translations

Ramsey, B. (ed.) and M. Boulding (trans.) (2004) *Expositions of the Psalms* 121-150, WSA, 3/20 (Hyde Park, New York).

Ramsey, B. (ed.) and M. Boulding (trans.) (2003) *Expositions of the Psalms* 99-120, WSA, 3/19 (Hyde Park, New York).

Rotelle, J. (ed.) and M. Boulding (trans.) (2002) *Expositions of the Psalms* 73-98, WSA, 3/18 (Hyde Park, New York).

Rotelle, J. (ed.) and M. Boulding (trans.) (2001) *Expositions of the Psalms* 51-72, WSA, 3/17 (Hyde Park, New York).

Rotelle, J. (ed.) and M. Boulding (trans.) (2000b) *Expositions of the Psalms* 33-50, WSA, 3/16 (Hyde Park, New York).

Rotelle, J. (ed.) and M. Boulding (trans.) with M. Fiedrowicz (intro.) (2000a) *Expositions of the Psalms* 1-32, WSA, 3/15 (Hyde Park, New York)

Augustine, *Epistulae*

Divjak, J. (ed.) (1987) *Les lettres de S. Augustin, Lettres* 1*-29*, Bibliothèque Augustinienne Oeuvres de Saint Augustin 46b (Paris).

Augustine, *De moribus ecclesiae Catholicae et de moribus Manicheorum*, L. Alici and A. Pieretti (eds./trans.) (1997) NBA, 13/1 (Rome).

Augustine, *Sermones*, NBA, vols. 29-35/2 (1979-2002).

Serm. de disc. christ., CCSL, 46

Serm. de utilitate jejunii, CCSL, 46

Montefiore C.G. and H. Loewe (eds./trans.) (1974) with foreword by R. Loewe, *A Rabbinic Anthology* (New York).

Possidius, *Vita Augustini*

A.A.R. Bastiaensen (ed.) (1975) *Vita di Cipriano. Vita di Ambrogio. Vita di Agostino*, Introduzione di C. Mohrmann, Testo critico e commento a cura di A.A.R. Bastiaensen, Traduzioni di L. Canali e C. Careno (Fondazione Lorenzo Valla), 127-241.

Rotelle, J. (trans.) and M. Pellegrino (intro. and notes) (1988) *The Life of Saint Augustine by Possidius Bishop of Calama*, The Augustinian Series, vol. 1 (Villanova, PA).

Secondary works

Allen, P. and E. Morgan (2009) 'Augustine on poverty', in P. Allen, B. Neil, and W. Mayer (eds.), *Preaching Poverty in Late Antiquity.*

Perceptions and Realities, Arbeiter zur Kichen- and Theologiegeschichte P. Allen, B. Neil, and W. Mayer (Leipzig, 2009).

Bolkestein, H. (1939) *Wöhltatigkeit und Armenpflege im vorchristlichen Altertum* (Utrecht).

Bonner, G. (1999) 'Anti-Pelagian works', in A.D. Fitzgerald (ed.), *Augustine Through the Ages. An Encyclopedia* (Grand Rapids, MI – Cambridge), 41-47.

Brown, P.R.L. (2000) *Augustine of Hippo. A Biography* (new ed.) (London).

Brown, P.R.L. (2002) *Poverty and Leadership in the Later Roman Empire,* The Menahem Stern Jerusalem Lectures (Hanover – London).

Brown, P.R.L. (2005) 'Augustine and a crisis of wealth in late antiquity', Saint Augustine Lecture 2004, *AS* 36, 5-30.

Bruck, E.F. (1956) *Die Kirchenväter und soziales Erbrecht. Wanderungen religiöser Ideen durch die Rechte der östlichen und westlichen Welt* (Berlin – Göttingen – Heidelberg).

Burnaby, J. (1960) *Amor Dei. A Study of the Religion of St. Augustine,* The Hulsean Lectures for 1938 (London).

Canning, R. (1993) *The Unity of Love for God and Neighbour in St Augustine* (Heverlee – Leuven).

Cohen, J. (1999) *Living Letters of the Law. Ideas of the Jew in Medieval Christianity* (Berkeley CA).

Di Berardino, A. (2003) 'La défense du pauvre: saint Augustin et l'usure', in P.-Y. Fux, J.-M. Roessli, O. Wermelinger (eds.), *Augustinus Afer: Saint Augustin, africanité et universalité.* Actes du colloque international Alger-Annaba, 1-7 avril 2001, (Fribourg, Switzerland), 257-63.

Fiedrowicz, M. (1997) *Psalmus vox totius Christi: Studien zu Augustinus 'Enarrationes in Psalmos'* (Freiburg i.B. – Basel – Vienna).

Finn, R.D. (2006) *Almsgiving in the Later Roman Empire: Christian Promotion and Practice (313-450)* (Oxford).

Finn, R.D. (2006a) 'Portraying the poor: descriptions of poverty in Christian texts from the late Roman empire', in M. Atkins and R. Osborne (eds.), *Poverty in the Roman World* (Cambridge), 130-44.

Fitzgerald, A.D. (1989) 'Almsgiving in the works of St. Augustine', in A. Zumkeller (ed.), *Signum Pietatis: Festgabe für Cornelius Petrus Mayer OSA zum 60. Geburtstag,* Cassiciacum 40 (Würzburg), 445-9.

Fitzgerald, A.D. (1999) 'Mercy, works of mercy', in A.D. Fitzgerald (ed.), *Augustine Through the Ages. An Encyclopedia* (Grand Rapids, MI – Cambridge), 557-61.

Grodzynski, D. (1987) 'Pauvres et indigents, vils et plebeians. (Une étude sur le vocabulaire des petites gens dans le Code Théodosien)', *Studia et documenta historiae et iuris* (Rome).

Hanson, C.L. (1988) 'Usury and the world of St. Augustine of Hippo', *AS* 19, 141-64.

Harmless, W. (1995) *Augustine and the Catechumenate* (Collegeville, MI).

Harrison, C. (2006) *Rethinking Augustine's Early Theology: an argument for continuity* (Oxford).

Holman, S.R. (2001) *The Hungry are Dying: Beggars and Bishops in Roman Cappadocia* (Oxford).

Ihssen, B.L. (2009) '*That which has been wrung from tears.* Usury, the Greek Patristics and Catholic social teaching', in J. Verstraeten, J. Leemans, and B.J. Matz, and J. Verstracten (eds.), *Reading patristic Texts an Social Ethics. Issues and Challenges for Twenty-First Century Christian Social Thought*, CUA Studies in Early Christianity (Washington, DC, 2011), 124-60.

Jones, A.H.M. (1960) 'Church finances in the fifth and sixth centuries', *JTS* NS 11, 84-94.

Kamimura, N. (2008) 'The emergence of poverty and the poor in Augustine's early works', in G.D. Dunn, D. Luckensmeyer, and L. Cross (eds.), *Prayer and Spirituality in the Early Church*, vol. 6 (Strathfield), 283-98.

Kessler, A. and Krause, J.-U. (1996-2002) 'Eleemosyna', in C. Mayer (ed.), *Augustinus-Lexikon*, vol. 2 (Basel), 752-67.

La Bonnardière, A.-M. (1971) 'Les *Enarrationes in Psalmos* prêchées par saint Augustin à l'occasion de fêtes de martyrs', *RA* 7, 73-103.

— (1971/72) 'Les trente-deux premières *Enarrationes in Psalmos* dictées par saint Augustin', *AEPHE.R* 79, 281-84.

— (1976) 'Les *Enarrationes in Psalmos* prêchées par saint Augustin à Carthage en décembre 409', *RA* 11, 52-90.

— (1977/78) 'La predication d'Augustin sur les Psaumes à Hippone', *AEPHE.R* 86, 337-41.

— (1978/79) 'Recherches sur les grandes Enarrationes in Psalmos dictées d'Augustin', *AEPHE.R* 87, 319-24.

Lenski, N.E. (2001) 'Evidence for the *audientia episcopalis* in the new letters of Augustine', in R.W. Mathisen (ed.), *Law, Society and Authority in Late Antiquity* (Oxford).

Lepelley, C. (1981) *Les cités de l'Afrique romaine au Bas-Empire*, 2, *Notices d'histoire municipale* (Paris).

Lepelley, C. (2006) 'Saint Augustin et la voix des pauvres. Observations sur son action sociale en faveur des déshérités dans la region d'Hippone', in P.-G. Delage (ed.), *Les Pères de l'Église et la voix des pauvres*. Actes du IIᵉ colloque de La Rochelle 2, 3 et 4 septembre 2005 (La Rochelle), 203-16.

Lepelley, C. (2007) 'Facing wealth and poverty: defining Augustine's social doctrine', Saint Augustine Lecture 2006, *AS* 38, 1-17.

Maloney, R.P. (1973), 'The teaching of the Fathers on usury: an historical study on the development of Christian thinking', *VC* 27, 241-65.

Marino, M. (1987) 'La pobreza de Cristo en los sermons de san Agostín', Congresso Internazionale su S. Agostino nel XVI centario della conversione, Roma 15-20 settembre 1986, Atti II: Sezione di studio II-IV = *Studia Ephemeridis Augustinianum* 25 (Rome), 295-311.

Mayer, C. (ed.), (1996-2002) *Augustinus-Lexikon* 2 (Basel).

Mayer, W. (2009) 'Homilies as a source – the problematic' in P. Allen, W. Mayer, B. Neil, and (eds.), *Preaching Poverty* details as on p. 201.

Moser, T. (1997) *Die patristische Zinslehre und ihre Ursprünge: vom Zinsgebot zum Wucherverbot* (Winterthur).

Neil, B. (2010) Models of gift giving in the preaching of Leo the Great, *JECS* 18.2, 225-59.

Neri, V. (1998) *I marginali nell'occidente tardoantico. Poveri, 'infames' e criminali nella nascente società cristiana*, MUNERA. Studi storici sulla Tarda Antichità 12 (Bari).

Olivar, A. (1991) *La Predicación Cristiana Antigua* (Barcelona).

Pétré, H. (1948) *CARITAS. Étude sur le vocabulaire latin de la charité chrétienne*, Spicilegium Sacrum Lovaniense, Études et Documents 22 (Louvain).

Ramsey B. (1982) 'Almsgiving in the Latin church: the late fourth and early fifth centuries', *TS* 43, 226-259.

Rondeau, M.-J. (1983), 'L'Elucidation des interlocuteurs des Psaumes et le développement dogmatique (IIIᵉ – Vᵉ siècle' in J. Becker and R. Kaczynski (eds.), *Liturgie und Dichtung* II (St. Ottilien) 509-577.

Rondet, H. (1958) 'Notes d'exégèse augustinienne. Psalterium et cithara', *RSR* 46, 408-415.

Rondet, H. (1960) 'Essais sur la chronologie des <<Enarrationes in Psalmos>> de saint Augustine', *Bulletin de littérature ecclésiastique* 61, 111-127 and 258-286.

Swift, L. (2001) 'Giving and forgiving: Augustine on *eleemosyna* and *misericordia*', *AS* 32, 25-36.

Vismara Chiappa, P. (1975) *Il tema della povertà nella predicazione di Sant'Agostino*, Università di Trieste Facoltà di Scienze Politiche 5 (Milan).

Abbreviations

AEPHE.R	*Annuaire de l'École Pratique des Hautes Études. Section des Sciences Religieuses*
AS	*Augustinian Studies*
CCSL	*Corpus Christianorum (Series Latina)*
CSEL	*Corpus Scriptorum Ecclesiasticorum Latinorum*
JTS	*Journal of Theological Studies*
NBA	*Nuova Biblioteca Agostiniana*
RA	*Recherches augustiniennes*
RSR	*Revue des Sciences Religieuses*
TS	*Theological Studies*
WSA	*The Works of Saint Augustine: A Translation for the* 21ˢᵗ *Century*

CAROL HARRISON

ENCHANTING THE SOUL: THE MUSIC OF THE PSALMS

From angels tilting on the heavenly spheres to earthworms burrowing through the soil, in antiquity the world was understood as a finely tuned instrument: it was a unified whole, ordered by cosmic harmonies, formed by equal ratios, held in tension by numerical proportion, structured by symmetrical form.[1] Most importantly, it was an instrument that sounded: it was 'en-chanted' – eternally resonating with a measured music.[2]

However poetic this might sound, classical philosophers, follow-ing Pythagoras, did not turn to the literary disciplines of the trivium (grammar, dialectic, dialectic) to describe this measured music, but to the mathematical disciplines of the quadrivium – to arithmetic, geometry, music and astrology – for they believed that the music of the cosmos was best grasped by means of the rational analysis of its numerical form, order, proportion, ratio and symmetry.[3] These were

[1] Augustine *Tractatus in Johannem* 1.13 'He who made the angel, the very same made the worm also...for every creature in the universe was made by Him; the greater and the less; by Him were made things above; beneath; corporeal; incorporeal; by Him they were made. no form, no structure, no harmony of parts, no substance whatsoever, that is capable of being weighed, or numbered, or measured, exists but by and from that Creator Word to whom it is said, thou has ordered all things, in measure, and number and weight (Wisdom 11:20)'.

[2] Chua (1999), 12-28 who describes the 'disenchantment' of the world as it has been progressively secularised, demystified and rationalised. He describes what he calls the 'Midas touch of reason': 'everything the sovereign touches turns into facts; and these facts can only be used as a means without meaning; they are truths drained of their sacred and moral substance. Instrumental knowledge only knows *about* the world; it can never *know* the world'.

[3] Chua (1999), 15 'In Plato's account of creation [*Timaeus* 34b-47e] music tunes the cosmos according to the Pythagorean ratios of 2:1, 3:2 and 9:8, and scales the human soul to the same proportions. This enabled the inaudible sounds of the heav-ens to vibrate within the human soul, and, conversely, for the audible tones of human music to reflect the celestial spheres, so that heaven and earth could be harmonised within the unity of a well-tuned scale. This scale came to be pictured as a monochord that connected the stars to the earth like a long piece of string that vibrated the struc-ture of the universe...so music, as the invisible and inaudible harmony of the spheres, imposed a unity over creation, linking everything along the entire chain of being.'

the eternal, immutable truths which structured, unified and harmonised every part of reality, from the microcosm of the human soul to the macrocosm of the stars and spheres. Music (and poetry, for that matter; the two were often considered together in this context) was above all a mathematical discipline, analysed in terms of order, rhythm, harmony and measure. And yet it could never simply be a matter for the mind, or for the philosopher: it resonated in time and space; it was heard and felt; it en-chanted the whole of reality, rational and sensible.

In a Christian context we encounter much the same understanding, though with an important addition. Without exception, the fathers of the church shared the classical mind-set fostered by the disciplines. For them, God is, as it were, the one who tunes the instrument of the cosmos: it is from Him, in Him and through Him that it receives, maintains, and reveals its eternal and immutable unity, form, order and harmony.[4] Their distinctive contribution was the doctrine of creation from nothing, which emphasised not only the radical, ontological divide between creation and Creator but also the complete dependence and contingency of the former upon the latter. In this context, there would, of course, be no instrument if God had not brought it into being, but most importantly, it would not sound if it did not respond to, and resonate with, the one who created it, tunes it, and plays it;[5] without whom it would be an inanimate, mute object which would quickly deteriorate into a heap of broken strings around a fallen sound post. The analogy should not, of course, be pressed too far, but, whilst taking over the classical world picture, we should realise that the fathers stressed the absolute contingency of all reality upon the divine Creator, and of its nothingness without its conversion towards, and participation in, Him. For them, the cosmos was not structured according to an eternal realm of forms which remained immutably fixed, whatever disorder and disharmony human behaviour brings about; rather they stressed the importance of the creature's response to, or conversion towards, the Creator, for existence itself. It is here

[4] eg. Clement *Protrepticos* I; Origen *Contra Celsum* 8.67 ; Athanasius *Contra Gentes* (McKinnon (1989), 55); Augustine *De trinitate* IV.2.4 (where he uses the analogy of the monochord); Basil *On the Hexaemeron* Homily 1, 7 'Moses almost shows us the finger of the supreme artisan taking possession of the substance of the universe, forming the different parts in one perfect accord, and making a harmonious symphony result from the whole'.

[5] A better, and more biblical, analogy might be that of a wind player, who blows or breaths into the instrument, rather than a string player who plucks it.

that I think they, too, move beyond the realm of the rational and mathematical into the realm of time and mutability, and of what is heard and felt. Cosmic harmony is maintained only through participation and response.

Both the classical philosophers and the fathers agreed that the form or music of the cosmos had aesthetic and ethical, as well as philosophical, implications: it was not only true, but was also compellingly beautiful, and a model or pattern for human behaviour. Human beings could not simply ignore, or go against it; its beauty could inspire and inform their souls; moreover they had to acknowledge its form and act in accordance with it if human society and the human body and soul were not to become chaotic, fragmented and discordant. A measured music therefore en-chanted the whole of reality, cosmos and microcosmos; the whole of human thought and action, philosophical, aesthetic and ethical; the entire spectrum of human relations, to the gods/God, society, the body, and the soul.[6]

In this paper I would like to look at one aspect of this music in microcosm, and examine how the fathers thought that the Psalms, and in particular hearing or singing the Psalms, could en-chant the soul, unifying, harmonising, and ordering it so that it converted towards, participated in, and resonated with the cosmic harmony of the Creator.

It would not be an exaggeration to say that it was the Psalms, more any other text, that shaped, informed, and both literally and metaphorically, en-chanted early Christian thought and practice. The words of the Psalms, and above all, their sound, resonated within the early Christians' ears and minds, shaping their understanding of their faith, informing their thoughts, feelings and language, inspiring their prayers and motivating their actions at every turn and in every place, circumstance and context. This is well summed up in the following (anonymous) text:

> In the churches there are vigils, and David [=the Psalms] is first and middle and last. In the singing of early morning hymns David is first and middle and last. In the tents at funeral processions David is first and last. What a thing of wonder! Many who have not even made their first attempt at reading know all of David by heart and recite him in order. Yet it is not only in the cities and the churches that he is so prominent on every occasion and with people of all ages; even in the

---

[6] Boethius *De Institutione Musica* – 3 levels of reality *musica instrumentalis, musica mundana, musica humana*

fields and the deserts and stretching into uninhabited wasteland, he rouses sacred choirs to God with greater zeal. In the monasteries there is a holy chorus of angelic hosts, and David is first and middle and last. In the convents there are bands of virgins who imitate Mary, and David is first and middle and last. In the deserts men crucified to this world hold converse with God, and David is first and middle and last. And at night all men are dominated by physical sleep and drawn into the depths, and David alone stands by, arousing all the servants of God to angelic vigils, turning earth into heaven and making angels of men.[7]

One small example: it is sometimes said that Augustine of Hippo wrote not in Latin, but in the Psalms, and there is some truth to this: like so many of the early Christians it was the psalter which first shaped his Christian imagination and it was through the language of the psalter that he found a voice with which to express his faith and to address his God. If one reads an edition of his *Confessions* in which the editor notes allusions to, or citations of, the Psalms, then one finds them occurring in almost every line: the psalms allowed Augustine to express the movements of his soul. He was by no means alone.

The anonymous text we have just cited sums up the various contexts in which the psalms were sung. The list is clearly meant to be exhaustive of all aspects of early Christian life and practice, and is confirmed by a multitude of other patristic texts. The psalms were everywhere: they were the grammar of the faith which punctuated everyday life and its significant events (meals, weddings, funerals), they sounded throughout the night,[8] formed part of the Church's liturgy,[9] alternated with the prayers of the monks[10] in an unceasing cycle,[11] accompanied their manual labour, and rose up from the monasteries at the ninth hour in such a way that they allowed the hearer to imagine he or she

---

[7] Pseudo-Chrysostom *De poenitentia* (cited by McKinnon (1989), 90

[8] Basil *Epistula* 207 . Nicetas of Remesiana *De uigiliis seruorum Dei*

[9] McKinnon (1989) 8-10, however notes that although there is evidence for the widespread use of psalmody at Christian meals ,there is no evidence for their use in the liturgy until the fourth century, when he observes that there was a 'wave of enthusiasm for psalmody'

[10] This practice became especially prominent in ascetic circles in the fourth century where the cycle of prayer, psalmody and scriptural meditation formed the background to monastic life, and was formally practiced in the monastic offices. See Dysinger (2005), 48-57.

[11] There are many references to unceasing psalmody in a monastic context, eg. *Apophthegmata Patrum* , Epiphanius 3 (McKinnon (1989), 62); Eusebius of Vercelli *Epistula* 63.82 (McKinnon (1989), 132).

was participating in the heavenly choir.[12] They sounded wherever pagan music had sounded, driving out, and replacing, instrumental music and singing directed towards the gods, with Christian chant, inspired by and offered to God.[13]

Carmen and *Canticum*

The terminology which the early Church used to refer to the psalms likewise reflects the effect they were thought to have, and directly relates to the way in which they were believed to en-chant every aspect of Christian life and devotion. The Greek for the psalms is *psalmoi*, or songs. In Latin, too, they were commonly referred to as 'songs' (*carmina*), the 'songs of David'. The other meaning of 'song/ *carmen*' in Latin is 'charm'. Ambrose combines these two senses when he refers to the charm of his hymns as *hymnorum carminibus* : 'They also say that people are led astray by the charms of my hymns. Certainly; I do not deny it. This is a mighty charm (*carmen*), more powerful than any other'.[14] The en-chanting charm of the psalms is further revealed in the other word commonly used for them in Latin: *canticum* or chant. Again, Ambrose plays on the word, this time to suggest its relation to the one who charms or enchants, the enchanter or *incantator*. No doubt with the music of the pagan cult, as well as the common belief that music had power over the demons, at the back of his mind, he writes: 'Many provoke the church, but the charms (*carmina*) of the soothsayer's art are not able to harm her. Those who enchant (*incantatores*) avail not where the chant (*canticum*) of Christ is sung (*decantatur*) daily. The Church has her own enchanter (*incantatorem*), the Lord Jesus, by whom she has voided the spells of the magical charmers (*magorum incantantium carmina*) and the venom of serpents'.[15]

---

[12] Palladius *Lausiac History* 7.1-5

[13] See Quasten (1983) for a full consideration of this.

[14] *Sermo contra Auxentium de basilicas tradendis* 34 ; (McKinnon (1989), 132). Cf. Quasten (1983), 45 n.18 where he notes that Homer describes the effect of music as 'bewitching' (*thelgein*) and uses the same word to describe the effect of a magic wand (Odyssey 1.337).

[15] *Hexaemeron* IV, 8.33 (McKinnon (1989), 130). Cf. Chrysostom *Homilia in Ps* 41 who also observes that through the psalms Christ drives out demons: 'For just as those who invite actors, dancers and lewd women to their banquets also invite demons and the devil and fill their house with numberless enemies, so those who invite David with the cithara through him invite Christ into their home' (cited by Quasten (1983),130).

In an extraordinary treatise on the *Usefulness of Hymns* (*De Utilitate Hymnorum*) Nicetas of Remesiana (fourth/fifth century) observes that the healing potion which the psalms offer the sick is likewise rendered sweet by means of their melody (*cantionem*). Most significantly, when he briefly describes how this potion takes effect, so that the soul is enchanted, what he describes is in fact and the way in which sense perception was generally understood to operate in antiquity: in the case of hearing, something is heard by the ear, transferred to the mind as a mental image, stored in the memory, where it has an effect on the soul, or 'enchants' it, through being recollected. He notes that this is most especially the case if the recollection occasions pleasure, observing that:

> since human nature rejects and avoids what is difficult, even if ben-
> eficial, and accepts virtually nothing unless it seems to offer pleasure,
> through David the Lord prepares for men this potion which is sweet
> by reason of its melody (*cantionem*) and effective in the cure of dis-
> ease by reason of its strength. For a psalm is sweet to the ear when
> sung, it penetrates the soul when it gives pleasure, it is easily remem-
> bered when sung often, and what the harshness of the Law cannot
> force from the minds of men it excludes by the suavity of song. For
> whatever the Law, the Prophets and even the Gospels teach is con-
> tained as a remedy in the sweetness of these songs.[16]

The psalms, therefore, impress themselves on the soul most effectively when they are sung, when they occasion pleasure, when they penetrate the heart, are recollected by being repeated, and bring about through delight what the Law could not achieve by its harsh ordinances. The supreme enchanter, Christ, offers them as a sort of healing potion which drives out the demons, enchants and charms the soul through hearing, thereby prompting virtuous action. As we shall see in what follows, many in the early church shared Nicetas' experience.

Enchantment through song

Perhaps the most well known and influential attempt to address the importance of the psalms in the early Church comes from Athanasius, in his letter to Marcellinus (*Epistula ad Marcellinum de interpretatione*

[16] *De Utilitate Hymnorum* 5.

psalmorum).[17] In this treatise he famously describes the psalms as a 'mirror for the soul'. What he means by this is that in the psalms Christians can find every aspect of their inner selves reflected, or more tellingly, revealed; every thought, every emotion, every feeling, every longing, every desire, every failing, foible and weakness. The psalms provided a sort of physiognomy of the human mind and heart in which all Christians, of all different types, characters and ages,[18] could recognise and contemplate themselves. Many of the fathers liken this natural resonance to that of an instrument being played: the psalms gave the soul a voice, and in singing them the soul found itself in complete harmony with their every movement and motion. This was at once a process of self-awareness, and of self-reformation: seeing itself in the Psalms, or more precisely, being 'en-chanted' by the psalms, the soul was able to identify not only its virtues and a model to encourage them, but also its vices so that they could be reformed and remedied. The psalms gave the soul a means to express its every movement, whether this be joy or fear, hope or despair, and a means to articulate them, and thereby address them to God appropriately, in praise or petition, desire or repentance.[19] As Athanasius puts it: ' it is as though it were one's own words that one read; and any one who hears them is moved at heart, as though they voiced for him his dearest thoughts'.[20]

Athanasius' description of the natural resonance which exists between the soul and the Psalms is clearly based on his conviction that both are the work of God and that both therefore resonate, in microcosm, with the measured music of his entire creation. The fact that the psalms are songs or chants is of the utmost significance, and brings them closer than any other work in Scripture to the harmony which reigns throughout the cosmos. Athanasius is insistent therefore, that they must to be sung or chanted, and not just read, in order to have full effect. This has a number of implications, all of which relate to the psalms' ability to en-chant, or unify, harmonise and order, both those who sing them and those who listen to them.

---

[17] Hereafter referred to as Athanasius, followed by page references to Athanasius *On the Incarnation* and *To Marcellinus on the Interpretation of the Psalms* (1963) transl. and ed. A Religious of CSMV (London).

[18] Ambrose *Explanatio psalmi* I.9 (McKinnon (1989), 126).

[19] Athanasius 103 Among many other examples, see Cassian *Conferences* 10.11.6 and 10.11.15 who, describes the monk singing the Psalms: ' he will begin to sing them not as if composed by the prophets; but as if spoken by him as his own prayers, drawn forth from the deepest compunction of heart' (quoted by Dysinger (2005), 58-59).

[20] Athanasius 104-105.

Enchanting soul and body

Firstly, the singing or chanting the psalms naturally unifies, focuses and concentrates the attention of the soul; it brings harmony to the operation of reason and will, and thereby enables it to resist distraction or division[21]. We will return this, but it is important to note here that the soul and body are similarly unified in singing the psalms: concentrated and focussed on the same object, the rational, spiritual attention of the mind is channelled, in singing, through the physical movements of the lungs, tongue and lips, so that they operate in unison. The resultant sound is, in turn, nothing less than an expression of the inner harmony of the soul, and of the soul with the body – a microcosm of cosmic harmony and unity. Athanasius observes: 'to sing the Psalms demands such concentration of a man's whole being on them that, in doing it, his usual disharmony of mind and corresponding bodily confusion is resolved, just as the notes of several flutes are brought by harmony to one effect … it is in order that the melody may thus express our inner spiritual harmony, just as the words voice our thoughts, that the Lord has ordained that the psalms be sung and recited to chant'[22] Basil, interestingly, attributes the same effect to the practice of antiphonal chant in Caesarea, in which two choirs sang alternate verses: 'At first they divide themselves into two groups, and sing psalms in alternation with each other, at once intensifying their carefulness over the sacred texts, and focusing their attention and freeing their hearts from distraction'.[23]

En-chanting Christian Culture

There is a sense in which any text which was as popular and influential as the psalms in the early Church, could not fail to become part of the collective consciousness of the Church and function as one of

[21] This is something Augustine examines at length in *Confessiones* 1 when he considers how the soul's attention is unified in its hearing or speaking the first line of a hymn by Ambrose (Deus Creator Omnium). In order to hear it enunciated in time it must remember, attend to, and anticipate what is being said, so that the mind's attention is both drawn out to encompass the whole (*distentio*) and focussed on the whole (*intentio*).

[22] Athanasius 114-115. Evagrius, *De oratione* 82, similarly emphasises that the psalms should be sung with what he calls 'good rhythm': 'Pray gently and without getting disturbed, sing psalms with understanding and good rhythm, and you will be like a young eagle, soaring on high'.

[23] Basil *Epistula* 207. 3 (McKinnon (1989), 68).

factors that created and maintained that consciousness. We might call this collective consciousness a Christian 'culture', 'society', 'subjectivity', 'paradigm', 'rhetoric', 'tradition'... or what we will, but whatever term we use, the psalms clearly became one of those tacit, customary, habitual practices which informed early Christian faith and imagination. In this sense, their power in shaping Christian identity, the charm they exercised, and the en-chantment they effected, cannot be over-estimated. The fathers most often articulate this effect in relation to the power of the psalms to unify those who heard and sung them together: to unify their attention (as we have seen) but also to harmonise their hearts and minds. First of all, the singing of the psalms by one person, could, as it were, hold up a mirror for the soul of another; the listener could be moved by what they heard, they might find it resonating with their own soul, and be moved to make the words their own – in other words to be harmonised with and transformed by them. In doing so, they would simultaneously be unified with all other Christians who had fallen under the same enchantment. Athanasius sums this up when he reflects that, 'It seems to me, moreover, that because the Psalms thus serve him who sings them as a mirror, wherein he sees himself and his soul, he cannot help but render them in such a manner that their words go home with equal force to those who hear him sing, and stir them also to a like reaction'.[24] That the Psalms are sung, rather than read, is again a significant factor in this context in order to express and effect not only the heart but also the mind and understanding of singer and listener: 'those who do sing... so that the melody of the words springs naturally from the rhythm of the soul and her own union with the Spirit, they sing with the tongue and with the understanding also, and greatly benefit not themselves alone but also those who want to listen to them'[25] Cassian acutely observes that the *manner* in which the psalms are sung by another is also important: 'sometimes the musical phrasing by the brother chanting will arouse dull minds to focussed supplication. We also know that the enunciation and reverence of the one chanting the psalms can very much increase the fervour of those who stand by [listening]'.[26]

Athanasius' reference to the 'rhythm of the soul and her own union with the Spirit' is the key to understanding the unifying effect of the

[24] Athanasius 105-6.
[25] Athanasius 115.
[26] *Conferences* 9.26.1-2 cited by Dysinger (2005), 61.

Psalms: just as the Holy Spirit was believed to have inspired the whole of Scripture, so that it is nowhere discordant, but unified in every part, so the Spirit's presence in the souls of those singing and listening within the Church ensures that what is enunciated and received by them will be heard in unity and without disagreement or discord. The magical experience of singing as one, of becoming part of the larger body of those with whom one sings, which is familiar to anyone who has sung in a choir, is something that the fathers identified in their congregations as they sang or listened to the Psalms, en-chanted by the Spirit. Ambrose sums up numerous reflections on this insight when he writes: 'A psalm joins those with differences, unites those at odds and reconciles those who have been offended, for who will not concede to him with whom one sings to God in one voice? It is after all a great bond of unity for the full number of people to join in one chorus. The strings of the cithara differ, but create one harmony (*symphonia*). The fingers of a musician (*artificis*) often go astray among the strings though they are very few in number, but among the people the Spirit musician knows not how to err'[27] Using an image widely employed by the fathers he comments elsewhere that their unity is like that of the waves of the sea; the Church 'hums with the prayer of the entire people like the washing of waves, and resounds with the singing of psalm responses (*responsoriis psalmorum cantus*) like the crashing of breakers'.[28]

Enchanting Scripture

The spirit-inspired and spirit-filled unity which the Psalms embody in Scripture, and re-embody in the congregation, in being sung or heard, is another way of expressing the way in which they en-chant. Here it is the Holy Spirit who is the en-chanter, the *incantator* or the magician, who harmonises, orders and unifies the hearts, minds and souls of the congregation through the Psalms. One of the ways the fathers emphasise this quality of the psalms is to insist that the Psalter contains within itself *all* the books of Scripture – the law, the

---

[27] Ambrose *Explanatio psalmi* 1,9 (McKinnon (1989), 126-7) See Quasten (1983) 67-69; 77-78 on the Fathers' insistence on singing with 'one voice', as signifying and embodying unity, harmony, peace, concord and love as against disharmony and fragmentation. He also (somewhat questionably) interprets this as a rejection of polyphony.

[28] Ambrose *Hexaemeron* III,V,23.

prophets, history... This might at first seem rather an odd claim, but it seems to rest, first of all, on the obvious point which we have just mentioned, that the psalms were inspired by the same Spirit which breathes through the rest of Scripture, and are therefore, in a fundamental sense, in harmony with all the other books of Scripture, but it is clearly also based on the fathers' shared conviction that the psalms, because they were songs or chants, were unique among the books of Scripture in being a microcosm of cosmic unity and harmony: they were not only a mirror for the soul and its movements but a mirror of the whole of creation and divine revelation: they contained *all* truth, in other words, the whole of reality, including the whole of Scripture, and therefore, in a sense, unify or harmonise it, too, in microcosm.[29]

Enchanting the Soul

Another consequence of the Spirit's inspiration of the psalms was the fathers' belief in their ability, in turn, to inspire or convert the soul towards spiritual things. They often use the metaphor of the psaltery to elaborate on this. It was an instrument which was distinctive because, as Basil puts it, 'it alone among musical instruments has the source of its sound in its upper parts'. While other instruments, such as the cithara and lyre, were played with a plectrum from below, the psaltery he observes, 'has the source of its harmonious strains from above...so that... [the soul] might be anxious to pursue higher things, and not brought down to the passions of the flesh by the pleasure of song (melous).'[30] We mentioned the importance of response and participation in the creature's relation to its Creator: having been drawn from nothing it can only remain in existence if it continually converts, or turns back towards its Creator in order to receive form (or harmony, measure, order and unity); if it turns away, it will become de-formed, dissonant, disordered and fragmented, and fall back into nothingness. It is this crucial conversion of the soul which the psalms are able to effect because of their resonance with the soul. Their en-chantment by the

---

[29] Athanasius 102; Ambrose *Explanatio Psalmi* I,7 (McKinnon (1989), 126).

[30] Basil *Homilia in Psalmum* I,2; Cf. Hilary *Instructio Psalmorum* 7 (McKinnon (1989), 123).

Spirit – in other words, their form – their harmony, measure, order and unity – resonates with that of the soul: the words, and most importantly, the unique harmonies of the Psalms, are imprinted/impressed on the soul of the one who sings or listens to the psalms, and in recollecting, re-presenting and repeating them to itself, it is formed and reformed according to them.

A good deal of patristic reflection on the practice of prayer, meditation, reading or singing the Scriptures is based upon these insights. Because of their unique form the Psalms become a sort of magical potion, a universal panacea – 'a kind of balm of human salvation' [31], as Ambrose puts it, for all the soul's needs. We have seen that the psalms' power to en-chant allows the soul to resonate with cosmic harmony, to identify its needs and address them appropriately to God, to focus and concentrate its attention in relation to its body, to become one with the body of Christ, the Church, to apprehend the whole of the Christian revelation throughout sacred history and Scripture, and to form and reform itself by conversion towards its Creator. In line with classical philosophy[32] these various en-chantments are often expressed by the fathers in terms of 'music therapy': of the healing, therapeutic effect they have on the passions (thumoi – check) which might otherwise disturb, distract or fragment the soul and body. As Evagrius puts it, 'Psalmody calms the passions and reduces to quietness the imbalance of the body'.[33] Anger, grief, fear, sadness, pain...are calmed soothed, alleviated and assuaged by the psalms' measured music. It is as if in singing, recalling, and repeating them, the even temperament of the psalms serves to correct any imbalances in the body's humours and to render body and soul in tune, so that they, in turn, can be free to outwardly express their inner harmony.[34] The first reason Athanasius has to offer to Marcellinus for why the psalms are written in poetry rather than prose, and should be sung rather than just read, is perhaps also the most telling: the poetry of the psalms allows the singer to 'express

---

[31] Ambrose Explanatio Psalmi 1.7.

[32] eg. Plato Timaeus 47 c-d ; Republic 4.441e-442a ; Aristotle Politics 1340a18; Galen De placitis Hippocratis et Platonis 5.6.20 – all cited by Dysinger (2005), 128-129.

[33] Evagrius Praktikos 83. See Dysinger (2005), 88-92 who considers the fathers' widespread use of the Greek word, kateunazo (lit. to put to bed; to lull to sleep), in an ascetic context, to describe the calming effect of psalmody on the passions.

[34] As Dysinger (2005), 128 comments in relation to Praktikos 69-71, Evagrius claims that 'undistracted psalmody' contributes to the establishment of a new krasis, an anakrasis, or 'complete blending' of the self with the virtues.

their love to God with all the strength and power they possess'[35] He
later adds that,

> When, therefore, the Psalms are chanted, it is not from any desire
> for sweet music but as the outward expression of the inward har-
> mony obtaining in the soul, because such harmonious recitation is
> in itself the index of a peaceful and well-ordered heart. To praise
> God tunefully upon an instrument...is, as we know, an outward
> token that the members of the body and the thoughts of the heart
> are, like the instruments themselves, in proper order and control, all
> of them together living and moving by the Spirit's cry and breath...
> he who sings well puts his soul in tune, correcting by degrees its
> faulty rhythm so that at last, being truly natural and integrated,
> it has fear of nothing, but in peaceful freedom from all vain imag-
> inings may apply itself with greater longing to the good things
> to come. For a soul rightly ordered by chanting the sacred words
> forgets its own afflictions and contemplates with joy the things of
> Christ alone.[36]

The psalms thereby initiate and facilitate the healing of the soul both
before the incarnation of Christ, the divine physician, and also through
Him, as he is prophetically and proleptically encountered in them.[37]

In expounding these ideas the fathers drew not only upon classical philosophy concerning the therapeutic effect of music upon the
soul, but also upon classical mythology: Orpheus, plucking his lyre in
order to tame the wild beasts, is likened to Christ taking up flesh and
playing 'odes' and 'epodes' through it in order to heal rational beings
of their 'wild passion and bestiality' with his inspired teaching.[38] Likewise, Odysseus tied to the mast, resisting the sirens' song, is likened to
Christ bound to the cross, resisting his tempters.[39]

Perhaps the most interesting of such figurative interpretations is,
however, found among the many patristic references to David, who
as a young boy sang and played the cithara for Saul, in order to quiet

---

[35] Athanasius 114

[36] Athanasius 115-16; See Dysinger 100-103 for similar observations in Evagrius, for
whom the psalms work not only on the passionate part of the soul (*pathetikon*) but on
the reason or *nous*, which is thereby able to apprehend the meaning, or inner *dunamis*
of what is being sung, without the distractions of imagery.

[37] Athanasius 106-7; Dysinger (2005), 104, on Evagrius.

[38] Eusebius *Tricennial Oration* 14. 5 (McKinnon (1989), 101).

[39] eg. Clement *Protrepticos* 12.1.18; 6.89.1; 1.41.3 – Odysseus' encounter with the
Sirens prefigures the temptation of Christ, who Justin calls the 'true Orpheus'.

and banish the demons that disturbed him. This episode, too, is interpreted by Nicetas as a figure of the incarnation. He writes, 'he [David] subdued the evil spirit which worked in Saul – not because such was the power of the cithara, but because a figure of the cross of Christ was mystically projected by the wood and the stretching of strings, so that it was the Passion itself that was sung and that subdued the spirit of the demon'.[40]

The ambiguity of enchantment

The power of the psalms to enchant the soul, although widely attested in patristic literature, was not, however, without its ambiguities. The fathers unanimously rejected pagan music on almost exactly the same grounds as they praised the effects of singing the psalms: both were able to 'wound the soul',[41] and impress the mind with images which, when recollected, imagined and re-presented could mould and motivate it to act in ways which conformed to them. This was acceptable when it was divine form, order, unity and harmony which were being impressed by the measured music of psalms, but wholly unacceptable when it was the immoral, licentious, chaotic and unruly exploits of the pagan gods which were being re-enacted and recounted in pagan cult and theatre, accompanied by instruments and song, inducing frenzy, madness, ecstasy and demon possession in the hearer.[42] Part of the challenge the fathers faced in attempting to identify for their congregations what could rightfully be identified and claimed as Christian within the pagan culture and society which constituted the everyday, tacit, conventions and habits of the culture and society in which they had hitherto lived, thought and behaved, and what was harmful and hostile to Christian faith and must be rejected and avoided, was their consideration of poetry and music. It was abundantly clear, from their education in the liberal arts, and above all, from their own experience as human beings, that poetry and music had unquestioned powers to beguile, en-chant and form the heart, mind and soul. Like rhetoric,

[40] Nicetas *De utilitate hymnorum* 3-4.

[41] Jerome *Epistula* 128 ad Pacatulam 4.3 'the sweetness of the voice wounds the soul through the ear'.

[42] Quasten (1983) 45 n.18 refers to Plato *Symposium* 215c who observes that flute music causes frenzy; Aristotle *Politeia* 8.5.55.1340a who notes its power to induce ecstasy.

this power needed to be harnessed, tamed and directed for Christian purposes, whilst avoiding the harmful effects the same practices could have in a pagan context. What was therapeutic in one context could be a deadly poison in another. Thus, patristic literature is replete with attacks on pagan music, and especially on instrumental music. The fathers tend to advocate – and even then, in a guarded and uneasy manner – only the use of the human voice, a simple, unadorned chant, a concentration on understanding and the meaning of the words in order to instruct and inform rather than to move or persuade, or afford delight and pleasure.[43] And yet, like rhetoric, they are more than aware of the voice's power to effect – naturally, unselfconsciously, intuitively and in an uncontrived way – precisely what they wished to avoid: the power not only to teach and inform the mind, but to en-chant, move, delight and persuade the heart and soul, the passions and emotions. Music could never simply be a matter for the mind and reason alone: because it sounded, resonated in time and space, and was received by the senses, it must always involve the sensible as well as the rational. What we have seen of their treatment of the psalms suggests that despite their reservations and misgivings, and despite their awareness of the dangers and pitfalls of music, the fathers were both aware of, and willing to harness and use, its power to en-chant: to unify, order, harmonise, focus, concentrate, sooth and heal the soul so that it can pray, meditate, convert and be conformed to its Creator.[44]

A few examples must suffice: Chrysostom, along with many of the fathers, concedes that although God does not need music he has nevertheless allowed it as a concession to human weakness, 'for nothing', he observes, 'so edifies and gives wings to the soul, looses it from the earth and the body's fetters and makes it to be contemplative and contemptuous of earthy things as the melody of music and a godly and rhythmic song'.[45]

---

[43] eg. Jerome *Epistula* 125 *Ad rusticum monachum* 15;(McKinnon (1989), 143); Augustine *De Doctrina Christiana* 4; Nicetas of Remesiana *De utilitate hymnorum* 15; Chrysostom *In Hebraeos Hom* 4.5; PL 63.43 (McKinnon (1989), 48); Canons of Basil 97 (McKinnon (1989), 120) sums up the fathers' attitude: 'Those singing psalms at the altar shall not sing with pleasure, but with understanding; they should sing nothing other than the psalms…'

[44] See Harrison (2011) forthcoming, for a discussion of these ambiguities and tensions in Augustine.

[45] Chrysostom *In psalmum* 49 cited by Quasten (1983), 92-3.

Various passages in Augustine's *Confessions* leave us in no doubt that Augustine was keenly aware of the beauty of music and profoundly sensitive to its effects. In the days following his baptism in Milan he recounts, 'How I wept during your hymns and songs! I was deeply moved by the music of the sweet chants of your church. The sounds flowed into my ears and the truth was distilled into my heart. This caused the feelings of devotion to overflow. Tears ran, and it was good for me to have that experience.'[46] In book 10, however, he reveals his divided mind on the subject.

> I feel that when the sacred words are chanted well, our souls are moved and are more religiously and with a warmer devotion kindled to piety than if they are not so sung. All the diverse emotions of our spirit have their various modes in voice and chant appropriate in each case, and are stirred by a mysterious inner kinship.

But he admits that he himself,

> fluctuates between the danger of pleasure and the experience of the beneficent effect, and I am led to put forward the opinion (not as an irrevocable view) that the custom of singing in Church is to be approved, so that through the delights of the ear the weaker mind may rise up toward the devotion of worship. Yet when it happens to me that the music moves me more than the subject of the song, I confess myself to commit a sin deserving punishment, and then I would prefer not to have heard the singer.[47]

The delight which the psalms undeniably occasion, whilst it can become an occasion for sin by being taken as an end in itself (as in Augustine's experience above) is also frequently attributed by the fathers to their inspiration by the Holy Spirit. The delight occasioned by rhythm, melody and harmony, as Augustine himself often observes in other contexts, can therefore also be an inspired means of communicating their meaning or truth more effectively to fallen, weak human beings, than the bald statement of truth could ever effect. Basil of Caesarea's comments are representative of a good deal of patristic reflection on this point when he comments:

---

[46] *Confessiones* 9.6.14 Cf. *Epistula* 9 (PL 33).
[47] *Confessiones*, 10.33.50.

What did the Holy Spirit do when he saw that the human race was not led easily to virtue, and that due to our penchant for pleasure we gave little heed to an upright life? He mixed sweetness of melody with doctrine so that inadvertently we would absorb the benefit of the words through gentleness and ease of hearing, just as clever physicians frequently smear the cup of honey when giving the fastidious some rather bitter medicine to drink. Thus he contrived for us these harmonious psalm tunes, so that those... while appearing only to sing would in reality be training their souls.[48]

Gregory of Nyssa similarly alludes to 'holy pleasure', and to the enchanted potion or medicine of the divine enchanter, but with far more daring – perhaps because he is drawing upon his own experience as a poet – and with a freer attitude to instrumental music and classical verse and chant than we ordinarily find in the fathers:

Second, I thought of youth,
And of the folk who find such joy in words:
My verse could be for them a pleasant potion,
Leading them towards the good by mild persuasion,
Sweetening by art the bitter taste of law.
Verse helps us to relax the tightened string,
If we but will, even if it be no more
Than lyric songs, musical interludes.
I write them simply, then, for your delight,
Lest other pleasures steal you from true Beauty
...The ancients sang instruction in their verse
Making delight the vehicle of beauty,
Forming the heart by virtue of song.
Saul is a prime example, whose troubled spirit
The music of the harp alone set free.
What harm then, if we lead the young
To share in God by means of holy pleasure?[49]

The end of this holy pleasure – of the en-chantment of the soul – is, of course, to move it beyond voices and words, beyond the senses, beyond

---

[48] Basil *Homilia in psalmum* 1; (McKinnon (1989), 65). Elsewhere Basil distinguishes between healthy and harmful tunes; between the music of David and flute music – *De legend.libr.gentil.*7. Cf. Chrysostom *In psalmum* 41.1 (McKinnon (1989), 79); Eusebius *Historia Ecclesiastica* 4. 29,1-3 (McKinnon (1989), 105); Plato *Politeia* 3(401 d.e. 402a Burnet) cited by Quasten (1983), 137.

[49] Gregory of Nazianzus *On His Own Verses* transl. Daley (2006), 164-165.

images, beyond measured music, to worship the unknowable, transcendent God – what Philo describes as 'songs of praise and hymns – not such as the audible voice sings, but such as are raised and re-echoed by the invisible mind'.[50] When Cassian and Augustine attempt to describe this end they are, as temporal human beings, reduced to words to describe the end of words. Cassian writes:

> And so our mind will attain that incorruptible prayer… which does not consist wholly in averting our inner gaze from images, but rather is characterised by the absence of any need for voice or word: for the focus of our minds is set ablaze through some indescribable eagerness of spirit, which our mind, beyond the senses or the effects of matter, then pours forth to God with inexpressible groans and sighs[51]

In the ascent at Ostia which he shared with his mother, Monnica, and which he recounts in book 9 of his *Confessions*, Augustine similarly describes how all the voices of earth and heaven fell silent; how God spoke directly, and in an unmediated way, to their souls; of how, having attained to this audition for a fleeting moment, the knowledge of it left them aching for more; of how, if such a state ever became permanent, it would be eternal life. Towards the end of the *Confessions* he looks towards, and yearns for, this heavenly life in words which closely echo Cassian's: 'I will enter my chamber and will sing you songs of love, groaning with inexpressible groanings on my wanderer's path and remembering Jerusalem with my heart lifted up towards it' (12.16.23).

Meanwhile, we are left with words -or better- music, to mediate the Divine – and the Fathers found none better but the songs of David.

Bibliography

Chua, D.K.L. (1999) *Absolute Music and the Construction of Meaning* (Cambridge)
Daley, B. (2006) *Gregory of Nazianzus* Early Church Fathers (London)
Dysinger, L. (2005) *Psalmody and Prayer in the Writings of Evagrius Ponticus* (Oxford)

---

[50] Philo *De uita Moysis* II (III) 239 (101 Cohn) cited by Quasten (1983), 54 who identifies this spiritualising tendency (what he calls the 'worship of the heart') in various pagan philosophers – see 50-57.

[51] *Conferences* 10.11.6 (Dysinger (2005), 61).

Harrison, C. 'Augustine and the Art of Music' in Jeremy S. Begbie and Steven R. Guthrie (eds) *Resonant Witness: Conversations Between Music and Theology* (Grand Rapids MI: Eerdmans, 2011) 27-45.

Kolbet, P. (2006) 'Athanasius, The Psalms, and the Reformation of the Self' *Harvard Theological Review* 99:1, 85-101

McKinnon, J. (1989) *Music in Early Christian Literature* (Cambridge)

Quasten, J. (1983) *Music and Worship in Pagan and Christian Antiquity* transl. B. Ramsay, NPM Studies in Church Music and Liturgy (Washington)

AUGUSTINE CASIDAY

'THE SWEETEST MUSIC THAT FALLS UPON THE EAR': TRANSLATING AND INTERPRETING THE PSALTER IN CHRISTIAN ANDALUSIA

Introduction

If recurrent themes in undergraduate essays count as anecdotal evidence, it is a tenet of common knowledge that from the Fourth Century a rift opened between the Christian East and the Christian West and was progressively widened by mutual ignorance and antagonism. Considerable knowledge of evidence from far-flung sources is needed for a more accurate understanding of the complex convergences and divergences that make up the history of Christianity. So it is a rare thing to encounter an overview of the period that discusses the advent of independent (and often competing) Christian societies with the dexterity and honesty found in Andrew Louth's *Greek East and Latin West: The Church AD 681-1071*. Louth's approach is deliberately intended to complement earlier similar volumes on the history of early medieval Christianity by taking as its point of departure an informed, Eastern Christian perspective. This is a commendable decision, but it does mean that some interesting episodes are left out; for instance, Spain is mentioned only as something like the far end of the world. Although it is noted that the expansive conquests by early Muslim forces, which transformed the Christian East, eventually came to incorporate Spain into the Umayyad Caliphate,[1] the comments about the emergence of Arabic-speaking Christian[2] culture overlook a fascinating, if historically marginal, phenomenon: the advent in Western Europe of a Christian Arabic society, complete with an

---

[1] Louth (2007), 4.

[2] Louth (2007), 163-66; a similar lack of emphasis on Arabic Christian literature from the West can be found in the standard reference for the subject: Graf (1944-53). But see Goussen and Monferrer Sala (1999).

orientation toward the Near East. Considering Louth's interests in the interactions of Christians across different cultures, in the historical transformations of Christianity, and in worship and sacred poetry as vehicles for theological reflection,[3] it therefore seems appropriate to contribute to this *Festschrift* a brief study of the Mozarabic Psalter that Hafs b. Albar al-Quti translated from Latin into Arabic in the late Ninth Century.[4]

It is impossible to understand the circumstances in which Hafs made his translation without attending first to some major social currents that flowed through (what we might anachronistically call) Spanish Christendom in the age of transition from Gothic to Umayyad rule. We shall look first to those circumstances, before turning to the attitudes about those events of Christians who were contemporaneous to them. Our attention will turn first to Paul Albar of Cordoba, whose attitude toward Arabic culture is adversarial to put it mildly. This is not to say that Albar inarticulately rages against all things Arabic, since he was in fact clear on his reasons for objecting to the loss of Romance culture. Albar's position needs to be considered before we turn to Hafs himself and to his translation. Preliminary attention to Albar will help us appreciate more clearly Hafs' background and his motivation in preparing the translation and his attitude as a Christian toward Arabic-language culture. These topics have received some attention already by scholars of early medieval Spain, whose lead will be important in the following pages. But because that earlier scholarship has been concerned above all with linguistic and historical aspects of Hafs' translation, earlier studies have paid scant attention to the *Preface* to the translation. Comparative analysis of the prose *Preface* and Hafs' verse introduction (the *urjûza*) has indicated that the *Preface* was not written by Hafs himself, but this hardly means that the *Preface* is without interest. The *Preface* gives evidence of a somewhat less well-spoken perspective from Mozarabic Christianity in Andalusia that still manages to adapt to Arabic culture without considering itself somehow compromised because of having done so.

The Arabization of Gothic Hispania

From the early Fifth Century, the Goths and other Germanic tribes who by force of arms stabilized Roman Hispania had gradually come to

---

[3] See, e.g., Louth (2002), 252-82.
[4] Urvoy (1994).

acquire political autonomy from the Roman Empire – even repelling the advances of Justinian's generals' re-conquest in the south – and to consolidate their own Visigothic kingdom. From Toledo, they ruled the Iberian Peninsula. Their kingdom flourished in the Seventh Century. During the second half of the same century a series of victories by the Umayyad armies in Egypt (641) and Persia (642) set the stage for expeditions into Roman North Africa. Success in North Africa provided a staging ground for the army of Caliph Walid I (668-715; regn. 705-15), under the command of Tariq ibn Ziyad, to turn its attention toward Europe in the early years of the following century. Tariq led his forces into Hispania in 711.

The earliest account of the invasion was written in Latin by a Christian contemporary to the events – the *Chronicle of 754*.[5] The anonymous chronicler relates how King Rodrigo led into battle troops whose loyalties were divided (*Chronicle of 754*, §52); it seems that Tariq chose his moment very wisely, because civil war was preoccupying the king. Rodrigo died in battle, his army was routed, and by 718 a Muslim rule was established that would endure within the Iberian Peninsula for seven centuries, known now as al-Andalus (or Andalusia). A redoubt of Christian control in the north of the peninsula formed in 722 under the leadership of Pelayo, the first king of Asturias.[6] Pelayo's victory and the continuation of a Christian dynasty among the Asturians promoted a distinctive level of self-confidence that is reflected in the *Chronicle of Alfonso III*, in which there breathes the hope of driving the Muslims from the land. Fairly representative is the response attributed to Pelayo when the prince and bishop Oppa (who colluded with the occupying forces) urged him to reconciliation with the Muslims. In his rousing speech, Pelayo claims,

> Christ is our hope that through this little mountain, which you see, the well-being of Spain and the army of the Gothic people will be restored. I have faith that the promise of the Lord which was spoken through David will be fulfilled in us: 'I will visit their iniquities with the rod and their sins with scourges; but I will not remove my mercy from them' (Ps. 89:32-33).[7]

---

[5] See Cardelle de Hartmann (1999). For the relevance of these chronicles as against the idea that Western Christians were ignorant of the Christian east, see Christys (2002), 28-51; for a more broad-based treatment of Mozarabic interaction with the Christian east in later times, see also Millet-Gérard (1984), 153-81.

[6] *The Chronicle of Alfonso III*, §§8-11.

[7] *The Chronicle of Alfonso III*, §§9 (trans. Wolf (1990), 166-67).

Whilst Pelayo's pious hope that Christ would liberate the faithful might have been shared by Andalusian Christians, it would have been difficult from them to express such hope in the belligerent tones used by Asturian Christians.

For, apart from the Kingdom of the Asturians, Muslim governance was consolidated and Umayyad sovereignty extended northwards for several decades until checked by the victory of Charles Martel's Frankish army at the Battle of Tours-Poitiers in October, 732. The stability of Islamic rule over al-Andalus provided a serious disincentive for separatist tendencies amongst the Andalusian Christians. This is not to say that all Christians in al-Andalus kept their heads down and themselves to themselves. In about 850, a Christian priest named Perfectus harangued an assembly of Muslims in Arabic with allegations of the moral inferiority of Islamic law and denounced Islam, with the result that he was executed – or, in the eyes of Eulogius who relates the tale, he was martyred.[8] Eulogius seems also to have been somewhat familiar with Arabic, at least in passing, since after relating a popular reaction against Perfectus he quotes a pious Muslim expression (صلي لله علي النبى وسلم, which Eulogius transliterated as 'Zalla Allah Halla Anabi Ua Zallen' and translated as 'psallat Deus super eum et saluet eum!').[9] The second martyr – a monk named Isaac – is specifically noted for being *doctus lingua Arabica* and formerly a public administrator, which would have required of him a working knowledge of the Arabic language.[10] Isaac's voluntary death inspired a dozen more Christians to come forward who for a variety of reasons were put to death. Over a period of some six further years, nearly fifty Christians in Andalusia (including Eulogius himself)[11] were executed.

A recent study suggests that particular attention should be paid to the assertion that Perfectus and Isaac spoke Arabic: 'Both these men were clearly Arabicized, but being Arabicized was one thing: being an Arabicized Christian was clearly another.'[12] It is highly probable that

---

[8] Eulogius, *Memoriale Sanctorum* II.1.1-6 (ed. Gil (1973), II: 397-401). For a detailed study of the martyrs of Cordoba with reference to contemporary Umayyad policy, see Gutiérrez (1994).

[9] Eulogius, *op.cit.* II.1.3 (ed. Gil (1973), II: 399).

[10] Eulogius, *op.cit.* II.2 (ed. Gil (1973), II: 402).

[11] Paul Albar, *Life of Eulogius* 12-15 (ed. Gil (1973), I: 337-40).

[12] Hitchcock (2008), 30.

they were not alone amongst the Cordoban martyrs in this respect.[13] Even so, it seems entirely reasonable to suppose that linguistic boundaries and religious convictions should be positively correlated – at least, that is the distinct impression conveyed by the literature that comes down to us. Although there were non-Arabic speaking Muslims, and Arabic speaking Christians, in much of the contemporary sources their presence (it has been suggested) is seen to offend against an expected order according to which identity of language implies identity of religion.[14]

There is evidence that the Arabic enculturation of Christians living elsewhere in Muslim domains was hotly contested in the so-called *Apocalypse of Samuel of Kalamun*. Samuel (c. 597-c. 695) was a prominent Egyptian monk and stalwart opponent of Byzantine Christology.[15] Though the *Life of Samuel of Kalamun* is largely silent regarding the Arabic conquest of Egypt, the *Apocalypse* is not so reticent: it speaks out strongly against the abandonment of Coptic in favour of Arabic. The claim that resounds most is that, not only are Coptic parents teaching their children Arabic, one can hear Arabic spoken by priests and monks, and even in the sacred precincts.[16] The tone of the sermon attributed to the great monk – for such it is – inclines us to think of linguistic displacement as a special problem for communities bound by a shared religion. The loss of Coptic is not merely the passage of a language, but even more the passage of a way of life – a *Christian* way of life. In the *Apocalypse of Samuel,* the change in language is a token which signifies problems that are social, moral, cultural, and liturgical. Given its trenchant opposition to Arabic, it is ironic that the Coptic original was lost long since and the *Apocalypse* now survives only in Arabic translation.

The fact that only a translation survives makes it difficult to date the *Apocalypse* with any precision. It would therefore be imprudent to make much of it as a contemporaneous source to a Latin document from al-Andalus that can be dated securely to 854 – and so to the midst

---

[13] See Millet-Gérard (1984), 53-62.

[14] Hitchcock (2008), 36-37.

[15] See Alcock (1983).

[16] Ziader (1915-17), 391-92: 'Ils commettront encore une autre action, dont vos cœurs seraient contrits de douleur, si je vous le disais, à savoir ils abandonneront la belle langue copte dans laquelle le Saint-Esprit s'est souvent exprimé par la bouche de nos pères spirituels; ils apprendront à leur enfants, dès leur jeunesse, à parler la langue de l'hégire et ils s'en glorifieront. Même les prêtres et les moines oseront eux aussi parler l'arabe et s'en vanter et cela à l'intérieur du temple.'

of the period of martyrdom in Cordoba. However, the similarity of concern between the *Apocalypse* and Paul Albar's *Indiculus Luminosus* is provocative.[17] Albar's tone is apocalyptic, his polemic against Islam sustained: he regarded Arabic enculturation by Spanish Christians as apostasy foreshadowed in the Revelation of St John. Albar rails against circumcision, working within the offices of an Islamic state, adopting Arabic clothing and culture more generally – but famously he lambasts young Christians who ignored Latin and enthusiastically studied Arabic instead:

> What intelligent person, I ask, is found amongst our laity, who intently looks to the Holy Scriptures and volumes of the doctors [sc., of the church] written in Latin? Who keeps himself aflame with evangelical, with prophetic, with apostolic love? Or rather, don't young Christian men – with fine countenance, distinguished in locution, conspicuous for deportment and posture, outstanding in classical education – transported by Arabic eloquence grapple most avidly with the volumes of the Chaldees, read them most intensely, discuss them most ardently and, collecting them with great interest, promulgate them with praises rich and precise, whilst being ignorant of churchly beauty and contemptuous of the rivers of the church that flow from Paradise as though they were utterly vile? Woe is me! Christians do not know their law, Latins do not attend to their own language, so that of the whole assembly of Christ scarcely one is found in a thousand who is able to write short letters correctly to a brother...[18]

In this period, some Christians evidently looked to safeguard their linguistic integrity in order to articulate for themselves a distinct social identity as Latin-speaking Christians. But whatever the *Indiculus Luminosus* and the *Apocalypse of Samuel* claim about the desirability to retain a traditional language, the very fact of their existence indicates that the perspective they advance was by no means universal. Indeed, the strident tones suggest that their authors were fighting a rearguard action. The issue of linguistic and social enculturation in these cases appears to have been very divisive, because language and society were seen as markers of religious commitment in such a way that

---

[17] Paul Albar, *Indiculus Luminosus* (ed. Gil (1973), I: 270-315); see further Sage (1943), 28-31.

[18] Albar, *Indiculus Luminosus* 35 (ed. Gil (1973), I: 314); see further Millet-Gérard (1984), 49-53.

assimilation to Arabic culture could be construed as a betrayal of religious fidelity.

Hafs the Goth

By his own account, Hafs b. Albar al-Quti's translation of the Psalter was prepared in the midst of a controversy about the propriety of Christians using Arabic – the sort of debate, that is, to which Albar's *Indiculus Luminosus* contributed. We will come to Hafs' allusions to the arguments (preserved in the *urjûza*) in due course. But first it is appropriate to introduce the translator himself. In the mid-Nineteenth Century, Hafs was presented as a Jewish translator since his Arabic style was positively evaluated in the *Kitab al-Muhadarah wal-Mudhakarah* by Moses ibn Ezra (c. 1055-1135), a rabbi, poet and scholar.[19] However, in a seminal article that briefly treats the fascinating question of Hafs' recognition by eminent Spanish Jews of the Eleventh Century, A. Neubauer establishes that this is implausible: Hafs' *urjûza* is replete with unmistakably Christian vocabulary. (For instance, his initial presentation of the Psalter states, 'These psalms are sung in the churches (البيع) / the sweetest music that falls upon the ear…')[20] Neubauer was on less sure ground in asserting that Hafs was 'an Arabic or Syrian Christian', perhaps from 'Qut… in the province of Balkh'.[21] Rather, as D.M. Dunlop has argued, Hafs was Mozarabic and 'al-Quti' does not indicate his place of origin, but rather his ethnic background: it means 'the Goth'.[22] Going further, Dunlop even ventured the intriguing opinion that 'b. Albar', Hafs' patronymic, may indicate that he was the grandson of none other than Paul Albar.[23] This is tentative and it would not do to put too much weight on such an opinion, however learned, especially since Dunlop later acknowledged that he had misinterpreted the dating system used within the *urjûza*, leading him later to modify his opinion (and state it even more guardedly); ultimately, he favoured the view that Hafs may have been

---

[19] Steinschneider (1857), 101.

[20] Hafs, *urjûza*, line 17 (ed. Urvoy (1994), 15; trans. Dunlop (1954), 140).

[21] Neubauer (1895), 67 and 66 n. 3. More recent consideration of the diffusion of Hafs' translation amongst the Jews of medieval Spain will be found in Urvoy (1991), 273-274.

[22] Dunlop (1954), 148.

[23] Dunlop (1954), 149.

Paul Albar's son.[24] Little has been made subsequently of the suggestive possibility that it might have been Albar's own son who took great pains to render the Psalter into respectable Arabic, although Dunlop's reconstruction regarding Hafs' background has met with general acceptance.

Our best source of information for Hafs is the *urjûza*, scattered across which we find points of orientation and autobiographical references. An example has already been mentioned: the dating of the document. In line 128, Hafs says that he made his translation in the year 889 A.D. (or, just possibly, 989); there is a reference in lines 106-7 to an otherwise unknown Bishop 'Balans' (بالنس), which might corroborate the earlier date, if we take it to refer to Valentius of Cordoba, bishop from 862.[25] Other indications enable us to extrapolate Hafs' perspective on contemporary events in the Christian community of al-Andalus. Here, the contrast with Albar is intriguing. Albar lamented the abandonment of Latin in favour of Arabic, with reference not only to the spoken languages but more generally to the culture, which Albar regarded as something like a dereliction of religious duties. An initial difference is that Hafs presents in summary form a theory of translation, as it were, that validates the cultural importance of Arabic as the target language.[26] If there is for Hafs a danger in the appropriation by Christians of Arabic culture, it is not the 'contamination' of Christian identity that might emerge from using Arabic as a vehicle for Christian prayer (as it appears to have been for Albar); to the contrary, Hafs' translation is noted for its 'adoption of a strongly Islamized vocabulary.'[27] Rather, the danger appears to be more akin to cultural embarrassment at the incompetence of an earlier Arabic translation of the Psalter:

> He who previously translated it in prose / spoiled its poetry and its interpretation
> So that the style of speech became absurd / and the charm of versified arrangement left it.

---

[24] Dunlop (1955), 211-213; Koningsveld (1991), 697, cautiously endorses Dunlop's claim that Hafs may have been Paul Albar's son. I am not aware, however, if anyone has previously noted the incongruity between that putative relationship on the one hand and, on the other hand, Albar's hostility to Christian use of Arabic names alongside the fact that Hafs itself is an Arabic name.

[25] Additional support for the earlier date is given in Koningsveld (1973), 315.

[26] See further Schippers (1996).

[27] Urvoy (1994), XIX.

Since he wished to produce in Arabic / word for word – the action of
  one inexperienced

And self-opinionated – he ruined the meanings / through his ignorance of the laws of the language.

He saw himself obliged to transpose / the words, till he spoiled the
  interpretation.

What he translated was not understood / since its meaning was not
  translated,

And what was in the translation was not understood, / from the
  absurdity of the artificial meanings.[28]

It is known that translations of the Bible into Arabic prepared in
the east circulated amongst Mozarabic Christians, so the possibility that Hafs may have had access to them cannot be discounted
entirely (though his relationship to such versions is at present speculative and therefore a matter requiring further research).[29] More
economical is the assumption that Hafs was criticising a local
translation.

What is in any case clear from Hafs' own admission is that he
looked to St Jerome's Latin when preparing his own translation:

I have translated what Jerome (يرونم) interpreted / and he is given prec-
  edence for his learning –

The interpreter of the Law and the Gospel, / and they serve for text
  and commentary.

I have translated his words in verse form / in a correct translation,

Aiming at the meaning, without change / of the plain sense of the
  text and without alteration,

Translating letter for letter, / not interpreting it by changing it,

Without addition or subtraction, / except according to the need of
  the [Arabic] language.[30]

Comparative studies have revealed that Hafs did not in fact restrict
himself to a single text but in all likelihood availed himself of several
of St Jerome's Latin translations: points of comparison with the *Psalterium ex hebraico,* but also the *Psalterium Romanum* and the *Psalterium*

---

[28] Hafs, *urjûza* lines 28-34 (trans. Dunlop (1954), 140-141).

[29] Koningsveld (1977), 75-76 n. 245.

[30] Hafs, *urjûza* lines 63-68 (trans. Dunlop (1954), 142, slightly modified; ed. Urvoy
(1994), 17).

Romanum, have been evaluated.[31] But Hafs was evidently able to make critical use of other texts and commentaries, as comparison with a wider range of sources has demonstrated.[32]

Hafs makes clear his rationale for preparing a fluent translation of the Psalter into Arabic: 'These are', as we have already noted, 'psalms sung in the churches...

> / the sweetest music that falls upon the ear,
> More affecting that the song of the singing-women / and than the affecting strain of the cameleers,
> And than the complaint of the lute and reed-pipe / and than the different kinds of audition,
> Which melt the hard, unfeeling heart / and cause the praise-worthy tear to flow,
> To the number of a hundred and fifty songs, / as it is in every computation.[33]

The importance of attention to Arabic metrics is to allow the psalms to resonate fully when sung (presumably, liturgically) in the churches. The aesthetic quality of beautiful Arabic *ragaz* metre moves the audience, melting 'the hard, unfeeling heart' and causing 'the praise-worthy tear to flow'. Unlike the deficient earlier translation, Hafs' aims to elicit an emotional response that has spiritual value for the hearer. But he goes further. The earlier, defective translation was also problematical in that it did not promote understanding. By contrast, in his Psalter the believers will find 'instruction for them[selves] / and understanding of what was previously not understood'.[34] Hafs intends to promote not only feeling, but understanding as well. His translation will, he intends, be more readily understood. Precisely what its audience will understand is not a question Hafs addresses – but it is one taken up by the anonymous author (or authors) of the *Preface* attached to his work.

The Preface *to the Mozarabic Psalter*

In contrast to Hafs' *urjûza*, the *Preface* to his translation has been relatively neglected by scholars. Neubauer argued that it is unlikely to

---

[31] Urvoy (1994), p. V; Koningsveld (1972); id., (1977), 52-54; Schippers (1998).

[32] Monferrer Sala (2000).

[33] Hafs, *urjûza* lines 17-21 (trans. Dunlop (1954), 140; ed. Urvoy (1994), 15).

[34] Hafs, *urjûza* line 112 (trans. Dunlop (1954), 144; ed. Urvoy (1994), 19).

have been written by Hafs, on the basis that such an overtly Christian document probably could not have been an integral part of a work that received favourable comments from Jewish poets and rabbis; for the same reason, he presumed that the interpretative matter that appear before each Psalm (the 'titles') – which typically are strongly Messianic or Mariological in tone and content, and sometimes triumphantly anti-Jewish[35] – were the work of a later hand.[36] This observation seems to have been accepted and even advanced by scholars: the editor of the text, for instance, notes that the style of both the *Preface* and the titles is 'extremely heavy and the expression obscure', indicating their origins in a later period.[37] This lack of attention to the *Preface* is understandable amongst scholars whose primary interest in the Mozarabic Psalter is as a specimen of Christian Arabic poetry. However, since our interest lies in the evidence that the Psalter sheds on the cultural transformation by which (broadly speaking) culturally Latin Christians became culturally Arabic Christians, it would be sheer negligence to ignore these supporting features to Hafs' translation.

One difference between the *Preface* and Hafs' *urjûza* that can be identified immediately is the character of their respective messages. The *urjûza* is clearly a personal reflection on contemporary issues. Its historical interest is patent, since it presents the perspective of an articulate, sensitive and educated Mozarabic Christian. By contrast, the *Preface* is an anonymous, expansive argument for the overall importance of the Psalter for Christians under several headings. It will be convenient to survey those headings, but first a few other features of interest require our attention. A minor point worthy of notice is the global scope of the *Preface*'s vision: harking back, perhaps, to the account of Pentecost in Acts 2, the *Preface* registers the several peoples who use their own languages to pray to God (Greeks, Hebrews, Persians, Latins, Arabs, Syrians, Franks, Indians....) and asserts that the Psalter is the font of those prayers.[38] Although the Psalms are therefore presented as universal inheritance (a point expanded upon in the

---

[35] E.g., the title to Psalm 67: 'On the coming of Christ, the scattering of the Jews, and the joy of the blessed' (ed. Urvoy (1994), 107).

[36] Neubauer (1895), 68.

[37] Urvoy (1994), III.

[38] *Preface* to the Psalter, 'All peoples pray in psalms' (ed. Urvoy (1994), 3); N.B. these titles are not part of the original text, but since they provide the only breaks within the text, I cite them for convenience sake.

following sections of the *Preface*, where the history of the writing of the Psalms is related), it should not escape our notice that the balance of attention in that roster favours the East.

Given the *Preface*'s preponderant interest in Eastern peoples and languages, it is noteworthy that immediately following the opening invocation of the Holy Trinity it cites an opinion from 'Jerome the wise interpreter'[39] concerning the prophetic character of the Psalter as a document that announces Christ. In this matter, the *Preface* follows Hafs, whose *urjûza* as we have seen paid tribute to Jerome precisely as a translator and interpreter. But the *Preface* goes further by providing two more quotations attributed to Jerome.[40] After an excursus on the Bible itself (including the Apostle no less than the Psalter), the *Preface* goes further still as it launches into its theologically-informed endorsement of the Psalter with an extended citation from Augustine (أغشتين) on the moral benefits that accrue for one who 'recites the psalms day and night'.[41] The inclusion of this reference to the African saint, unprecedented by Hafs himself, widens the frame of theological reference for the *Preface* in a way that corresponds more satisfactorily to the range of earlier sources that continued to be studied and perpetuated by Mozarabic Christians.[42] For this reason, the *Preface* is a precious, if slight, witness to the ongoing relevance of Latin patristic sources for Arabic-speaking Christians in al-Andalus.

In much the same way, the *Preface* is a precious, if slight, witness to theological literacy amongst Andalusian Christians. With constant reference to the Psalter, the *Preface* asserts that Christ is the ultimate referent of the Psalter. Next, it introduces a theme that will be familiar from Hafs: the importance of interpretation. With abundant citations from 1 Cor 14, the *Prologue* repeatedly stresses that comprehension is necessary and, seizing the Apostle's references to many tongues (1 Cor 14:5) and to psalms (1 Cor 14:26), lays out principles for its case for understanding the Psalter. The Psalter is presented, as we have already noted, as a common heritage for Christians irrespective of their linguistic or cultural background. Moreover, the Psalter is a repository

[39] *Preface* (ed. Urvoy (1994), 1); this citation and the others, mentioned in what follows, have for the time being eluded my attempts at sourcing them, e.g. by using CLCLT-7.

[40] *Preface*, 'Believers should chant when praying' and 'Once more, on the conditions of the editing of the Psalter' (ed. Urvoy (1994), 8, 12).

[41] *Preface*, 'The virtues of the Psalter' (ed. Urvoy (1994), 6).

[42] See Millet-Gérard (1984), 67; on the possibility of Arabic Christians and their literature in the Maghreb, see also Dufourcq (1979), Prevost (2007), and Tabli (1990).

of knowledge both obvious and concealed – but for assistance there is available exegesis of the Psalter by learned men, 'in Greek and in Latin, in great books'.[43]

Significantly, this knowledge aims at moral improvement (rather than, say, esoteric speculation): it is here, shortly after the reference to learned Latin commentators, that the *Preface* cites St Augustine's opinions on the benefits that constant recitation of the Psalter conveys. The *Preface* elaborates on the moral beauties of the Psalter and in so doing picks up an earlier remark, made in passing, about the metrical beauty of its verse. The *Preface* presents the Psalter as compendium for spiritual reading: 'To recite the Psalter is to read the Gospel, the Torah, and the complete message of the sixteen prophets and twelve apostles…'[44] Not losing sight of its rationale as the introduction to a metric translation of the Psalms into Arabic, however, the *Preface* goes on to exhort the faithful to perform the Psalms by chanting them in an aesthetically pleasing way, without the accompaniment of instrumentation. Biblical precedents for singing to God are then adduced – the songs of Moses, Anna the mother of Samuel, and David are specifically mentioned – and instrumental accompaniment is interpreted allegorically (taking the lead from the second citation from Jerome) so as to reinforce the *Preface*'s stated preference for *a cappella* chant.

The *Preface* next reiterates the moral benefits of reciting the Psalms, this time pausing to consider that the consolations conferred by recitation of the Psalms are in fact evidence of the abiding presence of the Holy Spirit. Indeed, the *Preface* glosses the effects of chanting the Psalms as something like a continuation of the miracles that are described in the Psalm. Although supposing this goes further than the clear words themselves state, the engaged reader might think that this extension of the Psalms' miracles into the readers' lives indicates something of the depth of the readers' plunging into the text, so that their lives become thoroughly imbued with the Psalms and are transformed by them. Because the Psalter encompasses the scriptural message concerning the Messiah so comprehensively and because through the chanting of the Psalter the Holy Spirit comes to dwell in and among Christians, the *Preface* goes so far as to claim that 'Christianity, around

---

[43] *Preface*, 'The conditions of the editing of the Psalter' (ed. Urvoy (1994), 5) : في اللاطينية والرمية في أجزاء عظيمة.

[44] *Preface*, 'Panegyric on reading the Psalter' (ed. Urvoy (1994), 7).

the world, finds in the Psalter the foundation of its religion'.[45] After making this bold claim, the *Preface* reverts to an earlier theme (the composition of the Psalter), placing emphasis now on the involvement of the Holy Spirit in that process. These comments lead the *Preface* somewhat hurriedly to brief reflections on the conclusion of each book of the Psalms, and so to its own conclusion.

Without being overly specific, the *Preface* makes a case for the Psalter as a resource of enormous value for Christians. There is less emphasis in the *Preface* on understanding as such (rather than understanding the Psalter) than can be found in Hafs' *urjûza*, so that the *Preface* might be said to open fewer pathways for theological reflection rooted in the Psalms. The balance of interest in the *Preface* falls rather on the possibility of improving one's moral and spiritual life through encountering the Holy Spirit in the recitation of the Psalms. Perhaps it would be overly generous to construe this as theology applied, but in any case the clear indication that prayer (or, in this context, the praying of the Psalms in particular) is at its best an encounter with the living God is surely a theological claim that merits respect.

Conclusions

Andrew Louth's recent monograph on St John of Damascus, an eighth-century Greek-speaking theologian who lived under the jurisdiction of the Umayyad Caliphate, draws attention to a number of important factors of that saint's writings and legacy. Because John was safely removed from the reach of the emperor in Constantinople, he was able to dissent boldly and creatively from the imperial policy of iconoclasm (for which he is well-known in the Christian East). He was also able to attain a vast erudition which he synthesized into his *Fountainhead of Knowledge* or *De fide orthodoxa* (for which he is well-known in the Christian West), which places him again at a watershed – this time, chronological rather than political: John's compendium of orthodoxy, though it did not initiate a phase of eastern scholasticism, nevertheless marks a period during which theological consolidation becomes more prominent than the writing of creative theological works. In terms of culture, John's writings also stand at a crossroad. After his time, Arabic increasingly

---

[45] *Preface*, 'The Psalter is the foundation of religion' (ed. Urvoy (1994), 11).

displaces Greek as the theological language of Christians living in regions under Islamic control. These aspects of John's influence are easily appreciated, but Louth also draws attention to the relatively neglected influence of John's liturgical poetry,

> in which this harvest of patristic theology is turned into song and celebration. This is not a matter of mere poetical embellishment; rather, in this disciplined praise and confession, theology finds its most fundamental role, in interpreting, as it were, the return of the whole human being, both body and soul, to God, the beginning and the end, the alpha and omega.[46]

These appreciative remarks about sacred verse and its indispensability for theology are vital for understanding the Damascene as a complex figure and elucidating his importance for the history of Christianity. That it is deeply fitting for the beauty of God and God's handiwork to be praised and confessed through a form that is beautiful – through songs and poems – is, of course, no modern insight. It is intriguing to consider, then, John of Damascus' twin concern for truth and beauty since these concerns were shared by Hafs the Goth, who also lived under the jurisdiction of the Ummayad Caliphate, albeit a century or so later and in Western Europe. Hafs stands midway (so to speak) through a process that we have considered here, during the course of which attitudes toward Arabic culture within the Christian community of the Iberian Peninsula gradually developed.

Taking Paul Albar's *Indiculus Luminosus,* Hafs' *urjûza,* and the anonymous *Preface* to the Mozarabic Psalter as our points for comparison, we can observe important changes expressed in terms of Christian identity when Christians encountered Arabic culture. Albar's position implies that Arabic culture (including its language) is separated only with huge and difficult effort from Islam, which by implication is Arabic religion. Even as merely the language of daily transactions and high culture, Arabic poses a threat to Christian culture in the view of Albar, who therefore laments the steady decline of Romance culture – understood, unsurprisingly, as *Christian* culture. Albar does not make a distinction between faith and language and for that reason has enormous anxiety when confronted with the Arabic enculturation of Christian youth. Hafs, who might or might not have been Albar's son, certainly had a more nuanced

---

[46] Louth (2002), 288.

view of how religion and language relate. Hafs expressed no misgivings that Arabic was already being used to translate holy texts for Christian use, but objected seriously when he found their efforts entirely unsatisfactory. In his *urjûza,* he advanced a cultural and aesthetic argument for preparing a good Arabic translation (though he knew this to be still controversial). Hafs considered the Psalter an irreplaceable resource for Christian prayer and regarded understanding – the understanding of the Psalms themselves, but also it would seem understanding as promoted by the Psalter – as hugely important. Finally, when the *Preface* was written, the existence of Christian liturgical Arabic was already taken for granted. The basic argument of the *Preface* is for the importance of the Psalter as a foundation for the whole of Christian faith and moral praxis. The three different attitudes expressed in these documents appear to indicate that the extension of daily language (Arabic) into the Christian community of early medieval al-Andalus appears to have progressed much more quickly on the social level than on the religious level. Even so, it is reassuring to see that an appreciation of the need to worship with beauty and understanding eventually overrode the rather more sectarian impulse to maintain inviolate the purity of ethnic religion.

Bibliography

Alcock, A., ed. (1983), *The Life of Samuel of Kalamun by Isaac the Priest* (Warminster).

Cardelle de Hartmann, Carmen (1999), 'The Textual Transmission of the Mozarabic Chronicle of 754', *Early Medieval Europe* 8, 13–29.

Christys, Ann (2002), *Christians in al-Andalus (711-1000)* (London).

Dufourcq, Ch.-E. (1979), 'La coexistence des chrétiens et des musulmans dans Al-Andalus et dans le Maghrib du Xe siècle,' in *Occident et Orient au Xe siècle* (Paris), 209–24.

Dunlop, D.M. (1954), 'Hafs b. Albar – the last of the Goths?', *Journal of the Royal Asiatic Society* 1954, 137–51.

— (1955), 'Sobre Hafs ibn Albar al-Quti al-Qurtubi,' *Al-Andalus* 20, 211–13.

Gil, J., ed. (1973), *Corpus Scriptorum Muzarabicorum*, 2 vols (Madrid).

Goussen, Heinrich, ed., trans., and augmented Juan Pedro Monferrer Sala (1999), *La literatura árabe cristiana de los mozárabes* (Cordova).

Graf, Georg (1944-53), *Geschichte der christlichen arabischen Literatur*, 5 vols (Vatican).

Gutiérrez, Eva Lapiedra (1994), 'Los Mártires de Córdoba y la Política antic-ristiana contemporánea en Oriente,' *al-Qantara: Revista de estudios árabes* 15, 453–62.

Hitchcock, Richard (2008), *Mozarabs in Medieval and Early Modern Spain: Identities and Influences* (Aldershot).

Koningsveld, P. Sj. van (1977), *The Latin-Arabic glossary of the Leiden University Library: A contribution to the study of Mozarabic manuscripts and literature* (Leiden).

— (1991), 'La literatura cristiano-árabe de la España Medieval y el significado de la transmisión textual en árabe de la Collectio Conciliorum,' *Concilio III de Toledo: XIV Centenario. 589–1989* (Toledo), 695–710.

— (1973), 'New quotations from Hafs al-Quti's translation of the Psalms,' *Bibliotheca Orientalis* 30, 315.

— (1972), 'Psalm 150 of the Translation by Hafs ibn Albar al-Quti (fl. 889 A.D. [?]) in the Glossarium Latino-Arabicum of the Leyden University Library,' *Bibliotheca Orientalis* 29, 277–80.

Louth, Andrew (2007), *Greek East and the Latin West: The Church,* AD 681–1071 (Crestwood, NY).

— (2002), *St John Damascene. Tradition and Originality in Byzantine Tradition* (Oxford).

Millet-Gérard, Dominique (1984), *Chrétiennes mozarabes et culture islamique dans l'Espagne des VIIIᵉ–IXᵉ siècles* (Paris).

Monferrer Sala, Juan Pedro (2000), 'Salmo 11 en versión árabe versificada. Unas notas en torno a las fuentes de la traducción del Psalterio de Hafs b. Albar al-Quti,' *Miscelánea de estudios árabes y hebraicos,* sección Hebreo 49, 303–19.

Neubauer, A. (1895), 'Hafs al-Qouti,' *Revue des études juives* 30, 65–69.

Prevost, Virginie (2007), 'Les dernières communautés chrétiennes autoch-tones d'Afrique du Nord,' *Revue de l'histoire des religions* 224, 461–83.

Sage, Carleton M. (1943), *Paul Albar of Cordoba: Studies on his life and writings* (Washington, DC).

Schippers, Arie (1998), 'Hafs al-Quti's Psalms in Arabic *raǧaz* metre (9ᵗʰ Century): A discussion of translations from three Psalms (*Ps.* 50, 1 and 2),' in U. Vermeulen and J.M.F. van Reeth, eds., *Law, Christianity and Modernism in Islamic Society* (Leuven), 133–46.

—— (1996), 'Medieval Opinions on the Difficulty of Translating the Psalms: Some Remarks on Hafs al-Quti's Psalms in Arabic *rajaz* Metre,' in Janet Dyk *et al.*, eds., *Give Ear to My Words. Psalms and other Poetry in and around the Hebrew Bible* (Amsterdam), 219–26.

Steinschneider, Moritz, trans. by W. Spottiswoode (1857), *Jewish Literature from the Eighth to the Eighteenth Century* (London).

Tabli, Mohamed (1990), 'Le Christianisme maghrébin: De la conquête musulmane à sa disparition' in Michael Gervers and Ramzi Jibran Bikhazi, eds., *Conversion and continuity* (Toronto), 313–51.

Urvoy, Marie-Thérèse, ed. and trans. (1994), *Le Psaultier mozarabe de Hafs le Goth* (Toulouse).

___ (1991), 'La culture et la littérature arabe des Chrétiens d'al-Andalus,' *Bulletin de Littérature Ecclésiastique publié par l'Institut Catholique de Toulouse* 112, 259–75.

Wolf, K.B. (1990), *Conquerors and Chroniclers of Early Medieval Spain* (Liverpool).

Ziader, J. (1915–17), 'L'apocalypse de Samuel, supérieur de Deir-el-Qalamoun,' *Revue de l'Orient chrétien* 20, 374–404.

NORMAN RUSSELL

THE 'GODS' OF PSALM 81 (82) IN THE
HESYCHAST DEBATES

Psalm 81 (82 in the Hebrew numbering) was important in the early
Church for helping the Fathers articulate the place of human beings
in the divine economy. 'I said, you are gods, sons of the Most High,
all of you' (v. 6) was taken to indicate our coming to share in the
divine life through our being incorporated into Christ by baptism.
The implications of this teaching remained entirely uncontroversial
until the fourteenth century. It was then that the psalm came under
fresh scrutiny in the context of issues arising out of the hesychast controversy. Palamas took the scriptural designation of men as gods (*theoi*)
for granted as implying our potential for participation in the divine
energies through the contemplative life. His opponents understood
this divinity more as an eschatological reward for a life of virtue. These
different interpretations of *theoi* prompted the hesychasts to review the
patristic exegesis of the psalm and eventually reappropriate some of its
hitherto neglected features.

Patristic approaches to the 'gods'

The first Fathers to quote Psalm 81:6 relied on an already existing
Jewish exegesis.[1] In the Second Temple period the gods of the psalm
were identified with Adam and Eve, who were intended by God to
live for ever but fell and became subject to mortality. They also stood
for the Israelites in the Sinai desert who worshipped the golden calf
after the giving of the Law and likewise forfeited eternal life. In both
cases the Israelites came under the power of death through disobedience. Jesus himself, according to John, drew on this exegesis when he

[1] The fullest treatment of the topic is now Mosser (2005); see also my discussion
in Russell (2004), 71-6, 96-101, 105-10.

243

was accused of making himself God (Jn 10: 33-6). Jesus quotes Psalm 81:6 to draw the attention of his audience to their potential sonship and immortality. In the past the predecessors of his hearers 'to whom the word of God came' had died like men (as verse 7 went on to state) and now they themselves were in danger of doing the same for the same reason, the rejection of the word of God.

The earliest Fathers develop the Jewish exegesis independently of John's Gospel. Justin Martyr quotes Psalm 81:6 in the 160s in his *Dialogue with Trypho* to prove that it is the Christians, not the Jews, who are the gods and sons of the Most High addressed in the psalm because it is they who keep God's commandments and have therefore inherited the divine promises.[2] Writing a decade or so later, Irenaeus of Lyons goes one step further and connects the gods and sons of the psalm with the baptized.[3] The gods are those who have received the grace of adoption by which we cry 'Abba, Father!' (Rom 8:6). It is baptism that enables us to participate in incorruption and immortality, which are properly divine attributes. Irenaeus also connects the gods with the attainment of the divine likeness through moral progress. Building on this insight, Clement of Alexandria expands the reference of the word 'gods' in a number of ways that go well beyond its baptismal associations.[4] He does this by adapting the standard philosophical ascent to God to a Christian perspective – for does not Plato, he asks, say that a person who devotes himself to the contemplation of the Ideas will live as a god among men?[5] Thus by the end of the second century the word 'gods' can be applied not only to the baptized but also to those who have regained humanity's divine likeness by conquering the passions, attaining gnosis, and entering into the contemplation of God.

The later Fathers expand the meaning of 'gods' still further. The reference to the baptized always remains central. Christians are 'gods by adoption'; there is no innate divinity in them waiting to be brought out. They became gods in an equivocal sense through putting on Christ, who is God properly and unequivocally. 'For he is a true Son,' says Cyril of Alexandria, 'who has his existence from the Father, while we are sons who have been adopted out of his love for us, and are

---

[2] *Dialogue with Trypho* 123-4. Cf. Mosser (2005), 35-41; Russell (2004), 98-101.

[3] *Against Heresies* 3. 6. 1; 3. 19. 1; 38. 4. Cf. Mosser (2005), 41-54; Russell, (2004), 105-10

[4] Mosser (2005), 54-8; Russell (2004), 121-40.

[5] *Stromateis* 4. 155. Plato nowhere says this explicitly; Clement is summarizing the general tenor of Plato's thought.

recipients by grace of the text, "I have said, you are gods and all of you sons of the Most High".[6] Such gods are also 'gods by grace', which becomes a compendious expression applicable to those who have appropriated the fruits of baptism. By the fifth century the role of the Holy Spirit begins to be emphasized. It is through having God dwelling and abiding within us through the Spirit, 'not simply by grace because we are winging our way towards the glory that transcends us' that we are made 'partakers of the divine nature' (2 Pet 1:4) and are said to be born of God.[7]

The work of the Holy Spirit is brought to fulfilment in us through our participation in the Eucharist. The Eucharist, according to Cyril, restores us wholly to incorruption and fills us with the energy of the Word, 'through which all things are given life and maintained in being'.[8] Maximus the Confessor claims that through the Eucharist those who are gods by adoption through grace become such both in name and in reality 'because the whole of God fills them entirely and leaves no part of them empty of his presence'.[9] Gregory of Nazianzus sums up this approach succinctly when he says that the Christian priest is one who through the Eucharist 'will become a god and will make gods'.[10]

Alongside this sacramental approach the Fathers also speak of our becoming gods through participation in the divine attributes. This more philosophical approach was introduced by Origen, who distinguishes between a strong sense of the divine (that which is living, immortal and rational of itself) and a weak sense (that which participates in these attributes in a dependent manner). Human beings can become gods in the latter sense. The Son is also God in a dependent manner because he is subordinate to the Father. But he has a unique mediatory role. He communicates the attribute of divinity (i.e. life and immortality) to those who accept him as God. The 'gods' are therefore 'those to whom the word of God came' (Jn 10:35). By participating in God through the Son they cease to be ordinary human beings and ascend the scale of being from men to gods so that they come to share in the divine life. In Origen, unlike Clement, such participation in the divine attributes is the result of Christian discipleship rather than

---

[6] Cyril of Alexandria, *Comm. on John* 1. 9, 91c (on Jn 1:12) (ed. P. Pusey, i. 133).

[7] Cyril of Alexandria, *Comm. on John* 1. 9, 93d (on Jn 1:13) (ed. P. Pusey, i. 136-7).

[8] Cyril of Alexandria, *Comm. on John* 3. 6, 324e (on Jn 6:35) (ed. P. Pusey, i. 475-6).

[9] Maximus the Confessor, *Mystagogia* 21 (PG 91. 697A).

[10] Gregory of Nazianzus, *Oration* 2. 73 (ed. C. Moreschini, 56).

philosophical contemplation. Later writers, while correcting Origen's subordinationism in the light of later Christological orthodoxy, retain his fundamental approach. When Dionysius the Areopagite comes to consider the meaning of the Scriptural 'God of gods' (Deut 10:17) he interprets the 'gods' as those whose minds have become deiform or deisimilar because, reproducing in themselves the unity of the one God, they have become sharers in the imparticipable cause of unity.[11] For Maximus a god is one who lives with the life of God and thus comes to share in his attributes. The final state is one in which the human is interpenetrated by the divine. Maximus calls this the state of eternal well being, in which the soul is nourished by God in a way that grants it Godlike perfection: 'Then the infinite splendours inherent in this nourishment are revealed to the soul, and it becomes a god by participation in divine grace, ceasing from all activity of intellect and sense, and at the same time suspending all the natural operations of the body.'[12]

Here Maximus touches on the eschatological dimension of theosis. This is a dimension that has been present since the fourth century when Athanasius refers to human beings as gods to emphasize the glorious destiny originally intended for the human race but forfeited through the Fall.[13] Some Fathers prefer to see the gods solely in eschatological terms. The 'gods' for (Ps.-) Macarius, for example, are those who after the resurrection 'put on the heavenly dwelling not made by human hands, the glory of the divine light'.[14] For Maximus, too, becoming a god by deification is essentially an experience which belongs to the Eighth Day which, while it can be tasted in this life, belongs properly to the time when the intellect has transcended created things and has entered into the repose of God.[15]

In our patristic texts the word 'gods' is always applied to human beings in a relative, nominal or analogous sense. The Fathers were perfectly aware that whether considered as the baptized or as partakers in the divine attributes, the 'gods' were only divine in a manner of

---

[11] (Ps.-) Dionysius the Areopagite, *Divine Names* 2. 8, 645c; 2. 11, 649c; 12. 4, 972B (ed. B. Suchla, 132, 136, 226); Russell (2004), 259.

[12] Maximus the Confessor, *Chapters on Theology* 2. 88 (PG 91. 1165D-1168A); trans. G. E. H. Palmer, P. Sherrard and K. Ware, *The Philokalia, the Complete Text* (London and Boston, 1981) ii. 160.

[13] Athanasius the Great, *On the Incarnation* 4. 30-3 (ed. R. Thomson, 144).

[14] (Ps.-) Macarius, Collection II, *Homily* 34. 2 (ed. H. Dörries, E. Klostermann and M. Kroeger, 261).

[15] Maximus the Confessor, *Chapters on Theology* 1. 54 (PG 91. 1104AB).

speaking.[16] Yet initially on the authority of Psalm 81, and later independently of the psalm, they found reference to human beings as gods a useful shorthand expression for those who were either in the process of appropriating the divine life or else had entered definitively into its eschatological enjoyment.

Gregory Palamas's references to Psalm 81

Gregory Palamas is fully aware of the later patristic tradition on human beings as gods. He takes it as a datum accepted by his readers which ought to compel their acknowledgement of the energies: without the latter 'the deified would be gods even by nature'.[17] He rarely, however, quotes Psalm 81, perhaps because in his technical treatises bare reference to the psalm would not have established anything of value against his opponents. The way the Fathers draw on the psalm is more important to him than the fact that there is biblical support for calling human beings 'gods'. In the dialogue *Theophanes*, for example, he quotes Maximus, 'we all become gods but without identity of essence,' and (Ps.-) Athanasius, 'we become gods but not by nature' to enlist patristic support for the divine energies.[18] If we become gods, as the Fathers say, it is by participation in God's attributes or energies. The alternative is to say we share in his essence, which is Messalianism.

In this dialogue Palamas aligns himself with the philosophical approach to the 'gods' of Psalm 81. In a letter written shortly afterwards to one of his supporters, Athanasios of Cyzicus, he takes up the ascetical approach.[19] Athanasios has inquired whether Gregory Akindynos adopts the same position as Barlaam on the light of grace. Palamas responds with a short treatise on the hesychast reception of the divine light and how this is related to the experience of the apostles on Mount Tabor. Akindynos, he says, holds that the body of the Lord was a symbol of the divine light just as the dove that was seen at his baptism was a symbol of the Spirit. But Akindynos also claims that the light is a symbol, which would make the body of Christ, claims

---

[16] Gregory of Nazianzus, for example, uses *theoi* with five different senses in the course of his *Orations*. For a discussion see Russell (2004), 222-3.

[17] Gregory Palamas, *Triads* 3. 3. 8 (ed. J. Meyendorff, 709. 26-7).

[18] *Theophanes* 16 (ed. E. Perrella, 1276), quoting Maximus, *Letters* 1 (PG 91. 376AB) and (Ps.-) Athanasius, *Questions to Antiochus* (PG 28. 613D-616A).

[19] Sinkewicz (2002), 148, dates the letter to 1343-4.

Palamas, a symbol of a symbol.[20] Behind his argument lies a difference of opinion on the nature of symbols. For Palamas a symbol was not simply something which stood for something else. It could also be 'enhypostatic', actually conveying that which it symbolized.[21] The light of the Transfiguration experienced on Mount Tabor was such a symbol, for it was 'the brilliance of the divine nature, by which God communicates with the worthy'.[22] In support of his point he cites a passage from Gregory of Nazianzus' celebration of God as light: 'Light is also the brilliance of heaven to those who have been purified here, when the righteous shall shine forth as the sun, and God shall stand in the midst of gods (cf. Ps. 81:1).'[23] But he transposes Gregory's gods from the end of time to the present. Purificatory virtue makes us gods even in this life because it renders us receptive to the divine light and enables God to dwell within us through unceasing prayer.

The anti-Palamite response

Gregory Akindynos was outraged that the Palamites expected to become gods. Writing to an old friend in 1345, he recalls how Satan brought about Adam's fall precisely by holding out the hope of divinity and thus deprived him even of immortality: 'Just as the present apostles do, no less, to those who trust in them, both boasting that they have themselves become uncreated gods without beginning and promising that they will make such those who are obedient to them.'[24] Akindynos is protesting against Palamas's characterization of the worthy not only as 'gods' (*theoi*) but as 'wholly one with God' (*homotheoi*)[25] and even as 'without beginning' (*anarchoi*) and 'without end' (*ateleutoi*).[26] In a letter of the same period to Hyakinthos of Corinth he expresses his hope

---

[20] *To Athanasios of Cyzicus* 12 (ed. G. Mantzarides, N. Matsoukas and B. Pseutogkas, 2, 423. 17-33).

[21] Palamas *Triads* 3. 1. 18 (ed. J. Meyendorff, 591-2). For a discussion see Russell, (2006a), 367-8.

[22] *To Athanasios of Cyzicus* 13 (ed. G. Mantzarides, N. Matsoukas and B. Pseutogkas, 2, 424. 20-1).

[23] Gregory of Nazianzus, *Oration* 40:6 (ed. C. Moreschini, 926).

[24] Akindynos, *Letter to Tzakonopoulos* (ed. A. C. Hero, Letter 49. 49-52).

[25] Palamas, *Letter to Athanasios of Cyzicus* 33 (ed. G. Mantzarides, N. Matsoukas and B. Pseutogkas, 2, 443. 16).

[26] Palamas, *On Divine Energies* 37 (ed. E. Perella, 1036).

that for his unyielding opposition to Palamas he will be crowned by Christ 'when He will stand as "God in the midst of gods" (Ps 81:1) and distribute the prizes to each of his followers according to the degree of one's love for Him'.[27] For Akindynos the 'gods' of the psalm can only have an eschatological reference.

In his *Refutations* of Palamas's *Dialogue between an Orthodox and a Barlaamite*, Akindynos develops his opposition to Palamas's version of *theoi* in more detail. The Fathers teach us that nobody is a god by nature. So how does Palamas dare to describe as uncreated and uncircumscribed 'those who have become partakers not of the divine nature but of the energy which according to you [Palamas] is a secondary and lesser divinity?'[28] If these are 'uncreated' (*aktistoi*), 'without beginning' (*anarchoi*) and 'uncircumscribed' (*aperigraptoi*), the difference between Christ and ourselves is abolished. In spite of Palamas's denials, God is assimilated, in Akindynos's, view to those who are gods by adoption and grace. Or alternatively, his doctrine results in the multiplicity of those who are gods by nature.[29]

Akindynos returns to these points in an address he delivered before the Patriarch John Kalekas during the same period when he was the patriarch's chief theological adviser. He recognizes that in the Dionysian tradition of apophatic theology God is essentially beyond divinity. But

> even if we accept that he is called 'more than divine' (*hypertheon*),[30] that is not because he is superior (*hyperkeimenon*) to other uncreated and supraessential divinities or gods – for that is what the Hellenes [the Neoplatonists] say – but because he is superior to the gods about whom it is said: 'I said you are gods and all of you sons of the Most High' [Ps 81:6] and 'God stood in the congregation of gods, he judges in the midst of gods' [Ps 81:1] …[31]

The holy Fathers have handed down to us that these gods are not co-eternal with God 'whether one calls them "gods" or "divinities" or "graces" or "theoses" or "illuminations" or "works" and "energies" or "wisdom" or anything similar, but are rather all creatures created by God and perfected by him'.[32] Akindynos is right that Fathers such as

---

[27] Akindynos, *Letter to Hyakinthos of Corinth* (ed. A. C. Hero, Letter 67. 35-8).

[28] Akindynos, *Refutation* III. 76. 72-5 (ed. J. Nadal Cañellas, 284).

[29] Akindynos, *Refutation* III. 77 (ed. J. Nadal Cañellas, 284-5).

[30] Cf. Dionysius the Areopagite, *Divine Names* II. 3, 640B (ed. B. Suchla, 125).

[31] Akindynos, *Discourse before John Calecas* 24. 791-5 (ed. J. Nadal Cañellas, 277).

[32] Ibid., 798-802.

Athanasius, Gregory of Nazianzus and Cyril always emphasize that the 'gods' are gods in an analogous sense by adoption or grace. But there is another strand of tradition represented by Maximus the Confessor which Akindynos ignores. It is this strand that the Patriarch Philotheos Kokkinos draws on for his defence of Palamas.

The Palamite defence

Philotheos, who was *hegoumenos* of the Great Lavra and then metropolitan of Heraclea before becoming patriarch (briefly) in 1353, and again from 1364 to 1376 is the author of fourteen chapters against Akindynos and Barlaam and two treatises against Akindynos.[33] These have not yet been published. But in his *Antirrhetics Against Gregoras* he addresses the problem of how we are to think of the 'gods' of Psalm 81, whether as partakers of divine eternity, as Palamas taught, or merely as eschatological recipients of the reward for virtue as Akindynos and Gregoras held. Gregoras had protested in his own *Antirrhetics* at Palamas's claim that human beings by participating in the divine light can share in God's eternity and uncreatedness: 'Palamas both calls himself "without beginning" (*anarchos*) and promises to make those who want to study with him "without beginning" (*anarchous*).'[34] This Gregoras identifies as 'the root of his own evil', for Palamas 'maintains that those who live in virtue become unoriginate (*anarchous*) and at the same time uncreated (*aktistous*) human beings.'[35]

In his response Philotheos relies on Maximus the Confessor, particularly on the excerpts from his works quoted in the Tome of 1351.[36] Maximus teaches that theosis is uncreated; it describes the operation of divine grace, not the created effect in those who participate in it.[37] It therefore remains incomprehensible (*akatalēptos*), infinitely beyond the finite limitations of the human mind. The deifying grace of the Holy Spirit is an uncreated and natural property of God. In spite of

---

[33] For a discussion of Philotheos's life and writings see Russell (2009).

[34] *Antirrhetics* I. 3. 2. 4 (ed. H.-V. Beyer, 369. 11-12).

[35] Ibid., I. 3. 2. 6 (ed. H.-V. Beyer, 369. 21-2). Cf. Palamas, *Triads* III. 1. 31 (ed. J. Meyendorff, 617. 10, 617. 24).

[36] This was the Tome issued by the third Synod to exonerate Palamas of any taint of heresy (PG 151. 718-74). The author was Philotheos himself.

[37] Philotheos, *Logos* 10. 85 (ed. D. B. Kaimakis, 366); cf. Maximus, *To Thalassius* 61, scholion 18 (PG 90. 644D-645A).

human participation in it, it remains incomprehensible. Gregory Palamas is in harmony with Maximus. To confirm this Philotheos quotes a passage from the *Ambigua*: 'the man who has in all things become obedient to God, in accordance with the text, "I said, you are all gods" (Ps 81:6), is not a god, nor is he called such, in accordance with [the category of] nature or relation, but has become a god and is called such in accordance with [the category of] adoption and grace.'[38] Yet while a god only by adoption and grace, he is so thoroughly interpenetrated by God that he partakes of the divine attributes pertaining to eternity and infinity. His natural properties are overwhelmed by the superabundance of God's glory.

Renewed opposition

The opponents of Palamism continued to find this promotion of humanity to divine uncircumscription and uncreatedness unacceptable. In the late 1360s, during Philotheos's second patriarchate, Prochoros Kydones, an Athonite monk and brother of the famous statesman, Demetrios, wrote a treatise *On Essence and Energy* in which he sought to refute the premise on which such promotion was based, the division of God into participable and imparticipable elements.[39] In his discussion of the Taboric light he finds a light which is divine yet other than the essence of God an absurdity. A perceptible light can only be divine by analogy. Dionysius the Areopagite testifies that Scripture speaks of 'saints', 'kings', 'lords' and 'gods' as beings sharing in the attributes of one who far outstrips them as their unparticipated cause. Prochoros therefore infers that it is through a divinity utterly transcending their own that human beings can become gods and then only in a subordinate and partial sense. Things that share in the attributes of another must be inferior to the attributes themselves.[40]

---

[38] Maximus, *Ambiguum* 20 (PG 91. 1237A), quoted by Philotheos at *Logos* 10. 395 (ed. D. B. Kaimakis, 375).

[39] The treatise, in six books, has not yet been published in its entirety. Books I and II are in PG 151. 1191-1242 (where they are wrongly attributed to Gregory Akindynos); Book VI has been edited by M. Candal.

[40] Prochoros, *On Essence and Energy* VI. 10 (ed. M. Candal, 270-1). The passage Prochoros cites is from the *Divine Names* XII. 4 (ed. B. Suchla, 225-6). Prochoros's comments are quoted for censure in the *Synodal Tome* of 1368 (PG 151. 700AB). On his debates with the hesychasts, see further Russell (2006b).

Later in the same book, Prochoros returns to the scriptural designation of human beings as gods. These uses, he insists, are analogous and homonymous. If human beings are called 'gods' or 'divinities', this refers to the one divinity which is their causal principle. The light of Tabor may be called 'divinity' (*theotēs*) either as manifesting the archetypal divinity as if in an image, or as being the deifying power adapted to the limitations of the body.[41] For 'theosis is that movement by which we become gods, which is not in God but is in the subject, and in consequence is not uncreated.'[42] Prochoros can only see a deep gulf between created and uncreated, in the manner of Athanasius the Great, Gregory of Nazianzus, or Cyril of Alexandria. He has also been influenced by the Thomist texts he had been translating which emphasize that we can know God not directly but only by analogical reasoning. The Maximian vision of the created shot through with the uncreated in the Christian filled with the grace of theosis is quite alien to him.[43]

The Hesychast Response

Prochoros's views provoked a strong reaction. They were not only condemned by a Constantinopolitan synod in 1368 but also elicited two responses from leading hesychasts, one from the former emperor, John Cantacuzenos, now the monk Joasaph, the other from Theophanes, metropolitan of Nicaea. Cantacuzenos singles out Prochoros's discussion of the Dionysian reference to the 'gods' in sacred Scripture for special comment.[44] He points out that both angels and human beings are called gods at several points in Scripture, including verses 1 and 6 of Psalm 81. There is therefore nothing strange or novel about created gods.[45] According to theologians such as Gregory of Nyssa, the word 'god' can be applied to the divine or angelic or human hypostasis (that is, to the agent), and 'divinity' to energy (that is, to the action).[46] Therefore since 'the energy

[41] *Essence and Energy* 25 (ed. M. Candal, 285-6).

[42] Ibid. 27 (ed. M. Candal, 288. 2-4).

[43] Although Prochoros frequently cites (Ps.-) Dionysius, I have not come across any reference to Maximus the Confessor in his printed works.

[44] *Refutation* I. 40-44 (ed. E. Voordeckers and F. Tinnefeld, 56-65).

[45] Ibid., 41. 40-51 (ed. E. Voordeckers and F. Tinnefeld, 38-9). He also cites Ex 7:1.

[46] Cantacuzenos paraphrases Gregory of Nyssa's *To Ablabios*.

is an efficacious and essential movement of nature, and the angel or human being becoming a god is an acquired (*epiktētos*) grace, and since 'the divinity is an energy', it follows that 'the latter is a natural and essential movement and as such can deify the person who is experiencing deification'. The deified person is not just a god by analogy but really has been transformed by the divine energy, though of course he does not possess a natural divinity, for then he would be able to deify others, which is an impossibility.[47] Cantacuzenos concludes his discussion by offering the (originally Christological) image of red-hot iron – at the same time wholly iron and wholly fire – to convey how a person can be simultaneously both human and divine without any obliteration of his humanity.

The second response came a few years later from Theophanes of Nicaea. Theophanes takes a different approach from Cantacuzenos. Instead of working systematically through his opponent's text, he organizes his material around key questions raised by him.[48] One of these concerns the nature of participation in Christ: how was Judas admitted to the Last Supper but not to the Transfiguration if the former was the more intimate experience of participation? In his reply Theophanes develops the eucharistic significance of the Christian's designation as a god.

Judas was able to partake of the Last Supper because Christ gave of himself there only in symbolic form, whereas at the Transfiguration he unveiled his divinity to the direct gaze of the apostles. This does not imply that the eucharistic experience of Christ is in any way inferior to the hesychast vision of the divine light. Both forms of participation in Christ require the attaining of likeness to God so far as possible. In his first *Discourse* Theophanes says that it is this conforming of ourselves to the divine likeness that results, in Palamite terms, in our living with the power and energy of God (i.e. becoming *homodynamoi* and *homoenergeis* with him) and as a result becoming equal in glory with God (*homodoxoi*) and wholly one with him (*homotheoi*), we may even be said to become consubstantial (*homoousioi*) with God, which would be absurd if we partook of the divine essence rather than the energies.[49]

---

[47] *Refutation* I. 43. 5-11 (ed. E. Voordeckers and F. Tinnefeld, 60).

[48] Prochoros is not mentioned by name as the opponent, but he is clearly the person to whom Theophanes is responding. For an excellent discussion and analysis of Theophanes' *Discourses* see Polemis (1996).

[49] *Discourse* I. 525-30 (ed. Ch. Sotiropoulos, 189).

For this last statement Theophanes appeals to patristic support without specifying his authorities. What he means is that when we are raised to consubstantiality with Christ's deified humanity, we also share by the *communicatio idiomatum* in his humanized divinity. This is made explicit in the third *Discourse*, where (referring to Leo's *Tome*) he describes the theosis of human beings as a twofold partaking of Christ in virtue of his dual nature. By partaking of his deified body we become gods by grace 'and thus we are united to him according to both [natures]'.[50]

Theophanes is keen to emphasize that it is not simply the vision of the divine light that deifies the hesychast. It is the Christian life as a whole – faith, moral effort and participation in the Eucharist:

> It is not simply seeing the divine glory that makes blessed but first conforming to it and experiencing it, which is and is called theosis. It is impossible for anyone to participate in this without sincere faith and without first purifying himself by scrupulous observance of the commandments; for this is what it is to become sons of God, to put on the Lord Jesus as the body of Christ and as members individually, to be perfected as temples of God, dwelling places of the Spirit, and gods by grace.[51]

Theophanes unites contemplation with communion, the philosophical ascent to God with sacramental participation in Christ, bringing the hesychast idea of 'gods by grace' to full maturity.

Conclusions

As a result of these debates the 'gods' of Psalm 81 re-entered hesychast discourse enriched by their earlier baptismal associations, the philosophical aspect of the attainment of deification being strengthened by a reappropriation of the sacramental dimension. In formulating his arguments Gregory Palamas had developed to the furthest limit a line of thought first adumbrated by Origen – the attainment by rational creatures of a relative divinity through participating in that

---

[50] *Discourse* 3. 240-51 (ed. Ch. Sotiropoulos, 234-5).
[51] *Discourse* 5. 77-86 (ed. Ch. Sotiropoulos, 288-9).

which is divine in itself.[52] Like Origen, Palamas's emphasis is on participation, through contemplation, in the glory of God, that is to say, in the eternal rather than the incarnate Word.[53] This is to be achieved through sharing in the divine attributes understood as energies. Participation in the attributes/energies of *theotēs* (divinity), *anarchia* (causelessness), *ateleutotēs* (eternity), and *aktitikotēs* (uncreatedness) renders human beings correspondingly *theoi, anarchoi, ateleutoi* and *aktistoi*. This was not thought by Palamas to compromise our essential createdness and finitude because the fact that we possess them by participation means that our divinity, causelessness, eternity and uncreatedness are only relative. But his opponents could not see it that way. Theophanes' great merit lies in his looking again at the Palamite account of the ascent to God and rooting it in our relationship with the *incarnate* Christ. We attain divinity by putting on Christ in baptism and by receiving him in the Eucharist; it is only 'in Christ' through his deified humanity that we can participate in the divine energies and thus become 'gods by grace'. These reflections mark the retrieval of a tradition going back to the Church's earliest exegesis of Psalm 81 which by the fourteenth century, if not forgotten, had been largely obscured in the anxiety to give the energies a philosophical rationale.

Bibliography

Primary

Beyer, H.-V. (ed.), *Nikephoros Gregoras Antirrhetika* I, Wiener Byzantinistische Studien, 12 (Vienna, 1976).

Candal, M. (ed.), 'El libro VI de Prócoro Cidonio (sobre la luz taborica),' *OCP* 20 (1954), 247-96.

Dörries, H., E. Klostermann and M. Kroeger (eds.), *Die* 50 geistlichen Homilien des Makarios (Berlin, 1964).

Hero, A. C. (ed.), *Letters of Gregory Akindynos*, Corpus Fontium Historiae Byzantinae, 21 (Washington, 1983).

---

[52] On Origen's references to human beings as gods see Russell (2004), 144-7. This approach came to Palamas not directly from Origen, of course, but through (Ps.-) Dionysius and Maximus.

[53] Palamas's pastoral sermons do take account of the role of the Incarnation in our deification but, curiously, this aspect does not appear in the technical treatises; see Russell (2006a), 377-8.

Kaimakis, D. B. (ed.), *Philotheou Kokkinou Dogmatika Erga* I, Thessalonian Byzantine Writers, 3 (Thessaloniki, 1983).

Mantzarides, G., N. Matsoukas and B. Pseutogkas (eds.), *Grēgoriou tou Palama Syggrammata* (Thessaloniki, 1966).

Meyendorff, J. (ed.), *Grégoire Palamas, Défense des saints hésychastes* (Louvain, 1959).

Moreschini, C. (ed.), *Gregorio di Nazianzo, Tutte le Orazioni* (Milan, 2000).

Nadal Cañellas, J. (ed.), *Gregorii Acindyni Refutationes Duae*, Corpus Christianorum Series Graeca, 31 (Turnhout, 1995).

Nadal Cañellas, J. (ed.), 'Discurso ante Juan Kalekas,' in Giuseppe Carmelo Conticello and Vassa Conticello (eds.), *La théologie byzantine et sa tradition II* (Turnhout, 2002), 258-84.

Perella, E. (ed.), *Gregorio Palamas, Atto e luce divina: Scritti filosofici e teologici* (Milan, 2003).

Pusey, P. (ed.), *Cyrilli Archiepiscopi Alexandrini in D. Joannis Evangelium* (Oxford, 1872).

Sotiropoulos, Ch. (ed.), *Theophanous III episkopou Nikaias peri Thabōriou Phōtos logoi pente* (Athens, 1990).

Suchla, B. (ed.), *Corpus Dionysiacum I. Pseudo-Dionysius Areopagita De Divinis Nominibus* (Berlin, 1990).

Thomson, R. (ed.), *Athanasius*, Contra Gentes *and* De Incarnatione (Oxford, 1971).

Voordeckers, E. and F. Tinnefeld (eds.), *Iohannis Cantacuzeni Refutationes Duae Prochori Cydonii*, CCSG, 16 (Turnhout, 1987).

Secondary

Mosser, Carl (2005), 'The Earliest Patristic Interpretations of Psalm 82, Jewish Antecedents, and the Origin of Christian Deification,' *JTS* 56/1, 30-74.

Polemis, I. D. (1996), *Theophanes of Nicaea: His Life and Works*, Wiener Byzantinische Studien, 20 (Vienna).

Russell, Norman (2004), *The Doctrine of Deification in the Greek Patristic Tradition* (Oxford).

— (2006a), 'Theosis and Gregory Palamas: Continuity or Doctrinal Change?,' *St Vladimir's Seminary Quarterly* 50/4, 357-79.

— (2006b), 'Prochoros Cydones and the fourteenth-century understanding of Orthodoxy,' in Andrew Louth and Augustine Casiday (eds.), *Byzantine Orthodoxies* (Aldershot), 75-91.

— (2009), 'The Patriarch Philotheos Kokkinos and his Defence of Hesychasm,' in Eugenia Russell (ed.), *Spirituality in Late Byzantium* (Newcastle upon Tyne).

Sinkewicz, Robert E. (2002), 'Gregory Palamas,' in Giuseppe Carmelo Conticello and Vassa Conticello (eds.), *La théologie byzantine et sa tradition II* (Turnhout), 131-88.

CAROLINNE WHITE

ALLEGORY AND RHETORIC IN ERASMUS' EXPOSITIONS ON THE PSALMS

Scattered over the period between 1515 and 1536, the year of Erasmus' death, are eleven separate works of varying length, dedicated to different friends and patrons, in each of which Erasmus focused on the interpretation of a particular psalm. The eleven psalms which he chose, or was asked to comment on, are Psalms 1, 2, 3, 4, 15, 24, 29, 34, 39, 84, and 86 (according to the numbering of the English version), produced in the following order (with date of composition): 1 (1515), 2 (1522), 3 (1523), 4 (1525), 86 (1528), 23 (1529), 29 (1530), 34 (1531), 39 (1532), 84 (1533) and 15 (1536). Why did he choose to write about these psalms? Given that he started with the first four psalms, was his original intention to produce a complete set of commentaries on all the psalms? The commentary on Psalm 1, written as Erasmus was finishing off his version of the Latin New Testament, as well as an extended edition of the *Adagia* and his edition of Jerome, is in fact his first work of Scriptural exegesis: Erasmus says that he chose to write it as an appropriate gift for his friend Beatus Rhenanus, because the psalm starts with the word 'beatus' in the Latin version. 'And so I send you yourself, a *Beatus* for a Beatus. What else could be more fitting – especially as you are blessed with a nature not prone to faults and try hard to keep both life and reputation free from the stain of any fault?'[1] Seven years later, when he came to the end of the next commentary, on Psalm 2, he speaks of it being time to go on to the next psalm[2] as if he is planning to work through the psalter, and in the dedicatory letter to Psalm 4 he refers to his dedicatee's insistence that he should produce a commentary for the complete psalter.[3] But by 1528 when he broke the sequence and leaped forward to Psalm 85, any such plan seems to have been abandoned as

[1] Letter 327 (CWE 63:7)
[2] CWE 63:144
[3] CWE 63:174

an impossible task. In a letter of 1530[4] Erasmus says he was asked, even by the King of England, to write on all the psalms but he was put off by the need to be a good Hebrew scholar to undertake such a project, and by the fear that an excess of psalm commentaries would actually obscure the message of the psalms. From 1528, then, the choice of psalm was determined either by the dedicatee's request or by Erasmus' decision to select a psalm which he felt was particularly relevant to the contemporary situation.[5]

If Erasmus ever considered dealing with every psalm in the psalter, it would seem that such a plan was never more than tentative and inchoate. Such a supposition is supported by the fact that he gave different titles to each of the first four works, characterizing them respectively as *enarratio, commentarius, paraphrasis* and *concio*.[6] Although he was happy enough writing paraphrases – a form of interpretation that fell between a translation and a commentary – of the books of the New Testament during the years 1517 to 1524, when it came to applying the genre to a psalm, Erasmus decided it was unsuitable as being too restrictive;[7] he also rejected the term *commentarius* but returned to *concio* for Psalm 86, and *enarratio* for Psalms 15, 23, 29, 34, 39 and 84. Such different designations are an indication of Erasmus' varying, and seemingly inconsistent, attempts at finding a literary form that would enable him to bring out the meaning of the psalm most effectively. The variety of title also reflects varieties of form, though the form he devised cannot necessarily be guessed at from the title. Erasmus rejected the idea of a verse by verse treatment of Psalm 29, which turned out as an essay on the question of whether Christendom should go to war against the Turks; the works on Psalms 15 (*De puritate tabernaculi*) and 84 (*De sarcienda ecclesiae concordia*) also deal with a single, contemporary theme (namely the state of the church) while remaining more traditional in their commentary-like form, with the individual psalm verses strung like necklace beads along the thread of the dominant theme. It will not surprise us that the *enarratio triplex* of Psalm 23 involves a tripartite investigation of the historical, typological

---

[4] Letter 2315 (Allen VIII 433).

[5] See the dedicatory letter preceding each psalm in the CWE volumes 63-5. Only in the case of Psalm 34 did he express dissatisfaction: in Letter 2443 he says that 'few [psalms] seem to me more barren than this one' (quoted in CWE 64:268).

[6] see Baker-Smith in the Introduction to Erasmus' *Exposition of the Psalms* (CWE 63:xvi-xviii) for a discussion of these terms.

[7] CWE 63:152; cf. the dedicatory letter to Psalm 4 (CWE 63:174).

and tropological senses, but in the *enarratio* of Psalm 1 Erasmus concentrated on the tropological sense, but on the typological sense when discussing Psalm 2. This is a level of meaning which, he says, is 'almost inexhaustible in the Psalms'.[8] It is also, as he admits, the most difficult kind of interpretation: once the application to the Head has been established, by reference to other passages in Scripture but particularly to the Gospels, it is relatively easy to go on to apply the same words to the sinful and suffering members of Christ's body.

However, such differences of title and form should not prevent us from seeing the consistency, over a period of over twenty years, of Erasmus' intention in writing these works. Although each of them is a free-standing work, there are a number of themes that recur throughout this corpus. Moreover, all eleven works should be considered in the light of the concerns he discussed in the *Ratio seu Methodus compendio perveniendi ad veram theologiam* of 1519[9] and the *Ecclesiastes*[10], finally published after a long process in 1535: both these works develop ideas already put forward in the *Enchiridion* of 1503, ideas that recur also in his psalm commentaries. As for the various forms Erasmus adopts, they can be seen as based on different combinations – often at different points in the same work[11]– of elements of the commentary, sermon and essay, all of which reflect his desire to instruct, inspire and persuade his readers.[12] In this he reveals his conviction that the ancient rules of rhetoric were the perfect instrument for conveying the divine truth and transforming those who heard it. In this he also remains true to the main aim of so much of his writing: as Dominic Baker-Smith has written, 'the real motive of all his religious writings is to reanimate the forms of the church, to restore the prophetic vision which should drive them.'[13]

This was an aim about which Erasmus was indeed passionate, and the situation in Europe during the last twenty years of his life accorded it a particular urgency. It is against the background of

---

[8] CWE 63:145.

[9] LB V:75-138 to which references in this article are made; cf. also the edition of Holborn (1933).

[10] Latin text in ASD V 4-5.

[11] See Psalm 86 (CWE 64:13) where Erasmus writes that each psalm contains different elements e.g. of thanksgiving, glorification and prayer.

[12] 'ut doceat, ut delectet, ut flectat', writes Erasmus in *Ecclesiastes* II (ASD V 4:274) Cf. Cicero *De optimo genere oratorum* 1.3 and *Orator* 21.69.

[13] CWE 63:lx.

Erasmus' involvement with and changing attitude to Luther's increasingly radical suggestions as to how to deal with abuses in the Catholic church, as well as his engagement with the question of the political and military situation regarding the Turks who were threatening to fight their way through Vienna into Western Europe, that we should understand the way in which he interprets the Psalms. The issues that Luther and the Turks forced Erasmus to deal with and to set in the context of his wider beliefs about Christian society and the spiritual life of the individual, were primarily that of the relative importance for salvation of faith, grace and good works, the unity of the church, and the importance of peace. Underlying his reaction to the difficult theological and political issues of the 1520s and early 1530s is Erasmus' belief in the necessity of making moral improvements to Christian society. In his essay on Psalm 29, on the Turkish war, Erasmus laments the state of contemporary society at every level,

> 'How terribly far the shepherds of the church have fallen below their archetype! How completely ... ambition and avarice have corrupted us! ... for how many years have we seen foreign princes striving against one another with implacable hatred? ... what province is there now where the common people are not poor and miserably afflicted by an incredible shortage of every commodity? ... what age ever saw fraud, violence, rapine and imposture practised so freely?'[14]

Even when the Islamic threat receded as the Turks withdrew towards the end of 1529, Erasmus' desire for moral reform and peace in the church remained as strong as ever. In the last few years of his life he was to suffer much at the sight of the church being torn apart by the increasingly entrenched and mutually hostile views of Luther and the Catholics, between whom Erasmus was seen to be sitting on the fence, a position for which he was much vilified, although it was a position not so much of weakness as the manifestation of his view of Christian society and theology.

In any attempt to remove discord and sinfulness, a study of the Psalms, Erasmus believed, can be very effective. Firstly, the Psalms were 'the traditional expression of corporate prayer in the church' and 'also a basic element in the lay piety encouraged by the reformers'[15] and as such there was the hope that they could bring people with

---

[14] CWE 64:241
[15] Baker-Smith in CWE 63:xiii-xiv

different interests and allegiances together in harmony and a common purpose. Then, with regard to content, the Psalms 'express nothing trivial, nothing earthly' as Erasmus writes in his explanation of Psalm 86.[16] Like the rest of the Old Testament they are relevant to Christians, though they might need to be interpreted figuratively. The conviction that David points forward to the mysteries of Christ and his church means that the Psalms in a sense form a bond between the Old Testament and the New. Furthermore, the Psalms contain a large part of what the Christian needs to know: the first psalm alone contains a useful summary of what the life of a good Christian ought to be: 'it begins by offering a great reward, bliss; it appeals to everyone to shun vice and turn to the pursuit of virtue, and by obeying divine law to be renewed, to flower again in Christ, in whom they are already engrafted through baptism [and]… it reveals the happiness which awaits the pious in the Last Judgement and the punishment which awaits the impious.'[17] If Erasmus was convinced of the value of the Psalms for the Christian life, this was something which he and Luther were in agreement on. Luther had lectured on the Psalms in the years 1513 to 1515, developing his view of them as prophecies of Christ which, interpreted allegorically, encompass also the body of Christ, as represented by the church, as well as each individual Christian. In this they were developing a view of the Psalms already found in Scripture, in Christ's words at Luke 24:44 and in Peter's interpretation of Ps 16:8-11 as a prophecy of the risen Christ (Acts 2. 22-36). In the person of the incarnate Christ, so Luther and Erasmus believed (influenced by the theories of their contemporary, the French scholar Lèfevre d'Étaples), are brought together the material events of history as well as their spiritual purpose, with Christ acting as the key. As Erasmus puts it, 'each of us in his own way can be both David and Christ'[18]. To be sure, the whole of Scripture has a mystical meaning vital to the Christian life – does not Christ say, 'Look at the Scriptures in which you believe you have life'?[19] – but the Psalms are particularly suited to the human spiritual and moral condition because of the wide range of universal situations and feelings they deal with. What is needed in order to start such a personal transformation is an interpretation that brings out the mystical and spiritual sense. The role of the exegete is not so much

[16] CWE 64:13
[17] CWE 63.11-12
[18] CWE 64:17
[19] John 5:39, Erasmus on Psalm 34 (CWE 64:281)

to inform as to transform, by showing how the individual believer, at whatever level, can interact dynamically with the received body of divine teaching and to inspire others to engage in shared interpretative activity which will encourage cohesion within the church as well as encouraging each person to become more like Christ.

Both Luther and Erasmus had of course learned not only from their contemporaries but also, indeed primarily, from the patristic writers and in this context, particularly from those who wrote on the Psalms such as Origen, Hilary, Jerome, Augustine and Arnobius the younger.[20] In broad terms one might say that from Origen Erasmus derived the idea that was in various forms to dominate Scriptural interpretation down to the Enlightenment, of different senses of Scripture reflecting the different parts of man – body, soul and spirit, or just body and soul. Hilary, in his prologue to the tractates on the Psalms, expressed the idea that all the Psalms were prophetic of Christ and therefore of our resurrection. It was primarily from Jerome's dealings with Scripture that Erasmus learned to discuss the meanings of individual words where necessary, often with reference to the Greek Septuagint version and the Hebrew original. For example in his work on Psalm 4 he writes with reference to verse 7, 'There is no mention in the Hebrew of oil, which was added by the translators of the Septuagint and is retained by our church. I do not know where the idea came from but I certainly do not think that it should be rejected since the Septuagint has a traditional authority.'[21] But it was arguably from Augustine's *Enarrationes in Psalmos* that he took most. Like Augustine he reads the Psalms largely in the light of St. Paul, while also bringing in many references to the Gospels to reinforce the Christological interpretation which, both believe, lies at the centre of the Psalms. However, he does sometimes disagree with Augustine over particular passages, or indeed apply the whole psalm differently: for example, Augustine takes Psalm 3 to refer to Christ's passion and resurrection, while Erasmus takes this as his starting point but then applies the psalm to the limbs of Christ's body, taking the first verse, 'O Lord, how have my tormentors been multiplied!' to apply to the sufferings of himself and his fellow Christians, drawing the conclusion that all Christians must put all their trust in God (a recurring theme in these writings), not in their own resources or in anything worldly. With regard to Psalm 4

---

[20] In Letter 2315 (Allen VIII 432), mentioned above, Erasmus gives a brief summary of those who have written on the Psalms.

[21] CWE 63:207.

which Augustine famously wove into his text in Book 9 of the Confessions, Erasmus expresses doubt over whether Augustine gave the correct interpretation, but if he was wrong 'he erred as a beginner and erred happily, since this misconception led him on to better things'.[22]

To be sure, Erasmus' expositions on the Psalms are in some ways very different from those of his patristic predecessors. Most obviously they tend to be much longer: by far the shortest is the paraphrase on Psalm 3, being about 15 pages, the longest the *enarratio* on Psalm 86 which runs to about 100 pages, while most are roughly 50 pages long. This allows for more Scriptural allusions deemed to relate to the psalm in question, giving a dense Scriptural texture; it allows more detailed treatment of tricky passages and broader treatment of themes that Erasmus decides are particularly important, even to the point of lengthy digressions or rather of perfectly controlled and rhetorically adept developments of a particular idea: indeed, it is easy for the reader to lose track of which particular psalm verse Erasmus is discussing and in the case of Psalm 29 on the war with the Turks, it is easy to forget that the piece has any connection with a psalm! There is also space for references to classical literature and philosophy (often as a foil to the Christian position), for proverbs (many of which are also collected in the *Adagia*) as well as contemporary allusions, indeed for criticism of contemporary society. Like much of the best satire, such criticism is both psychologically perceptive and relevant to every age for it attacks or laments tendencies in human behaviour that are universal and not limited to a particular society. In the sermon on Psalm 4, for example, he asks,

'Now why do Christians, who profess the gospel truth, live lives of such vanity? We sail, we trade, we wage war, we make treaties (and break them again), we contract marriages, we have children, we write wills, we buy and sell land, we make friends, we build and knock down; we are tonsured, anointed, and take the cowl; we are schooled in the various arts or … we seek degrees in the two kinds of law or in theology … In the long years we spend on them we lose the single most precious thing of all, which cannot be regained. And now the day of death has dawned and we must go before that judgment-seat where truth alone, not vanity, will find a place – and then as if waking from a dream, we realize that it has all been an empty simulacrum of reality.'[23]

[22] CWE 63.265.
[23] CWE 63:243.

In the same work he uses a more specific example to make his point regarding the importance of placing one's trust in God, using a method characteristic of much satirical writing:

> 'To make money, a wine merchant knows a hundred ways of adulterating wine, and sells expensive poison to his neighbour instead of wine. When his conscience pricks him, he replies, 'I am forced to do it, otherwise I could not look after my family or satisfy my creditors.' What should be our answer to him? 'Good man, you have only to make the sacrifice of righteousness, and place your hopes in the Lord; make up your income by being thrifty; parsimony can be very profitable. Stop cheating your neighbour, help him rather, in time of need, and leave the rest to God. He will not abandon you, unless you have abandoned your trust in him.'[24]

Despite such differences in his treatment of the Psalms Erasmus has no qualms about using a method of interpretation which is so typical of patristic writers, namely allegory. The adoption of such a method was not a matter of simply following in the footsteps of his patristic heroes. Nor was it something to be taken for granted in Erasmus' day, despite the interest of contemporaries such as Luther and Lefevre d'Etaples: Erasmus writes that 'the theologians of the present day either practically despise allegory or treat it very coolly'.[25] Erasmus marks himself off from such people in his enthusiasm for allegory, which as we shall see, is an exegetical method that accurately mirrors his theological and philosophical beliefs.

With Erasmus as with each of his predecessors, the exact way he uses allegory is peculiar to him, and indeed varies from psalm to psalm. Erasmus is clearly aware of the fourfold scheme – of literal, allegorical, moral and anagogical senses – which had become the classic scheme, used by many of the scholastic exegetes. In Book 3 of his *Ecclesiastes*, for example, Erasmus shows how the traditional fourfold scheme is applied to the story of Abraham in Genesis 18, as a kind of textbook example,[26] and he frequently uses the terminology of this scheme. Erasmus would not have had a problem with the accepted definition of these senses but he did not think it right to stick rigidly to such a scheme or to feel it essential to force every verse to bear

---

[24] CWE 63:195.
[25] *Enchiridion* (CWE 66:69).
[26] *Ecclesiastes* III (ASD V 5:222-226).

either an historical or an allegorical sense.[27] When he himself refers to a fourfold scheme in his exposition of Psalm 23, he applies it in a different way for it soon becomes clear that here he is not keeping to an interpretation according to the literal, allegorical, moral and anagogical senses. Instead, he writes that the Scriptures

> 'may be applied to Christ as the head of the church, or to his mystical body the church, or to both together, or to each separately. It deals with each separately when the whole prophetic passage applies equally well to head and body and with both together when one part of the passage applies to Christ but cannot have reference to his body, while another will fit the body but cannot properly be spoken of the head.'[28]

Having made such distinctions he then goes on to say,

> 'There is also a distinction to be made in the use of the word 'church'. Sometimes this word signifies the whole gathering of those who profess the name of Christ. ... On other occasions 'church' means that uniquely loved bride ... in whom we believe by faith, whom we do not discern with our eyes. ... Again the word refers sometimes to the assembly now triumphant in heaven and sometimes to the assembly here, which is divided, being physically on earth but spiritually in heaven. On occasion a biblical passage may refer to both these entities jointly.'[29]

All these possibilities are really just variations on the typological form of allegory, in which what we find in the Old Testament is interpreted as relevant to Christ and Christians. One sees from this example that the important thing is for the exegete to be sensitive and flexible so as to bring out the true sense of a particular word, phrase, verse or passage.

With regard to what is usually referred to as the literal sense, the status of which was often a bone of contention among exegetes, one should distinguish between the historical sense and the 'literalistic' sense where what should be taken as figurative is interpreted literally[30], thereby obscuring the true message. Erasmus does not deny the importance of the historical sense and of establishing a basic text,

[27] CWE 63:144, 64:301; cf. *Ratio* (LB V:127).
[28] CWE 64:127.
[29] CWE 64:127.
[30] cf. Augustine, *De Doctrina Christiana* III 5.

for 'how can you understand an idea unless you know exactly what the words mean?'[31]. Like Augustine and Jerome he will often discuss the meaning of a particular word. He believed, too, that the literal sense is as it were the foundation supporting the mystical sense[32] and he was wary of over-fanciful allegorical interpretations such as those he sometimes detects in the work of Origen or Ambrose[33]. However he felt that more recent scholars such as Nicholas of Lyra had thrown out the baby with the bath water in their determination to keep to the literal sense. Erasmus disapproves of such an emphasis as much as he does of the recitation of large numbers of psalms which was the practice in the monasteries of his time, as a superficial and almost meaningless liturgical task, for neither allow for spiritual development. As he writes in the *Enchiridion*,

> 'let this rule ever be in readiness, that we do not linger over temporal matters ... but rise up to the love of spiritual things. ... The same rule applies for all spiritual works which are made up of a literal sense and a mysterious sense ... The writings of all the poets and the Platonist philosophers belong to this category but especially the sacred Scriptures which like those images of Silenus enclose unadulterated divinity under a ludicrous appearance. Therefore you must reject the carnal aspect of the Scriptures and ferret out the spiritual sense.'[34]

Here we see an essential element of Erasmus's Scriptural interpretation, namely the division between literal and spiritual, reflecting the dichotomy between the material and the spiritual, between body and soul – a dichotomy on which Erasmus' anthropology and sacramental thought are based.[35] The implication of such a dichotomy is, so Erasmus believes as a keen Platonist, that humans must move away from the world of the senses, from what is mere outward form, as for example liturgical ritual can easily become, to the truth and beauty that lies hidden. In general terms he had of course learned not only from the exegetical examples of the Fathers but also from such works as Augustine's *De Doctrina Christiana* as to the value of allegory not only for interpreting passages of Scripture that did not on the face of

---

[31] CWE 63:47.
[32] CWE 64:19.
[33] *Ecclesiastes* III (ASD V 5:230).
[34] *Enchiridion* (CWE 66:67-9).
[35] Grant (1969), 17-23.

it make much sense, but also, more positively, for bringing out a sense compatible with Christian truth. Erasmus seems to have absorbed into his method of interpretation not only much of what he learnt from the Fathers, but also, by way of the earlier Humanists, elements from Ciceronian rhetoric and from Stoic and Platonist philosophy.[36] From the rhetoricians he learned how to recognize allegory, how to apply ethical criticism to texts, how to compare a passage to other contexts and how to convey truth effectively in order to bring about moral transformation, while the philosophies strengthened his belief in the value of allegory for the discovery of spiritual truth which brings us closer to God. But if Erasmus learned certain things about rhetoric and some aspects of ancient philosophy from the Italian humanists and from John Colet, these were ingredients, too, in patristic exegesis. Indeed, already in the *Enchiridion* Erasmus had said that two of the reasons why the Fathers are better than the scholastic writers on Scripture are their eloquence and their Platonism.[37]

For Erasmus allegorical interpretation is not principally a means of twisting the apparent meaning of Scripture to give a more acceptable sense to apparently absurd or shocking passages or to passages that conflict with what the reader wants to believe, which is how it is often regarded by modern critics. Erasmus believed on the one hand that divine wisdom uses allegory to veil the truth, thus preserving its mystery (a factor that is very important to Erasmus) while on the other, the fact that Scripture is regarded as full of allegory also shows that God wishes us to seek a hidden meaning under the layers of metaphor. In the New Testament Christ challenges his listeners by using parables in the Gospels, but even more effort is required of the reader of the Old Testament in order to find a meaning that is relevant to Christ. Erasmus believed strongly that Scripture must be made to penetrate the feelings of each individual and not just remain in the intellect. As he writes in the *Ratio*, the principal aim of anyone who reads Scripture must be to be changed, carried away and transformed.[38] But the preacher or exegete is usually needed to help the reader to achieve this. It is on this point, he feels, that contemporary church leaders fail: they neither practice what they preach nor do they help their flocks to digest their food – Erasmus provides a lengthy exposition on this

---

[36] Hoffmann (1994), 25-7.
[37] *Enchiridion* (CWE 66:69).
[38] *Ratio* (LB V:77)

subject in dealing with Psalm 23, using the theme of shepherd and flock to discuss the way church leaders should spiritually nurture their congregation.[39] Exegesis is not a matter of coming up with clever displays of human reason and intricate arguments, intended to dazzle a few other brilliant minds or providing answers to frivolous questions but a process that can work for the salvation of many, a process that is dependent on an appreciation of allegory for its success. The effective exegete needs moral goodness[40] and an understanding of allegory as a nutcracker to extract the nutritious and tasty kernel. This is an image used several times by Erasmus, also in his writings on the Psalms as for example in his work on Psalm 1:

> 'Anyone who gets no further than the outer shell of the law is not 'meditating on the law of the Lord.' An outer shell is usually tasteless and, far from being nourishing, it can be poisonous ... You must therefore nibble away until you reach the centre, where at last you will discover true nourishment for the soul; eat and you shall be transfigured into the image of Christ'[41]

and on Psalm 4:

> 'In order to enjoy the kernel of a nut, you do not begrudge the small effort involved in removing the hard shell and bitter rind; you should not therefore be reluctant to concentrate your thoughts for a while in order to feed them with the wholesome and delicious nourishment which this psalm offers you.'[42]

Although much of the time Erasmus' allegorical interpretations extend over many pages, one can find the occasional succinct example. With regard to the image of the tree in Ps.1:3 he refers this to pious people who 'are watered by the secret gifts of divine grace, grow strong in purity, produce buds by their delight in charity, flower in anticipation of their good deeds and finally bear fruit, to the glory of God and for the salvation of their fellow man ... and enjoy the fruits of their good

---

[39] CWE 64:186-7.

[40] *Ratio* (LB V:76), cf. *Enchiridion* (CWE 66:34).

[41] CWE 63:30.

[42] CWE 63:175; this was a popular image among patristic and reformation exegetes used by e.g. Jerome in Ep.58.9, 'Everything that we read in Holy Scripture has a bright, attractive outer layer but the inside is sweeter. Anyone who wants to enjoy the kernel must crack open the nut'.

works.'[43] At the beginning of his work on Psalm 4 Erasmus writes with reference to the idea of music suggested by the psalm's title,

'We should realize that our music is sweetest to God when every part of our lives is in harmony with the commandments, when our words are in tune with our lives, when the mellifluous chorus of brotherly concord is not marred by the discords of conflict, ... when a plangent lyre bewails our misdeeds, when we give thanks with the clash of cymbals and the trumpet boldly sounds the gospel message.'[44]

But the most sustained and coherent use of a single theme for allegorical interpretation is found in his work on Psalm 23. As so often in his work on the Psalms Erasmus has no difficulty giving the psalm a sense that applies to the life of the individual Christian. This sense he summarizes thus:

'The first requirement of salvation is that we should be sheep, that is to say, simple and tractable, and that we should recognize our shepherd Jesus and permit ourselves to be pastured by him. Then we must let him lead us into the pastures of the church where the forgiveness of sins gives the soul peace and rest, and soon we are led by a more abundant knowledge of the Scriptures ... to the waters which refresh our spirits and add strength to our faith and love.'[45]

But he also applies the whole psalm to Christ, putting a paraphrase of the psalm into his mouth which matches each verse to aspects of Christ's redemptive work among men and the support given by the Father,[46] supplementing the psalm references with relevant references to the Gospels. Speaking for the most part as Christ, he writes,

'The Lord directs me and it is by his authority that I take on this role, by his protection that I remain undefeated, and by his power that all the prophecies regarding me have been fulfilled. 'He has placed me in fields of pasture': this pasture is the church, to which Christ was sent to perform the redemption of the human race. He continues: When my soul was sorrowful unto death, he sent his angels to restore it with solace from heaven. When I hungered and thirsted after men's

---

[43] CWE 63:42.
[44] CWE 63:176.
[45] CWE 64:198.
[46] CWE 64:128-9.

salvation, he looked on with favour and refreshed my soul, granting that through my teaching and death all my people should have that for which I so desperately hungered and thirsted. For this was the thirst that tormented me when I was weary at the well and said to the woman of Samaria, 'Give me water to drink'; this was the thirst that made me cry out on the cross, 'I thirst'. These waters alone, where my Father gave me to drink, could cool that burning thirst. Then my Father was appeased and overturned the walls, opening heaven to those who believe in me and 'turned my soul' from the grief of the cross to rejoicing for those redeemed through the cross. When he had refreshed me with this hope, he led me by the paths of righteousness as I alone can walk the narrow path of the gospel's righteousness without straying. ... I lived among the dead, for sin is death and I went willingly to death on the cross. My soul descended into hell, ... the pains of death surrounded me, yet by my death I conquered death.'

If allegory is a form of metaphor whereby different things are brought together and one is interpreted in terms of the other,[47] there is also another rhetorical trope associated with metaphor that Erasmus frequently mentions, namely accommodation[48] (also referred to by the term synecdoche)[49] whereby words or ideas are adapted to make them more fitting or comprehensible to the reader. Accommodation is used in dealing with the text to decide to whom the words of a particular passage apply or who is speaking them: this is a rather more complex form of the accommodation of classical rhetoric which aimed at fitting the proper language to the matter or person. In Erasmus these rhetorical methods are reflected on a theological level: does not divine wisdom accommodate itself to the human condition by, for example, speaking in human terms even of God? As he writes in his exposition of Psalm 34, 'The word was made flesh for us: are we surprised that the Holy Spirit tailors his discourse to human understanding?'[50] Often Erasmus, following Origen, speaks of God using baby language to communicate with us: in the explanation of Psalm 86 he writes with reference to the opening verse 'Incline your ear, O Lord, and listen to me, for I am poor and needy' that we must not think of God really inclining his ear – rather, 'Scripture, by lisping indistinctly

---

[47] *Rhetorica ad Herennium* IV 34.46.
[48] *Ratio* (LB V:85); *Rhetorica ad Herennium* I 2.3.
[49] CWE 63:111; cf. *Rhetorica ad Herennium* IV 33.44-5.
[50] Psalm 34 (CWE 64:313), cf. Psalm 2 (CWE 63:102).

with the words of men so that it may be understood in a less forbidding way, accommodates itself to human weakness, like a nurse or a mother using baby language.'[51] 'Divine wisdom speaks to us in baby talk. … It lowers itself to your lowliness but you on your part must rise to its sublimity.'[52] Despite the gulf separating God and man, God accommodates the spirit to the flesh. By means of accommodation he lowers himself to man in the Incarnation, bringing out the similarities and enabling man to rise up and become similar to God. Here Christian and Platonic ideas are combined. In a parallel manner, allegory draws the reader in, encouraging him to penetrate the text in his attempt to understand what is said and this in turn allows the text to penetrate the reader and transform him.[53]

Another rhetorical trope related to allegory and metaphor is the comparison of a large number of texts taken from all over the Scriptures to reinforce the message of the original psalm passage. For example, in writing about Psalm 4 Erasmus takes the phrase 'they have been multiplied by the ripening of their [or 'his'] corn, their wine and their oil' in verse 7 as the starting point for an impressive and lengthy series of comparisons of this verse with other Scriptural passages involving corn or bread, wine and oil which can be interpreted allegorically to apply to many different aspects of the life of the Christian. He takes the phrase to apply firstly to spiritual regeneration through Christ which allows us to reach the stage 'when our minds are strengthened by the bread of sounder doctrine and our hearts are gladdened by the wine of love'[54]. Then alluding to the words from Ps 104:15, 'wine gladdens the heart and oil makes the face shine', he writes that the strength of this wine ensures that in the midst of suffering the mind exults with spiritual joy and the oil ensures that however burdened with cares we may be, we are still affable towards our fellow men. Meanwhile, the Jews, says Erasmus, go hungry; they spit out the grain of gospel teaching and drink the stagnant water of the letter. But the bread of the Christians, better far than manna, comes down from heaven to give us immortality. He goes on to allude to many other Scriptural passages to contrast those Christians who are strengthened by Christ's spiritual wine, with those who eat nothing but the empty husks of ritual and drink

[51] CWE 64:20-1.
[52] *Enchiridion* (CWE 66:35); cf. also *Ratio* (LB V:124).
[53] Hoffmann (1994), 112, Chomarat (1981), I 690.
[54] CWE 63:266.

the water of the letter. Erasmus then extends the relevance of the psalm verse to take in the bread and wine of the sacraments which unite us in one body, thereby introducing briefly one of his favourite themes, that of the unity of the church, before bringing this long section devoted to half a verse to a close, skillfully moving on to the next verse with the exhortation,

'If you truly eat the bread of sacred doctrine, truly drink of the wine which the divine wisdom has pressed for us, and are truly anointed with the oil of spiritual joy; if you promote harmony in the church, working evil against no man, rejoicing in the success of the good and ignoring the insults of the wicked, then you will be able to say, 'I shall sleep in peace and take my rest in it.'[55]

Here Erasmus produces an exegetical and rhetorical tour de force somewhat reminiscent of Jerome's Letter 22 to Eustochium on the subject of virginity, with its similarly dense and wide-ranging use of Scriptural passages; but whereas Jerome plucks together large numbers of quotations which he considers relevant to a particular theme, Erasmus brings together quotations verbally related to the original verse but bearing a wide variety of theological meanings.

What is striking as he discourses on the *philosophia Christi* in his writings on the Psalms is that he chooses to concentrate on the Christological and the tropological senses of allegory. But what happens to the dichotomy at the heart of Erasmus' thought if, when it comes to his interpretation of the Psalms, we most often find not just two senses, the literal and the spiritual reflecting body and soul, but three? For Erasmus divides the spiritual sense in two to give the typological or prophetic which interprets the psalm as relevant to Christ, and the tropological or moral which applies it to the members of Christ's body. That Erasmus does think in terms of these three senses (historical, typological and tropological) is very clear from an allusion to Psalm 144 made in the commentary on Psalm 2. Erasmus describes the psalm thus,

'There can be no doubt that this psalm is a song of praise to God with whose aid David ... struck down with his slingshot that boastful giant Goliath and cut off his head with his own sword. But this

[55] CWE 63:270.

historical sense does not in any way obstruct the allegorical; on the contrary it ensures that the rays of mystical knowledge, as if caught in a mirror, shine all the more brightly and clearly before our mind's eye. ... You will surely see ... how Christ, our David, overthrew the boastful prince of this world and his uncircumcised people with him, not with the weapons of this world but by a new method. ... After feasting our eyes on this divine spectacle we turn them inward and realize that we must follow his example and fight against the passions of this world, which struggle in our bodies against God's law.'[56]

So why two allegorical senses, or two aspects to the spiritual sense? Allegory may be seen as providing a bridge between the literal and the spiritual, just as Christ provides a bridge between the human and the divine but why should there be a need for two aspects to the allegory? One reason may be that it allows the psalm to reflect both aspects of the aim of the life of a Christian, namely Christ's glory and man's salvation.[57] The Christian needs to see Christ everywhere in the Scriptures and to learn about Christ who is both the source of his salvation, through the passion and resurrection, and should also be the model for his attitudes and behaviour. The Psalms, like the Gospels and the Pauline Epistles, can teach us about Christ and what he means for our lives and our salvation. It is as if, while working on his Paraphrases on the books of the New Testament, Erasmus came to see the Psalms as providing the opportunity for further understanding and as offering plenty of material in support of his most deeply held beliefs. It is perhaps significant, too, that the tropological and typological forms of allegory can be linked to the two criteria used by Augustine when deciding whether a text should be interpreted figuratively i.e. anything that cannot be related either to good morals or to the true faith should be accorded a figurative explanation.[58]

However, the two aspects of allegory, the Christological and moral, so prominent in Erasmus' work on the Psalms, may perhaps be regarded not as two separate senses but as in fact forming a single sense. Is it not the case that the two aspects are inextricably linked in the doctrine of the Body of Christ where Head and Body (whether

---

[56] CWE 63:78-9.

[57] *Enchiridion* (CWE 66:10).

[58] Augustine, *De Doctrina Christiana* III 10.

representing the corporate Church or the individual Christian) are themselves inextricably linked? Erasmus usually only deals with the moral sense once he has established the historical (if only to dismiss it) and the Christological senses, and the moral sense itself always brings the reader back to Christ as the model and the anchor. The two senses also combine in the fact that only by attempting to imitate Christ in the performance of acts of love can the Christian attain the moral purity which will allow him to gain an increasingly clear understanding of Scripture and its hidden meanings regarding the nature of the divine. Such an understanding will allow him to see that the only true happiness for a Christian lies in total commitment to Christ, a realization that will transform his life in every way, thereby bringing about the gradual transformation of society, both that of this world and the next.

Taking all Erasmus' individual works on the Psalms together one sees how, by choosing different literary forms to express what he wanted to say about the Psalms, Erasmus shows what his main concerns are. His choice of the *concio* points to his belief in the usefulness of rhetoric for analyzing the text, conveying the truth and affecting the listener. The choice of the paraphrase indicates that he felt that the Psalms could offer similar truths to those of the New Testament, whose books Erasmus had treated as paraphrases. The choice of *commentarius* for one psalm reveals Erasmus attracted to a form which was useful for the clear expression of philological and theological facts. The form that turned out to be his favourite in elucidating the Psalms, the *enarratio*, combined elements of the sermon and the commentary, allowing the author to focus on the text while also keeping in his sights the spiritual transformation of his audience.

Abbreviations used

Allen Opus Epistolarum Desiderii Erasmi Roterodami ed. P.S. Allen, H.M. Allen and H.W. Garrod (Oxford 1906-58)

ASD Opera Omnia Desiderii Erasmi Roterodami (North-Holland Publishing Company, Amsterdam 1969-)

CWE Collected Works of Erasmus (University of Toronto Press, Toronto 1974-)

LB Desiderii Erasmi Roterodami opera omnia ed. J. Leclerc (Leiden 1703-6)

Bibliography

Chantraine, G. (1971) *Mystère et philosophie du Christ selon Érasme* (Namur).

Chomarat, Jacques (1981), Grammaire et rhétorique chez Érasme (Paris).

Grant, J.B. (1969), *The Hermeneutics of Erasmus*, in J. Coppens (ed.) Scrinium Erasmianum (Leiden), vol. II 13-49.

Hoffmann, M. (1994) *Rhetoric and Theology: the hermeneutic of Erasmus*, (Toronto).

Holborn, H. and A.-M., (1933) Desiderius Erasmus Roterodamus, Ausgewählte Werke (Munich).

Pollet, J.V. (1969) Origine et structure du De Sarcienda Ecclesiae Concordia (1533) d'Érasme, in J. Coppens (ed.) Scrinium Erasmianum (Leiden), vol. II 183-95.

DIMITRI CONOMOS

ELDER AIMILIANOS ON THE PSALTER AND THE REVIVAL OF MELODIOUS PSALMODY AT SIMONOPETRA[1]

In 1999 the Convent of the Annunciation at Ormylia published the third of its multi-volume series entitled, *Spiritual Instructions and Discourses of Archimandrite Aimilianos*. Six volumes have so far appeared in Greek and translations are currently being produced in French, English, Romanian and Russian. These books contain many of the hundreds of speeches delivered over a thirty-five year period, and to highly diverse audiences, by Elder Aimilianos, Abbot and Founder of the monastic communities at Simonopetra on Mount Athos and Ormylia in Halkidiki. This third volume, entitled 'Let Us Exult in the Lord'[2], contains homilies on fourteen psalms. Now, as with all of his sermons and addresses, whether to the wider public beyond the Athonite peninsula or at smaller monastic *synaxes*, these psalm commentaries were never written down as texts to be circulated in printed form. Nevertheless, all of them have been recorded on cassette tapes and even now a team of dedicated nuns at Ormylia sits for hours each day listening to ancient, crackling, scratchy tapes, painstakingly transcribing those words of beauty and wisdom that years before had led them to the monastic life.

Eleven of the fourteen homilies were delivered between March 1962 and October 1973. These were the early years, the salad days, before the relocation to Athos and Sithonia, when Father Aimilanos's monks, nuns and novices – around fifty in all – were at the Meteora: the men at the Monastery of the Transfiguration (the so-called 'Great Meteoron')

---

[1] This paper was first delivered at the 2005 Cambridge Conference of the Friends of Mount Athos (UK), which had as its general theme the adage, 'Beauty will save the world', from Dostoevsky's *The Idiot*. A shortened version in Greek was published in *Synaxis* 101 (2007), 42–55.

[2] *Agalliasometha tō Kyriō*, cf. Psalm 94:1.

and the women at the Monastery of the two Saints Theodore. The last three discourses were given in Halkidiki: two at Simonopetra (January 1976 and July 1987) and one at Ormylia (July 1988).

It should come as no surprise when I say that it is one thing to read a book of the Elder's speeches or listen to them on tape and quite another to have heard them live. I still remember clearly, during my student days at Oxford, when on research trips to northern Greece, I would join the throng at one of his public sermons or addresses in Thessaloniki – in the University, at the cathedral of Saint Dimitrios during Lent, or in the course of a vigil service at Simonopetra's metochion of Saint Haralampos. Nothing short of electrifying was the impact one experienced simply by being in Father Aimilianos's presence – listening and watching. Sometimes I was fortunate enough to sit with the fathers or sisters at the more intimate monastic assemblies in the monasteries. Whether in city cathedrals – filled to capacity to hear the Elder – or at smaller informal gatherings in a Synodikon, he exuded a holiness that was palpable, provocative and altogether irresistible. In this respect, as in many others, Father Aimilanos compares very favourably with the Metropolitan Antony of Sourozh of blessed memory.[3]

It must be said, however, that there are certain benefits in having Father Aimilanos's talks enshrined in print. I say this because it now becomes possible to have another look at parts that require a second reading. One has only to sample a few sentences of his style, even in translation, to see that it is of a totally different order than the general run in theological or homiletic exposition. A true orator, the Elder's presentations are invariably models of clarity and economy. He has a lively distaste for discussions that straddle issues and stir theories about without a solid result in sight. And he has no use for expressions that are wordy, or laden with conditionals, or that make their points with rhetoric instead of reasoned sequence. Father Aimilianos speaks leanly; his observations are muscled with cogent insights and salted with applications of the *mot juste*. There is, at the same time, an extraordinary flair for the graceful turn of phrase as well as for the unpredictable stinging metaphor. The Elder's illuminations, both in the psalm commentaries, and in his other discourses, are precise and subtle; they must be savoured at *tempo andante*, never *allegro* or *presto*.

---

[3] Precisely *how* irresistible has been graphically detailed by Golitzin (2005), 201–42, and in (1996), esp. 161–67.

What this volume of psalm commentaries offers, then, is witness of an exceptional theologian's ability to penetrate time and again, and in a manner that radiates effortlessness, to the heart of complex and provocative spiritual matters. And it is precisely about spiritual matters that Elder Aimilianos devotes all of his energies.

There are three master themes in these addresses and these unify their content: (a) the yearning for God, (b) self-awareness, and (c) a profound sense of the ecclesial community. At the same time there is no doubt that the Elder derives much spiritual inspiration from Old Testament figures and from the history, genius and destiny of the Hebrew nation. Having immersed himself in the study of ancient Israel, Father Aimilianos demonstrates an intimacy not only with the Septuagint but also with the Massorah. When he comments on the Jewish legacy in Christian thought and worship, something that occurs very frequently, he does so with an astonishing versatility and theological competence that puts him in a class by himself among Athonite and Greek Orthodox teachers of his generation. To the specialist eye, the Elder reveals himself clearly as a deeply-read scholar not only of Biblical but also of Patristic texts. He is well aware of more recent interpretations and often surprises us with his own hermeneutic approach, from which it appears quite naturally that he lives the psalms as 'serenity for the soul, dispersing demons and drawing down help from the angels'[4]. With respect to these psalm commentaries, what is so unusual and unique is the author's acceptance of the Psalter as poetic literature, texts intended for the communal singing of the faithful, and not necessarily in a liturgical context.[5] There are, he insists, spiritual riches to be gained by singing the Psalms. Together with C. S. Lewis[6], the Elder clearly understands that the poetry of the Psalter is eminently lyrical, with all the formalities, the hyperboles, the emotional rather than logical connections, which are proper to lyric poetry. What is more, he adds, the themes covered embrace the entire range of the relations between God and man. This is a topos that can also be found in the writings of the early patristic authors, such as St Basil and St Ambrose[7] who find Christ or His Church prefigured in almost every psalm.

[4] Basil, PG 29, 212 CD.
[5] On the non-liturgical context of psalm-singing, see below, 284–285.
[6] C. S. Lewis (1958).
[7] Basil, *ibid*, Ambrose PL 14, 924–5.

Eight years before Ormylia's compilation of Elder Aimilianos's psalm homilies, that is to say in 1991, the monastery of Simonopetra itself published a musical anthology entitled *Psalterion Terpnon*, 'The Joyful Psalter'[8]. It comprises 640 pages of original musical settings (in all but one instance) for 51 of the 150 psalms in the Psalter, in addition to several other pieces. The ordering of the psalms in this music book is numerical, bearing, for the most part, no connection to liturgical requirements. The compiler, editor, composer, rubricist and calligrapher of this collection is the celebrated singer and composer of the monastery, Hieromonk Grigorios, whose hand-written music scores and rubrics are photographically reproduced. The selection of the psalms and the progressive style of the music have much to say about the book's compiler, the musical ability of the monastery, Simonopetra's perceptions of the liturgical and non-liturgical function of psalmody, and the spiritual milieu in which the community lives out its life of prayer and work.

The volume is divided into three parts. Section A (pp. 1–363), contains 77 chants, that is to say, 26 more melodies than there are psalm texts. The reason for this is that Father Grigorios has chosen to set eighteen of the psalms to more than one melody.[9] The settings are arranged according to the sequence of the eight church modes. Section B (pp. 365–605), is a miscellany entitled *Eklogai*, or 'Selections', comprising a further sixty compositions, this time not of complete psalms but of verses from different psalms chosen for their common subject matter. Each composition in Section B contains from between five and twenty psalm verses. Essentially what we have here is a collage, a re-grouping of sundry psalm verses that together create new songs. These are divided into two groups (a) according to the oktoechos (b) in the order of the major feasts in the liturgical year. They are designed to be used as proper verses at Communion for feast days since the theme of each verse in every grouping relates to the nature of the particular occasion being commemorated. Section C (pp. 60–640) is an Appendix with five unrelated pieces – only the first is from the Psalter: a setting of Psalm 135, known as the *Polyeleos*; a selection of tropes on the Salutations to the Mother of God; a new setting of the Great Doxology; a religious song in five strophes entitled *One is Lord*

---

[8] Psalm 80:2.

[9] Pss 1, 15, 18, 22, 23, 46, 64, 65, 94, 96, 115, 117, 148 receive two settings; Pss 97, 103 and 138 have three; Ps. 111 has four; Ps. 8 has five.

and finally the highly popular – some would even say notorious – Marian carol, *O Pure Virgin and Lady*.

We shall return to *The Joyful Psalter* and to the significance of its musical idiom in a little while. We shall also return to Elder Aimilianos and his expositions on the psalms in the Ormylia publication. Before doing so, however, I would like us to look at the wider picture in order to appreciate the background from which these new musical settings and these new analytical commentaries have emerged. I shall start by considering the role of the Book of Psalms in Christian worship – that is to say, in both urban and monastic contexts – and to rectify some commonly-held but unsubstantiated views about the history of psalm singing. Finally, in drawing together the evidence, I shall make two observations. First, that there may be ideological connections between the perceptions of Elder Aimilianos on the Psalter on the one hand, and the melodic style and artistic message of Father Grigorios's musical settings of the psalms in his 1991 publication on the other. Second, that the appearance of *The Joyful Psalter* some seventeen years ago and the immense appeal of its melodious psalm settings among church and lay choirs in and beyond Greece signals a revival of the Psalter's ancient role as a songbook for the community of the faithful with a relevance in situations both liturgical and domestic.

Psalmody in early Christian Worship

It is generally held by music and liturgical historians that psalmody – singing from the Book of Psalms – flourished in the Synagogue at the time of Jesus and that the practice was adopted by the Early Christian Church: not an unreasonable assumption considering that Jesus and his followers regularly attended the Synagogue. It is, however, a supposition that cannot be supported by any source known today. This does not mean that, broadly speaking, Jewish beliefs and practices had no influence on early Christianity. That they did is incontestable. But from this one cannot automatically draw congenial though unwarranted conclusions in specific liturgical and musical detail. And if one were to consult Jewish liturgical historians on the subject of ancient Synagogue psalmody, one might be surprised to note that they have maintained a cool objectivity in dealing with the evidence. They have not had much to say on the subject one way or the other, because the primary sources, quite simply, have given them little occasion to do so.[10]

Indeed, the absence of references in the sources to regular Synagogue psalmody constitutes a resounding argument from silence against the practice. Not only is the New Testament unforthcoming on the subject, but what is more telling, so is the Mishnah, the source from which we are able to construct the Synagogue service of c. 200 AD. Indeed, the entire Talmud fails to mention daily or weekly psalmody, which extends the period of silence to c. 500 AD. Finally, in the tractate Sopherim, redacted sometime in the mid 8th century, we *do* read of the daily recitation of psalms in the Synagogue. Thus the practice must have developed sometime between the close of the Temple period, c. 500, and the production of the Sopherim, c. 750.

To summarise the entire question of psalmody in the early Synagogue, all the evidence strangely suggests that at the time of Jesus there was no regular practice of psalmody in early Jewish worship. There is no documented evidence for the existence of established synagogue services of congregational prayer and singing which could have been taken over by the Christian Church in the decades following the Resurrection. There is no documented evidence for the existence of regular psalmody in synagogues during the first 600 years of the Christian era. The daily recitation of psalms was a development of the period between 500 and 750 AD, and even then it probably was not analogous, in a musical sense, to contemporary Latin or Byzantine chant. The highly-structured, instrumentally-accompanied, Levitical singing of psalms in the Temple contrasted markedly with the simple, unceremonious, unaccompanied singing performed at religious gatherings away from the Temple. The formal and ceremonial requirements of the Temple, and consequently its music, were unique to it and died with it in 70 AD. And although the Hallel (Psalms 113-118) can be traced in the Synagogue at the Passover as far back as the 2nd century AD, its performance appears to have resembled scriptural declamation more than song in the proper sense.

With respect to the early Christian context, I can at this time only summarize certain conclusions (support for these conclusions comes

---

[10] James McKinnon has written extensively about early Christian music and, in particular, the place of psalmody in early Jewish celebrations in and away from the Temple and in primitive Christian worship in and away from church. I am indebted to his outstanding scholarship in the foregoing discussion. See especially (1986), 159–91; (1990), 68–87 and (1994), 505–21.

from the New Testament and from a number of third-century Christian writers, such as Justin, Tertullian, Clement of Alexandria, Hippolytus and Cyprian of Carthage). First, the New Testament evidence suggests the spontaneous singing of individuals, probably of newly-composed hymns rather than Old Testament psalms; secondly, for the 2nd and 3rd centuries there was little if any genuine psalmody in the Eucharist service, but the primitive Christian tendency to sing was fostered in less formal circles, particularly in ritual meals; and thirdly, the 4th century witnessed a dramatic outburst of psalmody, one that rivalled the contemporary architectural revolution.[11]

There is no documented evidence for the existence of psalmodic chant in the Christian liturgy before the end of the 4th century AD – a time that coincides with the first appearance of the cantor (*psaltis*) who replaces the older lector *(anagnostes)*. Psalms, if used at all, were treated as one of the variable Old Testament readings (parallel to the aforementioned use of the Hallel in the early Synagogue). A document known as the Apostolic Tradition, which in chapters 25–26 describes the Roman liturgy of the third century, refers to the singing of psalms with Alleluia at the agape.[12] Here at last we have a verifiable link between Jewish and Christian practice in psalmody at ceremonial meals – a fact considerably significant for the question of Jewish and Christian musical links and one that is emphasised by Elder Aimilanos on a number of occasions.

As for the early singing of psalms in an unequivocally liturgical context, the first testimonials are later than normally imagined. The earliest description of the pre-Eucharistic 'Liturgy of the Word' appears in a mid-second century document, Justin Martyr's *First Apology*.[13] Reading and discourse are presented there, as is prayer. Psalmody is absent altogether and in fact we lack indisputable evidence for it in this service until the last quarter of the fourth century when it is to be associated with the monastic psalmody which eventually came to influence and finally to dominate urban popular praise both within and beyond the Church. Psalm-singing as practised in the pre-Constantinian period was incontrovertibly an expression of *koinonia*, the enhancement of community life. This is a point to keep in mind when I pick up where I left off with Simonopetra's *Joyful Psalter*.

[11] McKinnon (1993) is a valuable resource for patristic and other early Christian statements on music (New Testament times to the late fifth century).

[12] Hiley (1995), 486.

[13] Extract in McKinnon (1993), 20.

Monastic Psalmody

Turning now to the fourth century and its most crucial development: the rapid rise of monasticism. The monastic movement is best understood as a reaction to the triumph of the Church. Factors such as mass conversions, freedom from persecution and political ascendancy were responsible for a goodly measure of laxity and even corruption among fourth-century Christians. Numerous idealistic individuals, as a result, fled to the deserts and other remote areas hoping to re-establish the ideal of Christian life in eremetical solitude or in communities of like-minded souls. And in what sacred pursuits did they occupy the long hours of the day and night? Needless to say they maintained the regular Christian liturgical activities, but these consisted in not much more than Saturday and Sunday morning Eucharist, and perhaps morning and evening offices. They filled the vacuum, evidently, with the more formal observance of the traditional hours for private prayer; their device for doing so was the remarkable institution of the *cursus psalmorum*, that is, the recitation of the Book of Psalms from beginning to end. Indeed some monks were known to have recited the entire Psalter more than once in a single nightly vigil. Now we must not imagine this to have been a musical development at first; a case has been made, though is doubted by some scholars, that there were some fiercely antagonistic attitudes towards the frivolities of melodious psalmody.[14] Monasticism, however, was a broad and pervasive movement: it spread rapidly from its Egyptian cradle to the deserts of Palestine and Syria, finally making its way to the cities. There religious communities were established in close proximity to urban cathedrals. In this environment, apparently, monastic recitation of the Psalter took on the character of genuine psalmody, and here, in turn, their singing inspired the late fourth-century surge of popular psalmody.[15]

In trying to imagine what this psalmody was like from a musical point of view, we must not confuse it with the well-registered choral psalmody of medieval monasticism. It was an aid to the meditation of an individual rather than a corporate act of praise, more private prayer than public liturgy. For example, we read of Abba John 'that while

[14] Quasten (1930), 94–9 and Dekkers (1960), 120–37 quote passages expressing antagonism toward the musical elaboration of psalmody but it is likely that these issues were not consciously addressed by the early monks with their informal approach to liturgy. See Veilleux (1968), 162–63.

[15] On the general spirit of monastic prayer and psalmody, see Mateos (1963), 53–88; (1965), 107–26; (1967), 477–85 and Taft, (1986), 66–72.

returning from the harvest or from meeting the elders, he devoted himself to prayer, meditation, and psalmody until he had restored his mind to its original order'.[16]

Encomiums of psalmody have been penned by as many as five of the outstanding ecclesiastical figures of the time: Athanasius, Basil, John Chrysostom, Ambrose and Niceta. These remarkable documents share a number of intriguing commonplaces, but the point that is of particular interest here is that they reflect genuine aesthetic response to the musical attractiveness of psalmody. These authors make no apology for this. It gladdens them that psalms are sung to pleasant melodies and that the faithful are thereby enabled to recall their texts, something they fail to do with other books of the Scriptures. For example, Saint John Chrysostom writes: 'For nothing so arouses the soul, gives it wing, sets it free from the earth, releases it from the prison of the body, teaches it to love wisdom and to condemn all the things of this life, as concordant melody and sacred song composed in rhythm.'[17] Similarly Niceta declares that 'a psalm is sweet to the ear when sung, it penetrates the soul while it gives pleasure, it is easily remembered when sung often, and what the harshness of the Law cannot force from the minds of man it excludes by the suavity of song.'[18] One could say that, with its continuous psalmody, monasticism made a quantitative contribution to the song of the fourth century church, and received in exchange the gift of musicality.

It is no exaggeration to say that psalmody remained the hallmark of monasticism; no invocation of the monastic way of life could fail to mention it. Chrysostom reflected that experience when he wrote: 'As soon as they are up, they stand and sing the prophetic hymns. Neither cithara, nor syrinx, nor any other musical instrument emits such sound as is to be heard in the deep silence and solitude of those holy men as they sing'.[19] Basil, writing to his friend Gregory of Nazianzus, recommended the attractions of his monastic retreat at Pontus: 'What is more blessed than to imitate the chorus of angels here on earth; to arise for prayer at the very break of day and honour the Creator with hymns and songs?'[20] When spiritual advisers advocated a monastic way of life to their charges, they emphasized the role of psalmody. Jerome

---

[16] John the Short, *PG* 65, 216.

[17] *Homily on Psalm* 41, PG 55, 156.

[18] *De utilitate hymnorum* 5, in McKinnon (1993), 136.

[19] *Homily on I Timothy*, PG 62, 576.

[20] Letter 2,2, PG 32, 225–28.

wrote of Paula that 'when still tender her tongue must be imbued with sweet psalms,'[21] and of Pacatula, 'Let her learn the Psalter by heart'[22]; while Gregory of Nyssa said of his young sister Macrina, in the biography he composed after her saintly death, 'Everywhere she had the Psalter with her, like a good companion which one forsakes not for a moment'.[23] Finally, there is the stirring paean to Davidic psalmody attributed to John Chrysostom which concludes:

> If the faithful are keeping vigil in the Church,
> David is first, middle and last.
> If at dawn anyone wishes to sing hymns,
> David is first, middle and last.
> In the holy monasteries, among the ranks of the heavenly warriors,
> David is first, middle and last.
> In the convents of virgins, who are imitators of Mary,
> David is first, middle and last.
> In the deserts where men crucified to this world hold converse with
>   God,
> David is first, middle, and last.
> And at night when all men are dominated by physical sleep and
> David alone stands by, arousing all God's servants to angelic vigils,
> Turning earth into heaven and making angels of men.[24]

The 'Joyful Psalter'

This brings us back to the legacy of Simonopetra: to the publications of the *Joyful Psalter* and of the Psalm commentaries of Archimandrite Aimilianos. For many years this monastery alone has employed full double choirs rather than solo chanters for every service, each day of the year. Its example has recently been followed by Vatopedi and some other houses. This more traditional performance practice is gaining popularity in convents, monasteries and more progressively-minded parish churches both on the mainland and abroad. Moreover, use of the Book of Psalms – the ancient song book of the early monasteries – has been revived, as a result of the new melodious

---

[21] Epistle 107, PL 22, 871.
[22] Epistle 128, PL 22, 1098
[23] *Life of Macrina*, PG 46, 961–64.
[24] PG 64, 12–13 (selected lines).

settings by Father Grigorios of Simonopetra. In his own words Elder Aimilianos relates that 'The *Joyful Psalter* is the fruit of the experience of the brotherhood, already from when they were young at the Meteora and now as monks at our monastery' and adds that the faithful in the world who use the Psalter as a prayer book will become more familiar with it from its fruits *through* the musical settings.

But aside from its devotional value there are clearly also practical and pedagogical issues behind Father Aimilianos's promotion of psalm singing. For many reasons the Book of Psalms, so predominant in the services of the early Church, has from the ninth century onwards, taken second seat to musically more sophisticated and varied hymnography; that is to say, to anthems, motets and stanzas whose words are the non-Scriptural compositions of inspired monastic poets. This shift went hand in hand with developments in the liturgy, church architecture, post-iconoclastic artistic elaborations, and the rising popularity of new monastic practices in the city cathedrals and churches. In the face of the aesthetically-pleasing troparia and kanons, as well as of the evocative vocal displays in long drawn out processional chants, simple, popular psalm singing was demoted to dry reading by a soloist, or at best recitative. The results of this tendency are seen – or rather heard – today in renditions of the Psalm of Introduction at Vespers (the *Prooimiakos*), the psalm selections, or *kathismata*, the Six Psalms, the canonical Hours, Compline, the Midnight Office, and elsewhere. Where psalms continue to be sung – I am thinking of the antiphons and the ferial psalmody of Vespers and Lauds – their verses are drastically reduced. The new trends in sacred chant, made fashionable by the kalophonic masters of the Palaeologian era, ushered in the practice of performing highly artistic renditions of only a restricted number of verses or refrains, much to the detriment of the integrity of the psalm text which, to all intents and purposes, disappeared. This demotion of psalmody is most notable in the current renditions of Prokeimena (or Graduals), the Alleluia antiphons, the Trisagion and Cherubic hymns, and the Communion chants.

The achievement of Simonopetra has been to restore psalmody to its ancient seat of primacy in public and private worship. For this reason alone, the monastery's new musical settings are highly commendable. Using traditional, semi-traditional and contemporary techniques Hieromonk Grigorios has sought to adorn not mere verses, but entire psalms, in order to reinstate the Psalter to its rightful place in religious life.

At the same time, we may again note that many of these psalmodic compositions bear no direct application to the specific requirements of the Church's rites: the *Joyful Psalter* is not meant to be a service book; its intention is not simply to introduce more options for musical diversity. Uniquely, what we have in this anthology is a paraliturgical music book that paves the way for a renewed entry of the psalms into the devotions of the faithful. The settings here are meant for use beyond the Church's formal liturgies: for prayers at home, for Sunday Schools and Catechism classes; for youth camps and pilgrimages. Here the melody is a means and not an end; it serves essentially to be a sonic vehicle that conveys the Psalter's sacred message to the people of God, for His glory and for that of His Church. The *Joyful Psalter* revives the ancient tradition of popular, communal psalmody which was so highly praised and recommended by the writers of the early Christian centuries – a tradition, which we have seen, hearkens back to primitive Jewish domestic practice.

Psalm 83: Words and Music

Let us turn our attention now to Psalm 83 – its explanation by Elder Aimilianos and its musical dress by Father Grigorios[25]. I have chosen this psalm, not because I think it is the most beautiful of the musical compositions in the anthology, but because it relates to a poignant moment in the very early life of Fr Aimilanos's first two communities. The psalm begins with the well-known utterance: *How delightful are thy tabernacles, O Lord of Hosts.* Its interpretation by the Elder was delivered on 10 July 1973, during the last months of the communities' life among the holy megaliths of the Meteora. Having re-established monastic life there in the late 1960s at the behest of the saintly Bishop Dionysios of Trikkala, Elder Aimilianos realised, in the early 1970s, how impossible it was for him to remain there. Circumstances, especially the increase in tourism, the death of Dionysios in 1970, and an unhelpful new local hierarchy forced him to search for another dwelling-place, another tabernacle. Providence would eventually lead the monks to a new pinnacle, this time to a place on the rock of St Simon the Athonite. The nuns, too, would, in due course, find a home in neighbouring Sithonia.

---

[25] *Agalliasometha tō Kyriō*, 150–172 and *Psalterion Terpnon*, 165–69, respectively.

In July 1973 neither destination was certain; many obstacles had to be overcome. This was a time of great insecurity. The point behind the Elder's choice and analysis of Psalm 83 at that time was to give encouragement and to insist that openness to the will of God was the only way forward.

For the end, concerning the wine-presses; a psalm of the Sons of Korah. According to Father Aimilianos, the first part of the superscription, *For the end*, indicates the importance of this psalm, the particular pains that were needed for its execution, and its connection with the appearances of God at the end of the journey. The psalmist here, he says, is 'presenting himself' before God. The second part, *concerning the wine-presses*, is, the Elder observes, normally attributed to psalms linked to the Church of Christ, to the local churches, to the wine-presses the Lord left on the earth. The psalm therefore bears a prophetic echo of events that will take place in the future: a detail of obvious significance for the unsure destiny of the young communities.

The third part, *of the Sons of Korah*, he maintains, creates an air of confidence, because all the psalms of the sons of Korah[26], especially those of Kore, who followed David, are full of feeling and strength. This fact, argues the Elder, makes it easy 'for us young émigrés' to put ourselves into the position of the psalmist'. Finally, the word *psalm* in the title makes it clear that this is not merely a poem referring to certain historical events but rather that it deals with events of the soul. It is a lyrical song expressing religious feelings and spiritual experiences. Thus, he affirms, in Psalm 83 we have already in the superscription all the features we need for the journey on which *we* are about to embark: openness to the will and revelation of God; prophecy and confidence.

Like Psalm 41, this one was probably sung by David seeking God in the wilderness, after he had fled beyond the Jordan to escape his son, Absalom, when his adviser Ahitophel had deserted him[27]. 'The tabernacles', in this case, are the tent, and the space around it, which David had set up in Zion[28]. The psalm was sung when the caravans were preparing to set off or when they had arrived at the temple and were about to ascend Mount Moriah[29]. The singer is either in exile

---

[26] I Chron. 9, 19; II Chron 20, 19.
[27] II Kings (=II Sam.) 15, 1 ff; 17, 1-4; 22; 24.
[28] II Kings 6, 17; I Chron. 15, 1.
[29] II Chron. 3, 1.

or approaching the temple. The 'Lord of Hosts', suggests the Elder, is either a reference to David's personal history or to the history of his people. What is certain is that he still sees God from some distance away. Father Aimilanos's explanation of the subsequent verses is both lyrical and rhapsodic. Below are some examples of his uniquely eloquent and expressive expository style:

> Note how he says *before* the courts of the Lord. He says neither '*in* the courts of the Lord' nor '*towards* the courts of the Lord'. The first would mean that he already dwelt there; the second that he was a long way off and had turned towards them. But here the syntax indicates that the courtyard of the Lord is before him and that he can see it. David has arrived at the courts of the Lord; now that I am here there is nothing left for me to do. In a sense, my existence has ceased to have any meaning, since I now *am* and dwell '*before* the gates of the Lord'. Therefore my life will fade away when I enter. I have done what I set out to do[30]…

> *My heart and my flesh exulted in the living God.* 'Exult' is a powerful verb and denotes the externalization of rejoicing. In the Hebrew text this is rendered by a verb meaning 'sing aloud for joy'. Jews are vibrant people and this is why their bodies are so involved in worship. Here they are clapping their hands and shouting aloud. 'Exult' corresponds to 'shout aloud'[31]….

> If we do not want to feel such disappointment in our lives, if our sojourn amongst so many difficulties and fears is not wasted, then let us prepare ourselves. The Psalmist gave his soul, he gave his heart, he gave his flesh and all this was stimulation, a shock, a struggle, a palpation, a spiritual, intellectual and bodily trial, so that he could come into direct contact with God Himself and be sated with Him.

> I would like our own progress, too, to be such a movement, such a palpation, such a shock, such a stirring of the heart and of the flesh.[32]

---

[30] *Agalliasometha tō Kyriō*, 154

[31] Op. cit., 156.

[32] Op. cit., 171–72.

(Musical Example 1, Vs. 1-2)

Psalm 83

Mode III Plagal (Barys) Enharmonic

Hieromonk Grigorios
Holy Monastery of Simonopetra

Father Grigorios's musical setting to this psalm of migration (Example 1) captures the images of longing, submission and peregrination that act as leitmotifs in the Elder's masterly discourse. The substance of his melody shows the typical rounded contours of Byzantine plainchant. There are gentle arches that billow upward to occasional peaks; then they settle gracefully downward. Notice the square brackets above the notes marked A, B and C. Phrase A, which ascends, is what I call the 'wanderer motif' – the exile in search of a home in the courts of the Lord. The element of craving or yearning is also here. Phrase B is the mirror of A. Its descent represents submission, openness to the call of God, obedience to His will. Phrase C is functional; it signals the end of each verse and leads into the pendant Alleluia refrain. 'Alleluia' means 'Praise the Lord': it is the ancient Western chant used to signify Resurrection, the appearance and revelation of God. These three musical gestures, therefore, correspond to the elements that the Elder sees first encapsulated in the superscription and then elaborated in verse during the course of the psalm: desire – coupled with openness to God, prophetic expectation, and revelation.

In this piece, we do not hear thrusting interval skips, or the jagged motions of two skips in a row. These are very rare in this suave, curvilinear style. Where a leap occurs, the melody tends to fold right back and fill in the vacant space with smooth step motion.

(Musical Example 2, Vs. 3)

Psalm 83

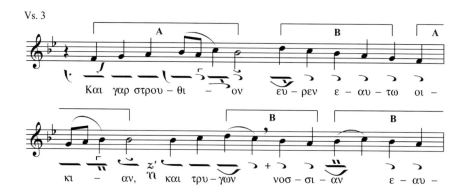

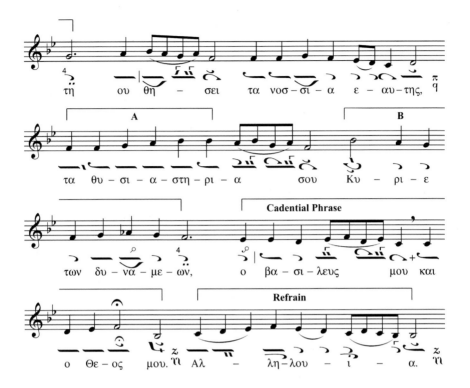

Here, in the next verse (Example 2), we see a different distribution of phrases A and B. They are ubiquitous and unpredictable in this musical tapestry. The piece's expansive lines, mellifluous flow and songlike contours make it more aria-like than conventional chant. The rhythms show the same tendency as the pitches to be gentle and rounded in their flow. Byzantine and Gregorian chants have meterless rhythms that lack any regular pulses or measures. There are no divisions in chant notation. Instead, the music moves in supple rhythmic waves that are free of conventional patterns. The chant's meterless rhythms have flexibility like that of an orator's declamation. For that reason they are sometimes described as 'oratorical rhythms'.

For all of its suave melodic flow and relaxed meterless rhythm, the psalmody before us is by no means a shapeless creation. Its gentle curves embellish an underlying plan that is as coolly rational as a medieval mathematical treatise, or as the design of a Byzantine basilica. The psalm verses are provided with musical turns that are on the whole, unambitious in their scope and variety and that exhibit an appreciable degree of thematic coherence and unity. Hence the musical statements, repetitions, and contrasts have an independent logic of their own – we see an effective balance between what is familiar and what is fresh. As with any piece of Byzantine church music, the composer has been concerned about projecting the sacred text and this is achieved by the creation of an alliance, elegantly and intimately balanced, between textual and musical ideas. Points of repose in the verse dictate the cadential phrases of the music with ingenious regularity, and embellishments, when they occur, are derived from a thesaurus of conventionalised ornamental patterns. These patterns are not applied mechanically, nor are they completely dependent upon incidences furnished by the psalm texts; their function is to inject a diversity of style welded into a carefully systematised verse-music scheme.

In terms of structure, the psalm's twelve verses are not set strophically. Instead, they are viewed as a single poetic unit which, accordingly, is treated in a lyrical manner. The music is through-composed, not a melody that is repeated in identical fashion over the course of the psalm. The musical leitmotifs (A, B, and C) are supple, never mechanically applied in the progression of the verses. The tune rises in ever-expanding parabolas of sonic brilliance while the alleluia, here integrated into the psalm text, pulls us down to earthly realities.

This type of music making is unusual – not because it departs from established traditional methods of composition, but rather because it revives an early popular and melodious style latterly superseded by the more virtuosic repertories for soloistic hymns and by the prevailing dry, hasty and tuneless recitation of the psalms.

Simonopetra's music publications constitute tradition in the making. There is no slavish imitation of a forgotten or imagined past. Modern sensibilities are catered for since there are clear influences of western harmonic theory (made evident by the moving bass note) and an evocative lyricism.

Summary

Allow me now to summarise what I consider to be the salient features of Simonopetra's psalmodic revival. First, the monastery's abbot, Elder Aimilianos, clearly appreciates the salutary beauty in the texts of the Psalter. This beauty, more interior than exterior, hearkens back to sentiments expressed by the fourth-century fathers in particular. Together with them he has placed value on musical execution. The addition of music makes the message of the psalms more alive and meaningful, and, as we remember from Saint Basil and Saint John Chrysostom, it also makes the words easier to remember. With respect to the inner beauty of music, Archimandrite Aimilianos takes this line of thought one step further:

> ...chant [he writes] touches the hearts of men, it reveals most expressively the meaning of the Psalter, it deeply engraves spiritual virtues, harvests grace, smoothes and clarifies Christological and dogmatic meanings. The Psalter through melody opens up the gates of heaven.[33]

In other words beauty is creative freedom, it liberates and opens up fresh possibilities. Secondly, with respect to the settings in the *Joyful Psalter*, their purpose is to return the Psalter to the community of the faithful. We have seen how the monastic initiative in the fourth century was eagerly appropriated by urban Christians who sang psalms not only at the vigils in Church but also on ceremonial occasions at home, while working in the fields, in centres of education, and at informal gatherings. With the advent of elaborate hymnody after the sixth century, and the highly virtuosic mannerisms of later times, the psalms, as musical items, largely fell into disuse. Now, the much more accessible and highly melodious compositions in the *Joyful Psalter* have re-established popular psalm singing. Since 1991, in Greece, Serbia, Bulgaria, the Middle East, Romania and Russia, Father Grigorios's psalm tunes with their unique sonorities are very widely sung and are regularly performed by lay choirs in diverse contexts. The *Joyful Psalter* has found a permanent place as a religious songbook for the 'Liturgy beyond the Liturgy'. This is its legacy to the Church.

It is significant that there is a noticeable resistance to Simonopetra's psalmody in many of the Athonite houses themselves as by some professional musicians. Its opponents, regarding the music as simplistic, even frivolous, echo the reactions of the early desert fathers to the new tuneful religious songs in the city churches.[34] It is interesting, too, that the monastery's musical initiatives have been embraced much more enthusiastically in urban contexts both religious and secular. Elder

---

[33] *Psalterion Terpnon*, viii.

[34] Recent negative expressions have been penned by K. Tserevelakis in two letters to the editor of *Synaxi*: vol. 102 (2007), pp. 88–90 and vol. 104 (2007), pp. 98-100. This author has responded to both: see *Synaxi* vol. 103 (2007), pp. 92–5 and vol. 105 (2008), pp. 85-90

Aimilianos is a pace-setter both in his monastic outlook and in his sensitivity to pastoral concerns. For him, as for Dostoevsky, the beauty that saves is a matter of confrontation not conformity; of creativity not custom.

What of the future? I believe that on the Holy Mountain we shall observe a greater degree of choral singing as opposed to soloistic virtuosity – though the latter will not disappear entirely for some time. Athonite music is also undergoing an observable commercialization. Some monasteries have lately been negotiating with the music industry. On the other hand, there has also been a recent tendency to examine the old manuscripts in order to re-discover earlier traditions and vocal practices[35]. Western musical tendencies, though perhaps never acknowledged as such, may continue to blend with the chant.

The Athonite musical tradition has adapted over the centuries to changing cultural tastes and conditions. This identifies it as an art that is living and accommodating. Because of its prestige, not only the spiritual message of Athos but also its artistic creations will constitute a leading force for trends well beyond its own territory.

Bibliography

Conomos, Dimitri (1996) 'The Musical Tradition of Mount Athos,' *Reports of the Friends of Mount Athos*, 29.

Dekkers, E. (1960) 'Were the Early Monks Liturgical?' *collectanea Ordinis Cisterciensium Reformatorum* 22, 120–37.

Golitzin, Alexander (2005) '*Topos Theou*: The Monastic Elder as Theologian and as Theology. An Appreciation of Archimandrite Aimilianos', in Dimitri Conomos and Graham Speake, eds, *Mount Athos, the Sacred Bridge: The Spirituality of the Holy Mountain* (Oxford), 201–42,

Golitzin, Alexander (1996) *The Living Witness of the Holy Mountain* (South Canaan, Pennsylvania).

Hiley, David (1995) *Western Plainchant* (Oxford).

Lewis, C. S. (1958) *Reflections on the Psalms* (London).

Mateos, Juan (1963) 'L'Office monastique à la fin du ive siècle: Antioche, Palestine Cappadoce', *Oriens christianus* 47, 53–88;

Mateos, Juan (1965) 'La Psalmodie dans le rite byzantin', *Proche-Orient Chrétien* 15, 107–26;

[35] The Fathers at Vatopedi have lately taken an interest in the monastery's oldest musical manuscripts which date from the eleventh century. See Conomos (1996), 29.

Mateos, Juan (1967) 'The Origin of the Divine Office', *Worship* 41, 477–85

McKinnon, James (1986), 'On the Question of Psalmody in the Ancient Synagogue', *Early Music History* 6, 159–91.

McKinnon, James (1990) 'Christian Antiquity', in James McKinnon, ed., (1990) *Music and Society: Antiquity and the Middle Ages. From Ancient Greece to the* 15th *Century* (London), 68–87.

McKinnon, James (1994) 'Desert Monasticism and the Later Fourth–Century Psalmodic Movement', *Music and Letters* 75, 505–21.

McKinnon, James, ed., (1993) *Music in Early Christian Literature* (Cambridge).

Quasten J. (1930), *Musik und Gesang in den Kulten der heidnischen Antike und christlichen Frühzeit* (Munster).

Taft, Robert (1986) *The Liturgy of the Hours in East and West* (Collegeville).

Veilleux, A. (1968) 'La liturgie dans le cénobitisme Pachômien au quatrième siècle', *Studia Anselmiana* 57 (Rome).

INDEX

Scriptural Index

Genesis 11, 36, 38, 41, 49, 80–81, 91–92, 97, 100, 102, 146, 150, 156, 168, 183, 264

Exodus 36, 37, 39, 40, 69, 102, 153, 170, 252

Deuteronomy 37, 100, 102, 105, 150, 183–184, 246

Numbers 35, 146, 150, 153, 156, 184

Leviticus 9, 35, 38, 83, 146, 183

1 Samuel 101, 145

2 Samuel 289

1 Kings 36, 43, 101

2 Kings 35, 289

1 Chronicles 101

2 Esdras 80

Tobit 102, 183

2 Maccabees 100

Job 80–81, 83–85

Proverbs 24, 36, 125, 183, 184

Wisdom 205

Song of Solomon 110

Sirach 36, 99, 101–102, 183

Hosea 148

Amos 35, 99

Micah 39, 100

Joel 103

Jonah 38–39, 42, 45–46

Habakkuk 145

Malachi 99

Isaiah 6, 26, 70, 80, 99–101, 148, 183

Jeremiah 80

Lamentations 99, 103

Ezekiel 101–102, 125

Daniel 99

Matthew 5, 6, 56, 60, 62, 68, 70, 73, 84, 99–100, 102, 108–110, 114, 117, 146, 153, 185, 189, 192, 194

Mark 1, 5, 48, 58, 69, 73, 103, 153

Luke 1, 46, 60, 62–63, 70, 84, 103, 108–109, 132, 143, 146, 187, 194, 196, 261

John 2, 3, 7, 26, 58, 73, 103–109, 117, 243–245, 261

Acts 26, 103, 108, 114, 235, 261

Romans 42, 45, 55–56, 60, 69, 70, 81, 85, 87, 101, 103, 114, 121, 125, 244

1 Corinthians 1, 20, 66, 68, 87, 101, 108–109, 112–113, 167, 236

2 Corinthians 7, 74, 100, 102, 104, 130, 194

Galatians 7, 45, 58

Ephesians 12, 122, 129, 172

Philippians 26, 27, 109, 122

Colossians 107, 109, 121, 172

Hebrews 17, 18, 20

1 Peter 102

2 Peter 245

Revelation 71, 114, 172, 178, 230

Index of Patristic and Medieval Authors

Ambrose of Milan 8, 86, 143, 148, 155, 163, 172, 177, 194, 196, 209, 211–212, 214–216, 279, 285

Athanasius of Alexandria 2–4, 9–10, 15, 17, 23–31, 91, 122, 135, 139, 176, 206, 210–213, 215–217, 223, 246, 249, 252, 256, 285

Augustine 4, 7, 11–14, 30–32, 44–46, 51, 66, 74, 79, 86–89, 91, 93–95, 131–132, 135, 161–183, 185–206, 208, 212, 219–220, 222–223, 236, 262–263, 265–266, 273

Basil of Caesarea 89, 126, 206, 208, 212, 215, 219–221, 279, 285, 295

Boethius 168, 177, 179, 207

Clement of Alexandria 65, 69, 75, 78, 81–82, 206, 217, 244–245, 283

Cyril of Alexandria 1, 4, 9, 87–88, 244–245, 250, 252

(Ps.) Dionysios the Areopagite 246, 249, 251–252, 255–256

Erasmus 257–275

Evagrius of Pontus 55, 75, 122–125, 129, 132–133, 135, 137–139, 212, 216–217, 222

Gregory the Great 8, 11, 45

Gregory of Nazianzus 245, 247–248, 250, 252, 285

Gregory of Nyssa 62, 65, 66, 68, 70, 89, 94, 126, 132, 136, 155, 221–222, 252, 286

Gregory Palamas x, 243–251, 254–256

Hafs ibn Albar al–Quti 226, 231–236, 238–242

Jerome 11, 44–45, 97–98, 113–114, 141–147, 155–158, 163–164, 218–219, 233, 236–237, 257, 262, 266, 268, 272, 285–286

John Chrysostom 44, 50, 68, 167, 209, 219, 221, 285–286, 295

John of Damascus ix, x, 114, 238–239, 241

Maximus the Confessor ix, x, 65, 78, 79, 88–95, 245–247, 250–252, 255

Origen 1, 5, 8–9, 17–23, 28, 30, 32, 44–45, 62, 70, 75, 78, 83–86, 94, 97–118, 132, 143–144, 155, 158, 206, 245, 254–255, 262, 266–270

Palladius 121–122, 137, 209

Philo of Alexandria 143, 146–147, 156, 158, 170, 222

Index of Main Authors

Kevin Andrews 53–54, 75

H. Bolkestein 183–184, 202

A. M. La Bonnardière 181, 190, 196–17, 203

Gerald Bonner 87, 93–94, 192–202

Peter Brown 87, 92–94, 182–184, 190–191, 196, 199–200, 202

Gabriel Bunge 122, 124–125, 133, 137

Robert Devreesse 2, 9–10, 15

D. M. Dunlop 231–234, 240

Luke Dysinger 122, 138, 208, 211, 213, 216–217, 222

Michael Fiedrowicz 12, 15, 181–182, 188, 201–202

R. D. Finn 189–190, 193–194, 199, 202

Balthasar Fischer 1, 3–4, 15

Allan D. Fitzgerald 31, 95, 190–194, 198–199, 202

J. N. D. Kelly 86, 142, 158

Jean-Claude Larchet 89, 95

C. Lepelley 186, 188, 191, 199–200, 203

Jon Levenson 40–41, 49, 51

Andrew Louth vii–xi, 31, 33, 50, 78, 93, 120, 132, 138, 157, 181, 225–226, 238–239, 241, 256

James McKinnon 123, 139, 164, 172, 180, 206–209, 211–212, 214–215, 217, 219, 221, 223, 282–283, 285, 297

John Meyendorff ix, 247, 248, 250

Jacob Milgrom 35, 51, 148, 158

Carl Mosser 243–244, 256

Harry Nasuti 38–39, 44, 46, 51

A. Olivar 182, 204

Erwin Preuschen 18–21, 31

Johannes Quasten 91, 95, 164, 166–169, 172–173, 176, 180, 209, 214, 218–219, 221–223, 284, 297

Boniface Ramsey 136, 191–194, 197, 199, 201, 204

Marie-Joseph Rondeau 2, 15, 122, 139, 182, 204

Henri Rondet 81, 83–85, 88, 95, 181, 190, 204

Christopher Stead 23, 31, 122, 139

Kenneth Stevenson 62, 65, 69, 74–75

Ephrem Urbach 37, 40, 51

Simon Wiesenthal 34, 49, 51

Charles Williams 48, 51, 64, 68, 73, 75

Rowan Williams 22–23, 25, 29, 31